Mastering
Intellectual Property

Carolina Academic Press Mastering Series

Russell L. Weaver, Series Editor

Mastering Bankruptcy
George W. Kuney

Mastering Civil Procedure
David Charles Hricik

Mastering Corporations and Other Business Entities
Lee Harris

Mastering Criminal Law
Ellen S. Podgor, Peter J. Henning, Neil P. Cohen

Mastering Evidence
Ronald W. Eades

Mastering Intellectual Property
George W. Kuney, Donna C. Looper

Mastering Legal Analysis and Communication
David T. Ritchie

**Mastering Negotiable Instruments (UCC Articles 3 and 4)
and Other Payment Systems**
Michael D. Floyd

Mastering Products Liability
Ronald W. Eades

Mastering Professional Responsibility
Grace M. Giesel

Mastering Secured Transactions
Richard H. Nowka

Mastering Statutory Interpretation
Linda D. Jellum

Mastering Tort Law
Russell L. Weaver, John H. Bauman, Ronald W. Eades,
Andrew R. Klein, Edward C. Martin, Paul J. Zwier II

Mastering
Intellectual Property

George W. Kuney
W.P. Toms Professor of Law and the Director of the
James L. Clayton Center for Entrepreneurial Law
University of Tennessee College of Law

Donna C. Looper
Adjunct Professor of Law
University of Tennessee College of Law

Carolina Academic Press
Durham, North Carolina

Library of Congress Cataloging in Publication Data

Kuney, George W.
  Mastering intellectual property / George W. Kuney and Donna C. Looper.
    p. cm. -- (Carolina Academic Press mastering series)
  Includes index.
  ISBN 978-1-59460-392-1 (alk. paper)
  1. Intellectual property--United States. I. Looper, Donna C. II. Title. III.
Series.

  KF2979.K86 2008
  346.7304'8--dc22

                                      2008035092

Carolina Academic Press
700 Kent Street
Durham, NC 27701
Telephone (919) 489-7486
Fax (919) 493-5668
www.cap-press.com

Printed in the United States of America

To Professor Margreth Barrett and memories of the Hastings College of Law Giles Sutherland Rich Patent Moot Court Team of 1989.

Contents

List of Figures

Table of Cases

Table of Statutes

Code of Federal Regulations

Uniform Commercial Code

Series Editor's Foreword

The Carolina Academic Press Mastering Series is designed to provide you with a tool that will enable you to easily and efficiently "master" the substance and content of law school courses. Throughout the series, the focus is on quality writing that makes legal concepts understandable. As a result, the series is designed to be easy to read and is not unduly cluttered with footnotes or cites to secondary sources.

In order to facilitate student mastery of topics, the Mastering Series includes a number of pedagogical features designed to improve learning and retention. At the beginning of each chapter, you will find a "Roadmap" that tells you about the chapter and provides you with a sense of the material that you will cover. A "Checkpoint" at the end of each chapter encourages you to stop and review the key concepts, reiterating what you have learned. Throughout the book, key terms are explained and emphasized. Finally, a "Master Checklist" at the end of each book reinforces what you have learned and helps you identify any areas that need review or further study.

We hope that you will enjoy studying with, and learning from, the Mastering Series.

Russell L. Weaver
Professor of Law & Distinguished University Scholar
University of Louisville, Louis D. Brandeis School of Law

About the Authors

George W. Kuney is a W.P. Toms Professor of Law and the Director of the James L. Clayton Center for Entrepreneurial Law at the University of Tennessee College of Law in Knoxville, Tennessee. He received his B.A. in 1986 from the University of California at Santa Cruz, his J.D. in 1989 from Hastings College of the Law, and his MBA in 1997 from the University of San Diego. He practiced law full time until 2001, last as a partner at the San Diego office of the Allen Matkins firm and previously with the Howard Rice and Morrison & Foerster firms in his hometown of San Francisco. At the University of Tennessee College of Law, he teaches business law courses. He is the author of SECURED TRANSACTIONS: UCC ARTICLE 9 AND BANKRUPTCY (Clayton Center for Entrepreneurial Law 2008, with Robert M. Lloyd); MASTERING BANKRUPTCY LAW (Carolina Academic Press 2008); LEGAL DRAFTING: PROCESS, TECHNIQUES, AND EXERCISES (West 2007, with Thomas R. Haggard); LEGAL DRAFTING IN A NUTSHELL (3rd edition West 2007, with Thomas R. Haggard); CHAPTER 11–101: THE ESSENTIALS OF CHAPTER 11 PRACTICE (ABI 2007, with Jonathan P. Friedland, Michael L. Bernstein, and Professor John D. Ayer); THE ELEMENTS OF CONTRACT DRAFTING WITH QUESTIONS AND CLAUSES FOR CONSIDERATION, 2nd Edition (text and teachers manual, West 2007); CALIFORNIA LAW OF CONTRACTS (University of California CEB Treatise 2007, with Donna C. Looper); and CONTRACTS: TRANSACTIONS AND LITIGATION (text and teachers manual, West 2006, with Robert M. Lloyd). http://www.law.utk.edu/Kuney. Professor Kuney is a member of the State Bars of California and Tennessee and consults and provides training for attorneys nationwide.

Donna C. Looper is an Adjunct Professor of Law at the University of Tennessee College of Law, Knoxville, Tennessee, where she teaches Legal Process and related courses. She received her J.D. in 1989 from the University of California, Hastings College of the Law and her A.B. in 1984 from Barnard College, Columbia University. She clerked for the Chief Judge of the United States District Court for the Eastern District of Louisiana and then for the United States Court of Appeals for the Ninth Circuit. Before teaching at the University of Tennessee College of Law, Ms. Looper was a Senior Attorney for the California Court of Appeal, Fourth District, Division One, and prior to that, was in private practice in San Diego and San Francisco. She is the author of CALIFORNIA LAW OF CONTRACTS (University of California CEB Treatise 2007, with George W. Kuney). Ms. Looper is a member of the State Bars of California and Tennessee and consults in matters nationwide.

Acknowledgments

This book would not have been possible without substantial contributions of time and effort on the part of Clayton Center for Entrepreneurial Law Research Associates Patrick Hawley, Melissa Hunter, Leah Walker, George Robert Whitfield III, and Emily Zibart. Special thanks and recognition go to Christopher William Sherman, the principal Clayton Center Research Associate and team leader on this project with the authors.

The authors also thank The American Law Institute for permission to quote the Uniform Commercial Code and various restatements of the law:

UNIFORM COMMRCIAL CODE, copyright 2007 by The American Law Institute of the National Conference of Commissioners on Uniform State laws. Reproduced with the permission of the Permanent Editorial Board for the Uniform Commercial Code. All rights reserved.

RESTATEMENT OF THE LAW, TORTS, copyright 1939 by The American Law Institute. Reprinted with permission. All rights reserved.

RESTATEMENT THIRD, UNFAIR COMPETITION, copyright 1995 by The American Law Institute. Reprinted with permission. All rights reserved.

Introduction

Intellectual property, which consists of property rights in innovations, is central to business and technological development in the global market. In the United States, the primary intellectual property rights are protected by state trade secret law, federal patent and copyright law, and state and federal trademark law. Each body of law protects different interests and operates in different ways. Further, these areas of law undergo frequent change due to the technological innovations they foster.

Intellectual property law is something of an anomaly in American law. In our society, competition and free markets are the norm, and the law generally disfavors monopolies, at least unregulated monopolies. Yet, one group of intellectual property laws—trade secret, patent, and copyright law—grants limited monopolies to induce inventors and authors to create new inventions and works. The key word here is "limited." In addition to granting property rights, intellectual property law is concerned with limiting the intellectual property monopoly and preventing its misuse. Thus, the scope and limits of the monopoly control the extent to which intellectual property law limits competition.

The other primary group of intellectual property rights covered in this book are state and federal trademark laws. These laws also grant a monopoly—but not in exchange for innovation or creation. Rather, trademark law is meant to prevent confusion about the source of goods and services in the market. These laws are more in keeping with the American conception of the competitive marketplace. Trademark law prevents confusion about the source of goods and services by allowing the goods and services to be branded. In this way, trademark law improves the information available to market participants and lowers transaction costs associated with information gathering. Thus, trademark law promotes competition even as it grants a monopoly on the use of a particular mark.

In addition, this book covers moral rights, somewhat foreign to the American pallet, a set of protections that secures artists' control over their work and allows them some control over their reputations. Traditionally, moral rights have not been widely recognized in the United States.

Intellectual property law has become increasingly important and increasingly pervasive in the practice of law. Although once considered to be a narrow specialty area, it is now critical that attorneys in the practice of general business law have at least a basic understanding of intellectual property law.

This book is intended to provide the intellectual property novice with a plain-language explanation of trade secret, patent, copyright, and trademark law.

Mastering
Intellectual Property

Chapter One

Trade Secrets

Roadmap

After reading this chapter, you should understand:

- The characteristics of a trade secret — information that is commercially valuable because of its secrecy, is not generally known or readily ascertainable, and is guarded by reasonable means to maintain its secrecy.

- The primary means of actionable misappropriation of trade secrets — acquisition by improper means, disclosure of an improperly acquired trade secret, or use of an improperly acquired trade secret.

- The primary defenses to claims of misappropriation — a valid licensing agreement, that the information was not actually secret, or discovery through proper means.

- The importance of trade secret licensing — the way for a trade secret owner to maximize benefit from their proprietary information without compromising its secrecy.

- The remedies available for trade secret misappropriation — injunctions, damages, attorneys' fees, punitive damages, and criminal penalties.

- How to gain and perfect a security interest in a trade secret.

---

1. Introduction

Trade secret law developed from state common law protections of proprietary information, unlike patent and copyright law, which are creatures of federal law. Trade secrets allow businesses to protect proprietary information and ideas that do not qualify for protection as a patent or copyright. A business may also choose trade secret protection instead of patent and copyright protection because it does not want to be subject to the limitations of patent and copyright laws. For example, as discussed in chapters two, three, and four of this book, a patent applicant must enter the content of its application into the public record in order to obtain a patent, but there is no such requirement to protect an invention or idea as a trade secret. Furthermore, common law trade secret protection may be broader than the finite terms of patent and copyright protections. Trade secrets remain protected as long as their holder takes the necessary steps to keep them secret, but once the information is no longer secret, trade secret protection is no longer available. Thus, precautions against the disclosure of trade secrets are very important.

Although almost any meaningful information can be protected as a trade secret, trade secrets are often overlooked and unrecognized business assets. In fact, the value of a business's trade secrets can be greater than the aggregate value of its other intellectual property holdings, such as copyrights and patents.

American recognition of trade secret protection began as early as 1868 in *Peabody v. Norfolk*, 98 Mass. 452 (1868). In *Peabody,* a mill owner (Peabody) had been developing machinery to manufacture a certain type of cloth. He employed an engineer (Norfolk), who signed a contract promising to only use the machinery for the benefit of Peabody and to prevent other persons from obtaining information that would enable them to use their machinery. About six months after signing his contract, Norfolk made arrangements to leave Peabody's mill to build a cloth-mill for a competitor using the secret information Norfolk had learned from Peabody. The court granted an injunction restraining Norfolk from using Peabody's secret information, stating that the policy of the law is to encourage and protect invention and commercial enterprise. Most importantly, the court held that:

> One who invents or discovers, and keeps secret, a process of manufacture, whether proper for a patent or not, has a property interest therein which a court of chancery will protect against one who in violation of contract and breach of confidence undertakes to apply it to his own use or disclose it to third persons.

This remains the essence of trade secret law today.

2. Defining Trade Secrets

Trade secret law in the United States developed from state common law based on various theories and policies. Some jurisdictions have adopted the position that trade secrets, like other forms of intellectual property, should be protected as a property interest. Other courts have rejected that approach, holding that trade secret protection is based on the theory of tortious breach of confidence. More recently, courts and state legislatures have taken the view that trade secrets should be protected by prohibitions against unfair competition. The Restatement (First) of Torts (1939) remains the most thorough treatment of trade secret law, although the Uniform Trade Secrets Act of 1979 and the Restatement (Third) of Unfair Competition are also authoritative sources of trade secret law.

Most states have followed a combination of three approaches in classifying a "trade secret." The first approach is provided in the Restatement (First) of Torts § 757 cmt. b (1939): A trade secret is any formula, pattern, device or compilation of information used in business that gives the user a competitive advantage over others that do not know the secret. The comments to the Restatement (First) of Torts explain that a trade secret is not simply information pertaining to single or short-lived events, but rather something that is continuously used in the business. Additionally, the comments specify that a trade secret must actually be secret and cannot be a matter of public knowledge.

The Restatement (First) of Torts expressly states that the policy underlying trade secret law is protection against bad faith and breaches of confidence, not protection of property rights to reward and foster invention and innovation. This is in contrast to, for example, the temporary monopoly granted to a patent holder in exchange for disclosing an invention—a reward for taking socially desirable action. The Restatement (First) provides six factors for determining whether something is a trade secret, paraphrased as:

(1) the degree that the secret is known to others;

(2) the degree that the secret is known to those involved in his business;

(3) the measures taken to guard the secret;

(4) the secret's value;

(5) the time, effort, and money invested to develop the secret; and

(6) how difficult it is for others to legitimately develop the information comprising the secret.

The Uniform Trade Secrets Act ("UTSA"), introduced by the National Conference of Commissioners on Uniform State Law in 1979, provides a second approach. The UTSA § 1(4) defines a "trade secret" as information, including a formula, pattern, compilation, program, device, method, technique, process, and the like that is secret and:

(A) derives independent economic value, actual or potential, from not being generally known to, and not being readily ascertainable by proper means by other persons who can obtain economic value from its disclosure or use; and

(B) is the subject of efforts that are reasonable under the circumstances to maintain its secrecy.

Ga. Code § 10-1-761 (mirroring UTSA § 1(4)). The UTSA thus departs from the Restatement (First) of Torts definition in that it does not limit a trade secret to "a process or device for continuous use in the operation of the business." This is intended to protect trade secrets not yet put to use. The UTSA definition also protects valuable information concerning what does *not* work, as discovering that a process or technique is not effective can be of great value to a business.

A third, and the most recent, definition of a trade secret is found in the Restatement (Third) of Unfair Competition § 39 (1995). Under this definition, "[a] trade secret is any information that can be used in the operation of a business or other enterprise and that is sufficiently valuable and secret to afford an actual or potential economic advantage over others." This is the broadest definition of the three.

3. Characteristics of a Trade Secret

A trade secret involves information that:

(1) is not a matter of general knowledge and is not readily ascertainable;

(2) is commercially valuable or gives the proprietor an economic advantage because of its secrecy; and

(3) is guarded by reasonable means to maintain its secrecy.

The essential characteristics of a trade secret vary from one jurisdiction to another, as do limitations on the availability of trade secret protection. For example, some jurisdictions that adopt the Restatement (First) definition refuse to extend protection to ideas alone. In other jurisdictions, however, ideas may be protected as trade secrets, though protection is often conditioned on a showing that the idea is novel, disclosed (if at all) in confidence, sufficiently concrete to be useable, and actually in use.

Technical information, business information, and even know-how are generally protectable as trade secrets.

- "Technical information" refers generally to scientific information such as formulas (including chemical formulas), manufacturing techniques, and software.

- "Business information" generally encompasses any other commercially valuable information, including financial data, market research, customer lists, vendor lists, uncompiled computer source code, and unannounced business negotiations.

- "Know-how" is factual knowledge not capable of precise description but which gives one an ability to produce something that they otherwise would not have known how to produce and knowledge necessary for commercial success. In other words, it is how to do something better, faster, or cheaper than a competitor.

Although technical information, as a category, generally encompasses subject matter eligible for patent protection, the Supreme Court has held that federal patent law does not preempt state trade secret protection even in regard to inventions that are clearly patentable. Rather, the Court has held that Congress's intent to use the patent law limited monopoly to encourage disclosure of genuinely novel inventions is not undermined by the availability of an alternative legal mechanism for fostering innovation, like trade secret law.

a. Not a Matter of General Knowledge or Readily Ascertainable

Common knowledge and readily ascertainable information cannot qualify as trade secrets. Further, if information is an industry custom or is known by even one competitor, trade secret protection may not be available. On the other hand, unlike other forms of intellectual property such as patents and copyrights, a trade secret need not be exclusive; thus multiple independent developers may have rights in the same trade secret if they develop the secret independently and each developer maintains secrecy.

Whether information is readily ascertainable is also significant in determining the availability of trade secret protection. According to the UTSA, a trade secret must not be readily ascertainable by "proper means." Proper means include discovery by independent invention, reverse engineering, discovery under a license from the trade secret owner, observation of the item in public use or on public display, and obtaining the trade secret from published literature. Generally, if information is discoverable within the bounds of commercial morality and reasonable conduct, it will not be protected as a trade secret.

For example, in *Nora Beverages, Inc. v. Perrier Group of America, Inc.*, 164 F.3d 736, 741–42 (2d Cir. 1998), the bottler of NAYA water claimed that Perrier Group misappropriated its trade secret by copying the design of a "convenience-size" plastic bottle originally introduced by NAYA. The court held that the shape of the NAYA water bottle was not a trade secret because it was readily observable in the marketplace.

Likewise, publication of information in trade journals, reference books, or even advertisements will undermine its status as a trade secret. Publication on the Internet may also cause information to become "generally known," unless the information is sufficiently obscure or is inaccessible to relevant parties, such as potential competitors.

In *Public Systems, Inc. v. Towry*, 587 So. 2d 969 (Ala. 1991), the Alabama Supreme Court refused to give trade secret protection to information contained in a commercially available software program because the information and software program were readily available to the public. The software used a basic third-party spreadsheet program, which was held not protectable as trade secret information. The information contained in the software was not a trade secret because it consisted of a map disseminated by the state, information from the 1980 census, and other information available to the public from government agencies. The development process consisted mainly of determining what information to obtain, requesting that information, and then plugging it into the computer — none of which required a substantial research investment. Although client lists often receive trade secret protection, here the plaintiff admitted that it distributed its client list to prospective clients, which defeated any claim that it was secret.

In many instances, trade secret protection is an alternative to patent protection, but the inventor's choice is exclusive: Publication in a patent destroys the trade secret, because (as discussed in chapters two, three, and four of this book) patents are intended to be widely disclosed. Moreover, trade secret protection will ordinarily be foreclosed by a patent application even if the patent is denied, because applications are published eighteen months after filing assuming that the patent applicant does not request otherwise and does not seek a foreign patent of the same invention.

Parties under a contractual duty of confidentiality will not be relieved of that duty, however, if a patent or application has disclosed information claimed as a trade secret. For example, in *Shellmar Products Co. v. Allen-Qualley Co.*, 36 F.2d 623, 623–25 (7th Cir. 1929), the defendant hired an attorney to conduct a patent search regarding the design of a candy-wrapping machine developed by the plaintiff, who had disclosed the design to defendant under a confidentiality agreement. When the attorney discovered a patent on which the design infringed, the defendant purchased the patent. However, the court held that defendant's breach of confidentiality by disclosing the design to the attorney gave rise to liability regardless of whether the information disclosed was actually secret.

b. Value

Information must be at least minimally commercially valuable to qualify as a trade secret. Actual or potential economic advantage conferred by the secret is sufficient. The Restatement (First) definition requires trade secret information to be in "continuous use," but modern trade secret law recognizes value in information or processes not yet put into use, and even "negative information" — knowledge of what will not work. Whether actual or potential, the economic advantage of keeping information secret need not be great, but must be more than trivial. Moreover, the advantage gained need not be competitive in the traditional sense, and many jurisdictions recognize economic value independent of competitors. For example, in *Religious Technology Center v. Netcom On-Line Communication Services*, 923 F. Supp. 1231, 1251–53 (N.D. Cal. 1995), the court found that unpublished materials used in an upper-level "course" taught for a fee by the Church of Scientology could be protected as trade secrets because parishioners were willing to pay for access to the material, despite the fact that the Church of Scientology had no competitors who could put the material to similar use.

Paralleling the value requirement, in many jurisdictions misappropriation of trade secret information is not actionable unless the information is at least minimally novel either to the world at large or to the misappropriator. Novelty shows that the idea was obtained from the trade secret holder and that the disclosure of the idea had some value.

c. Reasonable Means to Maintain Secrecy (PROTECTION MEASURES)

Information will not be protected as a trade secret unless its holder uses reasonable means to protect the information's secrecy. Proprietors must actively protect their trade secrets; merely describing information as "secret" is not enough. Absolute secrecy, however, is not required. Rather, "secrecy" is a relative term and is construed equitably, not absolutely. Although public disclosure undermines any claim of secrecy,

> [T]he holder of a secret need not remain totally silent: "He may, without losing his protection, communicate it to employees involved in its use. He may likewise communicate it to others pledged to secrecy.... Nevertheless, a substantial element of secrecy must exist, so that except by the use of improper means, there would be difficulty in acquiring the information."

Metallurgical Industries Inc. v. Fourtek, Inc., 790 F.2d 1195, 1200 (5th Cir. 1986) (quoting Restatement (First) of Torts § 757 cmt. b (1939)).

In essence, the means by which the trade secret holder protects his information need only be reasonable under the circumstances including the size of the company and the resources. For example, in *Metallurgical Industries*, the court held that the holder took reasonable security measures to protect against disclosure of its furnace design by hiding it from any public view, placing it in a restricted access area, posting restricted access signs and requiring any company employee with furnace access to sign a non-disclosure agreement. Other reasonable protective measures include securely locking secret files, guarding facility entrances, restricting access to certain areas, issuing identification to employees, requiring confidentiality or non-disclosure agreements, and using passwords to protect computer software.

The law does not require that extreme and unduly expensive procedures be taken to protect against flagrant industrial espionage. For example, *E.I. duPont deNemours & Co. v. Christopher*, 431 F.2d 1012, 1013 (5th Cir. 1970), duPont was constructing a plant to house its secret methanol-producing process when the defendant photographers (who had been hired by a competitor) obtained aerial photographs of parts of the process that were exposed to view from directly above the construction. (The photographers could not have obtained the photographs had construction been finished.) Under these circumstances, the court found that "[t]o require duPont to put a roof over the unfinished plant to guard its secret would impose an enormous expense to prevent nothing more than a school boy's trick." The court held that "[r]easonable precautions against predatory eyes we may require, but an impenetrable fortress is an unreasonable requirement, and we are not disposed to burden industrial inventors with such a duty in order to protect the fruits of their efforts."

Holders may, without destroying trade secret protection, divulge their processes or information to a limited extent. For instance, proprietors may make controlled disclosures to their employees and licensees without destroying secrecy. Many trade secret holders use confidentiality or nondisclosure agreements to prevent employees or licensees from further disseminating secret information. These agreements typically require employees to (1) acknowledge that during the course of employment they may be exposed to confidential or proprietary information that is the exclusive property of the company and (2) agree that they will not disclose that information to third persons without first having obtained written permission from the company. Confidentiality agreements provide employers with evidence that reasonable measures were taken to preserve secrecy. In addition, violation of a confidentiality agreement may permit a breach of contract claim against an employee who discloses proprietary information.

An implied duty of confidentiality may be imputed to employees, business partners, and even parties who gain knowledge of a trade secret through un-consummated contract negotiations. For example, an implied duty of confidentiality frequently arises where employees gain specialized knowledge during their employment that may qualify as a trade secret. Under such circumstances, an employee may be enjoined from disclosing or using trade secrets to compete with their employer. However, employees may use non-secret information to compete with a former employer.

In *Wright Medical Technology, Inc. v. Grisoni*, 135 S.W.3d 561 (Tenn. Ct. App. 2001), a former employee was allowed to create a product in direct competition with his former employer. Although the employee was exposed to trade secrets in his former employment, his subsequent use of the alleged trade secret was sufficiently distinct and was partially based on public sources and experience he gained prior to that job. In the absence of a non-competition agreement, he was allowed to market the competing product. The court observed that if a skill is beneficial across markets, it is a personal skill of the employee; however, if a skill is useful in only one particular industry then it is not a personal skill of the employee and is protectable by an employer as a trade secret. Similarly, in *Crocan Corp. v. Sheller-Globe Corp.*, 385 F. Supp. 251 (N.D. Ill. 1974), the court found an implied duty of confidentiality between a buyer and its supplier and held that either could be enjoined from using trade secrets obtained through their relationship. The trade secrets involved in the *Crocan* case related to tie-down straps and had aided the defendant in designing its own tie-down straps, avoiding the need for field or market testing, determining the best lengths for the straps, and related matters. Clearly, trade secrets need not be complicated or exotic to be valuable.

4. Misappropriation of a Trade Secret

The holder of a trade secret is entitled to recover under trade secret law only if the trade secret is misappropriated. Misappropriation of a trade secret gives rise to a variety of civil remedies and even criminal penalties. "Misappropriation" is defined as the:

(A) acquisition of a trade secret of another by a person who knows or has reason to know that the trade secret was acquired by improper means; or

(B) disclosure or use of a trade secret of another without express or implied consent by a person who:

(i) used improper means to acquire knowledge of the trade secret, or

(ii) at the time of the disclosure or use, knew or had reason to know that his knowledge of the trade secret was:

(I)   derived from or through a person who had utilized improper means to acquire it;

(II) acquired under circumstances giving rise to a duty to maintain its secrecy or limit its use; or

(III) derived from or through a person who owed a duty to the person seeking relief to maintain its secrecy or limit its use; or

(iii) before a material change of position, knew or had reason to know that it was a trade secret and that knowledge of it had been acquired by accident or mistake.

Ga. Code Ann. § 10-1-761 (mirroring UTSA § 1(2)).

In sum, misappropriation may be committed in three ways:

(1) by acquiring a trade secret through improper or wrongful means;

(2) by disclosing a trade secret that was acquired wrongfully, in breach of a duty, or by mistake; or

(3) by using a trade secret that was acquired wrongfully, in breach of a duty, or by mistake.

Where one person steals a trade secret and discloses it to another who uses the information knowing that it was stolen, three separate actions of misappropriation have occurred.

Actual misappropriation is not necessary for relief; the threat of misappropriation is sufficient. Although the requirement of misappropriation developed from law regarding breach of confidential relationships (such as information disclosed by an employer to an employee or under a confidentiality agreement), misappropriation can be committed by someone who had no confidential relationship with the trade secret holder.

a. Acquisition by "Improper Means"

It is difficult to precisely determine what constitutes "improper means." As broadly defined by the Restatement (First), improper means fall below the generally accepted standards of commercial morality and reasonable conduct. The UTSA defines improper means to include theft, bribery, misrepresentation, breach (or inducement of a breach) of duty to maintain secrecy, or espionage through electronic or other means. This definition includes any tortious or criminal act as improper means. Improper means could also include otherwise lawful conduct that is improper under the circumstances. The Restatement (Third) of Unfair Competition takes a flexible approach, defining improper means to include acquisition by "means either wrongful in themselves or wrongful under the circumstances of the case." Perhaps the epitome of circumstantially improper means was considered by the court in the *E.I. duPont* case, discussed previously, where a competitor of DuPont hired photographers to fly over a methanol plant during its construction to obtain pictures of DuPont's secret methanol-producing process. The court held that although it is otherwise lawful to fly over a plant during construction, it is improper to do so in order to obtain secret information of a competitor.

A party need not use or disclose improperly obtained information to be liable for misappropriation; acquisition of the trade secret is sufficient. The improper means of obtaining the secret are the basis for liability. For example, theft of a trade secret from an employee or other person entrusted with the secret is misappropriation. Additionally, to knowingly accept secret information procured through improper means is a form of misappropriation.

Improper means may even include memorization of secret information, particularly of confidential client lists, which generally qualify for trade secret protection. In *Ed Nowogroski Insurance, Inc. v. Rucker*, 971 P.2d 936, 946 (Wash. 1999), former employees of an insurance agency solicited clients using their former employer's confidential client list, which they had memorized. The Washington Supreme Court did not distinguish between written and memorized information, nor did it require the plaintiff to prove actual theft or conversion of physical documents embodying the trade secret information. This approach is at apparent odds with the Restatement (Second) of Agency, which allows former employees to use general information, including customer lists, that they remember. In contrast, in *DeGiorgio v. Megabyte International, Inc.*, 468 S.E.2d 367, 369 (Ga. 1996), the Georgia Supreme Court held that "only tangible lists of customers and suppliers are the property of the employer and warrant protection as trade secrets." Some jurisdictions do not protect client lists on the assumption that the contact information contained in the list is almost certainly easily ascertainable. *See, e.g., Iron Mountain Information Management, Inc. v. Taddeo*, 455 F. Supp. 2d 124 (E.D.N.Y. 2006). The value of memorization as a defense under trade secrets law is unclear. However, employees who, on their last day of work, peruse their employer's customer list with the intention of obtaining trade secret information will probably be found to have used memorization as an improper means of obtaining secret information.

b. Disclosure of Another's Trade Secret

A person who discloses trade secret information without the proprietor's knowledge or consent may be liable for misappropriation under certain circumstances. A person who discloses a trade secret obtained by improper means is liable to the trade secret holder. In addition, persons who obtain trade secret information by mistake, but who know that the information was obtained by mistake, are liable if they disclose the secret information. Likewise, a person who knowingly receives information from another who is bound by a nondisclosure agreement is liable for disclosure of a trade secret along with the person who disclosed it. Thus, if an employee discloses to his present employer a trade secret of his former employer, both may be guilty of misappropriation.

Disclosure of information obtained accidentally constitutes misappropriation if the disclosing party knew or had reason to know that it had accidentally or mistakenly acquired trade secret information. Thus, persons who receive trade secrets via fax to the wrong number or e-mail to the wrong address are liable for misappropriation if they disclose the secret information to a competitor of the sender.

c. Use of Another's Trade Secret

"Use" of a trade secret is a broad concept with no bright-line definition. According to the Restatement (Third) of Unfair Competition § 40 cmt. c, "any exploitation of the trade secret that is likely to result in injury to the trade secret owner or enrichment to the [misappropriator] is a 'use.'" For example, use may occur by operating under an expired license, contacting another's customers from a proprietary customer list, incorporating a trade secret into a production process, advertising a product that was manufactured using another's trade secrets, or even relying on another's trade secret in developing a business model. Furthermore, unauthorized use need not extend to every aspect or feature of the trade secret; use of a substantial portion of the secret is sufficient to subject the actor to liability. However, the use must be more than minor or inconsequential, and the trade secret owner must "demonstrate that the [misappropriator] received some sort of unfair trade advantage." *Omnitech International, Inc. v. Clorox Co.*, 11 F.3d 1316, 1325 (5th Cir. 1994).

An employer may, under certain circumstances, have a "shop right" to use trade secrets or even the patented inventions of its employees. A "shop right" is a common law right that entitles an employer to use an invention developed by one or more of its employees without charge and without liability for misappropriation when appropriate under principles of equity. For further discussion regarding shop rights see Chapter Four.

5. Defenses

The chief defense to a claim of misappropriation is discovery through "legitimate means," which, as stated in the comment to USTA § 1, include:

(a) Discovery by independent invention.

In *Greenberg v. Croydon Plastics Co., Inc.*, 378 F. Supp. 806 (E.D. Pa. 1974), the plaintiff accused the defendants of misappropriating its trade secrets, including the method for flavoring moldable athletic mouthguards. Prior to the use of this method, it was possible to flavor or mold mouthguards, but not both. A leading defendant testified that he was an experienced injection molder and already knew how to mix the flavoring into the plastic before the plaintiff's trade secret was disclosed to him. As evidence he introduced a plastic Christmas tree that had been scented by the same method and he referenced a flea collar he had developed in which poison was introduced to the plastic by the same method. Inconsistencies in his testimony and other credibility concerns led the court to find that the defendants had indeed misappropriated the trade secrets, but the court implied that if the process had been developed by the defendants independently, they could have successfully raised discovery by independent invention as a defense to misappropriation.

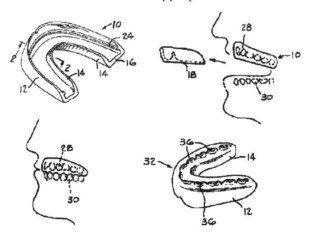

Figure 1-A
Greenberg v. Croydon Plastics Co., Inc., 378 F. Supp. 806 (E.D. Pa. 1974).
Flavored moldable athletic mouthguards.

In *Great Lakes Carbon Corp. v. Continental Oil Co.*, 219 F. Supp. 468 (W.D. La. 1963) the defendants successfully employed an independent invention defense. In *Great Lakes*, the plaintiff sought to enjoin the defendant's use of its superior method to refine tar and oil into "needle" coke, a product used to produce graphite electrodes used by the steel industry. The court found that, prior to the alleged misappropriation, the defendants had experimented with their own coke production methods and had already independently developed the process claimed by the plaintiffs as a trade secret.

    (b) Discovery by "reverse engineering," which involves starting with the known product and working backward to find the method by which it was developed. The acquisition of the known product must also be by a fair and honest means, such as purchase on the open market, for reverse engineering to be lawful.

In *Chicago Lock Co. v. Fanberg*, 676 F.2d 400 (9th Cir. 1982), the Ninth Circuit reversed the district court's holding of trade secret misappropriation against a locksmith who had published a list of serial number-combination correlations for the benefit of other locksmiths. The court found that a lock owner (and, by extension, the owner's locksmith) had the right to reverse engineer the lock to determine the tumbler code combination. The locksmith was under no duty of non-disclosure to the lock manufacturer because the information was obtained by the legitimate means of reverse engineering.

    (c) Discovery under a license from the owner of the trade secret.

Discovery under a license is generally a variation of reverse engineering: rather than deconstructing a product purchased on the open market, the product is licensed. Due to the risk of losing a trade secret in this manner, many license agreements explicitly prohibit reverse engineering. For example, the trade secret owner in *K & G Oil Tool & Service Co. v. G & G Fishing Tool Service*, 314 S.W.2d 782 (Tex. 1958), licensed its secret with an express prohibition on disassembly. The licensee did disassemble and thereby reverse engineer the magnetic fishing tool (used to recover broken drill bits and other metallic "junk" from wells) in contradiction to its promise in the license. The court held that there was improper acquisition, and therefore misappropriation, because the defendant discovered the trade secret in violation of the license. In its opinion, the court implied that there would not have been misappropriation absent the agreement not to disassemble the tool.

    (d) Observation of the item in public use or on public display.

In *Skoog v. McCray Refrigerator Co.*, 211 F.2d 254 (7th Cir. 1954), the plaintiff had designed a combination display case and freezer to save space and allow its grocery store customers to select meat self-service style. The plaintiff attempted to market the design to the defendant and mailed the defendant pictures and descriptions of the invention. The defendant declined to purchase the invention from the plaintiff and subsequently devised a similar combination freezer. The plaintiff then sued for misappropriation and use of its alleged trade secret combination design. The court held that the plaintiff's design could not be protected as a trade secret because the freezer had been on public display and in use for several months before the defendant obtained the supposed secret information.

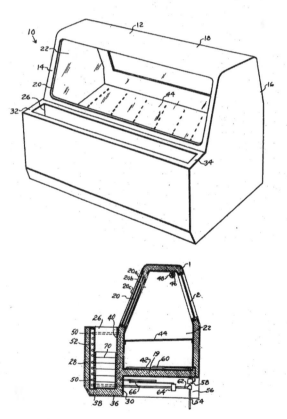

Figure 1-B
Skoog v. McCray Refrigerator Co., 211 F.2d 254 (7th Cir. 1954).
Self-service meat display case and freezer.

However, limited public display may not be enough to defeat trade secret protection. For example, in *K-2 Ski Co. v. Head Ski Co., Inc.*, 506 F.2d 471 (9th Cir. 1974), the plaintiff sued a competitor for trade secret misappropriation in replicating the specific design of its skis. The defendant claimed that secrecy was lost through public display and that there could be no misappropriation. The plaintiff had exhibited its skis, including an intact model and a model that had been cut lengthwise to reveal the inner materials and design, at a conference, but none of the defendant's personnel attended the conference and there was no evidence that any other competing ski manufacturer had attended. Also, the plaintiff allowed some members of the public to tour its manufacturing plant but did not permit competitor ski manufacturers to observe its manufacturing plant or other operations. The court held that these limited public displays did not destroy secrecy because there were sufficient precautions to prevent observation by competitors.

(e) Obtaining the trade secret from published literature.

In *Ferranti Electric, Inc. v. Harwood*, 251 N.Y.S.2d 612 (N.Y. Sup. Ct. 1964), the court held the plaintiff did not have a single protectable trade secret in the roughly forty-five allegedly secret processes it used to manufacture certain devices used in radar equipment. The court denied trade secret protection for several reasons, including the following: the manufacturer failed to put employees on notice as to the secrecy of the manufacturing process; a large number of the alleged secrets had been extensively published in trade journals; and some of the alleged secrets were too commonly known to claim as a trade secret (such as the manner in which the wire was cut—"in this case with scissors"). Information published in trade journals and known throughout the industry cannot be considered a secret, so its use could not be considered misappropriation.

In *DVD Copy Control Association Inc. v. Bunner*, 10 Cal. Rptr. 3d 185, 192 (Cal. Ct. App. 2004), the court reversed a preliminary injunction because the plaintiff was unlikely to succeed on the merits. The trade secret source code used to copy-protect DVDs had been widely published on the Internet and, due to a magazine report, potentially millions had seen and downloaded the code. Though the initial reverse engineering was likely in violation of the license agreement, the widespread publication effectively destroyed secrecy and those who subsequently obtained the former secret could not be liable for misappropriation because the information was no longer secret.

6. Remedies

a. Civil Remedies

A variety of civil remedies are available to the holder of a trade secret that has been misappropriated. These include damages, injunctions, accountings, and awards of profits, as well as destruction of objects embodying or incorporating the trade secret.

Injunctions are generally issued only if the trade secret remains a secret. An injunction usually lasts only as long as necessary to eliminate the commercial advantage or "lead time" obtained through misappropriation. Injunctions may be issued to prevent threatened use or disclosure of a trade secret. Further, under the inevitable disclosure doctrine, an injunction may be available to prevent former employees from performing the same job for a competitor of their former employer. The inevitable disclosure doctrine is based on the idea that in certain circumstances, trade secrets will inevitably be used or disclosed, regardless of a prior non-disclosure agreement by the employee.

The court may also award damages in addition to, or in lieu of, an injunction. Damages can include both compensation for actual loss and recovery for unjust enrichment. Alternatively, the court may order an accounting and award royalties lost because of unauthorized use or disclosure of trade secret information. The court may award attorneys' fees where the misappropriation was in bad faith, and exemplary or punitive damages are appropriate in cases of willful and malicious misappropriation.

b. Criminal Penalties

In addition to civil remedies, several jurisdictions have enacted legislation criminalizing misappropriation of trade secrets. States that impose criminal penalties for misappropriation generally do so either by expressly criminalizing misappropriation of trade secrets or by incorporating trade secrets within the coverage of larceny or robbery statutes. For example, in Georgia, misappropriation of a trade secret is a crime punishable by one to five years in prison and a fine of up to fifty thousand dollars. Ga. Code Ann. § 16-8-13 (2007). Minnesota, on the other hand, simply defines "property" under its theft statute to include "articles representing trade secrets." Minn. Stat. § 609.52 (2007).

Congress has also enacted federal legislation criminalizing the misappropriation of trade secrets. The Economic Espionage Act of 1996 mandates a prison sentence of up to ten years and a fine of up to $500,000 for any person (or up to $5 million for any "organization") who:

(1) steals, or without authorization appropriates, takes, carries away, or conceals, or by fraud, artifice, or deception obtains [trade secret] information;

(2) without authorization copies, duplicates, sketches, draws, photographs, downloads, uploads, alters, destroys, photocopies, replicates, transmits, delivers, sends, mails, communicates, or conveys [trade secret] information; [or]

(3) receives, buys, or possesses [trade secret] information, knowing the same to have been stolen or appropriated, obtained, or converted without authorization....

18 U.S.C. §§ 1832, 3571 (1996).

In one case, three co-conspirators stole product samples and other secret information from Coca-Cola and attempted to sell them to PepsiCo, in violation of the Economic Espionage Act. PepsiCo reported them and in May 2007 the three were sentenced to prison terms of between five and eight years. Where one misappropriates a trade secret with the intent to benefit a foreign government, 18 U.S.C. § 1831 provides a maximum senence of 15 years. Xiadong Meng was sentenced to twenty-four months imprisonment after pleading guilty to trying to sell fighter pilot training software to the Chinese Navy. Regardless of whether the information was actually secret, under the Economic Espionage Act the prosecution must prove only that "the defendant sought to acquire information which he or she believed to be a trade secret, regardless of whether the information actually qualified as such." *United States v. Hsu*, 155 F.3d 189, 203 (3d Cir. 1998).

7. Licensing of Trade Secrets

Trade secrets, like other forms of intellectual property, may be licensed. In fact, because a trade secret is only protectable while it remains secret, licenses are particularly useful in allowing trade secret holders to exploit the value of their proprietary information. Without a license, trade secret holders would likely be unwilling to share their secret with others and allow it to be used. As the Court in *Kewanee Oil Co. v. Bicron Corp.*, 416 U.S. 470, 486 (1974), explained: "The holder of a trade secret would not likely share his secret with a manufacturer who cannot be placed under binding legal obligation to pay a license fee or to protect the secret. The result would be to hoard rather than disseminate knowledge."

A license is a contract and, as such, may take many forms and encompass many different groupings of rights, duties, and remedies. Trade secret licenses are no more constrained than any other type of contract. By default, any right not specifically licensed from the trade secret holder to the licensee remains with the licensor. Thus, from the licensee's perspective, it is important to think through all the steps necessary to exploit the trade secret and protect the investment that it makes in doing so by including, for example, provisions regarding the right to use subsequent versions, updates, and innovations of the trade secret; to receive technical support if appropriate; and to define the scope of renewal rights in the secret. From the licensor's perspective, covenants of the licensee to protect the secrecy of the trade secret are perhaps as important as the consideration they are to receive in exchange for the license. Confidentiality agreements, non-disclosure agreements, and covenants to turn over material derived from the trade secret at the end of the contractual term are critically important.

In the absence of patent, antitrust, or other federal law issues, state law governs the assignment and licensing of pure trade secrets. Trade secrets can form the *res* of a trust and pass to a trustee in bankruptcy. Moreover, courts do not generally construe the parties' obligations under trade secret licenses as contingent on the continued secrecy of the subject. *Warner-Lambert Pharmaceutical Co. v. John J. Reynolds, Inc.*, 178 F. Supp. 655 (S.D.N.Y. 1959), *aff'd*, 280 F.2d 197 (2d Cir. 1960), provides an example: In 1883, Warner-Lambert licensed the unpatented but secret formula for Listerine from Dr. Lawrence, its inventor, under an agreement that called for royalty payments to be made by Warner-Lambert and its successors in interest. In 1931, an article published by the American Medical Association disclosed the formula for Listerine. Warner-Lambert thereafter sought a declaratory judgment foreclosing the licensor's right to ongoing royalties under the license. The court refused to reform the unambiguous contract on the grounds that the parties could have—and should have—allocated in the license agreement the risk that the formula would become known.

a. Exclusive v. Nonexclusive Licensing

One of the primary distinctions between types of trade secret licenses is whether they are exclusive or nonexclusive. An exclusive license is an express or implied covenant by the licensor not to use the trade secret themselves or grant others the rights contained in the exclusive license. A nonexclusive license is more limited and is treated merely as a covenant by the licensor not to bring suit to enjoin the licensee from using the trade secret within the scope of the license.

b. Residual Rights

Residual rights involve the licensee's responsibilities regarding non-tangible information that is retained by the licensee after the term of the license expires. If a licensee uses a particular formula or method of manufacture, for instance, the licensee will probably remember all or part of the trade secret, even once the license has expired. Unlike computers, licensees' minds cannot be "wiped clean" at the end of the license. Thus, licensors and licensees should contractually specify how the licensee may use (or not use) such information. The licensee has residual rights in the trade secret insofar as the licensee may use part of the secret after the term of the license has expired. Licensors take a dim view of residual rights and tend to view them as uses of the trade secret by the former licensee beyond the scope of the license. Licensees take the opposite view, and striking a balance between these two positions is complex in most situations.

c. Hybrid Trade Secret and Patent Licenses

Problems may result from the so-called "hybrid license" that licenses both trade secrets and patents. A patent typically has a term of twenty years, after which the patented subject matter becomes part of the public domain and is no longer subject to the patent-holder's monopoly. Licensing a trade secret and a patent together for a period longer than the patent's term constitutes a tying arrangement that violates antitrust laws. The solution is to (1) untangle the two licenses and give consideration for each so that they are separate—even if related—contracts, and (2) to provide for licensing of the trade secret alone once the patent has expired. In this way, the hybrid license problem is fairly easy to cure.

8. Security Interests in Trade Secrets

A security interest is a present, usually non-possessory, interest in property that may become possessory in the future if certain contingencies occur. An example is an automobile financing company's lien on a vehicle it has financed. When granted, the lien is non-possessory—the financing company does not possess or have the right to possess the vehicle. Upon default by the vehicle's owner, however, after complying with applicable foreclosure laws, the financing company may repossess the vehicle in satisfaction of all or part of the outstanding debt.

Trade secrets, along with other intellectual property such as copyrights and trademarks, often represent a significant portion of an entity's assets, and as such can be useful sources of collateral for secured loan transactions. To maintain priority, lenders must know how to properly create and perfect their security interests in intellectual property. Security interests in intellectual property are governed by both the Uniform Commercial Code and federal law. The extent to which the U.C.C. or federal regulations govern a particular security interest depends upon the type of intellectual property used as collateral. For trade secrets, only the state's enactment of the U.C.C. needs to be considered.

Article 9 of the U.C.C., which has been adopted by all fifty states, governs the creation and perfection of security interests in intellectual property—categorized by the U.C.C. as "general intangibles." A security interest in intellectual property is not enforceable (even against the debtor) and does not attach to the collateral unless:

(1) the secured party has given value in exchange for the collateral,

(2) the debtor has rights in the collateral, and

(3) the debtor has signed a security agreement that provides a description of the collateral.

Lenders must therefore ensure that the debtor has rights in the intellectual property collateral in order to obtain the security interest. When a security interest is properly granted it is said to have "attached" and is then enforceable against the debtor.

In a security agreement, a general description of the personal property used as security is sufficient if it reasonably identifies what is described. Therefore, a description of trade secret collateral in the security agreement as "general intangibles" or "trade secrets" is theoretically sufficient. However, it is best to also identify all important collateral as specifically as possible to avoid subsequent disagreement over what was included. The collateral description should, therefore, include all pending misappropriation claims; rights to income, profits, or other rights related to the trade secrets, including those arising under licenses; and all inventions and improvements related to the trade secrets. In addition, the agreement should both oblige the debtor to take all necessary measures to protect the collateral from infringement and guarantee the secured party's right to take any steps it deems reasonably necessary to maintain and protect its collateral.

"Perfection" of the security interest is the legal status that the security interest enjoys once the appropriate formalities have been complied with in order to make it good against the world rather than only enforceable against the debtor. Through perfection of its security interest, a secured party achieves and maintains the highest available priority for its security interest in collateral. An unperfected security interest may be effective against the debtor, but it is of little value against third parties. In bankruptcy, the difference between a perfected security interest and an unperfected security interest means the difference between a full recovery as a secured creditor and no (or minimal) recovery as a general unsecured creditor.

A security interest is perfected upon attachment if the applicable requirements are satisfied before attachment. A security interest in most types of personal property is perfected when a properly completed UCC-1 financing statement is filed with the appropriate state office, most often the office of the secretary of state. The financing statement must name both the debtor and the secured party, and must describe the collateral covered by the financing statement. The U.C.C. no longer requires the debtor to sign an electronically filed financial statement, although the debtor must authorize the filing.

The relative priorities of creditors holding conflicting security interests in most collateral are straightforward. Under the U.C.C.:

(1) if the conflicting security interests are perfected, they rank according to priority in time of filing or perfection;

(2) a perfected security interest has priority over a conflicting unperfected security interest; and

(3) if the conflicting security interests are unperfected, the first security interest to attach has priority.

Thus, perfecting a security interest in a trade secret is accomplished by obtaining a security agreement from the trade secret owner and properly filing U.C.C. financing statements at the appropriate state office. This perfection makes the security interest good as against other creditors and provides the creditor recourse against the trade secrets if the debtor defaults on its obligations.

Checkpoints

- Trade secret protection is derived from state common law and draws heavily from the following three sources: the Restatement (First) of Torts § 757, the Uniform Trade Secrets Act, and the Restatement (Third) of Unfair Competition § 39.

- Trade secret law protects proprietary information for as long as it remains secret (rather than for a fixed term like patents and copyrights).

- Eligible subject matter is information that: (1) is not a matter of general knowledge and is not readily ascertainable; (2) is commercially valuable or gives the holder an economic advantage because of its secrecy; and (3) is guarded by reasonable means to maintain its secrecy.

- Misappropriation can be committed by: acquiring a trade secret through improper or wrongful means; disclosing a trade secret that was acquired wrongfully, in breach of a duty, or by mistake; or using a trade secret that was acquired wrongfully, in breach of a duty, or by mistake.

- Defenses to misappropriation include a valid licensing agreement; that the information was not actually secret; and discovery by proper means, such as independent invention, reverse engineering, discovery under a license, observation of public use, and discovery through published literature.

- Remedies for trade secret misappropriation include injunctions, damages, attorneys' fees, and punitive damages. Misappropriation might also result in criminal penalties, including prison sentences and fines as high as $5,000,000.

- Licensing allows the trade secret holder to share and profit from the information without compromising its secrecy, and licensing agreements often include provisions related to updates and technical support, renewal rights, confidentiality and non-disclosure agreements, exclusivity of the license, and residual rights.

- Trade secrets can serve as collateral. Security interests in trade secrets attach and are perfected as "general intangibles" under Article 9 of the Uniform Commercial Code.

Chapter Two

Patent Law

Roadmap

After reading this chapter, you should understand:

- The characteristics of a patent — a patent is a limited monopoly that confers on the first inventor a right to exclude others from making, using, selling, importing, or offering an invention for sale.

- The limitations on patentable subject matter — any process, product, or design that meets the other criteria for patentability may be patented, but laws of nature, naturally occurring phenomena, and abstract ideas are not patentable.

- The types of patents and significant differences between them —

  - *utility patents*, the most common type, which cover both processes and products and expire twenty years from the date of the patent application;

  - *design patents* for non-functional ornamental designs, which expire fourteen years from the date the patent is granted; and

  - *plant patents* for asexually propagated plants, which expire twenty years from the date of the patent application.

- The *utility* requirement of 35 U.S.C. § 101 — the invention must be (a) capable of practical application or commercial benefit; (b) operable; and (c) reduced to practice.

- The *novelty* requirement of 35 U.S.C. § 102 — the invention must differ from prior art; a patent is prohibited if (a) there is an equivalent reference, (b) the patent applicant did not invent the claimed invention, (c) the applicant abandoned, suppressed, or concealed the invention, or (d) the statutory bar applies.

- The *statutory bar* as a way to defeat novelty — an invention patented, described in a printed publication, in public use, or sold prior to a certain date is unpatentable.

- The *non-obviousness* requirement of 35 U.S.C. § 103 — the invention must be more than an obvious advance over prior art as measured against a hypothetical person (or designer) with ordinary skill in the art.

- The role of *secondary considerations* and *synergism* as part of the non-obviousness inquiry —

  - secondary considerations include commercial success, long felt but unsolved needs, and the failure of others in the field;

- • synergism is the combination of obvious elements in such a way that the whole exceeds the sum of its parts;
- • either secondary considerations or synergism can lead to a finding of non-obviousness.
- • The basic concepts of patents as property interests and their use in secured transactions — patentees can assign or license their patents, and may use patents as valuable collateral in secured transactions.

1. Introduction

A patent—short for "letters patent"—is the government's grant to its holder of a limited monopoly that enables the holder to exclude others from making, using, selling, importing, or offering the patented invention for sale for a fixed period of time. In return for this grant of temporary exclusivity, patent applicants must reveal information that would allow the invention to be reproduced. Patents allow a compromise between the government's interest in promoting scientific and technological advances and inventors' interest in maximizing profit from their invention. The government, which normally discourages monopolies, gives inventors a limited monopoly over their inventions for a certain period of time (twenty years for most patents), and because of this temporary monopoly, inventors—who might otherwise keep their invention a (trade) secret—agree to reveal it to the public. At the expiration of the patent, the invention passes into the public domain and may be made, used, or sold by anyone. In this way, patent law stimulates technological innovation and spurs economic growth.

When a patent expires, the invention passes into the public domain and anyone may make free use of the invention. This advances the overall goal of patent law, to stimulate and reward technological innovation, because it allows current generations of inventors to advance technology by using older technology. An important corollary to this doctrine is that no patent should be granted that withdraws items already in the public domain.

2. Defining Patents

a. Basic Principles

American patent law is derived from Article 1, Section 8 of the United States Constitution and is governed solely by federal law. It is codified primarily in the Patent Act of 1952, as amended, in Title 35 of the United States Code. The

Patent Act allows inventors to obtain patents on "any new and useful process, machine, manufacture, or composition of matter, or any new and useful improvement thereof." 35 U.S.C. § 101. Additionally, an invention must be non-obvious in order to qualify for a patent. The key requirements for patentability are: (1) novelty (§§ 101–102), (2) utility (§ 101), and (3) non-obviousness (§ 103).

- For an invention to be new or "novel" under § 102, it must differ from previously known inventions and pre-existing knowledge in the field ("prior art").

- To be "useful" under § 101, an invention need only be minimally operable towards some practical purpose.

- To be "non-obvious" under § 103, the invention must be different enough from the prior art that it would not be obvious to "a person having ordinary skill in the art."

An invention may only be patented once; otherwise, an inventor could extend the monopoly beyond the specified statutory term (usually twenty years from the date of the patent application). In addition, only one inventor may patent the same invention. This requirement causes conflict when more than one inventor (or group of joint inventors) files a patent application describing the same invention. In such instances, the United States follows the *first-to-invent* rule: the first person to have actually invented the technology obtains the patent. This rule differs from the first-to-file rule, which is followed in most countries. The first-to-file rule awards the patent to the first person to file a patent application, regardless of whether that person was actually the first person to invent the technology. The United States' first-to-invent rule is arguably fairer in rewarding the pioneering inventor; however, the first-to-file rule is easier to administer, more certain, and encourages diligent, timely patent application filings.

b. Overview of Patent Applications

To obtain a patent, an inventor must file a patent application with the United States Patent and Trademark Office (the "PTO"). Section 112 of the Patent Act requires that the application describe the invention such that a person of ordinary skill in the particular field would be able to replicate and use the invention (this is the "enablement" requirement). A patent application must also contain "one or more claims particularly pointing out and distinctly claiming the subject matter which the applicant regards as his invention." 35 U.S.C. § 112.

The "patent claims" exclusively define the invention and are the most important part of the patent application. A patent's claims determine the scope of the patent in legal actions regarding the validity or infringement of the patent. Thus, the patent application must contain distinct, definite claims that clearly encompass the substance of the claimed invention.

In determining whether to approve a patent, the patent examiner compares the claims with existing technologies and inventions (collectively, the "prior art"). If the invention claimed in the patent application is useful, novel, and non-obvious, a patent will be issued.

c. Duration

Valid utility patents give patentees a monopoly over their invention for a twenty-year term, beginning on the date the patent application is submitted. 35 U.S.C. § 154(a)(2). This is a modification of the old rule, under which patents expired seventeen years after the date of issue. Design patents expire fourteen years from the date of issue. 35 U.S.C. § 173. (Note that the application date, which is used to determine the expiration of a utility patent, differs from the date of issue, which is used to determine the expiration of a design patent.) The term of a plant patent is not explicitly stated, however, under 35 U.S.C. § 161, "the provisions of this title relating to patents for inventions shall apply to patents for plants, except as otherwise provided." Thus, a plant patent's duration is the same as a utility patent's: twenty years from the date of application.

Under 35 U.S.C. § 156, the term of a patent for the substance, manufacture, or method of use of either a drug or a recombinant DNA technology (which are subject to regulatory review before they can be marketed) may be extended for up to five years for time lost due to regulatory review. This can be a trap for the unwary, as in *King Pharmaceuticals, Inc. v. Teva Pharmaceuticals USA, Inc.*, 409 F. Supp. 2d 609 (D.N.J. 2006), where the defendant filed a statement of intent with the FDA to begin manufacturing the drug claimed in the plaintiff's patent. Although the defendant waited twenty years after the plaintiff's patent was issued, it had failed to account for the nearly five-year extension obtained by the plaintiff due to regulatory delays after the date of issue.

Patent extensions are limited, however, and may be offset if the patent holder failed to exercise due diligence toward obtaining regulatory approval. In addition, only one patent related to a particular invention may be extended to offset time lost due to regulatory review. 35 U.S.C. § 156.

A patent may also be extended to offset delay in the issuance of an approved patent when the delay is attributable to interference proceedings, appeals from interference proceedings, secrecy orders, or the failure of the patent office to act in a timely fashion. 35 U.S.C. § 154(b). An extension is reduced by any delay caused by the patentee's failure to exercise due diligence. Amendments, reissues, and other modifications of patent applications are retroactively limited to the date of the original patent application.

A patentee can shorten the term of a patent by filing a "terminal disclaimer," which allows a patentee to "disclaim or dedicate to the public the entire term, or any terminal part of the term, of the patent granted or to be granted." 35 U.S.C. § 253. The terminal disclaimer is especially important where a patentee has substantially improved an earlier-patented invention, which could not be patented independently on the grounds of obviousness in light of the earlier patent. In *In re Deters*, 515 F.2d 1152 (C.C.P.A. 1975), a tool used to cut clay drain tile that had been slightly modified from the inventor's previous patent was unpatentable because it was obvious in light of the earlier patent. Had the inventor timely filed a terminal disclaimer, they would have been entitled to a patent on the tool as modified. Terminal disclaimers allow patentees to extend the monopoly on their invention with a patent that covers an improved version of the earlier patented invention. The second patent expires simultaneously with the first, so the public's right to use the invention after the first patent term expires remains unimpaired.

However, if the claims of the second patent application are substantially the same as those of the first, a terminal disclaimer cannot save the application. For example, in *In re Robeson*, 331 F.2d 610 (C.C.P.A. 1964), the patent for a chemical process for the production of trimethylolpropane was rejected as being obvious in light of the patent applicant's own prior patent. A terminal disclaimer did not change that this was, in essence, an attempt at double patenting.

A terminal disclaimer is different from a "statutory disclaimer," by which patent holders can disclaim a single invalid claim that might otherwise invalidate the whole of their patent. 35 U.S.C. § 253.

3. Patent Types

a. Patentable Subject Matter

The categories of patentable subject matter are found in 35 U.S.C. § 101. Categories include "any new and useful process, machine, manufacture, or composition of matter, or any new and useful improvement thereof." Patentable subject matter can be defined in two broad categories: "processes" and "products."

The breadth of patentable processes and products reflects congressional intent to make patentable "anything under the sun that is made by man." However, there are limits on the scope of patentable subject matter: laws of nature, physical phenomena, and abstract ideas are not patentable. Thus, new minerals discovered in the earth or new plants discovered in the wild are not patentable,

Einstein could not have patented E=mc2, and Newton could not have patented the laws of gravity. The rationale for this limitation is that natural things and natural laws have always existed in the environment and should not be subject to the exclusive rights of a single person. Natural things may be combined, however, to form a patentable invention. For example, in *Diamond v. Chakrabarty*, 447 U.S. 303 (1980), the Court held that a bacterium genetically engineered to break down crude oil was eligible for patent protection, even though it was a living organism, because it was not naturally occurring and was created by human invention.

b. Utility Patents

Inventions that fall into one of the four § 101 categories, "process, machine, manufacture, or composition," may qualify for a utility patent, the type of patent most recognized by laypersons and lawyers. A utility patent covers innovative products and processes for a twenty-year term and is the type of patent most frequently applied for. To be awarded a utility patent, an invention must meet the statutory requirements of: (1) utility, (2) novelty, and (3) non-obviousness.

i. Process

Courts have encountered some difficulty in defining the term "process" used in § 101, especially given the ever-increasing complexity of modern technology. Process is somewhat circularly defined in 35 U.S.C. § 100(b) as a "process, art or method, and includes a new use of a known process, machine, manufacture, composition of matter, or material." In *In re Durden*, 763 F.2d 1406 (Fed. Cir. 1985), the Court of Appeals for the Federal Circuit broadly described a process as "a manipulation according to an algorithm." In *Durden*, the court denied a patent for a process to recombine chemical compounds for use in a pesticide, even though the process yielded a new (although expected) result, because the application of an obvious process to a novel material is still considered obvious.

An abstract mathematical formula (sometimes called a mathematical algorithm) is not useful and is therefore unpatentable subject matter; however a mathematical formula may be patentable as an integral part of patentable subject matter (such as a machine or process) if the claimed invention is "useful." In *AT&T Corp. v. Excel Communications, Inc.*, 172 F.3d 1352 (Fed. Cir. 1999), the court held that a method of generating records of long-distance phone calls was patentable under § 101 because it was a combination of mathematical algorithms applied to a specific useful purpose.

The limitation on patenting mathematical formulas and concepts is narrowly applied to preserve the patentability of useful processes that depend on formulas, because all sequential processes depend in some sense on an algorithm. This narrow application makes it possible to patent computers and computer programs. In general, novel and useful inventions created with scientific knowledge or application of abstract ideas are patentable.

The patentability of mathematical processes is a question of law decided under a two-step analysis: The court first determines whether a mathematical algorithm is recited directly or indirectly in the patent claim. If the claim constitutes a mathematical algorithm, the court then determines whether the claim is directed toward a mathematical algorithm that is not applied to or limited by physical elements or process steps. If the algorithm is merely presented and solved by the claimed invention, patent protection is impermissible. Essentially, a step-by-step mathematical process is not patentable, but an invention that combines mathematical formulas with other discrete elements is patentable. Without a particular practical application, manipulation of an abstract idea or mathematical problem is not patentable. For example, in *State Street Bank & Trust Co. v. Signature Financial Group, Inc.*, 149 F.3d 1368 (Fed. Cir. 1998), the Federal Circuit considered the patentability of computer software designed to manage mutual funds pooled in a single portfolio. The court focused on the "practical utility" of the software, holding that the program was eligible for patent protection because the software produced a "useful, concrete, and tangible result" expressed in numbers such as price, profit, percentage, cost, or loss.

ii. Machine

A machine is a physical object, consisting of parts or devices. A machine's operation distinguishes it from other machines, but the machine itself is more than the abstract principles it employs. In *Burr v. Duryee*, 68 U.S. 531 (1864), the Court held that a machine used to make fur hats was a patentable invention. However, the court noted that if the patent attempted to claim the idea underlying the machine—that is, the concept of separating fur fibers from a pelt and attaching them to a hat mold—then it would be invalid as claiming unpatentable abstract concepts. Another example of a machine is found in *Gould v. Schawlow*, 363 F.2d 908 (C.C.P.A. 1966), where the court ruled on which party had priority in a machine commonly known as a "laser." (See Figure 2-A.)

In *Corning v. Burden*, 56 U.S. 252 (1854), the Supreme Court discussed the difference between a machine and a process in determining whether the claimed invention, a device for purifying iron during manufacture, was for a process or a machine. The Court held that "machine" includes every me-

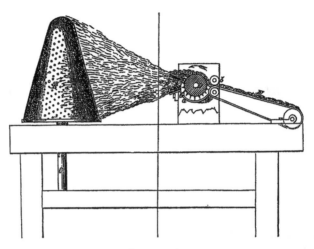

Figure 2-A
Burr v. Duryee, 68 U.S. 531 (1864). Fur hat making machine.

chanical device that performs a function and produces a result. If the result is produced by chemical action, however, it is a "process." As an example, the Court noted that one who discovers that combining rubber with certain salts at a certain temperature produces a better product would be entitled to a process patent, whereas one who invents an improved furnace that can efficiently carry out this process would be entitled to a patent for the machine. Additionally, the Court stated that a simple process (like iron being hammered) generally cannot be patented, but an improved machine that flattens iron generally can be.

iii. Manufacture

In *Diamond v. Chakrabarty*, 447 U.S. 303 (1980), the Supreme Court adopted the definition of manufacture as "the production of articles for use from raw or prepared materials by giving to these materials new forms, qualities, properties, or combinations, whether by hand-labor or by machinery." In *American Fruit Growers, Inc. v. Brogdex Co.*, 283 U.S. 1 (1931), the Court held that treating fruit with a borax solution to inhibit mold was not a patentable process because the fruit remained the same fruit and remained suitable for only the same purposes. In contrast, the applicant was entitled to patent cottonseeds treated with a gum product because the properties of the seeds — lint on the seeds that resisted flow — were transformed by the manufacture such that the treated seeds were capable of a smooth flow like that of corn or beans, which greatly increased their utility in the industry.

Following *Diamond v. Chakrabarty*, the Supreme Court in *J.E.M. Ag. Supply, Inc. v. Pioneer Hi-Bred International, Inc.*, 534 U.S. 124 (2001), held that utility patents could be awarded to genetically altered plants or seeds. The court concluded the *Chakrabarty* decision rested on the distinction between "products of nature whether living or not, and human made inventions" and thus plants containing human made inventions were eligible for utility patent protection.

iv. Composition of Matter

In *Diamond v. Chakrabarty*, 447 U.S. 303 (1980), the Supreme Court adopted the construction that a composition of matter includes "all compositions of two or more substances and … all composite articles, whether they be the results of chemical union, or of mechanical mixture, or whether they be gases, fluids, powders or solids." Patented compositions of matter are generally chemical compounds produced by chemists. Another example is found in *P. E. Sharpless Co. v. Crawford Farms, Inc.*, 287 F. 655 (2d Cir. 1923), where the court held that the process of combining cured and uncured cheeses to gain the physical qualities of one and the taste of the other was eligible for patenting as a composition of matter.

Compositions of matter require that some substance be combined with another. In *In re Nuijten*, 500 F.3d 1346 (Fed. Cir. 2007), the court held that variable electromagnetic signals, though useful, are not articles of matter but are instead fluctuations of electric potential. Therefore, the court determined that the process was not entitled to patent protection as a composition of matter.

c. Design Patents

Design patents, also called ornamental patents, are available for any "new, original and ornamental design for an article of manufacture" and have a fourteen year term. 35 U.S.C. § 171. Differences between the requirements for an ornamental patent and a utility patent are subtle, but significant. To be patentable, an ornamental design must be new, non-obvious, and original, as well as ornamental. 35 U.S.C. § 171. In *Barofsky v. General Electric Corp.*, 396 F.2d 340 (9th Cir. 1968), involving a challenge to a design patent for a television cabinet, the court observed that in order for a design patent to be valid, it must be:

(1) new,

(2) original,

(3) ornamental,

(4) non-obvious to a person of ordinary skill in the art, and

(5) not primarily for the purpose of serving a functional or utilitarian purpose.

The *Barofsky* court found that the cabinet was functional rather than ornamental and obvious in light of the prior art.

In the past, courts applied either the "ordinary intelligent person" or the "ordinary designer" standards in determining whether a design is obvious. For example, in *Schwinn Bicycle Co. v. Goodyear Tire & Rubber Co.*, 444 F.2d 295 (9th Cir. 1970), the court found that the slightly curved "banana-style" bicycle seat with a vertically disposed half-loop was sufficiently similar to earlier seat designs, which were slightly broader, flat, and had a horizontally disposed half-loop, as to be rendered obvious to the ordinarily intelligent person.

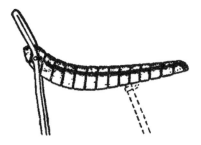

Figure 2-B
Schwinn Bicycle Co. v. Goodyear Tire & Rubber Co.,
444 F.2d 295 (9th Cir. 1970). Banana-style bicycle seat.

However, in *In re Nalbandian*, 661 F.2d 1214 (C.C.P.A. 1981), the predecessor court to the Federal Circuit noted that an ordinary person may have a "less discerning eye" than a trained designer, and that the ordinarily intelligent person standard made it easier to find invalidity. The *Nalbandian* court, recognizing the circuit split, elected to adopt the position of the Second, Third, Tenth, and D.C. Circuits, which required obviousness for design patents to be determined according to the ordinary designer standard. Although stating that the difference was basically semantics, the *Nalbandian* court found the ordinary designer standard to be more in line with the statute. Under this test, the *Nalbandian* court held that the designer's illuminated tweezers were rendered obvious by prior illuminated tweezers, and that the slight differences between the two—differing finger grips and straight rather than slightly curved pincers—

were *de minimis* modifications. The conflict regarding the appropriate standard for determining obviousness for design patents has not yet been conclusively resolved. This may not matter in practice, as courts will continue to find designs patentable or unpatentable according to their perceptions, regardless of the phraseology of the obviousness test.

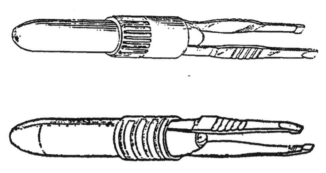

Figure 2-C
In re Nalbandian, 661 F.2d 1214 (C.C.P.A. 1981). Illuminated tweezers.

The application deadline for design patents is different than for other patents. Designers have only six months after filing a foreign patent application to apply for a United States design patent before the so-called "statutory bar"—a type of statute of limitations—forecloses patentability. In addition, non-provisional design patent applications do not relate back to the filing date of an earlier provisional application. The most conspicuous difference, however, is that designs may be protected for only fourteen years, rather than the usual twenty for utility patents.

d. Plant Patents

Plant patents are available for one who invents or discovers *and* asexually reproduces any new variety of plant. 35 U.S.C. § 161. Plant patents cannot cover tuber propagated plants and wild plants found in uncultivated areas. Tuber propagates like the potato and the Jerusalem artichoke were excluded because of their importance as basic food sources. As long as the plant is found in a cultivated area, it need not be the product of human work or intervention.

The basic requirements for patenting plants are slightly different than those for a utility patent. While an invention must be useful, novel, and non-obvious to be patentable, a plant need only be "distinct and novel" to be eligible for plant patent protection. Further, because the plant may be found in nature (as long as it is in a cultivated area), the novelty requirement is not as strict as that for a utility patent. Additionally, the patentee must asexually propagate the plant through cuttings or division rather than by seed. Otherwise, the patent provisions for other inventions apply in basically the same way to plant patents.

Characteristics that bear on whether a plant variety is "distinct" include habitat; immunity from disease; resistance to cold, drought, heat, wind, or soil conditions; color of flower, leaf, fruit, or stems; flavor; productivity, including ever-bearing qualities in the case of fruits; storage qualities; perfume; form; and ease of asexual reproduction. Patent protection is extended only to the direct, asexually produced progeny of the patented plant, and an infringement claim depends on a showing that the alleged infringement involved the asexual propagation of the patented plant's descendants — grafting, for instance, from patented stock — it is not enough that an allegedly infringing plant substantially resembles the patented plant. Thus, for example, in *Imazio Nursery, Inc. v. Dania Greenhouses*, 69 F.3d 1560 (Fed. Cir. 1995), which involved a new variety of *Heather persoluta* "particularly characterized by its profuse production of blooms over the entire length of the stem beginning in early December," a finding of infringement was reversed because a mere showing that the alleged infringing plant had the same essential characteristics does not prove lineage.

The Plant Variety Protection Act (PVPA) protects sexually reproduced or tuber propagate plants, but it is not actually a patent. The PVPA is administered by Department of Agriculture rather than the PTO. The eligibility requirements, found in 7 U.S.C. § 2402, are similar to that of a plant patent: the plant must be new, distinct, uniform and stable, and not sold in the United States more than one year before the filing. The PVPA allows the breeders of sexually reproduced plants to exclude others from selling, offering to sell, importing, exporting, or producing hybrids from their protected plant, 7 U.S.C. § 2483(a), and this protection lasts for twenty years from the date of issue (twenty five years for trees and vines), 7 U.S.C. § 2483(b).

New varieties of plants may also be eligible for a utility patent (rather than a plant patent) if they meet the more exacting standards required to patent a composition of matter. To obtain a utility patent, a plant breeder must show that the plant is novel, useful, and non-obvious and must also include a written description that satisfies § 112 as well as a deposit of seed that is publicly accessible. In *J.E.M. Ag Supply, Inc. v. Pioneer Hi-Bred International, Inc.*, 534 U.S. 124 (2001), the Supreme Court concluded that a sexually reproduced inbred and hybrid line of corn seed fell within the patentable subject matter of § 101 and was thus protectable by a utility patent not withstanding limitations found in the Plant Patent Act and the Plant Variety Protection Act.

e. Orphan Drug Act

Under the Orphan Drug Act, a manufacturer may receive a seven year exclusive license (which is not technically a patent) to manufacture medicine to treat a rare disease. 21 U.S.C. § 360cc(a)(2). A rare disease is one which affects fewer than 200,000 people in the United States or more than 200,000 people if there is no reasonable expectation that the cost of developing and marketing a drug for the disease can be recouped by United States sales. The purpose of the Orphan Drug Act is to encourage development of medicine to treat diseases that are so rare that it would not be profitable to develop drugs to treat them without this period of exclusivity.

4. Utility

The basic benefit of the patent monopoly contemplated in the Constitution and intended by Congress is the public benefit from an invention's substantial utility. To that end, § 101 of the Patent Code mandates that patents issue only to "useful" inventions. In reality, however, the utility requirement is rarely an obstacle to patentability. A finding of utility has long been held to require only a minimal showing that the invention is capable of practical application. The specifically claimed utility must also be "reduced to practice," a requirement intended to ensure that a patent does not "block off whole areas of scientific development" by asserting a claim that is too general.

For example, in *Brenner v. Manson*, 383 U.S. 519 (1966), the Court held invalid a patent that claimed a novel process for manufacturing a steroid with no known or likely useful application. Even though it worked—it produced the intended compound—and served as a catalyst for further research, the court concluded it lacked utility. In looking at the *quid pro quo* envisioned by Congress, the Court found this slight potential for future use to be an insufficient justification for permitting the patent applicant to close a whole field of research without providing anything useful to the public. The dissent, however, looked to the nature of chemistry and how it builds upon earlier discoveries; it would have found utility in the progression toward a commercially useful product, even if this particular invention itself lacked any practical application outside of further research.

To be patentable, an invention's utility must be more than purely speculative. The utility requirement is satisfied when an inventor has learned enough about the product to justify the conclusion that it is useful for a specific purpose. In *Estee Lauder Inc. v. L'Oreal, S.A.*, 129 F.3d 588 (Fed. Cir. 1997), which involved patents for sunscreen, the court found that positive test results were sufficient to show utility, but mere commencement of testing would not be.

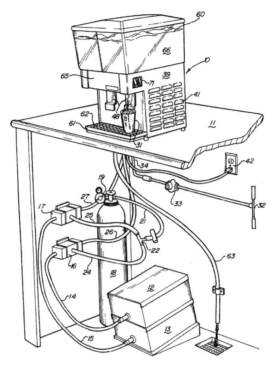

Figure 2-D
Juicy Whip, Inc. v. Orange Bang, Inc., 185 F.3d 1364 (Fed. Cir. 1999).
Deceptive beverage dispenser.

The required utility may be commercial rather than practical, and the fact that one product can be altered to make it look like another may itself be a specific benefit that satisfies the statutory utility requirement. For example, cubic zirconium simulates a diamond, imitation gold leaf imitates real gold leaf, and synthetic fabrics simulate expensive natural fabrics. In *Juicy Whip, Inc. v. Orange Bang, Inc.*, 185 F.3d 1364 (Fed. Cir. 1999), the court explicitly abandoned the rule that to be useful an invention must do more than make an article more salable. In *Juicy Whip*, the court recognized that the invention, a beverage dispenser, was deceptive, but that it still had utility within the meaning of the statute. The fact that the invention created the visual impression that it was a premix dispenser (while in actuality the beverage dispensed originated in a separate hidden postmix tank) provided utility in that it appeared more desirable to consumers and yet avoided commercial limitations by greatly increasing capacity and reducing the chance of bacterial contamination.

In order to be useful, the subject matter of the claim must be operable. This operability requirement is closely related to the § 112 enablement requirement. If the claim results in an impossibility then the invention as described is inoperable, not useful, and lacks enablement. Examples include perpetual motion machines and processes that prevent a person from aging. In *Process Control Corp. v. HydReclaim Corp.*, 190 F.3d 1350 (Fed. Cir. 1999), the invention measured the weight of individual ingredients entering a hopper and then measured the blend exiting the hopper to ensure consistent quantity and quality of the mixture. Proper construction of both claims indicated that the flow of ingredients leaving the hopper was different from the flow entering the hopper—a direct conflict with the law of conservation of matter, which states that matter can neither be created nor destroyed. Because of this impossibility, the court found that the claim was not operable, and that the invention therefore lacked utility. Consequently, the court held the patent invalid. (See Figure 2-E.)

5. Novelty

The novelty requirement requires that to qualify for a patent, an invention must differ from other inventions in the field known as "prior art." A patent for technology already known to the public would limit competition and raise prices on known devices and methods. Thus, the novelty requirement preserves information already in the public domain by preventing individuals from appropriating it for their exclusive benefit through a patent monopoly.

To avoid losing novelty, an inventor should avoid disclosing or selling the invention prior to filing her patent application. Although there is a one-year grace period in the United States between first disclosure or commercialization and the deadline for filing for a patent, this is not the case in most other nations and disclosure or commercialization prior to filing will bar patentability in those countries.

In determining whether an invention meets the novelty requirement, a patent examiner makes two distinct inquiries: First, the examiner determines which "references" (sources in the universe of available knowledge) are relevant to the novelty inquiry. The references are cumulatively known as "prior art." Second, the examiner determines whether the described invention is equivalent to any of the prior art. If the invention is equivalent to any reference, patent protection will be unavailable because the invention lacks novelty, but if the invention differs from the relevant prior art, the examiner will proceed

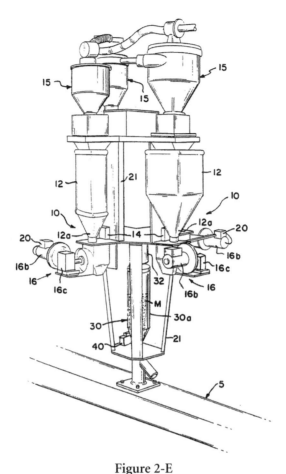

Figure 2-E
Process Control Corp. v. HydReclaim Corp., 190 F.3d 1350 (Fed. Cir. 1999).
Device to weigh ingredients entering and exiting a hopper.

under 35 U.S.C. §103(a) to determine whether the invention is obvious in light of the prior art.

Section 102 provides considerations relevant in determining whether a claimed invention is novel. Under 35 U.S.C. §102, a patent is to issue unless:

(a) the invention was known or used by others in this country, or patented or described in a printed publication, before the patent applicant invented it,

(b) the invention was patented or described in a printed publication or was in public use or on sale in this country, more than one year prior to the date of the application for patent in the United States,

(c) the patent applicant has abandoned the invention,

(d) the invention was patented by the applicant in a foreign country before applying for a patent in this country or an application for patent was filed more than twelve months before the filing of the application in the United States,

(e) if before the invention by the patent applicant, the invention was described in (1) another's published patent application before the invention by the patent applicant or (2) a patent granted to another,

(f) the patent applicant did not personally invent the subject matter sought to be patented, or

(g) (1) during the course of an interference proceeding, another inventor establishes that they invented it first and had not abandoned, suppressed, or concealed it, or (2) the invention was previously made in this country by another inventor who had not abandoned, suppressed, or concealed it.

The statute also specifies that courts determining priority under 35 U.S.C. § 102(g) consider (1) the respective dates of conception and reduction to practice of the inventions, and (2) whether the person who first conceived an invention exercised reasonable diligence in reducing the invention to practice.

The easiest way to analyze this section of the Patent Act is by dividing the seven subsections into two groups: subsections (a), (e), (f), and (g) specifically address novelty, and subsections (b), (c), and (d) address the "statutory bar." The primary difference between the two groups is that one regards events prior to the claimed invention, while the other concerns events prior to the patent application's filing.

The novelty provisions concern events that occurred prior to the date on which the applicant claims to have developed the claimed invention. Subsections (a) and (g) implement the first-to-invent rule by establishing that public knowledge of an earlier invention is prior art. Subsection (g) also serves as a basis for PTO priority contests known as "interferences." Interference proceedings are used to invalidate an existing patent for an invention first created by another inventor or to determine which inventor among several competing inventors is entitled to patent a particular invention. Section 102(e) disallows patent protection for inventions claimed in a previous patent or patent application. Section 102(f) specifies that a patent may not be issued to an applicant who did not invent the claimed subject matter.

The statutory bar provisions (subsections (b), (c), and (d)) address significant events that occurred prior to the patent application date. These provisions

encourage inventors to promptly apply for a patent for their inventions by pe-
nalizing inventors for undue delay. Section 102(b) is the most important and
most frequently invoked grounds for a statutory bar, as it requires inventors to
patent their inventions within one year of the invention's utilization in the United
States. Under § 102(b), the occurrence of certain activities (for example, sales of
the device described in the patent application or publication of written material
describing it) before the one-year critical date will bar the applicant from obtaining
a patent. This one-year period is often described as the "grace period."

Subsections (c) and (d) are straightforward and less frequently at issue.
Under § 102(c), abandonment of an invention by its inventor bars patentability. Subsection (d) bars issuance of a patent in the United States if a foreign patent
for the invention was issued over one year prior to the United States filing date.

An invention is novel unless the elements of a single earlier reference are
equivalent to all the elements of the challenged claim such that an expert could
produce the invention with knowledge only of the reference. This test is essentially the same for processes and products. The rationale behind this test is
to allow the public to utilize all prior art for technological development. To
that end, a patent should not be granted if it impedes the use of technology already available in the public domain.

"Anticipation" is a key concept in the novelty inquiry because an invention is
not eligible for patent protection if it has been "anticipated" by prior art. Whether
a reference is relevant as prior art is a question of law based on underlying factual determinations. If the prior art reference existed before the patent application was filed, it is presumed to defeat novelty; for purposes of the novelty
inquiry, the filing date is immaterial. However, the patent applicant or patent holder
can preserve novelty by proving that they reduced the invention to practice (or
conceived and diligently reduced to practice) before publication of the prior art,
or that they conceived of the invention prior to the publication and subsequent
to the publication they diligently reduced it to practice. Finally, knowledge of prior
art is presumed, and the inventor's actual awareness of prior art is irrelevant.

To bar patentability, relevant prior art must substantially anticipate the
claimed invention. There is no anticipation unless *all* of the elements in a
patent's claims are substantially identical to elements of a single prior art reference. For example, in *Canron, Inc. v. Plasser American Corp.*, 609 F.2d 1075
(4th Cir. 1979), the court held that printed publications disclosing all the elements of the patentee's lifting device used in railway tracks anticipated and therefore invalidated the patent. Complete anticipation is unnecessary, and if an
inferential step between the relevant prior art and the claimed invention would
be obvious to a skilled artisan, then the claimed invention has been anticipated
and is unpatentable. In *Deep Welding, Inc. v. Sciaky Bros., Inc.*, 417 F.2d 1227

(7th Cir. 1969), the court held that "anticipation may be found where achieving complete anticipation only required that one of ordinary skill in the art merely exercised that skill to complete the work." The court determined that the patent for an electron beam welding technique was anticipated by papers presented at a conference that described it sufficiently well that an expert could take the last step to produce the invention even though the publications did not amount to complete anticipation. In the ovular case of *Peters v. Active Manufacturing Co.*, 129 U.S. 530 (1889), an alleged infringer successfully defended itself by producing evidence of an unpatented device for attaching sheet metal moldings that predated, and met all the limitations of, the claims described in the plaintiff's patent application. Noting that the plaintiff would be infringing had the earlier device been patented, the court dismissed the complaint, holding that "[t]hat which infringes, if later, would anticipate, if earlier."

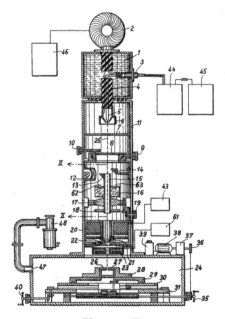

Figure 2-F
Deep Welding, Inc. v. Sciaky Bros., Inc.
417 F.2d 1227 (7th Cir. 1969). Electron beam welder.

Even substantially identical prior art will not anticipate a claimed invention if the qualities or characteristics claimed to be novel in the invention were not realized by the inventors or users of the prior art. In *Eibel Process Co. v. Minnesota & Ontario Paper Co.*, 261 U.S. 45 (1923), the patentee improved a papermaking machine by increasing the pitch or slope of a wire. Raising the pitch from three inches to twelve inches enabled paper to be produced twenty percent faster and without any reduction of quality. In retrospect, the improvement seemed to be a minimal step beyond the prior art, but the Court found that the improvement was novel as evidenced by paper manufacturers' initial reluctance to take the risk though eventually nearly all adopted the improvement. Put simply, prior art with an unrealized benefit does not constitute anticipation.

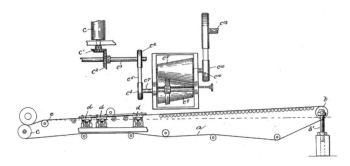

Figure 2-G
Eibel Process Co. v. Minnesota & Ontario Paper Co.
261 U.S. 45 (1923). Papermaking machine.

However, where the prior art was known and understood, although not appreciated or applied, it anticipates the claimed invention and undermines its patentability. Otherwise, it would be possible to patent a new use for an unchanged process; this is not permitted. For example, in *Research Corp. v. NASCO Industries, Inc.*, 501 F.2d 358 (7th Cir. 1974), the court invalidated a patent for a method of branding animals with a super-cooled material (such as dry ice or liquid nitrogen) because previously published articles had already discussed, and therefore anticipated, that the application of a super-cooled substance freezes pigmentation cells, causing hair to grow back without color. Although the patentee used this information for a specific purpose that was not disclosed in the articles, the court held that this method of branding was not a new invention.

Likewise, in *H.K. Regar & Sons, Inc. v. Scott & Williams, Inc.*, 63 F.2d 229 (2d Cir. 1933), the plaintiffs sued for infringement of their patented method for stitching a scalloped seam at the top of women's stockings. The court held the plaintiffs' patent invalid, noting that the stitching technique was not novel when patented, and concluded that "[i]f later, women came to prize a scalloped edge, it was not possible to monopolize it by claiming as an invention the discovery that they prized it." *H.K. Regar* remains good law and serves to illustrate this basic principle of novelty: patents protect new inventions, not new uses for old technology.

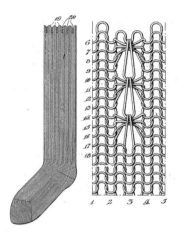

Figure 2-H
H.K. Regar & Sons, Inc. v. Scott & Williams, Inc.
63 F.2d 229 (2d Cir. 1933). Stocking with scalloped seam.

Abandonment, suppression, or concealment of an invention will also preclude patent protection of that invention. 35 U.S.C. § 102(g). Likewise, where an invention would otherwise anticipate some later invention, abandonment, suppression, or concealment by the first inventor will not bar a subsequent inventor from obtaining a patent on the grounds of lack of novelty. 35 U.S.C. § 102(g). Inventors may also forfeit their right to a patent by unreasonably postponing their patent application or attempting to conceal improvements from the public.

a. Statutory Bar

The statutory bar of 35 U.S.C. § 102 ensures that a patent will not issue if, more than twelve months before the patent application is filed with the PTO, the subject invention was (1) patented, (2) described in a printed publication, (3) publicly used in the United States, or (4) sold in the United States. 35 U.S.C. § 102(b). An invention is also statutorily unpatentable if a patent application was filed in a foreign jurisdiction more than twelve months before an application is filed with the PTO. 35 U.S.C. § 102(d).

The "critical date" is set at twelve months prior to the date of the patent application. The statutory bar is triggered if any prohibited activity occurs before this critical date. For purposes of the statutory bar, it is irrelevant whether the prior prohibited activity was authorized by the inventor. In other words, an inventor who is the victim of piracy is in the same position as one who has permitted the use of his process.

i. Publication Bar

The bar against patenting an invention disclosed by printed publication was designed to prevent an inventor from patenting an invention already in the public domain. "Publication" sufficient to trigger the statutory bar is minimal. The inquiry turns on whether a perceptible description of the invention was available to the "pertinent part of the public" more than twelve months before the application was submitted. In *In re Wyer*, 655 F.2d 221 (C.C.P.A. 1981), a patentee filed for a patent in Australia over a year before filing in the United States. Because the Australian Patent Office published the application and copies were available upon request, the court invoked the statutory bar to block patentability.

Claims disclosed in an earlier patent application (whether foreign or domestic) do not trigger the statutory bar unless (1) they share "substantial identity" with the claims disclosed in the earlier application and (2) the "new" invention is substantially the same invention as the old one described in the prior application.

A patent or patent application published in a foreign country may qualify as a "printed publication" within the meaning of § 102, but foreign patents are construed more strictly than domestic patents in determining anticipation. For example, in *National Latex Products Co. v. Sun Rubber Co.*, 274 F.2d 224 (6th Cir. 1960), the court refused to invalidate a patented process to mold hollow articles (such as toys) from vinyl plastisols under the statutory bar because the Italian patent that preceded the patent at issue was vague.

ii. Public Use Bar

The critical date and statutory bar encourage prompt filing of patent applications so that delay cannot be used to artificially extend a monopoly on an invention. The public use bar to patentability is triggered if an invention was used "publicly" prior to the critical date. The bar is triggered if the invention is used publicly by anyone—the inventor, their agent, or even an unauthorized third party—prior to the critical date. The use does not have to be broad or even overt; a single use of an invention for commercial purposes is enough. In other words, a commercial use is considered a public use, even if the use is kept secret.

The public use prior references must be enabling (i.e., it must allow others to make the invention), thereby placing the allegedly disclosed matter in the public domain. In *In re Epstein*, 32 F.3d 1559 (Fed. Cir. 1994), the court rejected patent claims for software designed to simplify the purchase of electronic parts because abstracts of the software submitted to the PTO listed "release" or "first installed" dates of more than one year before the patent application.

iii. On Sale Bar

The statutory bar is also triggered if the invention is sold or merely offered for sale by anyone (whether the inventor, their agent, or an unauthorized third party) prior to the critical date. Even free distribution of a prototype may raise the on-sale bar if the distribution is intended to solicit a sale. In *Pfaff v. Wells Electronics, Inc.*, 525 U.S. 55, 56 (1998), the Supreme Court concluded that:

> [T]he on-sale bar applies when two conditions are satisfied before the critical date. First, the product must be the subject of a commercial offer for sale.... Second, the invention must be ready for patenting. That condition may be satisfied in at least two ways: by proof of reduction to practice before the critical date; or by proof that prior to the critical date the inventor had prepared drawings or other descriptions of the invention that were sufficiently specific to enable a person skilled in the art to practice the invention.

In *Pfaff*, the patent for a computer chip socket was held invalid because the patentee accepted an order for sale and provided the manufacturer with detailed drawings sufficient to produce the invention before the critical date. The fact that the invention had not yet been reduced to practice was irrelevant because reduction to practice is not required to file a patent application. The invention, in patentable form, was sold more than a year before the patent application; therefore, the patent was invalid.

Whether a communication amounts to an offer to sell rests on the inventor's "present intent to sell" once the invention has been reduced to practice. If the circumstances show that the inventor intended to sell the invention in patentable form and prior to the critical date, the statutory bar is triggered, regardless of whether the sale was actually consummated.

What is sold (or offered for sale) must disclose and also *embody* the claimed invention in order to trigger the statutory bar. In *J.A. LaPorte, Inc. v. Norfolk Dredging Co.*, 787 F.2d 1577, 1583 (Fed. Cir. 1986), which involved a patent for cutter head extensions for hydraulic dredges, the court held that "the question is not whether the sale, even a third party sale, 'discloses' the invention at the time of the sale, but whether the sale relates to a device that *embodies* the invention."

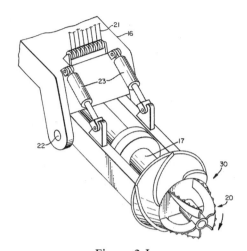

Figure 2-I
J.A. LaPorte, Inc. v. Norfolk Dredging Co.
787 F.2d 1577 (Fed. Cir. 1986). Cutter head extensions for hydraulic dredges.

The court will also consider whether the sale was intended to generate resources necessary for further testing because an inventor with limited means
should be able to test and refine the invention before filing for a patent, even if
that requires selling an interest in the invention. However, to maintain the experimental nature of the sale, the inventor must retain control over further sale
of the invention.

iv. Experimental Use Exception

A use that might otherwise constitute public use may be excused from the
statutory bar where its purpose is experimental and intended to enable the inventor to further refine his invention. However, the use must be *primarily*
experimental, however, not commercial. In *Baxter International, Inc. v. COBE
Laboratories, Inc.*, 88 F.3d 1054 (Fed. Cir. 1996), the court held that "[e]xper-
imental use negates public use; when proved, it may show that particular
acts, even if apparently public in a colloquial sense, do not constitute a public use within the meaning of section 102." *Baxter* involved a patent for a seal-
less centrifuge used to separate blood. The centrifuge had been used by a
third party—allegedly experimentally—to determine if it was useful to him,
more than one year prior to the date of the patent application. The *Baxter* court
held this use to be a primarily commercial, public use rather than an experimental use and invalidated the patent. The use must be primarily—but not
solely—experimental in order to be excused. This is a question of law, and

a court will consider the following factors in determining whether a use is primarily experimental:

- The length of the test period;

- Whether the inventor received payment for the testing;

- Any agreement by the user to maintain confidentiality;

- Any records of testing;

- Whether persons other than the inventor performed the testing;

- The number of tests; and

- The length of the test period in relation to tests of similar devices.

In *City of Elizabeth v. American Nicholson Pavement Co.*, 97 U.S. 126 (1878), the Supreme Court held that the inventor of an improved roadway surface did not abandon the invention to the public, even though the invention was exposed to the public before the critical date, because he installed it at his own expense, checked its status each day by observing it and poking it with his cane, and at no point let his invention out of his control. The inventor did not allow the city to install the roadway elsewhere, made no attempt to sell his invention, and did nothing to indicate that he intended to abandon the invention to the public domain. Rather, the Court held that the inventor had simply tested his invention in the only practical way: by installing a roadway in a high traffic area and repeatedly checking its durability.

In *Pickering v. Holman*, 459 F.2d 403 (9th Cir. 1972), a patent for a plastic blinker light used as a traffic warning device was invalidated because the claimed invention had been described in detail in a printed publication, and thus published prior to the critical date. The inventor unsuccessfully argued to extend the experimental use exception, but the court held that the experimental use exception is a part of the public use or sale doctrine and does not apply to publications. Publication places the invention in the public domain, and the public should be secure in their expectations that the invention may be freely used if not patented within a short time. (See Figure 2-J.)

Even an actual sale prior to the critical date will not trigger the statutory bar if the primary purpose of the sale was experimental and the end of the sale was to determine whether the invention could be improved, or reduced to operable, manufacturable, or useful form. A court will consider the same factors used to determine whether a public use was for experimentation in determining whether a sale was "primarily" experimental. In *In re Brigance*, 792 F.2d

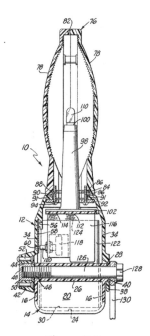

Figure 2-J
Pickering v. Holman, 459 F.2d 403 (9th Cir. 1972).
Plastic blinker light used as a traffic warning device.

1103 (Fed. Cir. 1986), the court considered whether a student testing and eval-uation method had been in public use more than one year before the patent application was filed. The court found that there had been a public, non-ex-perimental sale prior to one year before filing the application and held the patent invalid.

b. Abandonment

Whether an inventor has abandoned his claim is a question of law decided in consideration of equitable principles and public policy. Abandonment turns on the intent of the inventor, either as declared or implied from conduct in-consistent with an intention to claim a patent, and must be proven by clear and convincing evidence by the party challenging the patent. For example, in *Davis Harvester Co. v. Long Manufacturing Co.,* 252 F. Supp. 989 (E.D.N.C. 1966), the court invalidated several patents related to roller-clips used by a to-bacco harvester on alternative grounds: either Davis's patented device was in-vented by Long or, if Davis was the inventor, he abandoned it. Davis and Long developed several methods to move the tobacco leaves while harvesting, and the method Davis eventually patented was seemingly designed by Long. The court found that Long invented the roller-clips, but held that even if Davis had invented the roller-clips the patent would still be invalid because Davis completely abandoned the design for several years before claiming it as his patent. Davis had openly ridiculed the roller-clips, claiming they were incompatible with and inferior to his automated process. Davis had pursued other attempts at a similar invention, and his first patent did not include the roller-clips. After it became apparent (through Long's efforts) that roller-clips were commercially viable, Davis attempted to include them in his patent. The court held that Davis—if he was the inventor—had waited too late, and the patent was invalidated partially due to abandonment.

Inventors are typically presumed to have abandoned any aspect of their invention disclosed, but not claimed, in a patent or patent application. For example, in *PSC Computer Products, Inc. v. Foxconn International, Inc.*, 355 F.3d 1353 (Fed. Cir. 2004), the plaintiff patented clips used to secure a heat sink to microchips. The patentee disclosed plastic and molded metal clips in the patent application, as part of the prior art, but the patent claim was drafted narrowly to include only metal clips. The court held that by failing to claim the plastic clips, the patentee had abandoned any claim to plastic clips.

c. Suppression or Concealment

Inventors may forfeit patent rights if they fail to prosecute the patent application in a timely manner. In *Young v. Dworkin*, 489 F.2d 1277 (C.C.P.A. 1974), the inventor of a method to produce collapsible envelopes failed in their interference challenge—even though they invented and reduced to practice prior to the patentee—because they delayed filing a patent application for several years while upgrading their manufacturing equipment to produce the envelopes. The court acknowledged that delays due to testing and perfecting the invention are acceptable, but held that delays for commercial reasons not directly impacting the invention are unacceptable suppressions.

The requirement that inventors diligently and promptly pursue their right to a patent is founded on the theory that "inaction unduly postpones the time when the public would be entitled to the free use of the invention and thus defeats the policy of the patent law." In *Monsanto Co. v. Rohm & Haas Co.*, 312 F. Supp. 778 (E.D. Pa. 1970), the court invalidated a patent for a chemical used in herbicides for several reasons, including a twelve year gap between the time of invention and the patent application. Inventors who elect not to disclose their invention while waiting for a favorable commercial climate are particularly susceptible to a finding of suppression or concealment. For example, in *Woofter v. Carlson,* 367 F.2d 436 (C.C.P.A. 1966), the patent applicant lost priority for its improved electrical connector because it concealed the invention during a consumer downturn, awaiting an economic environment in which the patent would be more profitable.

Delay between completion of the invention and subsequent public disclosure is excusable if for a reasonable length of time under the circumstances. For example, in *Checkpoint Systems, Inc. v. United States International Trade Commission,* 54 F.3d 756 (Fed. Cir. 1995), a delay of four years after the invention of an anti-shoplifting device was first reduced to practice was not considered suppression because the time was used to develop necessary ancillary components (including a means of deactivation and a detection system) without which the invention was commercially useless.

d. Priority

Under the American first-to-invent rule, the inventor who is first to conceive of and reduce an invention to practice is generally awarded priority of invention. "Conception" is the formation of a definite and permanent idea of the complete and operative invention as the invention will be applied in practice. An idea need not be certain to work (which would amount to reduction to practice) but a general goal or research plan the inventor hopes to pursue is insufficient to constitute conception. The idea should be definite enough that it can be reduced to practice by applying ordinary skill and without extensive research or experimentation. In *Burroughs Wellcome Co. v. Barr Laboratories, Inc.,* 40 F.3d 1223 (Fed. Cir. 1994), the inventors conceived of certain drugs to treat HIV and then collaborated with another set of inventors to test the drugs. Six patents were granted as a result of their collaboration efforts. Some of the patents were granted solely to the first inventors because they had completed the conception phase, but the other patents were granted to all of the inventors because the tests yielded unexpected results that led to the conception of the methods used in the other patents, which were not even conceived prior to the testing.

To establish reduction to practice, an inventor must generally produce a prototype of the invention that meets all the limitations of the claim. At a minimum, the filing of a patent application serves as a constructive reduction to practice. Likewise, publication of a document that discloses the invention such that one skilled in the art could reproduce it may be considered a reduction to practice. For example, in *Bergstrom v. Tomlinson,* 220 F.2d 766 (C.C.P.A. 1955), a Swedish patent application served as evidence that a junior patent applicant had reduced the invention to practice prior to the United States patent application.

Under 35 U.S.C. § 102(g), priority of invention depends on both (1) the respective dates of conception and reduction to practice of the invention, and (2) the reasonable diligence of an inventor who was first to conceive and last to reduce to practice. If diligent, the first inventor to conceive of an invention, rather than the first to reduce it to practice, can establish priority of invention.

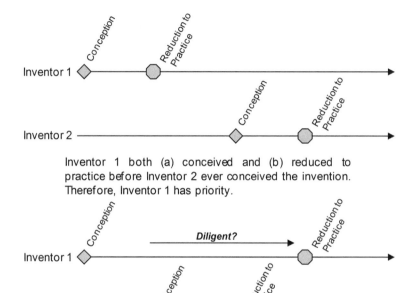

Inventor 1 both (a) conceived and (b) reduced to practice before Inventor 2 ever conceived the invention. Therefore, Inventor 1 has priority.

Here, Inventor 1 still has priority unless Inventor 1 failed to exercise reasonable diligence between the time Inventor 2 conceived and the time Inventor 1 reduced the invention to practice.

Figure 2-K
Priority of Invention under 35 U.S.C. § 102(g)

In *Cooper v. Goldfarb*, 154 F.3d 1321 (Fed. Cir. 1998), the Federal Circuit considered that situation: one inventor first conceived of an artificial vascular graft, but another inventor first reduced it to practice. The court remanded the case to the district court to determine if the junior inventor was acting on behalf of the senior inventor. The court held that if the junior inventor had not acted on behalf of the senior inventor, the senior inventor did not exercise proper diligence between conception and the eventual reduction to practice, in which case priority would be awarded to the junior inventor. Priority of invention, therefore, is awarded to the inventors who first reduce their invention to practice unless another inventor can show either (1) that they in fact conceived first and exercised reasonable diligence in later reducing that invention to practice or (2) that the first party to reduce to practice abandoned, suppressed or concealed the invention. Determinations of priority, conception, and reduction to practice are questions of law based on underlying facts, but diligence is a question of fact.

6. Non-Obviousness

Under § 103(a) of the Patent Act, an invention is not patentable:

> [I]f the differences between the subject matter sought to be patented and the prior art are such that the subject matter as a whole would have been obvious at the time the invention was made to a person having ordinary skill in the art to which said subject matter pertains.

The non-obviousness requirement is the most significant hurdle to obtaining a patent. It allows the PTO to deny a patent and the courts to invalidate a patent even if the claimed invention has never been made or the claimed process has not previously been performed. Section 103(a) requires courts and PTO examiners to decide whether an inventor's work product differs enough from the prior art to be patentable.

According to § 103(a), patentability is not affected by the manner in which the invention was made. In *Graham v. John Deere Co.*, 383 U.S. 1 (1966), the Supreme Court abolished the controversial "flash of creative genius" test, which was often previously used to test for obviousness. Accidental discoveries may yield non-obvious inventions, and unexpected beneficial results are evidence of non-obviousness. Presently, no weight is given to whether the claimed invention was derived at by experimentation rather than inventive genius. For example, in *Carter-Wallace, Inc. v. Gillette Co.*, 675 F.2d 10 (1st Cir. 1982), the court upheld a patented aerosol antiperspirant even though the claimed invention was the result of routine experimentation, which could have led any expert to the same results, rather than "inventive genius."

a. Primary Considerations

To evaluate the non-obviousness of an invention, courts and PTO examiners apply a three step analysis similar to the novelty inquiry:

(1) identify the relevant prior art;

(2) ascertain the differences between the prior art and the claims at issue; and

(3) resolve the level of ordinary skill in the art.

The standard for determining non-obviousness is the knowledge possessed by one with ordinary skill in the art, *i.e.*, a scientist or engineer in the relevant field. Secondary considerations such as commercial success, long felt but unsolved needs, and the failure of others are also relevant to the obviousness inquiry.

The patent examiner bears the burden of establishing a *prima facie* case of obviousness if denying a patent application for non-obviousness. In *In re Deuel*, 51 F.3d 1552 (Fed. Cir. 1995), the court reversed a rejection of claims on specific DNA sequences used in cell division and cell repair because the examiner's argument that similar genetic cloning was prior art failed to establish a *prima facie* case of obviousness for this specific set of genes. Issued patents are presumed valid, and any challenger bears the burden of proving the invention's obviousness by clear and convincing evidence. In *Vandenberg v. Dairy Equipment Co.*, 740 F.2d 1560 (Fed. Cir. 1984), the first and third claims on a radial arm hose support used for milking cows were invalidated as obvious, but the challenger could not overcome the presumptive validity as to the second claim, so the district court's order invalidating the entire patent was reversed as to the second claim.

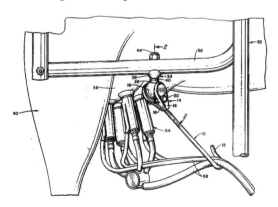

Figure 2-L
Vandenberg v. Dairy Equipment Co., 740 F.2d 1560 (Fed. Cir. 1984).
Radial arm support for hose used in milking cows.

Prior art relevant in determining an invention's non-obviousness will usually be the same as prior art relevant to the question of its novelty. However, several prior art references may be combined to show obviousness if the inventor combined the prior art references with a reasonable expectation that the combination would succeed. In *In re Rouffet*, 149 F.3d 1350 (Fed. Cir. 1998), the court reversed a finding of obviousness regarding a patent for a satellite network that used an elliptical-shaped footprint, which significantly reduced the number of "handovers" as the signal moved from one satellite to another. The lower court found that the invention was a combination of prior art that, when viewed together by someone highly skilled in the art, would have been obvious, but the lower court failed to show a motivation to combine the references and misapplied the requisite skill of the ordinary artisan. The fact that—in hind-sight—each aspect of the invention was present in other patents does not defeat the new invention unless the examiner shows that there was some motivation to combine the references that would have been apparent to one with ordinary skill in the art.

Under certain circumstances, it may be appropriate to use a hindsight analysis, however. For example, in *KSR International Co. v. Teleflex Inc.*, 127 S. Ct. 1727 (2007), a patent claimed an invention that solved a problem affecting the durability of electronic car-pedal assemblies that reassembled similar electronic car-throttle assemblies. The Federal Circuit held that the invention was not obvious because there was insufficient evidence that the pedal-related references motivated the inventor to combine the prior art references. The Supreme Court reversed, holding that the strong market incentive to develop workable electronic car-pedal assemblies made it inevitable that a skilled artisan would eventually look to the throttle technology, recognize the relevant reference, and develop the combination claimed by the patentee. (See Figure 2-M.)

Essentially an invention is unpatentably obvious where differences between the invention and the prior art are such that the invention would have been obvious at the time the invention was made to a person having ordinary skill in the art. However, an analysis based upon intuition is inappropriate, and the complexity of an invention does not necessarily affect obviousness. In *Roberts v. Sears, Roebuck & Co.*, 723 F.2d 1324 (7th Cir. 1983), the court remanded a finding of obviousness on a quick release socket wrench, reminding the lower court that the non-obviousness inquiry should not be distorted by hindsight. (See Figure 2-N.)

Inventors are presumed to have knowledge of all relevant prior art, both in their field and in all "reasonably pertinent" fields. For example, in *In re Wood*, 599 F.2d 1032 (C.C.P.A. 1979), the court held that the PTO had satisfied its

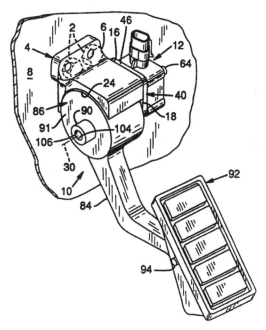

Figure 2-M
KSR International Co. v. Teleflex Inc.
127 S. Ct. 1727 (2007). Electronic car-pedal assembly.

burden of proof in rejecting an applicant's claimed invention (a sonic "venturi" carburetor) as obvious in light of prior art in the field of subsonic carburetors. Despite the applicant's argument that sonic and subsonic carburetors are not analogous technologies, the court found that the technologies were "reasonably

Figure 2-N
Roberts v. Sears, Roebuck & Co.
723 F.2d 1324 (7th Cir. 1983). Quick release socket wrench.

pertinent" to each other, and therefore relevant in determining the claimed invention's obviousness.

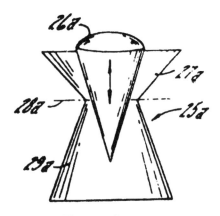

Figure 2-O
In re Wood
599 F.2d 1032 (C.C.P.A. 1979). Sonic venturi carburetor.

In comparing an invention to relevant prior art, the legal issue is not the obviousness of differences between the invention and the prior art, but the obviousness of the invention as a whole. For example, in *In re Schnell*, 370 F.2d 596 (C.C.P.A. 1967), a patent application for a new type of dentures was rejected as obvious because it used a known material and merely substituted one moldable thermoplastic material for another. The court held that, viewed as a whole, the entire invention was obvious.

In *Alexander Milburn Co. v. Davis-Bournonville Co.*, 270 U.S. 390 (1926), the Court held that an unclaimed disclosure in a patent application constitutes a constructive reduction to practice. The patent holder's claim for infringement failed because an earlier inventor published, but did not claim, the improved welding and cutting apparatus supposedly invented by the plaintiff. An unpublished, pending application therefore qualifies as prior art under § 102(g), and its disclosure renders later invention obvious under § 103. "Secret" prior art sufficient to undermine novelty under § 102(f) is also relevant to the obviousness inquiry. For example, in *OddzOn Products, Inc. v. Just Toys, Inc.*, 122 F.3d 1396 (Fed. Cir. 1997), the court held that confidential designs owned by a third party were part of the prior art to be considered when a patent for a specialty football was challenged. (See Figure 2-P.)

The scope of relevant prior art is determined based on the nature of the invention and the knowledge that a skilled person in the field would be expected

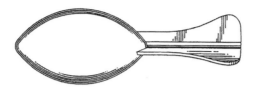

Figure 2-P
OddzOn Products, Inc. v. Just Toys, Inc.
122 F.3d 1396 (Fed. Cir. 1997). Specialty football.

to have. For example, in *Ryko Manufacturing Co. v. Nu-Star, Inc.*, 950 F.2d 714 (Fed. Cir. 1991), the court held that the prior art relevant in evaluating the obviousness of a keypad-operated carwash activation device (which was designed to replace a "mechanical insertion device") did not encompass all "car washing systems" technology in general, but only activation devices for such systems, including keypad technology garage-door openers. Therefore, prior art from analogous fields that may "by reason of that relation and similarity make an appeal to the mind" of the inventor may also be relevant. However, the more distant the prior art is from the patent's subject matter, the less persuasive or relevant it is. If inventors combine knowledge from multiple widely diverse fields, their inventions will likely survive the obviousness inquiry.

Slight structural variation from prior art may yield a novel result. An invention should be evaluated not only by the degree of change from a prior art reference but also by the purpose of the invention. Consider *Schering Corp. v. Gilbert*, 153 F.2d 428 (2d Cir. 1946), which involved a patented chemical compound used to dye gall bladder stones. Although the chemical was only a modest improvement over the prior art, its ability to illuminate only the gall bladder without harmful side effects that were common to previous dyes was sufficiently novel to render the chemical patentable.

To determine the level of ordinary skill in the art, as stated in *Environmental Designs, Ltd. v. Union Oil Co. of California*, 713 F.2d 693 (Fed. Cir. 1983), the court may consider factors including:

(1) the educational level of the inventor;

(2) the type of problems encountered in the art;

(3) the prior art solutions to those problems;

(4) the rapidity with which innovations are made;

(5) the sophistication of the technology; and

(6) the educational level of active workers in the field.

In *Standard Oil Co. v. American Cyanamid Co.*, 774 F.2d 448 (Fed. Cir. 1985), the court emphasized that ordinary skill in the art is measured by a hypothetical artisan with knowledge of all prior art; the inventor's actual knowledge is irrelevant. In *Standard Oil*, the court invalidated a claimed catalytic process used primarily to manufacture acrylamide because it was obvious: prior art suggested to those of ordinary skill in the art that copper would be an effective catalyst. In addition, hypothetical artisans interpret prior art in light of conventional wisdom; they do not operate with the drive of innovators.

For design patents, the hypothetical standard is that of the "ordinary designer." The ordinary designer differs from an ordinary person because their specialized knowledge brings more prior art into consideration. In *In re Rosen*, 673 F.2d 388 (C.C.P.A. 1982), a coffee table design that appeared to be a combination of prior art was nonetheless held non-obvious because each prior art reference had a slightly different design and appearance that gave them slightly different aesthetic appeal. The obviousness determination is not simply a regrouping of prior art; it involves analyzing primary references to determine what modifications would have been obvious given knowledge of the prior art.

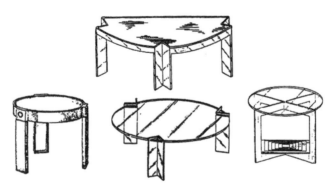

Figure 2-Q
In re Rosen, 673 F.2d 388 (C.C.P.A. 1982).
Coffee table design and prior art references.

On the other hand, in *Schwinn Bicycle v. Goodyear Tire & Rubber Co.*, 444 F. 2d 295 (9th Cir. 1970), discussed earlier, the court determined that Schwinn's popular "banana seat" was obvious to the ordinary intelligent person given earlier seat designs.

b. Secondary Considerations

In *Graham v. John Deere Co.*, 383 U.S. 1 (1966), the Supreme Court stated that secondary considerations such as "commercial success, long felt but unsolved needs, failure of others, etc.," may be relevant as "indicia of obviousness or non-obviousness...." There, a modification to a device designed to absorb shock from plow shanks was insufficient to overcome the non-obviousness requirements because it had the same claims as the prior art except for one significant difference, which the Court held was obvious to those skilled in the art. Since then, some courts have concluded that these considerations, while not dispositive, are a necessary inquiry.

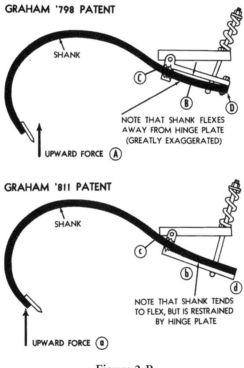

Figure 2-R
Graham v. John Deere Co.
383 U.S. 1 (1966). Plow shanks.

Other courts treat these secondary considerations as merely relevant. In *Ryko Manufacturing Co. v. Nu-Star, Inc.*, 950 F.2d 714 (Fed. Cir. 1991), the *Graham* considerations weighed in favor of non-obviousness, but were not enough to overcome the obvious combination of a keypad signal device used in electronic garage door openers with a carwash coin-activation system which were used to create the electronic keypad carwash activation system claimed by the patentee. Similarly, in *American Seating Co. v. National Seating Co.*, 586 F.2d 611 (6th Cir. 1978), which involved a patent for the base for seats used on passenger buses, the court held that the trial court's failure to account for secondary considerations was not reversible error and that "secondary factors may tip the scales toward patent validity, [but] they cannot save a patent [where] obviousness is clear." The court held that the inverted "T"-shaped base claimed in the patent was anticipated by a round base and that the inverted "T" design was an obvious adaptation.

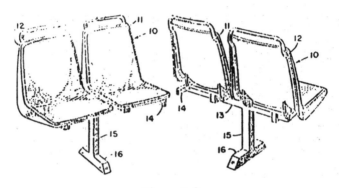

Figure 2-S
American Seating Co. v. National Seating Co., 586 F.2d 611 (6th Cir. 1978).
Bus seats with an inverted "T"-shaped base.

In *Environmental Designs, Ltd. v. Union Oil Co. of California*, 713 F.2d 693 (Fed. Cir. 1983), a patent for a process to remove sulfur from emissions was found valid and non-obvious, even though it was only a creative application of known chemical reactions and equations. The court concluded that secondary factors in the case—particularly the long-felt industrial need for the process and the disbelief of experts in the field regarding the viability of the process—overcame the apparent simplicity of the innovation and concluded that the invention was not obvious.

Courts give little weight to secondary factors that do not directly relate to the patent claims. For example, in *In re Vamco Machine and Tool, Inc.*, 752 F.2d 1564 (Fed. Cir. 1985), the court held that the commercial success of a product that barely resembled the patent claims was not a significant secondary consideration in the obviousness test. In *In re Vamco*, the self-contained feed roll for power punch presses was considered obvious in light of the prior art, and the secondary consideration of the power punch press's commercial success was not pertinent because the success was not significantly due to the self-contained feed roll. .

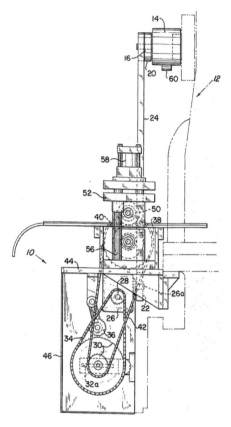

Figure 2-T
In re Vamco Machine and Tool, Inc., 752 F.2d 1564 (Fed. Cir. 1985).
Self-contained feed roll for power punch presses.

c. Synergism

Some courts have held that "synergism" is a prerequisite to patentability for inventions that simply combine obvious elements. Synergism is achieved when the combination of known elements as a whole exceeds the sum of its parts. For example, in *Bishman Manufacturing Co. v. Stewart-Warner Corp.*, 380 F.2d 336 (7th Cir. 1967), the patented invention consisted of an assembly of four prior art devices. The invention indicated the "light spot" on a car tire, allowing the tire to be balanced while remaining on its axle. The court upheld the patent, reasoning that although the elements of the assembly had been known, the combination claimed by the patent was novel and achieved a result that could not have been anticipated by others skilled in the art. In *Smith v. ACME General Corp.*, 614 F.2d 1086 (6th Cir. 1980), the court invalidated a patent for the bottom pivot assembly of a folding door that was merely a new combination of old elements. The court held that although that assembly was a good idea, it lacked the synergism required to overcome its obviousness to those skilled in the art.

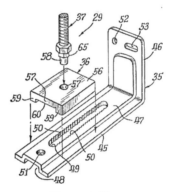

Figure 2-U
Smith v. ACME General Corp.
614 F.2d 1086 (6th Cir. 1980). Pivot assembly for a folding door.

Some courts have rejected a separate requirement of synergism, holding that the requirement is inconsistent with the non-obvious standard set forth in § 103 and is not a proper test to measure the patentability of combination inventions. In *Sarkisian v. Winn-Proof Corp.*, 686 F.2d 671 (9th Cir. 1981), which involved the design of a wind-resistant, light-weight road sign, the court rejected the notion that "synergism" is distinct from non-obviousness in general. The *Sarkisian* sign, although it used pre-existing elements, combined elements in a non-obvious manner to complete its windproof design.

7. Property Interest in Patents

The inventor or assignee named in the patent instrument is the initial owner. Where more than one inventor is named, each owns an undivided interest in the patent and each joint owner may exploit the patent without the consent of any other owner. However, courts have held that a joint owner of a patent must obtain permission from all other owners before commencing a patent infringement suit.

Patentees may assign (i.e., sell) or license their patent to others. 35 U.S.C. § 261. Pending patent applications and rights to future inventions are also assignable. It is common for employers to require employees to assign rights to work-related inventions as a condition of employment. Patentees may also use their patent as collateral in a secured transaction.

In contrast to an assignment, a license does not transfer ownership of the patent; rather, it permits a third party to use the patented invention, usually in exchange for royalties. The patent owner contractually specifies the specific rights granted under the license. A patent license agreement is simply a promise by the licensor to not sue the licensee, and regardless of the terms of the license, the licensor cannot convey an absolute right to the patent because their patent right is merely one of exclusion. For example, in *Spindelfabrik Suessen-Schurr Stahlecker & Grill GmbH v. Schubert & Salzer Maschinenfabrik Aktiengesellschaft*, 829 F.2d 1075 (Fed. Cir. 1987), a spinning device designed to aid in the production of yarn was licensed to the defendant. When sued by a third party for infringement of the third party's patent, the defendant argued that they should be entitled to legal estoppel against the infringement claim because they had legitimately licensed a different patent for virtually the same device. The court disagreed, holding that the license transferred only the right to use the licensed patent — not the general technology — and found that the defendant had infringed the related third-party patents.

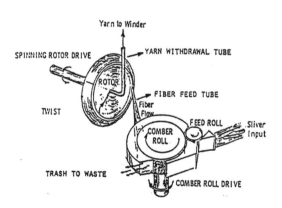

Figure 2-V
Spindelfabrik Suessen-Schurr Stahlecker & Grill GmbH v. Schubert & Salzer Maschinenfabrik Aktiengesellschaft, 829 F.2d 1075 (Fed. Cir. 1987)
Device used in the production of yarn.

The most important distinction between a patent assignment and a patent license is that an assignee is the sole owner of a patent and can bring suit for patent infringement under 35 U.S.C. §281, but a licensee usually cannot enforce a licensed patent. A licensee has only a promise that the licensor will not sue the licensee for patent infringement. Licensees can protect themselves by obtaining a covenant in their licensing agreement that requires the licensor to enforce the patent. Another distinction is that an assignment must be in writing, but a license need not be. 35 U.S.C. §261.

A license may even be implied. The Federal Circuit established a two part test to determine the existence of an implied license: first, a patent holder must have sold a product that had no non-infringing uses, and second, the circumstances of the sale must "plainly indicate that the grant of a license should be inferred." For example, the court implied a license in *Met-Coil Systems Corp. v. Korners Unlimited, Inc.*, 803 F.2d 684 (Fed. Cir. 1986), in which the patent assignee made and sold roll-forming machines that its customers used to bend flanges in the ends of metal ducts. The machines were not capable of a non-infringing use; therefore, the court held that the customers were impliedly licensed to use the machines to connect metal ducts in accordance with the patented process.

A valid license may also provide an affirmative defense to a suit for patent infringement. For example, in *Carborundum Co. v. Molten Metal Equipment Innovations, Inc.*, 72 F.3d 872 (Fed. Cir. 1995), the court found an implied license for customers who bought pumps used in a patented gas injection device. In a suit for contributory infringement, the court accepted that the implied license was a valid defense to direct infringement, without which there could be no contributory infringement. However, the court also held that the implied license existed only for the life of the pumps—not the life of the patent. Therefore, the implied license expired when the defendant replaced the pumps with different pumps manufactured by a competitor, and the defendant's continued use of the patented process without a license was infringement.

8. Security Interests in Patents

Patents, along with other intellectual property such as copyrights and trademarks, often represent a significant portion of an entity's value, and can be useful sources of collateral for secured transactions. To maintain priority, lenders must properly create and perfect their security interests in intellectual property. Security interests in intellectual property are governed by both the Uniform Commercial Code and federal law. The extent to which the U.C.C. or federal regulations govern a particular security interest depends upon the type of intellectual property used as collateral. For patents, both state and federal law must be considered.

Article 9 of the U.C.C., which has been adopted by all fifty states, governs the creation and perfection of security interests in intellectual property, which is categorized as a "general intangible." A security interest in intellectual property is not enforceable (even against the debtor), and does not attach to the collateral unless: (1) the secured party has given value in exchange for the collateral, (2) the debtor has rights in the collateral, and (3) the debtor has signed a security agreement that provides a description of the collateral. Lenders must therefore ensure that the debtor has rights in the intellectual property collateral prior to obtaining the security interest. When a security interest is properly granted it is said to have "attached" and it is then enforceable against the debtor.

In a security agreement, a general description of personal property used as security is sufficient if it reasonably identifies the property. Therefore, a description of patent collateral in a security agreement as "general intangibles" or "patents" should be sufficient. However, it is best practice to identify all patents by number, country, issuance or filing date, and expiration date. The collateral description should also include all pending patent infringement claims; rights to income, profits, or other rights related to the patents; all inventions and improvements described in the patents; and all continuations, divisions, renewals, extensions, substitutions, and reissuances of the patents.

A security agreement for which patents serve as collateral should address several additional issues. Because patents expire after twenty years and lapse unless maintenance fees are paid, 35 U.S.C. § 154(a)(2), a security agreement should require the debtor to make timely payments of all applicable fees prior to their due date and permit the lender to do so and recover reimbursement from the debtor should the debtor fail to pay the fees. The security agreement should also require the debtor to notify the secured party of patents acquired after the execution of the security agreement, and to execute and deliver any documents that must be filed with the PTO. However, the secured party should not rely exclusively on such provisions and should monitor its collateral to ensure that after-acquired patents are incorporated into the security agreement. The debtor should also warrant that all after-acquired patents are valid and enforceable. In addition, the agreement should both oblige the debtor to take all necessary measures to protect the collateral from infringement and guarantee the secured party's right to take steps necessary to maintain and protect the collateral.

"Perfection" of the security interest is the legal status that the security interest enjoys once the appropriate formalities have been complied with in order to make it good against the world rather than just enforceable against the debtor. Through perfection of its security interest a secured party achieves and maintains the highest available priority for its security interest in collateral. An unperfected security interest may be effective against the debtor, but it is of little value against third parties. In bankruptcy, the difference between a perfected security interest and an unperfected security interest means the difference between full recovery as a secured creditor and little or no recovery as an unsecured creditor.

A security interest is perfected when it attaches if the applicable requirements are satisfied before attachment. The process of perfecting a security interest in most types of personal property is accomplished when a properly completed UCC-1 financing statement is filed with the appropriate state office, most often the office of the secretary of state. The financing statement must name both the debtor and the secured party, and must describe the collateral covered by the financing statement. The U.C.C. no longer requires the debtor to sign an electronically filed financial statement, although the debtor must authorize the filing.

The relative priorities of creditors who hold conflicting security interests are straightforward. Under the U.C.C. (1) if the conflicting security interests are perfected, they rank according to priority in time of filing or perfection; (2) a perfected security interest has priority over a conflicting unperfected security interest; and (3) if the conflicting security interests are unperfected, the first security interest to attach has priority. However, under § 9-109(c)(1), Article 9 does not apply to the extent that it is preempted by federal law.

Filing a financing statement is neither necessary nor effective to perfect a security interest in collateral that is subject to a separate federal filing requirement. In such cases, compliance with such a federal requirement is equivalent to filing a properly completed UCC-1 financing statement, and compliance with federal law is the only means of perfection. U.C.C. § 9-311(b). However, even in cases where federal law governs the perfection of security interests, Article 9 governs the relative priorities of conflicting security interests unless federal law also establishes separate priority rules. Sections 9-109 and 9-311 of the U.C.C. raise distinct issues: under § 9-109, federal law preempts Article 9 where federal law governs ownership rights in the property secured as collateral, while under § 9-311 the U.C.C. defers to federal law regarding perfection if federal law has defined a filing requirement. The practical distinction between these sections is unclear and it is equally unclear whether security interests in intellectual property rights governed by federal law must be perfected in accordance with federal law or the U.C.C. Because of this uncertainty, security interests in patents, trademarks, and copyrights should be filed with both state and federal agencies.

Federal law provides that "[a]n assignment, grant or conveyance shall be void as against any subsequent purchaser or mortgagee for a valuable consideration, without notice, unless it is recorded in the Patent and Trademark Office within three months from its date or prior to the date of such subsequent purchase or mortgage." 35 U.S.C. § 261. This statute does not clearly satisfy the U.C.C. Article 9 preemption provisions and therefore does not displace the U.C.C. for purposes of perfecting security interests in patents. The case law in this area suggests that the U.C.C. controls the perfection of security interests in patents. Nevertheless, filing with the PTO provides important protections to the holder of a security interest.

The effect of 35 U.S.C. § 261 under Article 9's preemption provisions was first considered in *In re Transportation Design & Technology, Inc.*, 48 B.R. 635 (Bankr. S.D. Cal. 1985), in which the bankruptcy court held that a secured party was not required to file with the PTO to perfect its security interest in a patent. However, the court stated that filing under the U.C.C. only protects against competing lien creditors and does not protect against a bona fide purchaser or mortgagee who records with the PTO. In the court's view, a secured party must record its security interest with the PTO to protect against the subsequent transferring of the debtor's patent to either a bona fide purchaser or a mortgagee who properly records.

In *In re Otto Fabric, Inc.*, 55 B.R. 654 (Bankr. D.Kan. 1985), *rev'd*, 83 B.R. 780 (D.Kan. 1988), the bankruptcy court reached the opposite result and held that although the secured party had attempted to perfect its security interest by filing a UCC-1 financing statement, the Patent Act governed and required filing with the PTO. However, the district court reversed, holding that a federal filing was not required to perfect a security interest in patents as against a trustee in bankruptcy. The court emphasized that the Patent Act does not expressly state that filing with the PTO is necessary to perfect a security interest. It also noted that the Patent Act addresses assignments that are void against subsequent purchasers or mortgagees, but leaves open the area of protection against lien creditors. Finally, the district court questioned whether a security interest in a patent was an assignment at all. The court distinguished between a security interest and an assignment of title. (However, under an 1891 United States Supreme Court case, a federally recorded security agreement in a patent is considered an assignment and grants title to the secured lender. *Waterman v. Mackenzie*, 138 U.S. 252 (1891). This old precedent may raise additional confusion as the case law develops.)

In 2001, in *In re Cybernetic Services, Inc.*, 252 F.3d 1039 (9th Cir. 2001), the court held that the Patent Act does not preempt state regulation of security interests in patents under the U.C.C. and that a federal filing was not required for perfection. The court reasoned that a security interest in a patent, which does transfer rights of ownership, is a "mere license" rather than an "assignment, grant, or conveyance" within the meaning of 35 U.S.C. § 261. The court concluded that because the Patent Act only applies to transfers of ownership interests, U.C.C. Article 9 is not preempted by federal law.

Although Article 9 governs the perfection of security interests in patents under *Cybernetic Services*, the court also stated that the "record of a license, not being legally required, is not constructive notice to any person for any purpose." This raises the question of whether filing with the PTO serves any purpose at all. However, because most bona fide purchasers of patents search PTO records as part of their due diligence, filing a security interest with the PTO usually provides actual notice even if it does not constitute constructive notice.

The *Cybernetic Services* court also concluded that a security interest in a patent is a "mere license." However, a security interest (unlike a true nonexclusive license) may ripen into full ownership upon foreclosure if the debtor defaults. More recent cases have followed *Cybernetic Services* in holding that security interests in patents are governed by Article 9 rather than the Patent Act. *In re Tower Tech, Inc.*, 67 Fed. App'x 521 (10th Cir. 2003); *In re Pasteurized Eggs Corp.*, 296 B.R. 283 (Bankr. D.N.H. 2003). However, these cases have not adopted the "mere license" analysis.

In 2003, the Bankruptcy Court for the District of New Hampshire held that the filing of a security agreement with the PTO was insufficient to perfect a security interest in a patent. *In re Pasteurized Eggs Corp.*, 296 B.R. 283 (Bankr. D.N.H. 2003). Citing *Cybernetic Services*, the *Pasteurized Eggs* court concluded that the perfection of a security interest in a patent was a state law issue. Because the lender had not filed a UCC-1 financing statement pursuant to Article 9, its security interest was unperfected. Accordingly, the security interest was avoidable under § 544 of the Bankruptcy Code.

In sum, a security interest in a patent is perfected by properly filing U.C.C. financing statements at the appropriate state office, at least as against lien creditors and hypothetical lien creditors such as a trustee in bankruptcy. However, filing with the PTO may be necessary to protect against subsequent bona fide purchasers and mortgagees who properly record. No statute or case law specifically addresses the rights of a subsequent bona fide purchaser for value or of a mortgagee who has properly filed with the PTO, so secured parties should make appropriate filings under both U.C.C. Article 9 and Title 15.

Checkpoints

- Patent law provides inventors a limited monopoly on qualifying inventions that allows them to exclude others from making, using, selling, offering to sell, or importing their invention.

- Any process, product, design, or plant that meets the statutory requirements may be patented. However, abstract ideas, the laws of nature, and naturally occurring phenomena cannot be patented.

- *Utility patents*, the most common type of patent, expire twenty years from the application date, and are available for processes, machines, articles of manufacture, and combinations of matter.

- *Design patents* expire fourteen years from the date of issue and are available for non-functional ornamental designs.

- *Plant patents* expire twenty years from the application date and are available for asexually propagated plants.

- *Utility*, found in 35 U.S.C. § 101, requires that in order to be patentable, an invention must be capable of producing a practical or commercial benefit and must be operable and reduced to practice.

- *Novelty*, found in 35 U.S.C. § 102, requires that in order to be patentable, an invention must differ from prior art. Under § 102, inventors are not entitled to a patent if they did not personally invent the claimed invention, they abandoned, suppressed, or concealed the invention.

- The *statutory bar*, also found in 35 U.S.C. § 102, bars patenting if the invention was patented, described in a printed publication, in public use, or sold prior to the "critical date," which is one year before the patent application was filed.

- *Non-obviousness*, found in 35 U.S.C. § 103, is similar to novelty and requires that in order to be patentable, an invention must be more than a trivial advance over prior art. Obviousness is determined by whether the invention would be obvious to a hypothetical artisan of ordinary skill in the art given all of the prior art. Or, in the case of design patents, by the ordinary designer.

- *Secondary considerations,* such as commercial success, a long felt but unsolved need, and the failure of others, and *synergism,* the combination of obvious elements in such a way that the whole exceeds the sum of the parts, indicate nonobviousness and might enable a patent to issue in an otherwise close case.

- Patent holders can assign or license their patents and use them as collateral in secured transactions. Filing the necessary security documents under the applicable state-law Uniform Commercial Code and filing with the Patent and Trademark Office is prudent to ensure perfection of a security interest in a patent.

Chapter Three

Acquiring Patents

Roadmap

After reading this chapter, you should understand:

- The basics of provisional applications — provisional applications do not require claims and allow patent applicants to gain the priority of the provisional filing date, which will govern when they eventually file a non-provisional application.

- The important aspects of a patent application — the specification, claims, and drawings.

- The specification — discloses an invention, enables a skilled artisan to make the invention, shows that the inventor accomplished the invention at the time of the application filing, and sets out the best mode for carrying out the invention.

- Claims — specifically define the scope of a patent and distinguish the invention from prior art, inventions and things already disclosed at the time of the patent application.

- Claim construction — patents are construed according to the express language of the claims in light of the specification and by the application process history, also known as file wrapper estoppel.

- Drawings — when necessary, the patent application should also include drawings to illustrate the patent.

- Interference proceedings — when the claims contained in a patent application interfere with those of another application or an existing patent, that priority dispute is generally settled through an interference proceeding.

- The duty of candor — patent applicants are under a duty of candor toward the PTO and violations, by not disclosing known relevant prior art, for example, can invalidate the patent.

- Reissue patents — a patentee may obtain a reissue patent to correct innocent error but cannot use a reissue patent to correct a breach of the duty of candor or to extend the patent to cover improvements developed after the initial patent issued.

- Reexamination proceedings — there are two types of reexaminations, *ex parte* and *inter partes*, that allow a challenge to the validity of the patent after additional prior art is brought to light. *Ex parte* reexaminations have minimal participation from third parties while *inter partes* reexaminations require the challenger to actively participate in the proceedings.

1. Patent Prosecution

Patent rights, unlike other types of intellectual property rights, arise only after a formal application process and government review. "Patent prosecution" is the administrative process by which an inventor acquires a patent from the Patent and Trademark Office (PTO), a federal administrative agency within the Department of Commerce.

a. The Patent Applicant

As noted in *Beech Aircraft Corp. v. EDO Corp.*, 990 F.2d 1237 (Fed. Cir. 1993), only natural persons may qualify as "inventors." Inventors are presumed to own the patent application and patents issued for their invention unless they previously assigned their patent. In order to prosecute a patent, the patent's assignee must become an assignee "of record" by filing a copy of the executed assignment with the PTO.

Special restrictions apply when a patent is granted for an invention conceived by multiple inventors:

> When an invention is made by two or more persons jointly, they shall apply for a patent jointly and each make the required oath, except as otherwise provided in this title. Inventors may apply for a patent jointly even though (1) they did not physically work together or at the same time, (2) each did not make the same type or amount of contribution, or (3) each did not make a contribution to the subject matter of every claim of the patent.

35 U.S.C. § 116. Rather than defining joint inventorship, this provision defines a joint invention as the product of a collaboration between two or more persons. The existence of joint inventorship is a question of law determined in view of the underlying facts. There is no bright-line standard for determining whether a person is a joint inventor, but "to be a joint inventor, an individual must make a contribution to the conception of the claimed invention that is not insignificant in quality, when that contribution is measured against the dimension of the full invention." *Fina Oil & Chemical Co. v. Ewen*, 123 F.3d

1466, 1473 (Fed. Cir. 1997). "One who merely suggests an idea of a result to be accomplished, rather than means of accomplishing it, is not a joint inventor." *Garrett Corp. v. United States*, 422 F.2d 874 (Ct. Cl. 1970).

Joint inventorship arises only when two or more inventors collaborate and exercise concerted effort. In *Eli Lilly and Co. v. Aradigm Corp.*, 376 F.3d 1352 (Fed. Cir. 2004), the court held that Lilly's researchers could not be joint inventors of Aradigm's patented insulin inhaler using lispo, a modified version of regular insulin because there was insufficient evidence that Lilly's scientist communicated to Aradigm's scientist regarding the properties of lispo that made it ideal for use in an aerosol inhaler.

Every joint inventor must join in the patent application if possible, but if a joint inventor refuses to join or cannot be reached after diligent effort, then the missing joint inventor need not join in the application and the patent may issue in the name of all the inventors. Should an inventor be accidentally omitted from the application, the Director of the PTO may authorize an amendment to the application. 35 U.S.C. § 116.

Even if the inventors did not contribute equally to the invention, each co-inventor owns an equal undivided interest in the entire patent unless they have contracted otherwise, and each joint owner may exploit the patent without the consent of any other owner. However, 35 U.S.C. § 281, which grants patent holders a civil remedy for patent infringement, has been interpreted to require a joint owner to obtain permission from every other joint owner before bringing a patent infringement suit. For example, in *Ethicon, Inc. v. United States Surgical Corp.*, 135 F.3d 1456 (Fed. Cir. 1998), the patent at issue covered a medical device called a "trocar" used to make incisions during endoscopic surgeries. The patent holder sued another device manufacturer for infringement of the inventor's patent. However, a co-inventor of the device—who had contributed to only two of the patent's fifty-five claims—intervened in the suit and granted the defendant a license to use the invention. Although the co-inventor made only a minimal contribution to the invention, the court held that under § 116 he held an undivided one-half interest in the patent, which entitled him to grant a valid license for the entire patent. (See Figure 3-A.)

b. Patent Applications

The patent application describes the claimed invention and should include drawings (or diagrams) as necessary. Applicants are required to declare to the best of their knowledge that they are the original inventor of the invention they seek to patent. 35 U.S.C. § 115. An applicant also has a duty to disclose

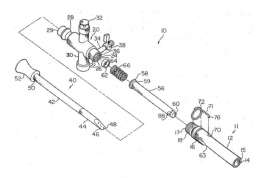

Figure 3-A
Ethicon, Inc. v. United States Surgical Corp., 135 F.3d 1456 (Fed. Cir. 1998).
Trocar used in endoscopic surgeries.

any prior art known to be material to the patentability of the claimed invention. 37 C.F.R. §1.56. The required elements of a patent application are listed in 37 C.F.R. § 1.77.

Under 35 U.S.C. § 122 patent applications are initially confidential, subject to limited exceptions. However, confidentiality is temporary; all applications must be published eighteen months from the filing date unless they are: no longer pending; subject to a secrecy order; provisional applications; or applications for design patents. Patent applicants may also request that their application not be published if they certify that the application will not be filed in a foreign country.

A non-provisional application must include a specification, a drawing, and an oath and be accompanied by the appropriate fee and signed by the inventor. 35 U.S.C. § 111. In a non-provisional application, the specifications must include one or more distinct claims about the invention. 35 U.S.C. § 112. Applicants must testify in the oath that they believe themselves to be the first inventor of the invention that they are seeking to patent. 35 U.S.C. § 115. Applicants must also state their country of citizenship. 35 U.S.C. § 115.

Patent applicants may instead file a provisional application to gain the benefit of the provisional filing date for priority purposes under a relation-back theory, provided they later file a non-provisional application. A provisional application must include a specification and drawing, but need not include a claim. 35 U.S.C. § 111(b). They are slightly less expensive to file than traditional, non-provisional applications. 37 C.F.R. § 1.16(a)–(d). Provisional applications are not examined by the PTO and are considered abandoned if the applicant takes no further action within twelve months of filing.

c. Specifications

The first paragraph of § 112 requires that the patent instrument disclose the invention. The "specification" or description called for by the first paragraph of § 112 is perhaps among the most difficult legal instruments to draft. The specification is subject to the three statutory requirements of 35 U.S.C. § 112:

- First, it must contain a written description of the invention sufficient to enable a skilled artisan to make and use the invention. This is often referred to as the "enablement" requirement.

- Second, the description must show that the inventor had accomplished the invention at the filing date.

- Third, the specification must detail the best mode contemplated by the inventor for carrying out his invention. That is, it must state the best way to work the invention claimed in the patent application. The "best mode" requirement restrains inventors from applying for a patent while concealing preferred embodiments of the invention.

d. Claims

Section 112 also requires that the specification "conclude with one or more claims particularly pointing out and distinctly claiming the subject matter which the applicant regards as his invention." While claims are technically part of the specification, patent practitioners commonly refer to the specification and claims as distinct portions of the patent instrument because claims are independently important. Claims both define the scope of the patent and distinguish the invention from prior art.

i. Claim Drafting

Claims define the scope of the protected invention. They must be adequate and definite as to the extent of legal protection afforded by the patent. A claim is adequate and definite if an expert in the field would understand all the language of the claim when read in light of the specification. The terms used in the claims are construed to have the ordinary and customary meaning as understood by a person of ordinary skill in the art unless the patent holder devises specific definitions or terminology in the application, in which case assigned meanings will be applied rather than the customary meanings. Applicants may phrase the claim however they wish, provided that the form and language particularly and distinctly claim the invention.

For example, patent no. 1,640,052 claims a transparent candy wrapper as follows:

1. A package of the character described comprising a bar of confection, a transparent pellicle in contact with and covering the face of the same, and a translucent waxed paper wrapper folded and sealed over the confection enclosing the same and provided with a cut-out over said pellicle.

2. A package of the character described comprising a bar of candy, a transparent pellicle in contact with and covering the entire face and edges only of the bar, and a waxed paper wrapper folded and sealed over the bar enclosing the same and provided with a cut-out over said pellicle within the marginal outline of the bar.

3. A candy package for a bar of candy in which the face of the bar is covered with a wrapping perfectly transparent over a portion of its face surface only and translucent over the remaining portion and being sealed thereover.

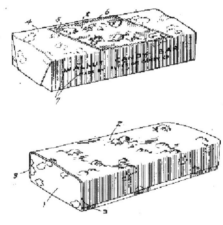

Figure 3-B
Patent No. 1,640,052
Transparent candy bar wrapper.

Claims are particularly important and must be drafted with care. In *In re Schwendler*, 115 F.2d 261 (C.C.P.A. 1940), the court stated that claims that are "unduly multiplied" and that cause confusion may be properly rejected solely for that reason. In *Schwendler*, the court rejected claims for a purified moisture-resistant plastic used in coffins because the claims did not clearly identify the invention, included multiple functional statements within a single claim, and were confusingly non-specific.

In *Consolidated Electric Light Co. v. McKeesport Light Co.*, also know as *The Incandescent Lamp Patent* case, 159 U.S. 465 (1895), the patent at issue claimed "carbonized fibrous or textile material" for use as an incandescent lamp filament. The inventors tested over 6,000 unsuccessful varieties of plant matter for use as a filament, and sought to claim the use of all plants even though only a handful were found to work. The Court found no common quality in the fibrous materials they claimed, and declared it unjust to allow them a monopoly over *all* plant material. Through another set of experiments, Thomas Edison found other species that were not disclosed in the patent claimed by the other inventors and that were commercially viable as filaments because of their parallel fiber structures and thick cell walls in particular, bamboo. The Court held that bamboo could not be claimed by the other inventors' previous patent.

In *Amgen, Inc. v. Chugai Pharmaceutical Co., Ltd.*, 927 F.2d 1200 (Fed. Cir. 1991), the court noted that it is well established that patent applicants are entitled to claim their invention generically, provided that the invention's description satisfies the requirements of 35 U.S.C. § 112. However, there are limits: in *Amgen*, the patentee attempted to claim 4,000 nucleotides, but only described the production of Erythropoietin (EPO) and a few analogs. In that case, the court invalidated the undescribed claims. Thus, an invention should be described with many claims of progressively broadening scope that differ by only one aspect or term so that, if challenged, some of the claims may be stricken without damage to the remainder.

ii. Types of Claims

There are three types of claims: "Independent claims" are integrated claims drafted to stand alone. "Dependent claims" incorporate by reference, build upon, or otherwise "depend" upon another claim. "Multiple dependent claims" are the same as dependent claims, but reference, build upon, or otherwise "depend" upon multiple other claims.

Independent claims are organized into three parts: a preamble that generally describes all the non-novel or obvious elements of the claim, a transitional phrase (such as "wherein the improvement comprises"), and a description of the "elements, steps and/or relationships" actually claimed as the subject of the invention. 37 C.F.R. § 1.75(e). For example, the J.M. Smucker Company applied for a patent, number 6,004,596, for its Uncrustables PB&J Sandwich (a sealed, crustless peanut butter and jelly sandwich). Their first claim was an independent claim that first generalized the invention and then claimed the actual sandwich, layer by layer:

1. A sealed crustless sandwich, comprising:

    [a] a first bread layer having a first perimeter surface coplanar to a contact surface;

    [b] at least one filling of an edible food juxtaposed to said contact surface;

    [c] a second bread layer juxtaposed to said at least one filling opposite of said first bread layer, wherein said second bread layer includes a second perimeter surface similar to said first perimeter surface;

    [d] a crimped edge directly between said first perimeter surface and said second perimeter surface for sealing said at least one filling between said first bread layer and second bread layer;

    [e] wherein a crust portion of said first bread layer and said second bread layer has been removed.

Dependent claims must reference an independent claim in the same application and are construed to incorporate by reference all the limitations of that claim. 35 U.S.C. § 112. Dependent claims that reference more than one claim are "multiple dependent claims." 37 C.F.R. § 1.75(c). Multiple dependent claims must reference underlying claims only in the alternative, may not reference another multiple dependent claim, and are "construed to incorporate by reference all the limitations of the particular claim in relation to which it is being considered." 35 U.S.C. § 112. In the same application for the Uncrustables PB&J Sandwich, the second and third claims were dependent claims that built upon the first claim and detailed the manner in which the edge was crimped. The sixth claim depended on the previous claims that described the sandwich:

6. The sealed crustless sandwich of claim 5, wherein:

    [a] said first filling is juxtaposed to said first bread layer;

    [b] said third filling is juxtaposed to said second bread layer; and

    [c] an outer edge of said first filling and said third filling are engaged to one another to form a reservoir for retaining said second filling in between.

The patent application must also include drawings that further describe and define the invention when needed to understand the invention claimed in the patent application. 35 U.S.C. § 113. Drawings supplement and give meaning to claims (i.e., they "illustrate" claims) but do not expand claims or other aspects of the patent.

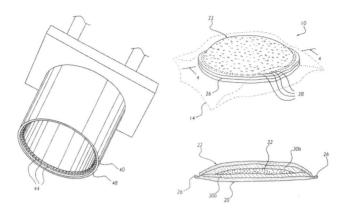

Figure 3-C

Drawings submitted to illustrate the Uncrustables PB&J Sandwich portray the sandwich itself and the machine used to produce the sandwich. Patent number 6,004,596 covering the Uncrustables technology was issued in 1999, but was reexamined and all if its claims were cancelled in 2006.

iii. Claim Construction

A patent is construed in light of its claims and its "file wrapper," the patent's prosecution history in the Patent Office. A file wrapper is the complete record of all PTO proceedings regarding a particular patent, including all representations and limitations made by the applicant during the approval process. In prosecuting their patent application, applicants may accept limitations on their claims to circumvent a prior art-rejection by the examiner. If a claim has been narrowed, the doctrine of "file-wrapper estoppel" (also called "prosecution history estoppel") will bar the patentee from later advocating a construction of that claim that is broader than the construction presented to the PTO. For example, in *Graham v. John Deere Co.*, 383 U.S. 1 (1966), the patent holder had designed an "overcap" lid intended to cover the sprayer heads on bottles of insecticide to prevent accidental spray leakage during shipment. The patentee later alleged that the entire mechanism was claimed by the patent, as it had been in the initial application, but the file wrapper reflected the examiner's approval of only two minor aspects of the design as patentable innovations. Therefore, the Court invoked the doctrine of file-wrapper estoppel and limited the claims to those aspects. (See Figure 3-D.)

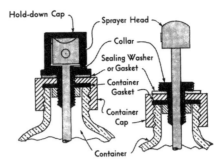

Figure 3-D
Graham v. John Deere Co., 383 U.S. 1 (1966).
Overcap lid to cover the sprayer heads on bottles of insecticide.

In *Narda Microwave Corp. v. General Microwave Corp.*, 675 F.2d 542 (2d Cir. 1982), the patentee had limited its claims to distinguish them from a prior, similar patent by excluding certain "radiation detectors," and the doctrine of file-wrapper estoppel later prevented the patentee from re-expanding its claims to include these items. File-wrapper estoppel is intended to ensure certainty as to a patent's scope and allow competitors to compete without fear of accidentally infringing on the patentee's monopoly.

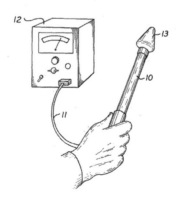

Figure 3-E
Narda Microwave Corp. v. General Microwave Corp.
675 F.2d 542 (2d Cir. 1982). Radiation detectors.

Claim infringement under the doctrine of equivalents is not necessarily foreclosed by file-wrapper estoppel. In *Festo Corp. v. Shoketsu Kinzoku Kogyo Kabushiki Co., Ltd.*, 535 U.S. 722 (2002), the Supreme Court reasoned that, although a limitation in the file wrapper is in fact a concession that the original claim exceeded the scope of patentable invention, narrowing limitations do not bar an inventor's claim to unanticipated equivalents not fairly surrendered by the limitation. For example, in *Warner-Jenkinson Co., Inc. v. Hilton Davis Chemical Co.*, 520 U.S. 17 (1997), the patent for filtering dyes claimed an upper limit pH of 9 and a lower limit pH of 6. The specification did not state why the lower limit was set at a pH of 6. In deciding whether a similar method conducted at a pH of 5 infringed under the doctrine of equivalents, the Court remanded the case for a determination of why the claim was limited to a pH of 6. If the claim was limited to gain approval from the patent examiner, then prosecution history estoppel would waive claims below a pH of 6; but if the lower limit was selected for another reason, then applying the doctrine of equivalents would not unreasonably expand the claims of the patent.

e. Duty of Candor

Given the non-adversarial *ex parte* nature of patent prosecution, the public interest is best served when the PTO is aware of and evaluates all information material to patentability. 37 C.F.R. § 1.56(a). Thus, every party associated with the filing and prosecution of a patent application — including inventors, attorneys, agents, and anyone else substantially involved with the application — is required to disclose all material information throughout the prosecution with "candor and good faith in dealing." The duty of candor ceases when the claim is withdrawn from consideration or the application is abandoned. Compliance is ensured by the policy that no patent will be granted for an application involving fraud or attempted fraud on the PTO or a violation of the duty of disclosure through bad faith or intentional misconduct.

The Federal Circuit has defined materiality to mean a substantial likelihood that a reasonable examiner would have considered the information important in deciding whether to issue a patent. In *Molins PLC v. Textron, Inc.*, 48 F.3d 1172 (Fed. Cir. 1995), for example, the patent applicant had invented a batch process to improve the efficiency of a machining system. While the patent application was pending, the applicant discovered — but did not disclose to the PTO — prior art that arguably anticipated the invention. In a subsequent infringement action, the patent was held unenforceable due to the applicant's lack of candor with intent to deceive.

Full disclosure of even adverse facts is prudent, since a breach of the duty of candor will render the patent unenforceable. On the other hand, as in *Lam, Inc. v. Johns-Manville Corp.*, 668 F.2d 462 (10th Cir. 1982), which involved interior lamp designs, if the inventor does not believe known technology to be relevant prior art and the PTO and a reviewing court agree, the patent will not be declared unenforceable for lack of candor or disclosure. Whether particular facts were material and whether an applicant intended to breach the duty of candor are questions of fact.

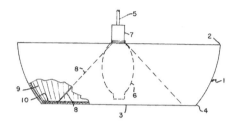

Figure 3-F
Lam, Inc. v. Johns-Manville Corp.
668 F.2d 462 (10th Cir. 1982). Interior lamp designs.

f. Rejection and Appeal

Under 35 U.S.C. § 134, an applicant whose claim has been twice rejected — whether for lack of novelty, lack of utility, or obviousness — may appeal the examiner's decision to the Board of Patent Appeals and Interferences. The Federal Circuit has exclusive jurisdiction over all appeals from the Board of Patent Appeals and Interferences regarding the denial of a patent application or the determination of an interference proceeding. 28 U.S.C. § 1295(a)(4)(A). However, by appealing to the Federal Circuit, the applicant or patentee waives the right to bring a civil action to compel the PTO to issue a patent or decide an interference differently. An appeal to the Federal Circuit must be taken within two months of the Board of Patent Appeals and Interferences decision unless the Director of the PTO grants an extension. 37 C.F.R. § 1.304.

2. Reissue

A patent holder may surrender a patent that, because of innocent error, is inoperative or invalid because of defective specifications, drawings, or the scope of its claims in exchange for a reissued patent for the invention disclosed in the original patent. 35 U.S.C. § 251. A reissued patent may also be available to the legal representatives or assigns of the patent holder. 37 C.F.R. § 1.172(b).

The reissue may even result in several reissued patents for distinct parts of the invention though none may exceed the balance of time remaining on the original patent. A reissued patent, to the extent that its claims are identical with the original patent, constitutes a continuation of the original patent and has effect from the date of the original patent. 35 U.S.C. § 252.

For reissue to be appropriate, a patent must be inoperative due to "correctable" error. For example, in *C.R. Bard, Inc. v. M3 Systems, Inc.*, 157 F.3d 1340 (Fed. Cir. 1998), the inventor initially failed to appreciate the full scope of their invention, a biopsy "gun" that fires a needle into tissue, by failing to claim the needle in the initial patent. The court held that the omission did not represent intent to not claim the needle, and that the omission was a remediable error that entitled the inventor to a reissued patent that also covered the needle. Likewise, nonjoinder or misjoinder of inventors may be cured by reissue. 37 C.F.R. § 1.324.

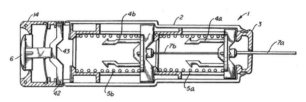

Figure 3-G
C.R. Bard, Inc. v. M3 Systems, Inc.
157 F.3d 1340 (Fed. Cir. 1998). Biopsy gun.

The reissue provision is based on principles of equity and, although construed liberally, reissue is not available to cure all errors. One significant limitation is found in 35 U.S.C. § 251: a reissued patent may not enlarge the scope of the original patent unless it is applied for within two years of the grant of the original patent. For example, in *Dart Industries, Inc. v. Banner*, 636 F.2d 684 (D.C. Cir. 1980), the patent holder filed an initial patent application claiming its engine carburetor design and two subsequent applications for amendments. In the initial application, the patentee disclosed—but did not claim—a particular feature of his invention: a "venturi" or flared tube that creates a pressure differential and assists in mixing fuel with air before it is sent to the pistons. The patent holder neither disclosed nor claimed this feature in the second application, but both disclosed and claimed the feature in the third application, arguing that it had been disclosed in the "grandparent" application and therefore was not "new matter" under § 251. The court rejected this argument, concluding that the patent holder's failure to maintain continuity of disclosure was uncorrectable.

Similarly, in *Hester Industries, Inc. v. Stein, Inc.*, 142 F.3d 1472 (Fed. Cir. 1998), the reissue patent for a steam cooker was invalidated because of the recapture rule. The recapture rule, which is similar to prosecution history estoppel, prevents a reissued patent's claims from broadening their scope to claim things abandoned in order to achieve the original patent.

Additionally, a reissue patent is not available to correct errors of judgment or to supply inventive concepts originating later. In *Dill Manufacturing Co. v. J.W. Speaker Corp.*, 83 F. Supp. 21 (E.D. Wis. 1949), the plaintiff had patented a device for vulcanizing rubber and later amended that patent to bring within its claims a device subsequently developed by its competitor. The court held that it was beyond the intent of the reissue statute to allow such an amendment under those circumstances unless the error arose from inadvertence, accident, or mistake.

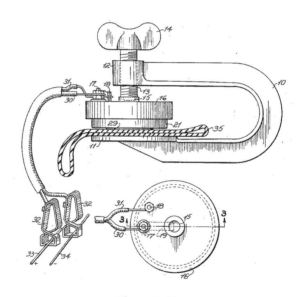

Figure 3-H
Dill Manufacturing Co. v. J.W. Speaker Corp.
83 F. Supp. 21 (E.D. Wis. 1949). Device for vulcanizing rubber.

Moreover, reissue cannot cure a defect caused by a breach of the duty of candor. As stated in *In re Clark*, 522 F.2d 623 (C.C.P.A. 1975), "[w]here inequitable conduct has occurred during prosecution, it cannot be purged or cured after the patent has issued." In *Clark*, where the patent applicant attempted to receive a reissue patent for a device used for quantitative chemical analysis with only trivial modifications from a patent application previously rejected for inequitable conduct, the court found that reissue could not cure that invalidity.

3. Reexamination

Reexamination allows "any person at any time" to question the validity of a patent in light of prior art. 35 U.S.C. §§ 302–18. In *McNeil-PPC, Inc. v. Procter & Gamble Co.*, 767 F. Supp. 1081 (D.Colo. 1991), the defendant accused of infringement moved for leave of the court to petition the PTO to reexamine the plaintiff's patent. The court held that under § 302 the defendant did not need to request leave and could seek reexamination.

In *Ethicon, Inc. v. Quigg*, 849 F.2d 1422 (Fed. Cir. 1988), the court held that a finding of a patent's validity means only that the party alleging invalidity failed to carry its burden of proof. Hence, the PTO cannot stay reexamination under § 303 simply because a court did not invalidate the patent. However, in *eSoft, Inc. v. Blue Coat Systems, Inc.*, 505 F. Supp. 2d 784 (D.Colo. 2007), the court held that, because a determination of invalidity by the PTO renders the patent invalid and unenforceable in any pending litigation, a district court may stay litigation pending a reexamination by the PTO.

In *Patlex Corp. v. Mossinghoff*, 758 F.2d 594 (Fed. Cir. 1985), the court held that the presumption of validity that arises in district court actions is a presumption of administrative validity that does not apply in a PTO reexamination because § 305 requires reexaminations to proceed in the same way as initial examinations (where there is no presumption regarding patentability of a claimed invention).

There are two types of reexamination: (1) *ex parte* reexamination and (2) *inter partes* reexamination. *Ex parte* reexamination involves minimal participation of a third party challenger of a patent's validity. A challenger may anonymously request the reexamination of a patent by producing relevant prior art and may reply to proofs adduced by the patentee in response, but may not otherwise participate or appeal. *Inter partes* reexamination is similar to *ex parte* reexamination, except that the challenger may not remain anonymous, must participate more extensively, and may appeal the final decision of the PTO.

To initiate an *ex parte* reexamination, under 35 U.S.C. § 303(a) the challenger must request the reexamination in writing and point to specific prior art that tends to raise a substantial new question of patentability of the challenged claim. The PTO must immediately notify the patent owner of a reexamination request and must decide within three months whether a substantial question of patentability exists. The PTO can also initiate a reexamination, regardless of whether the prior art cited was considered when the patent was originally granted. If the PTO determines that there is no substantial question of patentability, that decision is final and nonappealable. Under 35 U.S.C. § 304, if the PTO determines that a reexamination is warranted, both the challenger and patentee must be notified. The patentee has a reasonable time of at least two months to file a statement on the question, including any amendment to the patent and new claims. The patent holder must also serve a copy of its statement on the challenger, who may respond within two months. The patentee then proceeds under 35 U.S.C. § 305 and attempts to distinguish its patent from prior art, proceeding as if the patentee was protesting an initial rejection of the patent.

In an *ex parte* reexamination, participation of the requester and the patentee is limited to the submission of statements allowed under 35 U.S.C. § 304. For example, in *In re Opprecht*, 868 F.2d 1264 (Fed. Cir. 1989), the court held that the efficiency of a reexamination under § 304 would be undermined if a third party were allowed to intervene merely because it was concurrently defending a claim for infringement of that patent. However, in *In re Merck & Co.*, 800 F.2d 1091 (Fed. Cir. 1986), the court allowed an intervention on appeal because the third party sought to intervene in order to present evidence otherwise not before the PTO. The patentee is the only party that can appeal the PTO's *ex parte* reexamination of a patent under 35 U.S.C. § 306. For example, in *Syntex (U.S.A.) Inc. v. United States Patent & Trademark Office*, 882 F.2d 1570 (Fed. Cir. 1989), the court held that § 306 did not grant a right of appeal to the third party that requested the reexamination.

In an *inter partes* reexamination, the third party challenger participates more actively than in *ex parte* proceedings. Under 35 U.S.C. § 314, except for the initial reexamination request, any paper filed by either the patentee or the challenger is served on the other and, during the reexamination proceeding, the challenger has thirty days in which to respond to any filing of the patent holder. The challenger may appeal to the Board of Patent Appeals and Interferences under § 314 or to the Federal Circuit under § 141, and may be party to any appeal by the patentee under § 315(b). In any subsequent civil action on the patent, third party challengers are estopped from asserting the invalidity of any claim that they failed to raise during the reexamination, excluding assertions of invalidity based on newly discovered priority that were not available to the third party challenger or PTO at the time of the reexamination.

At the conclusion of a reexamination, the PTO publishes a certificate canceling any claim of the patent finally determined to be unpatentable, confirming any claim determined to be patentable, and incorporating any proposed amended or new claim determined to be patentable. 35 U.S.C. §§ 307(a), 316(a). The reexamination is not complete, and the examiner's decision is not final, until the PTO has issued the reexamination certificate required by § 307(a). That issue was critical in *In re Bass*, 314 F.3d 575 (Fed. Cir. 2002), where the examiner affirmed the patentee's claims before it issued a reexamination certificate, but later reconsidered and denied those claims when the certificate was actually issued. The court held that because the PTO had not yet issued the certificate, the examiner was allowed to change his finding.

Checkpoints

- Joint inventorship arises when two or more inventors collaborate or exercise concerted effort and the inventors have some open line of communication during their inventive efforts.

- Provisional applications do not require claims and allow patent applicants to gain the priority of the provisional filing date when they eventually file a non-provisional application.

- Patent applications are confidential at the outset but after 18 months are published (with some exceptions).

- The specification discloses the invention, enables a skilled artisan to make the invention, shows that the inventor accomplished the invention at the time of the application filing, and sets out the best mode for carrying out the invention.

- Claims specifically define the scope of the patent and distinguish the invention from the prior art and are construed in light of the specification.

- When necessary, the patent application should also include drawings to illustrate the patent.

- Patent applicants are under a duty of candor toward the PTO and violations can invalidate the patent.

- A patent holder may obtain a reissue patent to correct innocent error but cannot use the reissue process to correct a breach of the duty of candor or to extend the patent to cover improvements developed after the initial patent issued.

- There are two types of reexaminations, *ex parte* and *inter partes*, that allow a challenge to the validity of the patent after additional prior art is brought to light. *Ex parte* reexaminations have minimal participation from third parties whereas *inter partes* reexaminations require the challenger to actively participate in the proceedings.

- When the claims contained in a patent application interfere with those of another application or an existing patent, that priority dispute is generally settled through an interference proceeding.

Chapter Four

Enforcing Patents

Roadmap

After reading this chapter, you should understand:

- Patent law jurisdiction — United States district courts have original and exclusive jurisdiction of any civil action arising under the patent laws. On appeal, jurisdiction lies in the United States Court of Appeals for the Federal Circuit. The Federal Circuit applies its own law to patent matters and the law of the circuit in which the originating district court sits for non-patent matters in the case.

- Infringement — any unauthorized manufacture, use, sale, offer to sell, or import of any patented invention. It is a strict liability cause of action; the intent of the infringer is only relevant to the determination of damages.

- The infringement analysis — courts construe the claims of a patent and then determine if an alleged infringing device "reads on" every limitation of the claims, either identically or under the doctrine of equivalents.

- Claim construction — the construction of a patent's claims to determine infringement (which is similar to the construction used in the initial application process): claims are construed according to their express language in light of the specification, drawings, and the "file wrapper" or patent prosecution history. Extrinsic evidence may be considered unless it contradicts the express language of a claim.

- The doctrine of equivalents — the doctrine of equivalents broadens the scope of patent protection to cover insubstantial or trivial nonfunctional changes that do not literally infringe. An element is equivalent to a limitation of a patent claim if it performs substantially the same function in substantially the same way to obtain substantially the same result as the claim limitation.

- Direct infringement — the manufacture, use, sale, or import of the infringing device.

- Indirect infringement — includes both contributory infringement and inducement to infringement and requires direct infringement as a prerequisite to liability.

- Contributory infringement — contributory infringement occurs when one sells a material component of another's patented invention that is not itself a staple article or commodity of commerce suitable for substantial non-infringing use.

- Inducement to infringement — inducement to infringement occurs when one actively induces another to engage in direct infringement.
- The implied license to repair — the patent monopoly prevents users from reconstructing a patented device, but the users are given an implied license allowing them to repair a patented invention they were authorized to have or use (e.g., that they purchased from the patentee/licensee of the patent).
- Defenses to infringement — including patent invalidity, misuse, shop rights, prior use, safe harbors, and nonpatent defenses, such as non-infringement and running of the statute of limitations.
- The defense of invalidity — defendants asserting patent invalidity carry the burden of proof but may use any of the grounds required for patentability to make the challenge such as by negating novelty, non-obviousness, utility, etc.
- The defense of misuse — misuse is generally asserted as a defense when the patentee abused the patent monopoly with a tying arrangement by requiring the purchase of unpatented goods with the patent or conditioning the grant of a license upon acceptance of another different license or some similar tying arrangement or unlawful restraint of competitive trade.
- The defense of shop rights — shop rights grant an employer the right to use an invention patented by an employee under equitable circumstances, such as when the employer provided the material and the employee developed the invention in the course of their employment.
- The defense of prior use — a defendant that continuously used the patented method for at least a year prior to the date the patent issued may continue using the method if it was developed independently of the patentee.
- The equitable remedy of an injunction — injunctions are the most common remedy for patent infringement and are issued on equitable principles identical to those for nonpatent injunctions. To receive an injunction, patent holders are required to show (1) that they have suffered irreparable injury, (2) that money damages are inadequate, (3) a balance of the hardships, and (4) that the public interest would not be disserved.
- Monetary damages — infringed patent holders may also recover monetary damages for their lost profits if proven with requisite certainty but more often the measure of damages is a reasonable royalty. A reasonable royalty is calculated by what a willing licensor and licensee would bargain for in a hypothetical negotiation.
- Additional remedies — The court may treble the damages in a case of willful infringement or bad faith, but cannot increase damages as a compensatory measure. In exceptional cases, such as those involving willful infringement, inequitable conduct, or vexatious litigation, the prevailing party may receive an award of its reasonable attorneys' fees.

1. Patent Litigation in Federal Court

a. Choice of Forum

Federal district courts have original jurisdiction of any civil action arising under patent law. 28 U.S.C. § 1338(a). Therefore, the Federal Rules of Civil Procedure and the Federal Rules of Evidence govern discovery, exhibits, juries, motions, pleadings, presumptions, standards of proof, and witnesses. The United States Court of Appeals for the Federal Circuit has nationwide jurisdiction over cases arising under Title 35 Patent Law. 3 U.S.C. § 141. The Federal Circuit was created in 1982 to ensure a more consistent interpretation of patent law. Prior to 1982, patent appeals were heard by the court of appeals for the circuit in which the district court was located. This system led to circuit splits on important questions of patent law.

In some cases, the plaintiff's cause of action does not arise under patent law, but counterclaims or defenses raised in the defendant's answer do. In such cases, the Supreme Court has held that neither a counterclaim nor a defense can serve as the basis for the Federal Circuit's "arising under" jurisdiction. In *Holmes Group, Inc. v. Vornado Air Circulation Systems, Inc.*, 535 U.S. 826 (2002), a case involving a declaratory judgment on a possible trade-dress infringement, the defendant counterclaimed for patent infringement. The Supreme Court held that cases where patent questions arise only in a counterclaim are outside the appellate jurisdiction of the Federal Circuit. Courts apply the "well-pleaded complaint rule" to determine whether the plaintiff's complaint establishes that either (1) federal patent law creates the cause of action or (2) the plaintiff's right to relief necessarily depends upon the resolution of a substantial question of patent law. For example, in *Christianson v. Colt Industries Operations Corp.*, 486 U.S. 800 (1988), the plaintiff alleged that Colt had engaged in anti-competitive behavior and asserted the possible invalidity of several of Colt's patents. On appeal the Federal Circuit refused jurisdiction on the ground that the patent issue was not central and transferred the case to the Seventh Circuit, which refused jurisdiction because a patent issue, however slight, was raised in the complaint. Ultimately the Supreme Court held that because resolution of the patent issue was not determinative of the plaintiff's cause of action, those claims did not "arise under" patent law.

b. Choice of Law

Choice of law becomes an issue when the Federal Circuit hears cases that involve both patent issues and other matters over which the court lacks exclusive jurisdiction. When reviewing district court judgments in patent cases, the Federal Circuit applies its own law to patent issues and generally applies the law of the circuit in which the district court sits to non-patent issues. Moreover, an issue "that is not itself a substantive patent law issue is nonetheless governed by Federal Circuit law if the issue pertains to patent law, if it bears an essential relationship to matters committed to [the Federal Circuit's] exclusive control by statute or if it bears clearly implicates the jurisdictional responsibility of [the Federal Circuit] in a field within its exclusive jurisdiction." *Midwest Industries, Inc. v. Karavan Trailers, Inc.*, 175 F.3d 1356 (Fed. Cir. 1999) (en banc) (internal citations and quotations omitted). There the court applied Federal Circuit law to the issue of whether patent law preempted state causes of action or conflicted with Federal Trademark law.

2. Priority Disputes

Priority disputes are usually settled through "interference proceedings" which occur if the PTO determines that the claims of one patent application "interfere" with the claims of either another application or an existing patent. 35 U.S.C. § 135(a). They are conducted by the Board of Patent Appeals and Interferences and may be appealed to the Federal Circuit. Interference proceedings concern only priority and "ancillary issues." For example, during the interference proceeding *Walsh v. Davidson*, 101 F.2d 224 (C.C.P.A. 1939), the court stated that it had jurisdiction to establish priority, but refused to consider whether the junior inventor would be entitled to a patent.

Parties are permitted to settle interference disputes through arbitration, and the arbiter's decision is enforceable once the PTO is notified. 35 U.S.C. § 135(d). The PTO must be notified if the disputing parties settle their dispute so that the interference will be properly terminated. For example, in *Moog, Inc. v. Pegasus Laboratories, Inc.*, 376 F. Supp. 445 (E.D. Mich. 1974), a patent was issued for Moog's patented fluid control valve after an interference proceeding concluded under an oral agreement. The agreement was later formalized in writing, but it was not filed with the PTO as required by § 135(c) before the interference ended. When Moog later sued for infringement of that patent, the court held the patent unenforceable because of Moog's failure to comply with the filing requirement of § 135(c).

3. Patent Infringement

Patent infringement is the unauthorized use of a patented invention. Under 35 U.S.C. § 271, "[e]xcept as otherwise provided in this title, whoever without authority makes, uses, offers to sell, or sells any patented invention, within the United States or imports into the United States any patented invention during the term of the patent therefore, infringes the patent."

An individual may either directly or indirectly infringe upon a patent. A person directly (or "literally") infringes when engaging in an act granted exclusively to the patent holder under Title 35. A person indirectly infringes (or commits "dependent infringement") if the person encourages others to engage in direct infringement.

Although the intent of the infringer is relevant in determining damages, the infringer's intent is irrelevant to the issue of liability, as patent infringement is a strict liability cause of action. If a person has engaged in any of the statutorily prohibited acts, he/she is liable for direct infringement. 35 U.S.C. § 271(a). For example, in *Aro Manufacturing Co. v. Convertible Top Replacement Co.*, 377 U.S. 476 (1964), Ford Motor Company (without license) manufactured convertible cars with a patented retractable cloth-top design. In a subsequent action by the patent owner against the manufacturer of replacement cloth tops, the Supreme Court held that car purchasers, by using the infringing automobiles, had themselves committed direct infringement.

In an infringement case, a court first examines the scope of the claims describing the prior invention, and then decides whether those claims "read on" the alleged infringement. A claim is said to "read on" another product or process where that product or process embodies every limitation of the claim. So where a patented invention reads on a subsequent invention, the patent has been infringed. Even if an invention does not literally infringe, it might infringe under the "doctrine of equivalents" if the difference is minor and the invention performs the same function in the same way and with the same result as the patented invention. For example, in *Atlas Powder Co. v. E.I. duPont deNemourst & Co.*, 750 F.2d 1569 (Fed. Cir. 1984), the patent for a water-resistant emulsified blasting agent was infringed, even though the subsequent infringing blasting agent did not directly read on the claim. DuPont had claimed aluminum as an ingredient of the claimed compound in its first independent claim, whereas Atlas claimed aluminum in its fourteenth dependent claim. However, the court held that DuPont's claims infringed under the doctrine of equivalents, since regardless of where the additional ingredient was claimed, both it and the compound served substantially the same function in substantially same way to yield substantially the same result.

Once the claims have been construed, they are compared to the allegedly infringing product or process. If the court finds both that the defendant's invention is identical to a claim of the patent and that the defendant has performed one of the activities reserved to the patentee — making, using, importing, offering to sell, or selling the patented invention — then infringement will be found. The patentee must prove infringement by a preponderance of evidence, and the defendant may assert several defenses to infringement, including invalidity, misuse, and other equitable defenses. 35 U.S.C. § 282.

a. Claim Interpretation

Patent claims define the scope of a patentee's exclusive rights and are construed according to their express language, the specification, any drawings, the file wrapper, and the patent's prosecution history. In construing a claim, courts attempt to assign a fixed, unambiguous, legally operative meaning to the claim, which can then be compared to the accused device. There is a fine line between reading a claim in light of the specification and reading a limitation from the specification into the claim. For example, in *Liquid Dynamics Corp. v. Vaughan Co.*, 355 F.3d 1361 (Fed. Cir. 2004), the patent for a method and apparatus for handling waste water claimed a substantial helical flow path. The lower court, using the drawings to limit an unambiguous claim, misinterpreted the substantial helical to be a perfect helical path rather than an approximate path. On appeal, the Federal Circuit vacated the finding of noninfringement and remanded for determination under the proper claim construction.

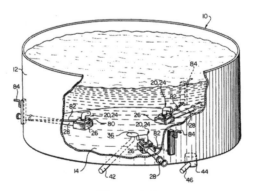

Figure 4-A
Liquid Dynamics Corp. v. Vaughan Co.
355 F.3d 1361 (Fed. Cir. 2004). **Apparatus for handling waste water.**

In *Markman v. Westview Instruments, Inc.*, 52 F.3d 967 (Fed. Cir. 1995), the Federal Circuit clarified and underscored a court's role in claim interpretation. *Markman* was a patent infringement suit involving an inventory control system used in the dry cleaning business that turned on the definition of "inventory." The *Markman* court held that claim construction is a matter of law, and that, even in a jury trial, the court has the power and the obligation to construe the meaning of the language used in patent claims. The *Markman* court also reviewed the types of evidence that can be considered in claim construction. Claims must be read in view of the specification and in consideration of the prosecution history. Extrinsic evidence, such as expert and inventor testimony, dictionaries, and treatises may be used to aid the court's understanding of the language employed in the patent but cannot be used to vary or contradict the terms of the claim.

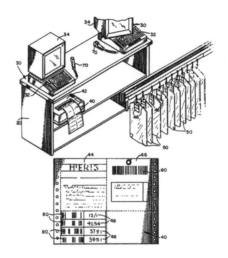

Figure 4-B
Markman v. Westview Instruments, Inc., 52 F.3d 967 (Fed. Cir. 1995).
Inventory control system used in the dry cleaning business.

b. Doctrine of Equivalents

The doctrine of equivalents broadens the scope of patent protection by providing that, even in the absence of literal overlap, a patent is infringed if "an equivalent ... correspondence of every limitation of the claim is found in the accused device." Whether the elements of a suspect device are equivalent to the limitations of a patent claim is a question of fact that turns on whether the differences between the suspect device's elements and the patent's claim limitation are insubstantial. For example, in *Graver Tank & Manufacturing Co. v. Linde Air Products Co.*, 339 U.S. 605 (1950), the trial court found that the plaintiff's patented formula for welding flux differed from the defendant's only in that the defendant had substituted manganese silicate, known from prior art to be an adequate equivalent, for magnesium silicate described in plaintiff's claim. The Supreme Court refused to reconsider the trial court's factual determinations, and held that because the difference between the elements used was "colorable only," the defendant's formula had infringed under the doctrine of equivalents and its product was the result of imitation, not experimentation or invention.

An element is equivalent to a limitation of a patent claim if—like the manganese silicate in *Grover Tank*—it performs substantially the same function in substantially the same way to obtain substantially the same result as the claim limitation. However, a conclusion that infringement has occurred requires that the accused device be either equivalent to or literally overlap each individual element of one or more of the patent claims, not the invention as a whole. As stated in *Seachange International, Inc. v. C-COR, Inc.*, 413 F.3d 1361, 1378 (Fed. Cir. 2005), the "all elements rule provides that the doctrine of equivalents does not apply if applying the doctrine would vitiate the entire claim limitation."

c. Direct Infringement

Direct infringement is the unauthorized manufacture, use, sale, or importation of any patented invention during the patent's term. 35 U.S.C. § 271(a). The infringing product must read on the patented device; therefore a patentee cannot prevail in an infringement claim without showing that the patent claims cover the alleged infringer's invention. For example, in *SEB S.A. v. Montgomery Ward & Co.*, 77 F. Supp. 2d 399 (S.D.N.Y. 1999), the court held that an importer of consumer deep fryers had infringed, either literally or by use of equivalents, on every element of the plaintiff's claimed invention where both the patented deep fryer and the accused device employed a high-temperature plastic ring to safely secure a plastic shell to the frying pan.

A similar device that performs a similar function as a patented invention does not infringe the patent unless the accused device infringes every claim, either literally or under the doctrine of equivalents. For example, in *Powell v. Allergan Medical Optics*, 868 F. Supp. 1217 (C.D. Cal. 1994), an accused intraocular lens performed the same function in a fundamentally similar way, but the patent holder could not establish infringement because a key limitation of the patent claim— that the lenses "have a socket recess entirely within the circumference of the optic"—was not met, even under the doctrine of equivalents. (See Figure 4-C.)

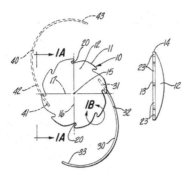

Figure 4-C
Powell v. Allergan Medical Optics
868 F. Supp. 1217 (C.D. Cal. 1994). Intraocular lens.

In *Transmatic, Inc. v. Gulton Industries, Inc.*, 53 F.3d 1270 (Fed. Cir. 1995), the court noted that a patent claim is not necessarily limited to the preferred embodiment disclosed in the patent and that limitations from narrow dependent claims cannot be cannot be used to limit broader independent claims. In determining that the patented cornice lighting fixture used inside public transit vehicles was infringed, the court noted that the lighting fixture housing, as mounted, had a different affect on airflow, but that difference did not matter because the infringing device embodied every term of the patent claims.

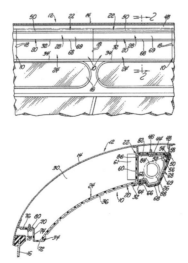

Figure 4-D
Transmatic, Inc. v. Gulton Industries, Inc., 53 F.3d 1270 (Fed. Cir. 1995).
Cornice lighting fixture used inside public transit vehicles.

d. Indirect Infringement

Indirect infringement includes both contributory infringement and inducement to infringement. Indirect infringement is dependent on direct infringement, meaning that until direct infringement is proven, indirect infringement cannot be established. Moreover, the plaintiff must show that the defendant was aware of the patent and actually intended for an infringement to occur, although circumstantial evidence may be sufficient to establish the requisite knowledge and intent. In *Hewlett-Packard Co. v. Bausch & Lomb Inc.*, 909 F.2d 1464 (Fed. Cir. 1990), the court found that defendant's use of certain X-Y plotters for drawing two-dimensional graphs infringed a prior patent, but refused to hold the defendant liable for inducement to infringement connected with the sale of its business (and the infringing articles) because the defendants sought only to sell their business and the requisite intent to induce infringement had not been established.

A person who sells or imports a component or device that constitutes a material part of another's patented invention for use in a manner that infringes a patent, commits contributory infringement unless the component or device is "a staple article or commodity of commerce suitable for substantial noninfringing use." 35 U.S.C. § 271(c).

Inducement to infringement occurs when one party actively induces another party to engage in direct infringement of a patent. In such a situation, both parties are liable for infringement. 35 U.S.C. § 271(b). For example, in *C.R. Bard, Inc. v. United States Surgical Corp.*, 258 F. Supp. 2d 355 (D.Del. 2003), the court upheld a jury's determination that by marketing a hernia plug with instructions to surgeons to alter the plug during surgery in a way that infringed on the plaintiff's patent, the defendant was liable for enhanced damages because it had willfully induced surgeons to commit infringement. (See Figure 4-E.)

Acts occurring entirely outside of the United States generally cannot give rise to an infringement claim, but under 35 U.S.C. § 271(f), a United States exporter of components may be held liable where those components are combined into an infringing device abroad. For example, in *Microsoft Corp. v. AT&T Corp.*, 127 S.Ct. 1746 (2007), Microsoft had developed a version of Windows for installation on personal computers built and sold abroad with a program that allowed users to record and compress speech on their home computers. AT&T claimed that Microsoft's software enabled users of those computers to infringe upon AT&T's patent for a computer designed to perform the same recordation and compression. The Court recognized that had Microsoft exported copies of the Windows software, the copies would have con-

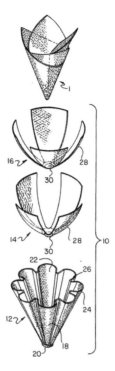

Figure 4-E
C.R. Bard, Inc. v. United States Surgical Corp.
258 F. Supp. 2d 355 (D.Del. 2003). Hernia plug.

stituted infringing components under § 271(f). However, the Court further held that because the "gold master copy" of the software exported by Microsoft was never directly installed onto the foreign computers, but was used only to generate copies which were installed onto the computers, Microsoft had not actually exported the infringing component and was therefore not liable under § 271(f).

Under the exhaustion doctrine, the authorized unrestricted sale of a patented product places the product beyond the reach of the patent, and the purchaser is free to use or resell the product without infringing the patent. For example, in *Quanta Computer, Inc. v. LG Electronics, Inc.*, 128 S.Ct. 2109 (2008), the Supreme Court held that method patents are subject to the exhaustion doctrine, and that, because LG's license to Intel did not limit the downstream use of the computer cips, the patent was exhausted by the sales to third parties. Therefore, the Court reversed the Federal Circuit's finding of infringement.

4. Repair v. Reconstruction

The purchaser of a patented invention has an implied license to use and repair the invention. However, the purchaser doe not have a right to reconstruct the invention. The line between repair and reconstruction, which separates permissible use from infringement of the patent holder's exclusive right to manufacture the invention, is often uncertain. In *Dana Corp. v. American Precision Co.*, 827 F.2d 755 (Fed. Cir. 1987), the court affirmed summary judgment in favor of a defendant who had allegedly infringed on the plaintiff's patent for heavy-truck clutches by repairing used clutches by substituting salvaged and new parts for parts that were worn out.

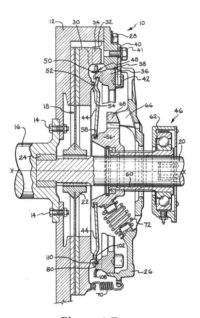

Figure 4-F
Dana Corp. v. American Precision Co.
827 F.2d 755 (Fed. Cir. 1987). Heavy-truck clutch.

In *Wilbur-Ellis Co. v. Kuther*, 377 U.S. 422 (1964), the defendant had bought four used fish-canning machines that embodied the plaintiff's combination patent. Three of the machines were inoperative due to rust and corrosion, and the defendant cleaned and modified the machines to pack five-ounce cans rather than one-pound cans. The patent owner sued for infringement, alleging that the defendant had "reconstructed" the machines. The Supreme Court held that repair of the machines to their original utility did not constitute reconstruction because the "machines were not spent; they had years of usefulness remaining though they needed cleaning and repair." The Court held that by adapting the old machines to a related use, the defendant had done more than simply repair the machines. However, the Court held that adaptation of the machine for use on a 5-ounce can was within the patent rights purchased, since size was not an invention.

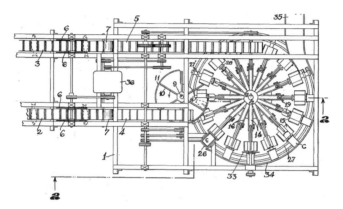

Figure 4-G
Wilbur-Ellis Co. v. Kuther
377 U.S. 422 (1964). Fish-canning machine.

5. Defenses

a. Invalidity

Patents are presumed valid, and any party asserting that a patent is invalid bears the burden of establishing its invalidity. 35 U.S.C. § 282 provides that invalidity of the patent or any claim on grounds of non-novelty, obviousness, lack of utility, statutory bar, inadequate specifications, improper amendment, or any other defense can, if proved by an alleged infringer, serve to defend against a claim of infringement. Thus, one accused of patent infringement may defend on the ground that the patented device allegedly infringed upon was not actually patentable.

In *MedImmune, Inc. v. Genetech, Inc.*, 549 U.S. 118 (2007), the Genetech holder of a patent for respiratory medication threatened to sue its licensee for infringement, alleging that the licensee's use involved not only licensed innovations, but also technology claimed in a different patent. In response, MedImmune sought a declaratory judgment that Genetech's patent was invalid. The Supreme Court noted that invalidity is a defense to infringement, not a cause of action. However, the Court held that the patent holder's threat to bring suit for infringement created a genuine controversy and that the licensee need not breach the license agreement before seeking a declaratory judgment of invalidity.

b. Misuse

A patent holder's misuse of the patent monopoly provides a defense for alleged direct or indirect infringers. Classic examples of misuse include:

- requiring the purchase of unpatented goods for use with patented apparatus or processes,

- conditioning the granting of a license under one patent upon the acceptance of another and different license, or

- prohibiting production or sale of competing goods.

The first two examples are called "tying arrangements," as they seek to tie other products to the patented invention. The availability of misuse as a defense to infringement reflects the public policy of preventing the patent monopoly from being extended beyond its appropriate scope.

A patent holder's use of license agreements to restrict unpatented products produced using a patented method constitutes misuse. For example, in *Robintech, Inc. v. Chemidus Wavin, Ltd.*, 628 F.2d 142 (D.C. Cir. 1980), the plaintiffs licensed their patented method for forming internal grooves in a pipe. The resulting grooved pipes and pipe fittings were not patented, but the license agreement limited where the licensee could export the pipes. The court held that the plaintiffs had misused their patent because the patent-license agreement restricted the licensee's freedom to sell unpatented goods produced using the patented method. However, not all license terms that affect non-patented goods constitute misuse. For example, in *Bayer AG v. Housey Pharmaceuticals, Inc.*, 228 F. Supp. 2d 467 (D.Del. 2002), the court considered a license for patented drug-development software and held that royalties due after the patent had lapsed were for the pre-expiration use of the claimed invention, and that the arrangement did not constitute misuse of the patent.

c. Shop Rights

Under certain circumstances, an employer may defend charges of infringement of an employee's patent on the ground that the employer has a "shop right" in that invention. A "shop right" is a common law right that entitles an employer to use an invention patented by one or more of its employees without liability for infringement.

Employers do not acquire a shop right in their employees' inventions as a matter of course, but only if the court determines that equity and fairness demands it in consideration of the contractual relationship between the employers and employee, whether the employee consented to the shop right, and whether the employee assisted the employer in the use of the invention. Whether the employer's resources contributed to the employee's development of the invention and whether the employee developed the invention in the course of employment are particularly relevant to the determination of a shop right. For example, in *Francklyn v. Guilford Packing Co.*, 695 F.2d 1158 (9th Cir. 1983), the court held that where the patent holder's former employer had sponsored the patentee's on-the-job development of a clam harvester and the patent holder had not later demanded royalties for the employer's use of the patented device, the employer had acquired a shop right in the harvester. However, the court also held that a third party could not avoid paying royalties to the patentee by purchasing one of the harvesters on the open market, selling it to the shop-right holder, and then leasing it back.

An employer's claim to a shop right may be undermined if, for example, the employer demanded reimbursement for resources expended in developing the invention. In *Mechmetals Corp. v. Telex Computer Products, Inc.*, 709 F.2d 1287 (9th Cir. 1983), the court refused to award a shop right in the patented capstan, a device used to accelerate magnetic tape used to store information in computers, to the corporation that produced the invention because it received reimbursement for development costs in the form of a contract to be the sole manufacturer of the capstan.

An employer may also forfeit potential shop rights if the employer enters into a licensing agreement with the employee. Shop rights are also non-assignable except to a successor in intrest in connection with a sale of a business.

d. Prior Use

35 U.S.C. § 273 provides a narrow "prior user" defense to defendants who had continuously used the plaintiff's patented method for at least one year prior to the date the plaintiff's patent issued. If the prior user proves they used the invention for more than a year before the patent application was filed, then the patent is invalid under the statutory bar. However, if the use first occurred within a year of the filing and before the patent issued, the prior use defense applies.

The prior use defense is unavailable if the use was abandoned then resumed within a year of the patent being issued. Only the specific methods previously used by the defendant are excepted, and only if the defendant developed the method independently of the patentee and persons in privity with the patentee. Moreover, the benefit of the exception is unassignable, except as a part of a good faith assignment or transfer of the entire line of business to which the defense relates, and even then only if the business continues to operate on the same physical site. A defendant must prove the prior user defense by clear and convincing evidence, and the court may award attorney fees if a defendant asserts, but fails to prove, this defense.

e. Regulatory Safe Harbor

A "safe harbor" provided by § 271(e) protects certain federal regulators, such as the FDA, and protects private researchers whose use of patented technology is reasonably expected to yield information that will be submitted to a regulatory authority. For example, in *Merck KGaA v. Integra Lifesciences I, Ltd.*, 545 U.S. 193 (2005), the defendant discovered that a substance claimed in plaintiff's patent was capable of reversing the growth of some tumors. Of the array of clinical experiments the defendant thereafter conducted, it reported only some in later applications for FDA approval of the substance for use in treating tumors. The Supreme Court found that the defendant's use of the plaintiff's invention in experiments reported to the FDA was clearly within the safe harbor of § 271(e). The Court further held that the defendant's use of the drug in experiments that were not reported to the FDA would qualify within § 271(e)'s safe harbor if the defendant had "a reasonable basis for believing" the results would be relevant to the FDA.

6. Remedies

Patent holders may seek an injunction and damages if their patents are infringed. The most common remedy for patent infringement is an injunction under § 283. The standard for receiving an injunction is the same as in non-patent cases. Under § 284, the patent holder may also receive compensatory damages, which may be tripled at the discretion of the court if the infringement was willful. An award of "reasonable royalty" payments is determined by what a willing licensee would pay after a hypothetical negotiation. Patent holders can also recover costs and prejudgment interest, and under § 285, the prevailing party can recover attorneys' fees in exceptional cases.

35 U.S.C. § 286 provides a six-year statute of limitations to the recovery for patent infringement. Under § 287, the patentee and any licensees must mark

products that embody the claimed invention with the word "patent" or the abbreviation "pat." and the patent number to notify the public that the article is patented. The patentee cannot recover monetary damages for the unauthorized manufacture of articles infringing on his patent where the authorized embodiments did not carry such notice. This requirement does not apply to process claims, which, because they are intangible, cannot be marked.

a. Injunctions

Injunctions are the most common remedy for patent infringement. The right to obtain an injunction is very important; without it, the patentee's right to exclude would lose much of its value. Courts enjoy considerable discretion in determining whether an injunction should be issued, and the appellate standard of review is abuse of discretion.

Injunctions enjoining infringement normally terminate with the expiration of the patent, although under certain circumstances the court may bar the enjoined party's use of an invention after the patent term has run on other grounds. For example, in *Hughes Tool Co. v. A.F. Spengler Co.*, 73 F. Supp. 154 (D.Okl. 1947), the plaintiff sought enforcement of an earlier decree that enjoined the defendant from infringing on the plaintiff's patent for earth-boring drills and incorporated a settlement agreement providing that the plaintiff would not seek damages if the defendant agreed not engage in the sale or manufacture of earth-boring drills for as long as the plaintiff remained so engaged. The court recognized that its "permanent" injunction necessarily terminated upon the expiration of plaintiff's patent, but further held that the defendant's noncompete agreement, entered into in connection with the sale of its business and goodwill, remained entirely enforceable.

In *eBay Inc. v. MercExchange, L.L.C.*, 547 U.S. 388 (2006), the Supreme Court held that the plaintiff's patented method for online market management software was infringed. In discussing the appropriate remedy, the Supreme Court stated that in patent litigation (as in other types of litigation) a plaintiff seeking a permanent injunction must satisfy the traditional four-factor test:

(1) that it has suffered an irreparable injury;

(2) that remedies available at law, such as monetary damages, are inadequate to compensate for that injury;

(3) that, considering the balance of hardships between the plaintiff and defendant, a remedy in equity is warranted; and

(4) that the public interest would not be disserved by a permanent injunction.

Prior to the *eBay Inc. v. MercExchange, L.L.C.* decision, irreparable harm was generally presumed once a clear showing of infringement was made. For example, in *W.L. Gore & Associates, Inc. v. Garlock, Inc.*, 842 F.2d 1275 (Fed. Cir. 1988), the court stated the grant or denial of an injunction is discretionary, that injunctive relief against an adjudged infringer is usually granted, and that an injunction should issue once infringement is established unless there is a sufficient reason for denying it.

Injunctive relief may be appropriate even if the defendant has already stopped infringing. This logic is fairly simple; if the defendant has truly stopped infringing then the injunction will cause no harm, and if the cessation of infringement was merely to hide future acts from the court then the infringer deserves to be enjoined.

An injunction may be granted whether the effect of the injunction is slight or drives the defendant out of business. For example, in *Du Bois v. Kirk*, 158 U.S. 58 (1895), which involved a patent on a portable dam used in the timber industry, the defendant needed to make only a minor change to cease infringement, but the plaintiff was nonetheless entitled to an injunction. In *Windsurfing International Inc., v. AMF, Inc.*, 782 F.2d 995 (Fed. Cir. 1986), the court reversed denial of an injunction to prohibit the manufacture and sale of patented "sailboards." The defendant's entire business involved the manufacture and sale of the infringing sailboards, so injunctive relief would effectively destroy its business. Nevertheless, an injunction was proper, and "[o]ne who elects to build a business on a product found to infringe cannot be heard to complain if an injunction against continuing infringement destroys the business so elected." (See Figure 4-H.)

Courts may also grant a preliminary injunction during the course of litigation to preserve the status quo and to protect the rights of the parties pending the outcome of litigation on the merits. In *Cordis Corp. v. Medtronic, Inc.*, 835 F.2d 859 (Fed. Cir. 1987), for example, the patent holder had successfully defended their patented tined leads used with cardiac pacemakers against a licensee who sought to invalidate the patent. Subsequently, the licensee filed a declaratory action to determine that their finned leads did not infringe the patented tined leads and requested a preliminary injunction to prevent the patent holder from terminating the license agreement. The court found that the license holder met its burden and therefore granted the preliminary injunction pending resolution on the merits. (See Figure 4-I.)

Although injunctions are normally routine, a court may refuse to grant a permanent injunction for a variety of reasons. For example, in *City of Milwaukee v. Activated Sludge Inc.*, 69 F.2d 577 (7th Cir. 1934), the plaintiff sought an in-

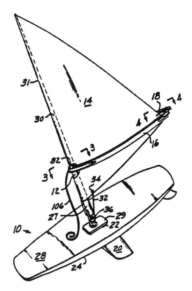

Figure 4-H
Windsurfing International Inc., v. AMF, Inc.
782 F.2d 995 (Fed. Cir. 1986). Sailboard.

junction to prevent Milwaukee from using its patented method of sewage treatment. Rather than requiring the city to dump large quantities of raw sewage into Lake Michigan, the court denied an injunction and instead awarded monetary damages. In *Foster v. American Machine & Foundry Co.*, 492 F.2d 1317 (2d Cir. 1974), the court upheld the denial of a permanent injunction for welding machinery. The court held that because the defendant was currently manufacturing the product, whereas the patent holder was not, it was inequitable to cause irreparable harm to the infringer without any benefit to the patentee. Instead, the court determined that a compulsory license with royalties provided adequate compensation to the patent holder.

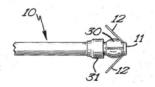

Figure 4-I
Cordis Corp. v. Medtronic, Inc., 835 F.2d 859 (Fed. Cir. 1987).
Tined leads used with cardiac pacemakers.

Courts may also delay the effective date of a permanent injunction. In *Schneider (Europe) AG v. SciMed Life Sys., Inc.*, 852 F. Supp. 813 (D.Minn. 1994), the court found infringement of a patented balloon dilatation catheter used to treat coronary artery disease, but delayed the permanent injunction for one year to allow health care providers ample time to switch over to non-infringing products. However, the court imposed a mandatory royalty on the sale and use of the infringing product that increased each quarter of the year pending the injunction to encourage a quicker transition.

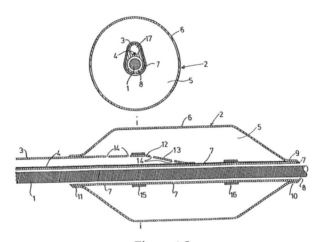

Figure 4-J
Schneider (Europe) AG v. SciMed Life Sys., Inc.
852 F. Supp. 813 (D.Minn. 1994). Balloon dilation catheter.

Contempt proceedings are used to ensure that an infringing party does not violate the injunction. A court will find a defendant in contempt only if the infringement continues or a similar modified article infringes under an analysis similar to the doctrine of equivalents. For example, in *KSM Fastening Systems Inc. v. H.A. Jones Co.*, 776 F.2d 1522 (Fed. Cir. 1985), the court vacated findings of contempt for an accused violation of an injunction because the enjoined party modified their product (a refractory anchor used in the linings of furnaces) such that it no longer infringed on a similar, patented device. The court reversed the finding of contempt because the modified device was not a trivial variation, but instead a legitimate non-infringing device. The lower court's injunction did not disallow competition; it only prevented the defendant from continuing to infringe.

b. Money Damages

35 U.S.C. §284 provides for monetary damages "adequate to compensate for patent infringement but in no event less than a reasonable royalty for the use made of the invention by the infringer," plus pre and post judgment interest and court costs. The court may accept expert testimony to aid in the determination of the damages or reasonable royalty. Damages are available to restore patent holders to the position they would have occupied but for the infringement. Patentees often seek lost profits, but a reasonable royalty is the default measure of damages.

i. Lost Profits

In *Panduit Corp. v. Stahlin Bros. Fibre Works, Inc.*, 575 F.2d 1152 (6th Cir. 1978), the court specified the four factors considered in determining whether a patent owner is entitled to recover for lost profits:

(1) The demand for the patented product,

(2) The absence of acceptable non-infringing substitutes,

(3) The patent holder's manufacturing and marketing capability, and

(4) The amount of profit the patent holder would have generated.

If the plaintiff cannot prove lost profits, or they are minimal, then damages are calculated based on a reasonable royalty. For example, in *Kearns v. Chrysler Corp.*, 32 F.3d 1541 (Fed. Cir. 1994), the plaintiff held a patent for intermittent windshield wipers. Because he was unable to meet the third part of the *Panduit* test (that is, he lacked the capability to produce or market the quantity of wipers sold by Chrysler), the court denied his request for lost profits and instead fixed damages at a reasonable royalty.

In *Kori Corp. v. Wilco Marsh Buggies and Draglines, Inc.*, 761 F.2d 649 (Fed. Cir. 1985), the court used the infringer's profits to calculate the patentee's lost profits. Ordinarily, a patentee is not entitled to the infringer's profits, but in this instance the defendant sold amphibious marsh craft incorporating the patent holder's patented pontoons in direct competition with the patent holder. The court inferred that the defendant's sales would have been made by the plaintiff but for the infringement, and therefore found it appropriate to award lost profits in the amount of the infringer's profits. In contrast, under §289, the holder of a design patent is automatically entitled to an infringer's profits, and the award may not be less than $250. (See Figure 4-K.)

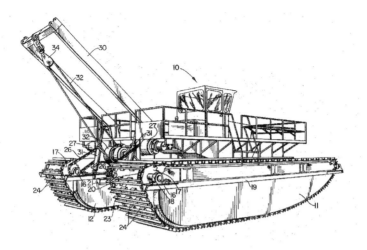

Figure 4-K
Kori Corp. v. Wilco Marsh Buggies and Draglines, Inc.
761 F.2d 649 (Fed. Cir. 1985). Amphibious marsh craft.

ii. Reasonable Royalty

In *State Industries, Inc. v. Mor-Flo Industries, Inc.*, 883 F.2d 1573 (Fed. Cir. 1989), the court stated that the determination of a reasonable royalty is not based on the infringer's profit margin, but on what a willing licensor and licensee would bargain for in a hypothetical negotiation. The court is allowed to consider the infringer's profits, but other factors — such as the value of collateral sales, alternatives to the patented invention, and existing royalties paid by others — should also be considered.

The reasonable royalty is a hypothetical rate used to measure damages, and the amount of the reasonable royalty may exceed what the infringer would have actually paid for a license or the infringer's profit margin on the infringing article. For example, in *Golight, Inc. v. Wal-Mart Stores, Inc.*, 355 F.3d 1327 (Fed. Cir. 2004), Wal-Mart infringed the plaintiff's patented remote-controlled portable searchlight. Wal-Mart objected to the reasonable royalty because it would force them to sell the product at a loss and argued that the reasonable royalty should be capped at their expected profit margin. The court held that even if Wal-Mart would lose money on sales, the royalty determined by the court was reasonable and further held that capping damages at the infringer's profit margin was not an appropriate method of determining damages.

In *Georgia-Pacific v. United States Plywood Corp.*, 318 F. Supp. 1116 (S.D.N.Y. 1970), the court compiled an often-cited, non-exhaustive list of factors used to determine reasonable royalties:

1. The royalties currently paid to the patentee by legitimate licensees.

2. The royalties paid for the use of patents comparable to the infringed patent.

3. The nature and scope of the license (for example, whether the license is exclusive or non-exclusive, and whether the license has territorial restrictions.

4. The patent holder's established licensing policy (for example, whether the patent holder has elected to maintain its patent monopoly by not licensing to others or by licensing only under special conditions designed to preserve that monopoly).

5. The commercial relationship between the licensor and licensee (for example, whether they are competitors in the same territory, in the same line of business or whether they are the inventor or promoter).

6. The patent holder's practice of selling the patented product in a manner that promotes sales of the patent holder's other products.

7. The duration of the patent and the term of the license.

8. The established profitability of the product made under the patent; its commercial success; and its current popularity.

9. The utility and advantages of the patent property over other similar products or methods.

10. The nature of the patented invention; the character of the product or method as owned and produced by the licensor; and the benefits to those who have used the product or method.

11. The extent to which the infringer has made use of the invention.

12. The portion of the profit or selling price that is customarily paid in the industry for a license on a similar invention.

13. The portion of the realizable profit that should be credited to the patented position of the invention as distinguished from non-patented elements, the manufacturing process, business risks, or significant features or improvements added by the infringer.

14. The opinion testimony of qualified experts.

15. The amount that a licensor (such as the patentee) and a licensee (such as the infringer) would have agreed upon (at the time the infringement began) if both had been reasonably and voluntarily trying to reach an agreement.

iii. Treble Damages

In cases of willful infringement or bad faith, under 35 U.S.C. §284, the court may increase the damages by up to three times the amount of compensatory damages. In *Beatrice Foods Co. v. New England Printing & Lithographing Co.*, 923 F.2d 1576 (Fed. Cir. 1991), the court emphasized that treble damages under §284 are appropriate to punish willful infringement or bad faith, but should not be used to increase a compensation award. The district court awarded compensatory damages of twenty-two million dollars, but the award was reversed on appeal because there was inadequate evidence to support the damages. The district court then found damages of eight million and tripled them to twenty-four million, but that award was also reversed. The Federal Circuit held that the treble damage provision of §284 is punitive—not compensatory—and, citing the district court's finding that there was not any evidence of bad faith or willful infringement, reversed the enhanced damages.

iv. Attorneys' Fees

35 U.S.C. §285 provides that "[t]he court in exceptional cases may award reasonable attorney fees to the prevailing party," a reversal of the traditional "American Rule" under which each party bears its own fees and expenses. Willful infringement, inequitable conduct before the PTO, misconduct during litigation, vexatious or unjustified litigation, and the filing of a frivolous suit are among the types of exceptional conduct that can form a basis for awarding attorneys' fees. Exceptional conduct must be shown by clear and convincing evidence. The compensation of expert witnesses may also be awarded under §285. In *Beckman Instruments v. LKB Produkter AB*, 892 F.2d 1547 (Fed. Cir. 1989), the jury found that the defendant infringed some of the patent's claims. The court issued an injunction, but the defendant repeatedly violated the injunction and engaged in a vexatious litigation strategy involving frivolous counterclaims and defenses and discovery abuses. The court found this to be an exceptional case and awarded attorneys' fees to the plaintiff. The policy reason for the award of attorneys' fees is not to further reward the prevailing party, but to compensate that party for costs that it would not have incurred but for the losing party's misconduct. *W. L. Gore & Associates, Inc. v. Oak Materials Group, Inc.*, 424 F. Supp. 700 (D.Del. 1976).

Checkpoints

- United States District courts have original and exclusive jurisdiction over any civil action arising under the patent laws. On appeal, jurisdiction lies in the United States Court of Appeals for the Federal Circuit. The Federal Circuit applies its own law to patent matters and the law of the circuit in which the originating district court sits for non patent matters in the case.

- Infringement includes any unauthorized manufacture, use, sale, offer to sell, or importation into the United States of any patented article. Infringement is a strict liability cause of action; the intent of the infringer is only relevant in the determination of damages.

- In conducting an infringement analysis, the court construes the claims of the patent and then determines if the allegedly infringing device "reads on" every limitation of the claims, either identically or under the doctrine of equivalents.

- The construction of the claims to determine infringement is similar to the construction used in patent prosecution; claims are construed according to their express language in light of the specification, drawings, and the file wrapper. Extrinsic evidence may be used, but not if it contradicts the express language of a claim.

- The doctrine of equivalents broadens the scope of patent protection to cover insubstantial or trivial nonfunctional changes that do not literally infringe. An element is equivalent to a limitation of a patent claim if it performs substantially the same function in substantially the same way to obtain substantially the same result as the claim limitation.

- Direct infringement is the manufacture, use, sale, or importation of the infringing device and requires that the accused device meet every limitation of the claim, either literally or under doctrine of equivalents.

- Indirect infringement includes both contributory infringement and inducement to infringement and requires direct infringement as a prerequisite to liability.

- Contributory infringement occurs when one sells a material component of another's patented invention that is not itself a staple article or commodity of commerce suitable for substantial non-infringing use.

- Inducement to infringement occurs when one actively induces another to engage in direct infringement.

- Common defenses to infringement include invalidity of the patent, misuse, shop rights, prior use, safe harbors, and nonpatent defenses including that the accused device did not infringe or lapse of the statute of limitations.

- Defendants asserting patent invalidity carry the burden of proof but may use any of the grounds required for patentability to make the challenge such as by negating novelty, non-obviousness, utility, etc.

- Misuse is generally asserted as a defense when the patent holder has allegedly abused the patent monopoly with a tying arrangement by requiring the purchase of unpatented goods with the patent or conditioning the grant of a license upon acceptance of another different license or some similar tying arrangement or unlawful restraint of competitive trade.

- Shop rights grant an employer the right to use an invention patented by an employee under equitable circumstances, such as when the employer provided the material and the employee developed the invention in the course of their employment.

- A defendant that continuously used the patented method for at least a year prior to the date the patent issued may continue using the method if it was developed independently of the patentee.

- Injunctions are the most common remedy for patent infringement and are issued on equitable principles identical to those for nonpatent injunctions. To receive an injunction, patent holders are required to show that they have suffered irreparable injury, that money damages are inadequate, balance of the hardships, and that the public interest would not be disserved.

- Patent holders may also receive money damages for their lost profits if they can prove them with requisite certainty but more often the measure of damages is a reasonable royalty. A reasonable royalty is calculated by what a willing licensor and licensee would bargain for in a hypothetical negotiation.

- The court may treble the damages in a case of willful infringement or bad faith, but cannot increase damages as a compensatory measure.

- In exceptional cases, such as those involving willful infringement, inequitable conduct, or vexatious litigation, the prevailing party in a patent infringement action may receive an award of its reasonable attorneys' fees.

Chapter Five

Copyright Law

Roadmap

After reading this chapter, you should understand:

- Common law copyrights — perpetual copyright protection for works that were created before 1978 and have not been published. The statutory copyright preempts common law copyrights once the work is published, and for works created after 1978 statutory copyright preempts the moment the work is fixed in tangible form, even if the work is never published.

- Copyrightable works — original works of authorship; 17 U.S.C. § 102 provides a nonexclusive list, which includes literary works; musical works; dramatic works; pictorial, graphic, and sculptural works; motion pictures and other audio-visual works; sound recordings; and architectural works.

- Expression — copyright protects only the expression of an idea, not the underlying idea, procedure, process, system, method of operation, concept, principle, or discovery. Facts themselves are not protected, although selection and organization of facts may qualify as expression.

- Fixation requirement — copyright protection extends to all original works of authorship fixed in any tangible medium of expression (now known or later developed) from which they can be perceived, reproduced, or otherwise communicated, either directly or with the aid of a machine or device.

- Originality requirement — to be copyrightable, a work must be the independent creation of the author and display at least minimal creativity.

- Utilitarian works — purely utilitarian works cannot be copyrighted, but if "conceptual separability" exists, then the aesthetic or expressive aspects of a utilitarian work can be copyrighted.

- Merger doctrine — when an idea necessarily involves certain forms of expression, those forms of expression cannot be copyrighted.

- Joint works — works prepared by two or more authors with the intention that their contributions be merged into inseparable parts of a whole. The authors' contributions need not be equal, but each must be independently copyrightable. Coauthors of joint works are treated as tenants-in-common, and each has the exclusive rights found in 17 U.S.C. § 106 and may independently license the work.

- Works for hire — works prepared by an employee within the scope of their employment or a commissioned work if the parties expressly agree that it is a work for hire.

- Duration of a copyright — for authors or joint authors, copyright protection lasts seventy years past the death of the last surviving author; for works created before January 1, 1978, copyright protection lasts twenty-eight years from the date the work was first copyrighted and may be renewed for an additional sixty-seven years; for anonymous, pseudonymous, and works for hire, copyright protection expires ninety-five years after the first publication or 120 years after their creation (whichever is earlier).

- Transfers of copyrights — authors may assign or license some or all of their rights. An exclusive transfer requires a written embodiment, but a nonexclusive transfer need not be in writing.

- Termination right — authors are allowed to recapture their work by cancelling assignments and licenses.

- Copyright holders can use their interest as collateral in secured transactions. Security interests in copyrights are perfected by a filing with the Copyright Office.

1. Introduction

Copyrights, like patents, are designed to foster a public policy. By protecting works from unauthorized copying, society motivates authors and artists to produce useful works that benefit society. The federal government's power to protect copyrights is derived from the same source as patent law: Article 1, Clause 8 of the United States Constitution. The vast majority of federal copyright law is found in Title 17 of the United States Code.

The first Congress enacted the first federal statutes on patent and copyright law in 1790. Since then, there have been a number of revisions to copyright law — primarily to increase the types of works that are eligible for copyright protection. The Copyright Act of 1976 overhauled United States Copyright law and replaced the Copyright Act of 1909. Among other things, the 1976 Act granted copyright protection from the moment a work is fixed in tangible form and extended the duration of copyright protection. In 1989, as part of the United States' decision to join the Berne Convention, Congress made substantial revisions to the notice provision and other formalities required by the 1976 Act. Congress continues to update copyright protection to adapt to changing technologies and an expansion in the public's perception of artists rights. For example, in 1990, Congress expanded architects' rights to their plans and buildings constructed based on their plans, and in 1992, the Act was amended to afford record companies and performers additional protection in response to the development of digital recording machines.

2. State and Common Law Copyrights

Two types of copyrights existed prior to 1978: statutory and common law. Statutory copyright protection extended only to works that were published, and common law copyrights protected unpublished works. Statutory copyright protection was limited to a term of years, and common law copyright protection was perpetual. However, common law copyright was largely abolished with the passage of the Copyright Act of 1976. Under § 302(a), works are copyrightable once they are fixed in tangible form. The preemption provisions of 17 U.S.C. § 301, preempt, as of January 1, 1978, all legal and equitable rights within the general scope of copyright as specified in § 106 with regard to all copyrightable subject matter, regardless of the date of publication. Likewise, §§ 106A pertaining to moral rights, 113(d), and related sections preempt all state law governing rights within the scope of § 106A with regard to "undertakings commenced" after § 106A became effective.

The preemption provisions of § 301 do not preempt state law regarding subject matter beyond the scope of §§ 102 or 103, state law governing the violation of rights beyond the "general scope" of § 106, and state or local landmark, historic preservation, zoning, or building codes. Moreover, state law "rights and remedies" regarding sound recordings made before February 15, 1972 are not preempted until February 15, 2067, and § 301 neither "annuls [nor] limits any rights or remedies" otherwise available under federal law.

State law is not preempted to the extent that it either grants rights that are not equivalent to those conferred by §§ 106 and 106A or governs activities violating legal or equitable rights that extend beyond the life of the author. Common law copyrights received before January 1, 1978, are entitled to protection only where the common law cause of action arose from undertakings commenced prior to 1978. § 301(b)(2). In *Klekas v. EMI Films, Inc.*, 198 Cal. Rptr. 296 (Cal. Ct. App. 1984), an author brought a common law claim of plagiarism against the producers of the film *The Deer Hunter*. The author contended that his claim was not preempted because he wrote his novel before 1978. However, the court, following federal circuit and district court authority, held the dates of the alleged acts of plagiarism were dispositive, and, thus, the alleged acts of copying that occurred in 1976 or 1977 were not preempted, but claims relating to the 1978 distribution of the film and subsequent novel were preempted.

3. Copyrightable Subject Matter

The Copyright Act protects "original works of authorship fixed in any tangible medium of expression, now known or later developed, from which they can be perceived, reproduced, or otherwise communicated, either directly or with the aid of a machine or device." 17 U.S.C. § 102(a). Under § 102(a), works of authorship include:

- literary works;
- musical works, including any accompanying words;
- dramatic works, including any accompanying music;
- pantomimes and choreographic works;
- pictorial, graphic, and sculptural works;
- motion pictures and other audiovisual works;
- sound recordings; and
- architectural works.

The types of copyrightable works expand as technology advances. For example, in *Williams Electronics, Inc. v. Artic International, Inc.*, 685 F.2d 870 (3d Cir. 1982), the defendants argued that a videogame was not a fixed expression because new images were displayed every time the game was played. However, the court held that videogames were suitably fixed and consequently were protectable by copyright. Similarly, the copyrightability of computer programs was uncertain in the last quarter of the twentieth century. Because computer programs cannot be expressed without the aid of a computer, there were doubts as to whether the programs were copyrightable. Congress concluded that computer programs should be eligible for protection and amended the Copyright Act to specifically include computer programs in 1980.

The Constitution uses two terms that are particularly important to determine the scope of copyright law: "authors" and "writings." From the earliest stages of copyright law, these terms have been given broad meaning. For example, in *Burrow-Giles Lithographic Co. v. Sarony*, 111 U.S. 53 (1884), responding to a challenge on the status of photographs as copyrightable works, the Supreme Court addressed the meaning of the term "writings." The Court concluded that "writings" encompasses all forms of writing, printing, engraving, etching, and the like whereby the ideas of the author are "given visible expression," including the somewhat mechanical process of photography. The Court also defined "authors" as any person to whom a writing owed its origin.

In § 102(b), the Copyright Act describes works to which copyright protection cannot be extended, including any "idea, procedure, process, system, method of operation, concept, principle, or discovery." This restriction reflects the constitutional grant of power to protect "writings," which has been construed to include only tangible expressions. Additionally, copyright protection is not available for works that are not original or that lack minimal creativity.

a. Fixed and Tangible

To qualify for copyright protection, a work must be "fixed in any tangible medium of expression, now known or later developed, from which [it] can be perceived, reproduced, or otherwise communicated, either directly or with the aid of a machine or device." 17 U.S.C. § 102(a). "Tangible medium of expression" is a broad category that separates copyrightable expressions from patentable processes and methods. For example, in *Baker v. Selden*, 101 U.S. 99 (1879), the inventor of a book-keeping system argued that the system was protected by his copyright in a book that described the system. The Supreme Court concluded it was not, because copyrights protect the author's expression of an idea, while patents protect the use of the idea itself. The idea of the book-keeping system had been placed in the public domain, precluding patent protection, but the book explaining it was protected under copyright.

Copyright attaches at the moment an idea is fixed as a tangible expression. Generally this requirement is easily met. For example, the idea for a book is fixed when it is written. In a more complex example, § 101 provides that a live broadcast "consisting of sounds, images, or both, ... is 'fixed' for purposes of this title if a fixation of the work is being made simultaneously with its transmission." For example, in *Trenton v. Infinity Broadcasting Corp.*, 865 F. Supp. 1416 (C.D. Cal. 1994), the court held that the live broadcasts of the "Loveline" radio program featuring Dr. Drew were copyrighted because they had been simultaneously recorded. Fixation of computer programs in a tangible medium includes their storage in computer memory chips, discs, magnetic tape, and the like. In *Apple Computer, Inc. v. Franklin Computer Corp.*, 714 F.2d 1240 (3d Cir. 1983), the court held that the computer program was fixed once it was stored in the computer's ROM.

b. Originality

To be copyrightable, a work must be "original," meaning it is: (1) the independent creation of its author, and (2) at least minimally creative. The requirement of creativity is minimal, and most works satisfy the requirement.

For a work to be creative, it needs only to possess some creative spark. In *Bleistein v. Donaldson Lithographing Co.*, 188 U.S. 239 (1903), the employees of a lithographer had produced and properly copyrighted a circus advertisement prepared for the circus owner, and the defendants produced further copies. On appeal, the Supreme Court held that even a "mere advertisement of a circus" displayed enough originality to warrant copyright protection.

Historically, the "sweat of the brow" doctrine justified a finding of originality for any compilation of factual information. The sweat of the brow doctrine required only that the author invest original work into the final product. As a result, maps, charts, and telephone directories were copyrightable works. The Supreme Court rejected the sweat of the brow doctrine in *Feist Publications, Inc. v. Rural Telephone Service Co.*, 499 U.S. 340 (1991), in which the Court denied copyright protection for a telephone directory. The Court held that the information was factual and not eligible for a copyright. The *Feist* Court was clear that originality—not sweat of the brow—is required for copyright protection in directories and other fact-based works. Originality can exist in the selection, coordination, and arrangement of public information, but the Court concluded that the "entirely typical" alphabetical organization of the telephone directory in *Feist* indicated that the "creative spark [was] entirely lacking or so trivial as to be virtually nonexistent."

However, even a copy of an original work (like an art student's painting of another artist's work) may satisfy the creativity requirement if it possesses sufficient variation. For example, in *Alfred Bell & Co. v. Catalda Fine Arts*, 74 F. Supp. 973, 975 (S.D.N.Y. 1947), the plaintiff commissioned and copyrighted eight mezzotints (oil-based ink prints produced using finely engraved, steel-coated copper plates) that accurately reproduced painted images that had passed into the public domain. The defendant produced and marketed lithographs of those mezzotints. The court held that the author's contribution of "something more than a 'merely trivial' variation" satisfied the requirement of originality. In sum, anything more than a direct copy is generally considered creative.

c. Expression Not Ideas

It is the expression of an idea that is copyrightable, not the underlying idea itself (but a patent can be used to secure an idea described in a copyrighted work). The difference between the "idea" embodied in a work of authorship and the particular "expression" of that idea is critical to this inquiry. For tangible articles, the difference between the useful and aesthetic elements of the article determine the boundary between aspects of the article that are copyrightable and aspects that are patentable.

For example, in *Continental Casualty Co. v. Beardsley*, 253 F.2d 202 (2d Cir. 1958), the plaintiff sought a declaratory judgment that, by modeling its own forms after those in the defendant's copyrighted book of insurance forms, it had not infringed on the copyright. The court held that the plaintiff had used the forms' language only incidentally to its use of the underlying idea and therefore did not infringe the copyright. In *Baker v. Selden*, 101 U.S. 99 (1879), the Court held that a book describing how to create a medicine could be copyrighted, but the right to produce the medicine described therein could be protected only by a patent.

d. Expressive Not Utilitarian

A work is not protected by copyright to the extent that it is purely utilitarian. If the work is utilitarian, but also has aesthetic or expressive qualities, it might be eligible for a copyright if these qualities are sufficiently separable.

Courts have used different approaches to distinguish between expressive and utilitarian elements. For example, in *Brandir International, Inc. v. Cascade Pacific Lumber Co.*, 834 F.2d 1142 (2d Cir. 1987), the court considered whether a bicycle rack inspired by abstract-expressionist sculpture qualified for copyright protection. The court concluded that because the design of the bicycle rack arose from substantially utilitarian considerations, the creative elements were not sufficiently separable to be copyrightable.

Figure 5-A
Brandir International, Inc. v. Cascade Pacific Lumber Co.
834 F.2d 1142 (2d Cir. 1987). Bicycle rack.

Contrast the outcome in *Brandis* with that in *Pivot Point International, Inc. v. Charlene Products, Inc.*, 372 F.3d 913 (7th Cir. 2004), where the plaintiff alleged that its copyright to a successful hair-stylist's mannequin had been infringed by the defendant's sculpturally similar model. The court concluded that the plaintiff's copyright protected the facial modeling of their mannequin, holding that conceptual separability exists when the artistic aspects of an article can be conceptualized as existing independently of their utilitarian function.

On the other hand, in *Galiano v. Harrah's Operating Co.*, 416 F.3d 411 (5th Cir. 2005), the plaintiff clothing designer alleged that the defendant casino had infringed upon her design for casino uniforms by continuing, after the expiration of their contract, to purchase uniforms manufactured according to her design. The court considered whether there was substantial likelihood that, even if the uniform had no utilitarian use, it would still be marketable simply because of its aesthetic qualities. The court found that the uniforms would not have been marketable but for their utility and held that the uniform design was therefore not copyrightable. The court stated that is utility test was somewhat subjective, but justified the test on the grounds that it was easy to administer.

e. Merger Doctrine

The merger doctrine is related to the utility analysis. It holds that when an idea necessarily involves certain forms of expression those forms of expression are not copyrightable. The idea behind the merger doctrine is that such a copyright would effectively copyright the underlying idea. For example, in *Herbert Rosenthal Jewelry Corp. v. Kalpakian*, 446 F.2d 738 (9th Cir. 1971), the plaintiff alleged that the defendants had infringed on its copyrighted design for a jewel-encrusted bee-shaped pin. The court held the design was non-copyrightable, noting that if the design were copyrightable, it would be impossible to make a jewel-encrusted bee-shaped pin without infringing upon the plaintiff's copyright. In such circumstances, protecting the expressions of the idea would confer a monopoly on the idea itself to the copyright owner.

Similarly, in *ATC Distribution Group, Inc. v. Whatever It Takes Transmissions & Parts, Inc.*, 402 F.3d 700 (6th Cir. 2005), the plaintiff had developed a parts-numbering system for its auto-parts catalog that reflected the sequence of parts necessary to build a transmission. When another auto-parts wholesaler re-designed its own catalog around a similar system, the plaintiff alleged copyright infringement. The court held that the plaintiff's numbering system was fundamentally an idea, and that ideas alone are not copyrightable.

i. Typeface

Mechanical typeface has been categorically denied copyright protection under the merger doctrine. For example, in *Eltra Corp. v. Ringer*, 579 F.2d 294 (4th Cir. 1978), the court held that an original typeface designed for use with a particular typesetter's presses could not be copyrighted because of the age-old rule that typeface is an industrial design that cannot exist independently and separately as a work of art. However, as noted by the court in *Adobe System Inc. v. S. Software Inc.*, 45 U.S.P.Q.2d 1827 (N.D. Cal. 1998), "scalable" computer generated fonts *are* copyrightable because they cannot be copied without an infringement upon the underlying (and independently copyrightable) source code.

ii. Computer Programs

Computer programs have also implicated the merger doctrine. A computer program is protected as a "set of statements or instructions to be used directly or indirectly in a computer in order to bring about a certain result." 17 U.S.C. § 117. The literal elements of the computer software (the source code) are copyrightable as a tangible medium of expression. In this way, computer programs are protected as literary works. For example, in *Apple Computer, Inc. v. Franklin Computer Corp.*, 714 F.2d 1240 (3d Cir. 1983), the court considered whether an operating system, which is written in binary code, is uncopyrightable as insufficiently literary. Noting that under § 101, the definition of "literary works" extends to numerical symbols or indicia, the court held that the instructions embodied in the binary code were protected by copyright. Additionally, the court concluded that the merger doctrine did not prevent Apple's operating system from being copyrightable because any number of variations could have achieved the ultimate result.

The non-literal elements of the computer program, "the structure, sequence and organization of the program, the user interface, and the function, or purpose, of the program," are also copyrightable as long as they are not the only possible expression of an underlying idea. For example, in *Johnson Controls, Inc. v. Phoenix Control Systems, Inc.*, 886 F.2d 1173 (9th Cir. 1989), the court found that the particular structure, sequence, and organization of the various elements of the plaintiff's software were arbitrary rather than dictated by the demands of its intended function, and that the software was therefore copyrightable as an expression.

The literal and nonliteral aspects of computer software are both subject to the same copyright limitations as are written works. For example, in *Lotus Development Corp. v. Borland International, Inc.*, 49 F.3d 807 (1st Cir. 1995), the court held that a particular feature of the plaintiff's user interface for a spreadsheet program was uncopyrightable because competitors could not achieve similar operability without duplicating the program's formal elements.

In *Apple Computer, Inc. v. Microsoft Corp.*, 35 F.3d 1435 (9th Cir. 1994), Apple claimed that Microsoft's Windows operating system had infringed on the look of its copyrighted user interface, but the court held that the idea of modeling an operating system's user interface after a working desktop could not be copyrighted. The "substantial similarity of expression" between Microsoft's desktop format and iconography did not therefore infringe on Apple's copyrighted operating system. Similarly, in *Lotus Development Corp. v. Borland International*, 49 F.3d 807, 815 (1st Cir. 1995), the court held that the plaintiff's "menu command hierarchy," whereby various keystrokes allowed users to prompt the software to perform particular corresponding functions, was merely a "means by which a person operates something" (in this case a computer program) amounting to an abstract "method of operation" specifically excluded from copyright protection by 17 U.S.C. § 102(b).

4. The Copyright Property Interest

A copyright arises automatically once a protective work has been fixed in a tangible medium of expression. Under § 201(a), ownership of a copyright initially vests in the author. Ownership of a material object that embodies the copyrighted work does not give the owner any copyrights in the work. For example, the owner of a reproduction of a painting does not thereby own the copyright to the painting, and the owner of this book does not own the copyright to it.

Authors possess the exclusive rights of § 106 and may exploit the copyrighted work themselves or may transfer all or some of those rights to others. The character of the author is important, and it is determinative of the duration of copyright protection. If the copyrighted work is the product of joint authors, each author may exploit it. A work for hire vests the copyright in the employer rather than the natural person who created the work.

a. Joint Authorship

All authors of a joint work have rights in the copyrighted work. A joint work is "a work prepared by two or more authors with the intention that their contributions be merged into inseparable or interdependent parts of a unitary whole." 17 U.S.C. § 101. Authors can manifest the requisite intent to create a joint work either by working together to produce the work or by acknowledging that their works will be merged together. The authors' independent contributions to the joint work do not have to be equal in any sense, whether measured by quality, quantity, or economic value. However, the contribution of each must be independently copyrightable. For example, in *Childress v. Taylor*, 945 F.2d 500 (2d Cir. 1991), the court held that an actress was not the joint author of a play, even though she had conducted research for and met regularly with the playwright, because she had not actually written any portion of the play.

To mitigate the possibility of abuse from subordinate authors, there must be evidence of a mutual intention to share authorship, such as shared credit or shared approval of revisions, if the authors did not collaborate directly. For example, in *Thomson v. Larson*, 147 F.3d 195 (2d Cir. 1998), the court considered whether the author of the Broadway musical *Rent* had intended that a university professor, who had helped to refine the work, be its coauthor. The court assigned special weight to the facts that the author alone had decision-making authority in writing the script, billing as author upon production and publication of the work, and credit as author in contracts with third parties regarding the musical, and concluded that the author never intended to share authorship with the professor, who had acted as his assistant.

Co-owners of joint works are treated as tenants in common. Each co-owner has an undivided, independent right to the entire work, subject only to a duty of accounting for profits to other co-owners. So, for example, in *Goodman v. Lee*, 78 F.3d 1007 (5th Cir. 1996), the previously unacknowledged coauthor of the song "Let the Good Times Roll" successfully sued her coauthor's heirs for entry in the Copyright Office's register as a coauthor, as well as an accounting for 50% of the royalties paid on the song. As the court noted in *Goodman*, the right to an accounting arises not from infringement by one coauthor against the other, but rather from the fact that coauthors have equal rights in the proceeds of a copyrighted work as tenants in common.

Each co-owner has the exclusive rights of § 106 and may license or authorize other persons to use those rights. However, absent agreement otherwise, any profits gained by licensing or assigning the exclusive rights are subject to the duty of accounting and must be shared between co-owners.

b. Works for Hire

When a work is made as part of employment or hire, "the employer or other person for whom the work was prepared is considered the author ... and unless the parties have expressly agreed otherwise in a written instrument signed by them, owns all of the rights comprised in the copyright." 17 U.S.C. § 201(b). A "work for hire" is:

(1) a work prepared by an employee within the scope of employment; or

(2) a work specially ordered or commissioned for use as a contribution to a collective work as a part, a motion picture or other audio-visual work, as a translation, a supplementary work, as a compilation, an instructional test, as a test, as answer material for a test, or as an atlas, if the parties expressly agree in a written instrument signed by them that the work shall be considered a work made for hire.

17 U.S.C. § 101. A work cannot be made into a work for hire by contract after it has been completed; rather, a prior or simultaneous contract is required.

Section 101(1) does not define "employee" or "scope of employment" and courts apply the federal common law of agency to make this determination. Many factors are considered, including:

1. The hiring party's right to control the manner and means by which the product is accomplished;

2. The skill required;

3. The source of the instrumentalities and tools involved;

4. The location of the work;

5. The duration of the relationship between the parties;

6. Whether the hiring party has the right to assign additional projects to the hired party;

7. The extent of the hired party's discretion over when and how to work;

8. The method of payment;

9. The hired party's role in hiring and paying assistants;

10. Whether the work s part of the regular business of the hiring party;

11. Whether the hiring party is in business;

12. The provision of employee benefits (or not); and

13. The tax treatment of the hired party.

In *Community for Creative Non-Violence v. Reid*, 490 U.S. 730 (1989), the plaintiff made arrangements with Reid, a sculptor, to create "Third World America," depicting the plight of homelessness. After the sculpture was completed, the plaintiff sued to establish copyright ownership of the work, alleging it was a work for hire. Considering the factors listed above, the Court concluded that

Reid was an independent contractor and not an employee of the plaintiff and, thus, the sculpture was not a work for hire.

An example of a work for hire prepared within the scope of employment is found in *In re Marvel Entertainment Group, Inc.*, 254 B.R. 817 (D.Del. 2000). Marvin Wolfman had created several comic book characters—including "Blade, the Vampire Hunter"—as a writer and editor for Marvel Comics. The court found that because the works were created while Wolfman was a Marvel employee and at his employer's instance and expense, the characters were works for hire. Therefore, the court held that Marvel was the works' author under §201(b).

An example of a work for hire commissioned by contract is found in *Playboy Enterprises, Inc. v. Dumas*, 960 F. Supp. 710 (S.D.N.Y. 1997). Playboy Magazine had purchased and published hundreds of artist Patrick Nagel's paintings and paid for many of the paintings with checks that described the works as "made for hire." The court held that the checks, which were endorsed by Nagel, satisfied the written agreement requirement, and that the works were therefore works for hire.

A work cannot be converted into a work for hire after its production. For example, in *Billy-Bob Teeth, Inc. v. Novelty, Inc.*, 329 F.3d 586 (7th Cir. 2003), a company that manufactured the prosthetic teeth featured in the *Austin Powers* movies claimed the teeth as works for hire, although the company's founders had actually designed the teeth prior to the manufacturer's incorporation. The court held that the teeth could not be works for hire because the corporation claiming them as such could not have employed or commissioned the designers prior to its legal existence.

c. Duration

The duration of copyright protection depends on when the work was created and the identity of the work's author. Currently, a copyright expires seventy years after the author's death or, in the case of a jointly authored work, seventy years after the death of the last surviving author. 17 U.S.C. §302(a). However, works created before January 1, 1978, expire twenty-eight years from the date they were first copyrighted and may be renewed for an additional sixty-seven years. 17 U.S.C. §304. For works created before January 1, 1978, but not published by that date, copyright subsists from January 1, 1978, and endures for the life of the author plus 70 years—the term provided for in §302(a). In no case, however, shall the term of copyright in those works expire before December 31, 2002; and, if the work was published on or before December 31, 2002, the term of the copyright does not expire before December 31, 2047. 17 U.S.C. §303. Anonymous works, pseudonymous works, and works for hire are protected for the shorter of ninety-five years after their first publication or 120 years after they were created. 17 U.S.C. § 302(c). At the end of a work's copyright term, the work enters the public domain.

Since passage of the fist copyright laws, Congress has repeatedly lengthened copyright duration. As amended, § 302(a) of the Copyright Act stated that the "[c]opyright in a work created on or after January 1, 1978, subsists from its creation and endures for a term consisting of the life of the author and fifty years after the author's death." In 1998, when the European Union added twenty years to its member nations' copyright terms, the United States amended the standard duration under § 302(a) to life plus seventy years.

When congress modifies copyright duration, problems arise in deciding what works will fall under the new provision. For example, in 1998, the Sonny Bono Copyright Term Extension Act extended the terms of works published in the 1920s and 1930s by an additional thirty years. These works had been caught in between the 1909 Copyright Act and the 1976 Copyright Act and would have expired in 1998 (less than seventy-five years after their publication) without the extension.

Other duration problems arise regarding works written under pseudonyms, jointly-authored works, works for hire, and works by authors whose dates of death are uncertain. Section 302(c) provides that copyrights in anonymous works, pseudonymous works, and works made for hire expire ninety-five years from the first publication or 120 years from the year of its creation, whichever expires first. In the case of joint works, the copyright term is the life of the last surviving author plus seventy years. 17 U.S.C. § 302(b). Sections 302(d) and 302(e) govern what is considered to be a death record and specify how to determine a copyright's expiration date in the absence of documentation of death.

Any interested person may file a statement with the Copyright Office regarding whether the author of a particular work is still living. 17 U.S.C. § 302(d). Ninety-five years after a work was first published, any person who obtains a certified report from the Copyright Office that fails to reflect whether the author is still living or has been dead for less than seventy years is entitled to a "presumption that the author has been dead for at least 70 years," which may be raised as a complete defense to infringement. 17 U.S.C. § 302(e).

d. Transferability

If the work for hire doctrine does not apply, ownership of a copyright initially vests in the authors, and the authors may transfer their rights to another person or entity. 17 U.S.C. § 201(d)(1). Any of the rights included in a copyright may be individually transferred or conveyed to another person or entity, and the new owner is entitled to all the protections and remedies afforded to that exclusive right. 17 U.S.C. § 201(d)(2).

The Copyright Act distinguishes between exclusive and nonexclusive copyright transfers. Section 204(a) requires a writing (similar to the statute of frauds) for exclusive transfers of copyrights or portions of copyrights. Section 101 defines "transfer of copyright ownership" to include both assignments and exclusive licenses. Therefore an assignment or exclusive transfer of any portion of the copyright must be evidenced by a properly executed writing. Without such a writing, signed by the assigning or transferring party, a transfer of copyright ownership (other than by operation of law) is not valid. 17 U.S.C. § 204(a).

In contrast, a nonexclusive license need not be in writing. In *Davis v. Blige*, 505 F.3d 90 (2d Cir. 2007), the court held that when a coauthor granted an oral license to use two songs without the plaintiff's consent, that license could not have been an exclusive license because that would have foreclosed the plaintiff's rights to even perform her own compositions.

The Copyright Act also addresses priority between competing transferees. Under 17 U.S.C. § 205(d), a first assignee can secure priority over later assignees by recording the assignment with the Copyright Office within one month of the execution of the assignment (extended to two months if the assignment was executed outside of the United States). A subsequent assignee can gain priority only if they satisfy three conditions:

(1) The earlier assignee must not have recorded their assignment within the one month allowed by § 205(d);

(2) The subsequent assignee must be the first to record their assignment with the Copyright Office; and

(3) the subsequent assignee must take their assignment in good faith, for value, and without notice of the earlier assignment.

In *Latin American Music Co. v. The Archdiocese of San Juan of the Roman Catholic & Apostolic Church*, 499 F.3d 32 (1st Cir. 2007), a musician had assigned the rights to his song to two different music publishers. The subsequent assignee had taken its assignment without actual knowledge of the earlier assignment only days after the first assignee had been issued a copyright registration certificate, and was also the first to record its assignment. However, the court held that registration by the first assignee resulted in constructive notice to the second, therefore the requirement that the second assignment be taken without notice was not satisfied. Additionally, the court held that the requirement of good faith was not satisfied because the subsequent assignee could have discovered the prior assignee's copyright by searching the Copyright Office's register prior to taking its assignment.

During a period of five years that begins thirty-five years after a transfer by an author of an interest in any particular work, the author or the author's successors-in-interest may terminate the transfer and recapture their rights in the work. 17 U.S.C. § 203(3). The termination is effected by serving advance notice on the copyright owners that, on a date within that five-year period, the copyright will revert to the author or his successors in interest, notwithstanding any agreement to the contrary. 17 U.S.C. § 203(4)–(5). 17 U.S.C. § 304, provides similar rights for works created before January 1, 1978.

At an author's death, the author's termination rights pass to his heirs in accordance with § 304(c). The rights are first divided equally between the author's surviving spouse (if any) and other heirs, and are apportioned thereafter among the author's lineal descendants on a per-stirpes basis. For example, in *Steinbeck v. McIntosh & Otis, Inc.*, 433 F. Supp. 2d 395 (S.D.N.Y. 2006), John Steinbeck's son and granddaughter successfully exercised the termination right against five publishers to whom Steinbeck had exclusively licensed his early works.

In *Music Sales Corp. v. Morris*, 73 F. Supp.2d 364 (S.D.N.Y. 1999), the nephew of composer Billy Strayhorn served as executor of his uncle's estate and exercised Strayhorn's inalienable termination rights to cancel assignments executed by Strayhorn. The court held that, under § 304, as executor, he was empowered to exercise the author's termination rights as a fiduciary for the benefit of the beneficiaries of the estate in whom the rights will ultimately vest.

5. Security Interests in Copyrights

Copyrights, along with other intellectual properties such as patents and trademarks, often represent a significant portion of an entity's value and can be a useful source of collateral for secured transactions. To maintain priority, lenders must properly create and perfect their security interests in intellectual property.

Article 9 of the U.C.C., which has been adopted by all fifty states, governs the creation and perfection of security interests in intellectual property, which is categorized as a "general intangible." U.C.C. § 9-102. A security interest is defined as "an interest in personal property or fixtures which secures payment or performance of an obligation." A security interest is not enforceable against either a debtor or third parties and does not attach to the collateral unless

(1) the secured party has given value in exchange for the collateral,

(2) the debtor has rights in the collateral, and

(3) the debtor has signed a security agreement that provides a description of the collateral.

U.C.C. § 9-203(b). Lenders must therefore ensure that the debtor has rights in the intellectual property collateral prior to obtaining the security interest.

Perfection is the method by which a secured party achieves and maintains the highest available priority for its security interest in collateral. An unperfected security interest may be effective against the debtor, but it is of little value against third parties. In bankruptcy, the difference between a perfected security interest and an unperfected security interest often means the difference between a full recovery as a secured creditor and either little or no recovery as an unsecured creditor.

A security interest is perfected when it attaches if the applicable requirements are satisfied before attachment. The process of perfecting a security interest in most types of personal property is accomplished when a properly completed UCC-1 financing statement is filed with the appropriate state office, most often the office of the secretary of state. The financing statement must name both the debtor and the secured party, and must describe the collateral covered by the financing statement. The U.C.C. no longer requires the debtor to sign an electronically filed financial statement, although the debtor must authorize the filing.

The relative priorities of creditors who hold conflicting security interests are straightforward. Under the U.C.C. (1) if the conflicting security interests are perfected, they rank according to priority in time of filing or perfection; (2) a perfected security interest has priority over a conflicting unperfected security interest; and (3) if the conflicting security interests are unperfected, the first security interest to attach has priority. However, under § 9-109(c)(1), Article 9 does not apply to the extent that it is preempted by federal law.

Filing a financing statement is neither necessary nor effective to perfect a security interest in collateral that is subject to a separate federal filing requirement. In such cases, compliance with such a federal requirement is equivalent to filing a properly completed UCC-1 financing statement, and compliance with federal law is the only means of perfection. U.C.C. § 9-311(b). However, even in cases where federal law governs the perfection of security interests, Article 9 governs the relative priorities of conflicting security interests unless federal law also establishes separate priority rules. Sections 9-109 and 9-311 of the U.C.C. raise distinct issues: under § 9-109, federal law preempts Article 9 where the former governs ownership rights in the property secured as collateral, while under § 9-311 the U.C.C. defers to federal law regarding perfection if federal law has defined a filing requirement. The distinction between these sections is unclear, and it is equally unclear whether security interests in intellectual property rights governed by federal law must be perfected in accordance with federal law or the U.C.C. Because of this uncertainty, financing statements in patents, trademarks, or copyrights should be filed with both state and federal offices.

The method of perfecting security interests in copyrights is substantially different from perfecting interests in patents and trademarks. The United States Copyright Act of 1976 provides for the recordation with the Copyright Office of "[a]ny transfer of copyright ownership or other document pertaining to a [registered] copyright...." 17 U.S.C. § 205(a). A "transfer of copyright ownership" is defined in § 101 of the Copyright Act as "an assignment, mortgage, exclusive license, or any other conveyance, alienation, or hypothecation of a copyright or any of the exclusive rights comprised in a copyright, whether or not it is limited in time or place of effect, but not including a nonexclusive license." The "mortgage" and "hypothecation" categories include pledges of property as security or collateral for a debt, which must be recorded to provide constructive notice of the facts stated in the recorded document. 17 U.S.C. § 205(c).

Some courts have held that, because the Copyright Act duplicates the state filing provisions of Article 9, a U.C.C. filing is neither necessary nor adequate to perfect a security interest in a registered copyright. *See In re Peregrine Entertainment, Ltd.*, 116 B.R. 194 (Bankr. C.D. Cal. 1990); *In re AEG Acquisition Corp.*, 127 B.R. 34 (Bankr. C.D. Cal. 1991); *In re Avalon Software, Inc.*, 209 B.R. 517 (Bankr. D.Ariz. 1997); *In re World Auxiliary Power Co.*, 303 F.3d 1120 (9th Cir. 2002). Perfection of a security interest in a copyright therefore requires only (1) proper registration of the copyright with the United States Copyright Office and (2) the filing of a security agreement or copyright mortgage with the United States Copyright Office.

In re Peregrine Entertainment, Ltd. is the ovular case regarding the perfection of security interests in copyrights. There, a lender had extended to the predecessor of National Peregrine a line of credit secured by National Peregrine's copyrights in various films. The lender filed U.C.C. statements in several relevant states, but not with the federal Copyright Office. National Peregrine thereafter defaulted, and as a debtor-in-possession filed a complaint against the lender asserting that because the lender's security interest was unperfected, it retained a judicial lien on the copyrights. The *Peregrine* court held that the Copyright Act preempted Article 9 of the U.C.C., and that any security interest in a registered copyright could be perfected only by an appropriate filing with the Copyright Office. The court reasoned that 17 U.S.C. § 205(a) "clearly" established a national system for recording transfers of copyright interests and identified a place for filing security interests different from that required by

Article 9. The court concluded that "[t]he federal copyright laws ensure 'predictability and certainty of copyright ownership,' 'promote national uniformity' and 'avoid the practical difficulties of determining and enforcing an author's rights under the differing laws and in the separate courts of the various States.'"

The *Peregrine* court further held that the federal transfer-priority scheme preempts that of Article 9. Under Title 17, the first transfer executed prevails if it is either recorded within one month after its execution in the United States, within two months after its execution outside the United States, or before recordation of the later transfer. 17 U.S.C. § 205(d). Thus, perfection under the Copyright Act may relate back as far as two months. Under U.C.C. § 9-322(a)(3), when conflicting security interests are unperfected, the first to attach has priority. However, neither Title 17 nor *Peregrine* addresses the relative priorities of multiple parties holding unperfected security interests in the same copyright. Arguably, if none of the conflicting security interests in a registered copyright have been perfected under Title 17, then the U.C.C.'s priority scheme would govern.

Because registration is not a prerequisite to copyright protection, many copyrights are never registered with the Copyright Office. However, only courts in the Ninth Circuit have addressed the issue of perfecting security interests in unregistered copyrights. A year after *Peregrine*, in *In re AEG Acquisition Corp.*, 161 B.R. 50 (9th Cir. BAP 1993), a bankruptcy court applied *Peregrine's* reasoning and held that perfection of a security interest in any copyright requires both registration of the copyright and recordation of the security interest with the Copyright Office. The court's decision necessarily implies that it is impossible to perfect a security interest in unregistered copyrights. If widely followed, *In re AEG Acquisition Corp.* would preclude unregistered copyrights from being used as collateral to support secured financing.

In 1997, the Bankruptcy Court followed the decision in *In re AEG Acquisition*, 127 B.R. 34 (Bankr. C.D. Cal. 1991), holding that a copyright must be registered with the Copyright Office before a security interest can be perfected in it. Courts in the Ninth Circuit shifted away from the position that unregistered copyrights are incapable of being subject to a perfected security interest. In 2002, the Ninth Circuit explicitly rejected *AEG Acquisition* and *Avalon Software*, holding that the federal perfection scheme does not preempt the U.C.C. regarding security interests in unregistered copyrights. *In re World Auxiliary Power Co.*, 303 F.3d 1120, 1130 (9th Cir. 2002). The court further held that recording a security interest in an unregistered copyright with the Copyright Office does not give "constructive notice" under 17 U.S.C. § 205(c), and will not operate either to perfect or to preserve the priority of a secured party's interest in an unregistered copyright. The court concluded that Title 17 did not address unregistered copyrights, and the court refused to infer from Congress's silence an intent to make unregistered copyrights useless as collateral. Regarding registered copyrights, the Ninth Circuit followed *Peregrine* and concluded that "there can be no question" that a security interest in a registered copyright can only be perfected by recording in the United States Copyright Office. Title 17 triggers the U.C.C.'s preemption provisions by providing a priority scheme that "governs the rights of parties to and third parties affected by transactions" in registered copyrights and creates a single "national registration" for security interests in registered copyrights. Therefore, the Copyright Act governs both the perfection and priority of registered copyrights. Although the Ninth Circuit has concluded that unregistered copyrights may be perfected under the U.C.C., contrary decisions in *AEG Acquisition* and *Avalon Software* raise concern as to how the issue will be resolved in other circuits.

At present, then, security interests in registered copyrights are properly perfected under Title 17 by recordation with the Copyright Office. Although unregistered copyrights are most likely perfected by filing a UCC-1 financing statement with the appropriate state office, a secured party should require the debtor to register all copyrights prior to obtaining a security interest in them. Ultimately, Congress may need to resolve the question of how unregistered copyrights are perfected.

A security agreement should reference copyrights as "general intangibles" and identify each copyright by title and registration number. To guard against unregistered copyrights, the agreement should oblige the debtor both to notify the secured party of all registered copyrights and to complete the registration of copyrights that are pending. Copyright Office filings under Title 17 relate only to existing copyrights, and blanket liens against subsequent registrations are not permitted. 17 U.S.C. § 205(c)(1). Therefore, the security agreement should also obligate the debtor to notify the secured party of all subsequent copyrights, to promptly register those copyrights with the Copyright Office, and to execute supplemental security agreements.

In the event of default, both the U.C.C. and the security agreement itself govern the rights of the parties. Under U.C.C. § 9-601(a), a secured party may reduce the claim to judgment, foreclose on the collateral, or enforce the claim or security interest by any other available judicial means. These rights are cumulative and may be exercised simultaneously according to U.C.C. § 9-601(c). If possible without a breach of the peace, a secured party may also take direct possession of the collateral without resort to the judicial process according to U.C.C. § 9-609(a)–(b).

However, the intangible nature of intellectual property gives rise to several practical difficulties when enforcing a security interest, primarily because the creditor cannot literally take possession of the collateral. Therefore, unless the debtor has signed an acknowledgment of surrender and transfer, the most efficient way for a secured party to foreclose upon intellectual property collateral is to sue for foreclosure or declaratory judgment.

Foreclosure can occur through either a public or private sale, or the secured party may enforce his rights through a strict foreclosure—the seizure of the collateral in satisfaction of the debt—and so acquire the debtor's interest in the collateral without a sale. U.C.C. §9-620, cmt. 2. A strict foreclosure requires the secured party to send its proposal to the debtor, any other secured creditors with perfected security interests in the collateral, and any guarantors of the security interest. U.C.C. §9-621(a)–(b). Prior to the Article 9 revisions in 2001, a secured party could accept the collateral only in full satisfaction of the obligation; however, under Revised Article 9, the secured party may accept the collateral as either full or partial satisfaction of the obligation it secures.

Acceptance of collateral by the secured party in either full or partial satisfaction of the debtor's obligation (1) discharges the obligation to the extent consented to by the debtor; (2) transfers to the secured party all of the debtor's rights in the collateral; (3) discharges the security interest and any subordinate security interest; and (4) terminates any other subordinate interest. U.C.C. §9-622(a). Subordinate interests are discharged even if the secured party does not comply with the requirements of Article 9. U.C.C. §9-622(b). However, the debtor, guarantors, and any other secured parties retain the right to redeem the collateral by satisfying the obligations secured by the collateral and paying any reasonable expenses (including attorney's fees) incurred by the secured party. U.C.C. §9-623(a)–(b).

A debtor may either consent to strict foreclosure or object to force a sale. U.C.C. §9-620(a). Additionally, all parties entitled to receive a proposal under U.C.C. §9-621 have the opportunity to object. If the secured party receives any objection, he must dispose of the collateral—either by sale, lease, license, or otherwise—though public or private proceedings. U.C.C. §9-610(a). Under Revised Article 9, every aspect of the disposition—including the method, manner, time, place, and other terms—must be commercially reasonable. U.C.C. §9-610(b). Under U.C.C. §9-610(c)(2), a secured party may purchase collateral sold at a private sale if it is either customarily sold on a recognized market or can be valued according to widely distributed standard price quotations; however, there is often no recognized market for particular intellectual property. Intellectual property is therefore usually disposed of through a public sale, although the secured party is often the only bidder.

If the debtor accepts the proposal for strict foreclosure, then the amount is deemed commercially reasonable. However, the debtor may object if the price for which the collateral is sold at either public or private sale is either too high or too low. U.C.C. § 9-615, cmt. 6. If the secured party foreclosing on the collateral is also the transferee receiving the collateral, he may lack the incentive to maximize the sales price. In such cases, if the sales price is significantly below what would have been realized if the interested party had not been involved in the transaction, U.C.C. § 9-615(f) provides for calculating the deficiency.

The purchaser at sale is entitled to a "transfer statement," authenticated by the secured party, stating (1) that the debtor has defaulted in connection with an obligation secured by the collateral purchased; (2) that the secured party has exercised his post-default remedies; (3) that, by reason of the exercise, the transferee has acquired rights of the debtor in the collateral; and (4) the name and mailing address of the secured party, the debtor, and the transferee. U.C.C. § 9-619(a). A transfer statement entitles the transferee to records of all the debtor's rights in the collateral, as well as any official filing, recording, registration, or certificate of title system covering the collateral. U.C.C. § 9-619(b). The transfer statement may be filed with the Copyright Office to document the transfer. 17 U.S.C. § 204.

In sum, it is better practice to require the debtor to register all copyrights prior to obtaining a security interest in them and to perfect under Title 17 by recordation with the Copyright Office and also perfect under the U.C.C. by filing a proper security agreement with the appropriate state office.

Checkpoints

- Common law copyrights provide copyright protection for works that were created before 1978 and have not been published, but for works since that date the statutory copyright preempts common law copyrights the moment the work is created, even if the work is not published.

- All original works of authorship are copyrightable. Section 102 provides a nonexclusive list of copyrightable works including literary works, musical works, dramatic works, pictorial, graphic, and sculptural works, motion pictures and other audio visual works, sound recordings, and architectural works.

- Copyright protects only the expression of an idea, not the underlying idea, procedure, process, system, method of operation, concept, principle, or discovery.

- Copyright protection extends to all original works of authorship fixed in any tangible medium of expression, now known or later developed, from which they can be perceived, reproduced, or otherwise communicated, either directly or with the aid of a machine or device. This is known as the "fixation" requirement.

- A work must be the independent creation of the author and display at least minimal creativity in order to be eligible for a copyright: the "originality" requirement.

- Purely utilitarian works cannot be copyrighted, but if conceptual separability exists then the aesthetic or expressive aspects of a utilitarian work can be copyrighted.

- The "merger doctrine" applies when an idea necessarily involves certain forms of expression, in which case those forms of expression cannot be copyrighted.

- Joint works are works prepared by two or more authors with the intention that their contributions be merged into inseparable parts of a unitary whole. The contributions need not be equal, but each must be independently copyrightable. Co-authors of joint works are treated as tenants in common and each has the exclusive rights found in § 106 and may independently license the work.

- Works for hire are works prepared by an employee within the scope of their employment or a commissioned work if the parties expressly agree that it is a work for hire; but they cannot make it a work for hire retroactively.

- For authors or joint authors, copyright protection lasts for the life of the last surviving author plus an additional seventy years; for works before January 1, 1978, copyrights last twenty eight years with an option to renew it for another sixty seven years; for anonymous, pseudonymous, and works for hire copyright protections expire after the earlier of ninety five years after the first publication or 120 years after the date of their creation.

- Some or all of the author's rights can be assigned or licensed. An exclusive transfer requires a written embodiment but a nonexclusive transfer need not be evidenced by a writing.

- The termination right allows authors to recapture their work and cancel any assignments and licenses.

- Copyright holders can use their interest as collateral in secured transactions and are perfected by a filing with the Copyright Office.

Chapter Six

Enforcing Copyrights

Roadmap

After reading this chapter, you should understand:

- Copyright registration — copyright protection of a work attaches upon the work's creation, but the copyright must be registered to enforce the copyright against infringers and to recover statutory damages or attorneys' fees.

- Notice — under the 1909 Copyright Act, the failure to place notice precluded protection, but under the 1976 Act, the lack of notice only limited remedies and reduced damages. After the revisions in the wake of the Berne Convention, notice is irrelevant to copyright protections and remedies for works created after 1989.

- Exclusive rights under the Copyright Act — these include the exclusive right to reproduce the work; prepare derivative works; distribute copies through sale, rental, lease, or lending of the work; perform the work publicly; display the work publicly; and perform the work publicly via digital audio transmission.

- The right to reproduction — this allows the copyright holder to prevent others from making an unauthorized copy or phonorecord.

- The right to derivative works — this allows the copyright holder to prevent others from making unauthorized translations, dramatizations, fictionalizations, motion picture adaptations, abridgments, and other transformative works.

- The right to distribution — this allows the copyright holder to prevent others from selling, renting, leasing, or lending the work.

- The "first sale doctrine" — this limits the copyright holder's right of distribution so that once a copyrighted article is sold without restriction, the distribution rights no longer prevent further distributions of that same article.

- The right to performance — this allows the copyright holder to prevent others from publicly performing the work, but there are exceptions for non-profit groups, religious services, and charity fundraisers.

- The right to display — this allows the copyright holder to prevent others from publicly displaying the copyrighted work, but the face-to-face exception allows the public display of the work at the place where the work is located.

- Copyright infringement — infringement occurs whenever another engages in activities otherwise reserved for the copyright owner without permission.

- Infringement suit — To prevail, the plaintiff must show that there is a valid copyright, one that is original and fixed in a tangible medium of expression. Also, the mark must be registered (or denied registration) in order to bring suit.

- Proving copying — this can be accomplished by direct or circumstantial evidence. To indirectly prove copying, one must show that the alleged infringer had access to the protected work and that the accused work is substantially similar to the protected work.

- Access — a reasonable opportunity to view, hear, or experience the protected work. Access can be shown by possession of a copy of the work, inferred based on interaction with those in possession of the work, presumed when the work has been widely disseminated or mass produced, or inferred when the two works are strikingly similar when considered against the diversity in the marketplace.

- Substantial similarity — determined through tests that objectively and subjectively compare the copyrighted work and the allegedly infringing work.

- Secondary infringement — liability for those who induce, cause, or materially contribute to the infringement of another.

- Defenses to infringement — these include fair use; independent creation; performance or display of a work for educational purposes, in the course of worship, or for free public concerts and charitable fundraisers; and copies for personal use and software backups, among others.

- Fair use — an equitable doctrine that acts as an affirmative defense. Fair use is determined by balancing four factors: the purpose and character of the use, including if it is a commercial or non-profit use; the nature of the copyrighted work; the amount and substantiality of the portion used in relation to the work as a whole; and the effect of the use upon the market for or value of the copyrighted work.

- Types of fair use — transformative works borrow from an earlier work to produce a new work and includes parody. Non-transformative works are those that are direct copies of the original work, *e.g.*, works reproduced for criticism or educational purposes.

- Copyright infringement remedies — include injunctions, impoundment, monetary damages, and attorneys' fees. Criminal penalties are also available in cases of willful infringement for commercial advantage or personal financial gain.

- Injunctions — issue after meeting the traditional four part test: a showing of irreparable harm; that money damages are inadequate; a balancing of the hardships; and that the public interest is not disserved.

- Other remedies — courts can order the impoundment and destruction of infringing articles.

- Monetary damages — available for lost profits, lost royalties, loss of goodwill, and the like.

- Infringers' profits — awards of profits may be ordered if they are greater than the actual damages; but double recovery of damages and profits is not allowed.

- Statutory damages — in lieu of actual damages or infringers' profits, statutory damages may be awarded in an amount of $750–$30,000 per infringement (as low as $200 for innocent infringement and up to $150,000 if willful infringement), as set by the court.

- Attorneys' fees and costs — awardable to the prevailing party if the infringement was willful or if the suit was frivolous or brought in bad faith.

1. Formal Requirements under the Copyright Act

The Copyright Act of 1976 provides that copyright attaches to the work upon creation; consequently the formal registration process is no longer the vital step that it once was under prior law. However, the formalities of publication, registration, and notice remain important because they allow the copyright holder the full gamut of rights, remedies, and means of enforcement.

a. Registration

Because the work is copyrighted from the moment of creation, registration is not required in order for a copyright to be valid. However, there are many incentives to register a work and registration remains a fairly important step in the copyright enforcement process. The registration process has several steps:

(1) application and payment of the required fee;

(2) deposit of a copy of the work in the Copyright Office;

(3) examination by the Register of Copyrights;

(4) registration, or denial of registration by the Register; and

(5) issuance of certificate of registration.

17 U.S.C. §§ 408, 410. Additionally, the copyright owner must deposit with the Copyright Office two copies of any published work or one compete edition of the work if it is unpublished, collective, or foreign work. 17 U.S.C. § 407(a).

The benefits of registration are substantial. Authors must have registered their copyright in order to commence an action for copyright infringement. There is an explicit exception to the registration requirement for works that were first published in other nations that adhere to the Berne Convention.

Furthermore, if a work is infringed upon before it is registered, the holder of the copyright will not be able to seek statutory damages or attorneys' fees from the infringing party unless registration is secured within three months of the work's first publication. Registration made within five years after the work's first publication constitutes *prima facie* evidence of the validity of the copyright. 17 U.S.C. § 410.

b. Notice

In 1989, as part of the United States' decision to join the Berne Convention, Congress revised the notice provision so that failure to include a copyright notice will not result in *any* loss of copyright. However, the absence of notice may allow a defendant to raise an innocent infringer defense, while the presence of notice forecloses that defense.

Under the 1909 Copyright Act, failure to place proper copyright notice on copies distributed to the public would generally be fatal to the copyright and the work would become part of the public domain. The Copyright Act of 1976 significantly softened the consequences of a failure to provide proper notice in 17 U.S.C. § 405.

With respect to copies and phonorecords publicly distributed by authority of the copyright owner before the effective date of the Berne Convention Implementation Act of 1988, the omission of the copyright notice described in 17 U.S.C. §§ 401 through 403 from copies or phonorecords publicly distributed by authority of the copyright owner does not invalidate the copyright in a work if—

(1) the notice has been omitted from no more than a relatively small number of copies or phonorecords distributed to the public; or

(2) registration for the work has been made before or is made within five years after the publication without notice, and a reasonable effort is made to add notice to all copies or phonorecords that are distributed to the public in the United States after the omission has been discovered; or

(3) the notice has been omitted in violation of an express requirement in writing that, as a condition of the copyright owner's authorization of the public distribution of copies or phonorecords, they bear the prescribed notice.

For example, in *O'Neill Developments, Inc. v. Galen Kilburn, Inc.*, 524 F. Supp. 710, (N.D. Ga. 1981), the plaintiff sought to cure its failure to include proper notice on brochures it distributed through registration of the work within five years after the publication without notice, and made a reasonable effort to add notice to all copies that were distributed after the omission had been discovered. The Court interpreted "discovery" in § 405(a) to include "'discovery' of the fact that the existence of a copyright has become an issue."

The notice requirements of §§ 401 and 402 apply only to "published" works—narrowly defined as the transfer of ownership or lease of copies or phonorecords, for purposes of distribution, public performance, or public display. 17 U.S.C. § 101. But, mere public performance or public display alone does not constitute publication.

If a copyright notice appears on a copy, it must consist of:

(1) the symbol ©, or the word "Copyright", or the abbreviation "Copr."; and

(2) the year of first publication of the work; and

(3) some clear identification of the copyright owner. 17 U.S.C. § 401(b).

The requirements are essentially the same for a phonogram, except that instead of bearing the symbol © or equivalent mark, it must bear a ℗ symbol. 17 U.S.C. § 402(b)(1). The copyright notice must be situated on the item in such a way as to give "reasonable notice of the claim of copyright" and otherwise as prescribed by the Register of Copyrights. 17 U.S.C. §§ 401(c), 402(c).

Fixing adequate notice to copyrighted computer software presents unique issues. Under Copyright Office regulations, notice is fixed and positioned so as to provide reasonable notice of the claim of copyright when it appears:

(1) either near the title or at the end of material printed from the software;

(2) displayed at the user's terminal when the user signs on;

(3) continuously on display on the computer terminal while the software is in use; or

(4) durably fixed to either the device on which the software is stored or on the container used as a permanent receptacle for the software storage device.

37 C.F.R. § 201.20(g).

The chief benefit of a properly affixed notice is that it negates any claim by an infringer that they did not know the work was copyrighted, foreclosing a defense of innocent infringement. 17 U.S.C. §§ 401(d), 402(d). Aside from its evidentiary value, the copyright notice serves to encourage copyright owners to either enforce their rights or allow material to slip into the public domain, to identify the copyright owners, and to allow users to calculate the term of the copyright by the date affixed to the item.

2. Exclusive Rights Protected under Title 17

a. Generally

The Copyright Act gives the author the exclusive right to:

(1) reproduce the copyrighted work;

(2) prepare derivative works based upon the copyrighted work;

(3) distribute copies of the work through sale, rental, lease, or lending;

(4) perform copyrighted works publicly;

(5) display the copyrighted work publicly; and

(6) perform the copyrighted work publicly through digital audio transmission (in the case of sound recordings).

17 U.S.C. § 106. The copyright owners may exercise these rights exclusively, or may authorize others to do so.

The first three of the exclusive rights listed in § 106 apply to all copyrightable works. The rights to perform and display copyrighted works are limited to works that can be performed or displayed. The right to perform copyrighted material publicly applies to literary, musical, dramatic, and choreographic works, pantomimes, and motion pictures and other audiovisual works. The right to display copyrighted work publicly applies to literary, musical, dramatic, and choreographic works, pantomimes, and pictorial, graphic, or sculptural works, including the individual images of a motion picture or other audiovisual work. Finally, the right to public performance through digital audio transmission is limited to sound recordings.

b. Reproduction

A copyright owner has the exclusive right to reproduce the work in the form of phonorecords or copies, which are terms of art. 17 U.S.C. § 106(1). Phonorecords capture and convey sound while copies capture images and convey those images visually. The parallel treatment of copies and phonorecords under Title 17 is purposeful. The statutory grant to the copyright owner of an exclusive right "to reproduce the copyrighted work in copies or phonorecords" reflects the distinction under Title 17 between "copies"—defined in § 101 as "material objects, *other than phonorecords*, in which a work is fixed by any method now known or later developed"—and "phonorecords"—defined as material objects in which sounds, other than those accompanying a motion picture or other audiovisual work, are fixed by any method now known or later developed.

The exclusive right to reproduce encompasses changing mediums for conveying copyrightable material. Thus, compact discs, digital video discs, and other newer forms of phonorecords and copies are protected in addition to vinyl records, paper photocopies, and other, older forms of recordation. For example, unauthorized fax copies and unauthorized uploading of images produced by a scanner are considered infringements. In *Pasha Publications, Inc. v. Enmark Gas Corp.*, (N.D. Tex. 1992), the court held that the defendant had violated the author's exclusive right to reproduction by faxing a copyrighted newsletter to its employees. Similarly, in *Playboy Enterprises, Inc. v. Webbworld, Inc.*, 991 F. Supp. 543 (N.D. Tex. 1997), the plaintiff's infringed upon Playboy's exclusive right to publish its copyrighted images by collecting images scanned and posted online by third parties, and re-posting them on its members-only website.

Likewise, the right to duplicate digital music files is protected in addition to vinyl records and other, older forms of recordation. For example, in *Metro-Goldwyn-Mayer Studios Inc. v. Grokster, Ltd.*, 545 U.S. 913 (2005), the Supreme Court reversed a lower court grant of summary judgment in favor of the defendants' peer-to-peer computer networks Grokster and StreamCast. The networks had been sued by a consortium of music publishers and copyright owners alleging inducement to infringement and contributory infringement. The defendants had advertised themselves as alternatives to Napster and had actively encouraged users to infringe on copyrighted material, conduct which the Court held unlawful.

Title 17 outlines several exceptions to the exclusivity of reproduction and performance rights otherwise reserved to copyright owners.

Sections 112 and 117 impose limitations on the exclusivity of a copyright owner's right to reproduce copyrighted works. Section 117 allows computer software licensees to back-up their software, and even to alter it if necessary to render the software functional for their needs. Section 112 provides a similar defense to broadcast-programming licensees who make backup recordings of copyrighted material for later rebroadcast and archival purposes.

Section 117 also specifically forbids software purchasers from reselling their backup or archived copies of copyrighted software except as "part of the lease, sale, or other transfer of all rights in the program"—and even then only with the copyright owner's permission. The safe harbor of § 117 for backup or archival purposes does not allow the software purchaser to actually *use* the copies they have made. For example, in *Wall Data Inc. v. Los Angeles County Sheriff's Department*, 447 F.3d 769 (9th Cir. 2006), the court held that where the Los Angeles County Sheriff's Department purchased

3,500 licenses to use a computer program, but installed and used the program on more than 6,000 computers, the copying fell outside of the § 117 safe harbor.

Rebroadcasters' freedom to make copies of performances and sound recordings for rebroadcast purposes under § 112 is an important right that gives broadcasters control over their programming schedules, provided that they comply with the restrictions imposed by the statute. In order to avail itself of the exception, a broadcaster must meet three conditions:

(1) the broadcaster must make only one copy, and that copy must be used only by its maker,

(2) the copy must be used only for rebroadcast within the maker's local service area, and

(3) the copy must be destroyed within six months unless preserved for archival purposes.

The importance of § 112 was evident in *Agee v. Paramount Communications, Inc.*, 59 F.3d 317 (2d Cir. 1995), in which defendant Paramount infringed upon the plaintiff's reproduction rights in copyrighted sound recording synched to the credits of the program "Hard Copy." The program was then transmitted to the codefendant affiliate stations, which complied with the requirements of § 112. The court held that although Paramount had infringed, the affiliate's compliance with § 112 insulated them from liability for unauthorized reproduction of the plaintiff's sound recordings.

Both the Audio Home Recording Act of 1992 ("AHRA") and the Intellectual Property and Communications Omnibus Reform Act of 1999 address the author's exclusive right of reproduction in the context of evolving technology. AHRA broadly prohibits the manufacture, importation or use of devices that are capable of serial copying—defined as "the duplication in a digital format of a copyrighted musical work or sound recording from a digital reproduction of a digital musical recording" 17 U.S.C. § 1001(11)—but not if they conform with recognized systems by which the unauthorized duplication of digital recordings can be restricted. 17 U.S.C. § 1002. AHRA provides for:

(1) a serial copy prevention system under which consumers are permitted to make an infinite number of copies directly from a lawfully purchased prerecorded tape but, due to digital code that is inserted into any initial copy of the purchased tape, are prevented from making further copies from any initial copy;

(2) a 2-percent royalty levy on the transfer price of digital recorders and a 3-percent royalty levy on the transfer price of blank recording media;

(3) the deposit of these royalties into the Copyright Office for distribution by the Copyright Royalty Tribunal under a sound recording fund and a musical works fund; and

(4) various civil remedies and the arbitration of certain disputes.

H.R. Rep. 102-873(II), at 3 (1992). The first provision described above is embodied in § 1008, which prohibits any claim of infringement "based on the noncommercial use of [a device capable of serial copying] by a consumer [to make] digital musical recordings or analog musical recordings." 17 U.S.C. § 1008. In providing this limited exception, Congress extended to licensees a right to copy recordings which would otherwise constitute infringement.

The Omnibus Reform Act prohibits both the circumvention of a "technological measure that effectively controls access to a work protected under this title," 17 U.S.C. § 1201(a), and any activity that would make available for use technology designed, anticipated or known to be used "for use in circumventing a technological measure that effectively controls access" to a copyrighted work. 17 U.S.C. § 1201(a)(E)(2).

However, several exceptions are specifically permitted. The Librarian of Congress has the authority to exempt from the general prohibition any class of work if the overly zealous protection of it might impede non-infringing use of protected works. 17 U.S.C. § 1201(a)(D). Furthermore, software licensees are permitted, where necessary, to develop, apply and disseminate the means to decode and decrypt any protections on licensed software for the purpose of enhancing the "interoperability" of the "independently created computer program with other programs...." 17 U.S.C. § 1201(f). There are also other narrower exceptions scattered throughout the text of section 1201.

c. Derivative Works

The exclusive right to make or authorize derivative works of a copyrighted work is especially valuable. Derivative works are those "based upon one or more pre-existing works, such as a translation, musical arrangement, dramatization, fictionalization, motion picture adaptation, sound recording, artistic reproduction, abridgment, condensation, or any other form in which a work may be recast, transformed, or adapted." 17 U.S.C. § 101. In addition, revisionary works, including those that consist of editorial revisions, annotations, elaborations, or other modifications which, as a whole, represent an original work of authorship, are derivative works. For example, authors have the right to convert novels into motion pictures, to translate articles into other languages, or to make orchestral arrangements of popular hits. Authors also have the right to license others to authorize the production of these derivative works.

The standard for proving that a work is derivative and therefore infringes upon the copyright-holder's rights is not as strict as the standard for copyrightability of a derivative work. A derivative work is copyrightable only if it satisfies 17 U.S.C. § 102, but infringing on another's exclusive right to create derivative works involves even less than infringing on the right to reproduce the work. A work is derivative if it has been substantially copied from prior copyrighted work. Further, a derivative work does not have to be "fixed in a tangible medium" in order to be an infringement upon the copyright owner's rights. In *Herbert v. Shanley Co.*, 242 U.S. 591 (1916), for example, the Supreme Court held that the live performance of a copyrighted arrangement of a comic opera was an infringement, even though no admission was charged to the audience. In addition, words do not necessarily have to be borrowed from the copyrighted work. In a classic derivative rights case, *Kalem Co. v. Harper Bros.*, 222 U.S. 55 (1911), the Court held that a silent motion picture adaptation of the novel *Ben Hur* was a derivative work of the book and constituted infringement.

Editing and abridging a work, along with expansion of a work, can infringe upon the exclusive right to derivative works. In *Gilliam v. American Broadcasting Companies*, 538 F.2d 14 (2d Cir. 1976), the network heavily edited television programs without the permission of the comedy group (Monty Python). The court concluded that the network had infringed upon the copyright to the program scripts held by the comedy group and *sua sponte* enjoined ABC from continuing to broadcast properly licensed but roughly edited episodes of Monty Python's Flying Circus, which the court described as "a mere caricature of [the group's] talents." Although the court briefly discussed moral rights, and even hinted at an "actionable mutilation" of the plaintiff's work, its opinion rested more securely on a traditional theory of the performer's copyright in the script, since the edits exceeded both reasonable expectations and the editorial rights ABC claimed under the license agreement.

d. Distribution

Under 17 U.S.C. § 106(3) the copyright owner has the exclusive right to distribute copies or phonorecords of the copyrighted work to the public through sale, rental, lease, lending, or other transfer of ownership. The classic example of infringement through distribution is that an infringer hands out copies of a copyrighted work, and thereby infringes upon the copyright owner's exclusive right of distribution. For example, in *Tangorre v. Mako's, Inc.*, 2003 WL 470577 (S.D.N.Y. 2003) (unreported decision), the plaintiff had photographed the defendant club's "girls" in anticipation of a promotional calendar. The defendant refused to pay the plaintiff, but published the calendar using the plaintiff's photographs, and distributed copies to patrons. The court held that by allowing its customers to take copies of the calendar containing unlicensed copies of the plaintiff's photographs, the defendant had infringed upon the plaintiff's right of distribution.

The rise of the Internet has provided increased low-cost opportunities for infringement and also somewhat altered the dynamic. For example, in *A&M Records, Inc. v. Napster, Inc.*, 239 F.3d 1004 (9th Cir. 2001), the court addressed whether the users of an online file-sharing network had infringed upon the plaintiff's exclusive rights in copyrighted music. Finding that the music was indeed copyrighted, the court held that users had infringed on the plaintiff's distribution and reproduction rights, in that: "Napster users who upload files to the search index for others to copy violate plaintiffs' distribution rights. Napster users who download files containing copyrighted music violate plaintiffs' reproduction rights."

Taken alone, 17 U.S.C. § 106(3) would make it an infringement for a bookseller to sell books or a person to loan a movie to a friend, but under the "first sale doctrine" these activities are not infringement. In *Bobbs-Merrill Co. v. Straus*, 210 U.S. 339, 350 (1908), the Supreme Court concluded that a person who has "sold a copyrighted article, without restriction, has parted with all right to control the sale of it." The first sale doctrine is codified in 17 U.S.C. § 109(a).

The purchaser of a book that was sold with permission of the owner of the copyright may sell it again, but cannot publish a new edition of it. Essentially, the first sale of a copyrighted work extinguishes the right of the copyright owner in that particular edition or embodiment of the copyright. Thus, a book dealer can resell antique book but she cannot remove the illustrations from those books and produce a new compilation of antique illustrations. For example, in *Nat'l Geographic Soc'y v. Classified Geographic, Inc.*, 27 F. Supp. 655 (D.Mass. 1939), the court held that where the defendant collected copyrighted materials from secondhand copies of the plaintiff's magazine and sold those materials to the general public as a compilation or arrangement of the copyrighted work, they violated the plaintiff's exclusive right.

Section 109(b) is an exception to the first sale doctrine. It forbids the "rental, lease, or lending" of music phonographs and copies of computer programs because Congress concluded that these works could be inexpensively copied by customers as an alternative to buying the works. This ban on rentals of sound recordings and computer programs applies only to for-profit operations and explicitly excludes nonprofit libraries. 17 U.S.C. § 109(2)(A).

Copyright infringement is a strict liability cause of action. It is irrelevant whether an infringer knew or had any reason to suspect that by purchasing or selling particular goods they infringed upon another's copyright. For example, in *Pinkham v. Sara Lee Corp.*, 983 F.2d 824 (8th Cir. 1992), the plaintiff Mary Ellen Pinkham had sold, to a subsidiary of Sara Lee Corporation, 13,000 copies of her book *Mary Ellen's Best of Helpful Hints* through the intermediary company Camex, which had also printed the books. When Camex sold an additional 300,000 copies of the book to Sara Lee, Pinkham sued Sara Lee alleging infringement. Sara Lee argued that it believed Camex was Pinkham's agent, and that its good faith reliance on their prior course of dealing should excuse it from liability. The court disagreed, holding:

> Once a plaintiff has proven that he or she owns the copyright on a particular work, and that the defendant has infringed upon those "exclusive rights," the defendant is liable for the infringement and this liability is absolute. The defendant's intent is simply not relevant....

In *Holsey Corp. v. Waldron Street Book Co.*, 2006 U.S. Dist. Lexis 61387, 2006 WL 2506592 (E.D.N.Y. 2006), the defendant booksellers purchased a shipment of books from a seller who had purchased them from a waste company entrusted with the task of disposing of the books on behalf of their publisher. When the publisher brought a claim of infringement against the defendant, the defendant argued that they were shielded from liability by the first sale doctrine as embodied in 17 U.S.C. § 109. The court disagreed, holding that "The first sale doctrine protects only those sellers who take possession as part of an innocent chain of title, and [the] first sale doctrine, therefore, does not shield the defendants."

e. Performance

The copyright holder has the exclusive right to performance for all works except for pictorial, graphic, sculptural works, and sound recordings. The exclusion of sound recordings from those works covered by the exclusive right to performance seems surprising, but that exclusion does not leave music unprotected. In *Lodge Hall Music, Inc. v. Waco Wrangler Club, Inc.*, 831 F.2d 77 (5th Cir. 1987), the court held that playing copyrighted records in a late-night bar would constitute infringement of the copyright holder's exclusive right to public performance. But, an author's right to exclusive performance of underlying musical compositions only applies to performance for a live audience. In 1995, Congress extended the ownership of a copyright in a sound recording to cover the public performance of the work by means of digital audio transmission. 17 U.S.C. § 106(6). This expansion of the performance right to sound recordings is of increasing importance as the popularity of the Internet and other digital music services grows.

To infringe on the copyright owner's exclusive right, the performance must be public. 17 U.S.C. § 106(4). To perform a work publicly means:

> [T]o perform or display it at a place open to the public or at any place where a substantial number of persons outside of a normal circle of a family and its social acquaintances is gathered or to transmit or otherwise communicate a performance or display of the work to [such a gathering] or to the public ... by means of any device or process....

17 U.S.C. § 101. A motion picture or other audio-visual work is performed by showing its images in any sequence or making the sounds accompanying it audible. With regard to movies and other "audiovisual" works, 17 U.S.C. § 101 defines the copyright owner's exclusive right as the right "to show [the movie's] images in any sequence or to make the sounds accompanying it audible." For example, in *Video Pipeline, Inc. v. Buena Vista Home Entertainment, Inc.*, 192 F. Supp. 2d 321 (D.N.J. 2002), Video Pipeline had produced a series of short, unauthorized movie trailers by editing movies for which Buena Vista held the copyrights, then posted the trailers on its website. Video Pipeline sought a declaratory judgment that its trailers did not infringe on Buena Vista's copyrights, but the court held that they clearly infringed upon Buena Vista's performance right. Although the trailers were so heavily edited that they often bore little resemblance to the underlying movies, the court held that by reproducing the films' "images in any sequence [with] the sounds accompanying" them, Video Pipeline had performed the copyrighted works. Moreover, because the trailers had been posted online, those performances were public and therefore an infringement.

The House Report that accompanied the 1976 revisions further explained that even "performances in 'semipublic' places such as clubs, lodges, factories, summer camps, and schools are 'public performances' subject to copyright control," but Congress concluded that "routine meetings of businesses and governmental personnel would be excluded because they do not represent the gathering of a 'substantial number of persons.'" H.R. Rep. No. 94-1476, at 64 (1976).

Prior to the Copyright Act of 1976, copyright owners were only protected against for profit public performances. The Copyright Act of 1976 did away with the "for profit" requirement, but created certain exceptions that benefit many non-profit groups. Section 110(3), for example, allows the performance and display of works "of a religious nature" in the course of worship services. In *F. E. L. Publ'n, Ltd. v. Catholic Bishop of Chicago*, 506 F. Supp. 1127, 1134 (C.D. Ill. 1981), the court held that singing hymns in a church service qualified for the non-profit exemption.

Section 110(4) provides a similar, although somewhat more limited, defense for the live performance of copyrighted work provided there is no cost of admission to the public, or the performance is for charitable purposes. However, the exception allowed by § 110(4) does not protect infringers if they obtain *any* commercial benefit from the infringement. For example, in *Morganactive Songs, Inc. v. Padgett*, 2006 U.S. Dist. Lexis 74099 2006 WL 2882521 (M.D. Ga.), the plaintiff alleged that three of its copyrighted songs had been performed in the defendant's club during a children's charity fundraiser. Despite the overall charitable character of the event, the court concluded that the defendant had obtained a direct commercial benefit from alcohol sales the night of the performance, and was therefore ineligible for the exception allowed under § 110(4).

Sections 111, 119, and 122 limit the exclusivity of a copyright owner's performance rights in favor of those who retransmit, for commercial purposes, programming copyrighted by the original broadcaster.

Section 111(a) allows hotels, educators, governmental bodies, and nonprofit organizations to retransmit broadcast programming. Section 111(c) allows for the simultaneous "secondary transmission" of broadcast signals by cable television providers. Section 111(e) allows U.S. cable providers operating outside of the contiguous 48 United States to make single recordings of broadcast programming for a single *non*-simultaneous retransmission subject to certain further conditions. Cable providers that retransmit broadcast signals under §§ 111(c) and (e) may not alter the programming or commercial content of the broadcast signals they retransmit, and are subject to statutory licensing requirements described in excruciating detail in § 111(d). Those requirements are too intricate to cover here, but amount to a requirement that cable providers pay royalties, collected and disbursed by the Copyright Office, for the copyrighted broadcast programming they carry. Sections 119 and 111 impose similar statutory licensing requirements on satellite television service providers.

Under § 114(a), the owner of a copyright in a sound recording has no exclusive right of performance with regard to that work, except as provided in § 106(6) with regard to "digital audio transmission." Section 114(d) provides that with the exception of "nonsubscription broadcast transmissions," digital audio transmissions are subject to statutory licensing requirements described in § 114(f). Under Federal Regulation, that "broadcast" exception is limited to traditional "over-the-air" broadcasts. *Public Performance of Sound Recordings: Definition of a Service, Final Rule*, 65 Fed. Reg. 77292 (Dec. 11, 200). In *Bonneville Intern. Corp. v. Peters*, 347 F.3d 485 (3d Cir. 2003), the National Association of Broadcasters sued the copyright office, challenging its definition of "nonsubscription broadcast transmission" in hopes of escaping statutory licensing requirements for their simultaneous online broadcast of "over-the-air" programming. The court rejected that interpretation, holding that "nonsubscription broadcast transmissions" include only over-the-air broadcasts, extended to include retransmissions and digital rather than more traditional analog signals, but not to include simultaneous streaming webcasts.

f. Display

The copyright holder's right of public display applies to all copyrighted works except sound recordings. 17 U.S.C. § 106(5). This right of public display compliments the right of public performance reserved to the owners of copyrights in sound recordings or other works with a temporal dimension, such as movies or pantomimes. With regard to audiovisual works, the copyright owner has both a performance right and a display right under § 106. 17 U.S.C. § 101 explains that displaying a work means showing, "a copy of it, either directly or by means of a film, slide, television image, or any other device or process or, in the case of a motion picture or other audiovisual work, to show individual images nonsequentially." Thus showing individual frames from a motion picture infringes upon the copyright owner's right of display, but not its performance right. The same definition of public that applied to the performance right applies to the public display right. Including a picture of a piece of artwork on a website that can be viewed by the public, even if they view it alone in a private setting, is therefore a public display and will constitute infringement unless the copyright owner has given permission for the display.

Congress created an exception to the general rule of public display to strike a balance between the copyright owner's rights and the interests of a person who owns a physical copy of a work. 17 U.S.C. § 109(c), provides that an owner of a lawful copy of a work or a person authorized by that owner may display that copy or an image of the copy publicly to viewers present at the place where the copy is located. This exception for face-to-face display is very narrow. Section 109(c) is intended to make it clear that 109(a) and 109(b) do not apply to someone who merely possesses a copy or phonorecord without having acquired ownership of it. Thus a person who rents a movie from the copyright owner has no right to rent the movie to someone else without first acquiring the copyright owner's permission—to do so would violate the copyright holder's right of display. Section

110(s) allows public venues, like restaurants and bars, to play the radio or television without violating the copyright owner's right of performance or display, subject to some restrictions regarding the size of the display system.

3. Copyright Infringement

Copyright infringement occurs whenever someone engages in activities otherwise reserved to the copyright owner under § 106 without permission from the copyright owner. To prevail in a claim for copyright infringement, copyright holders must show that they hold a valid copyright and that the alleged infringer impermissibly copied the work. Copying is usually difficult to prove by direct evidence and is most often proved by circumstantial evidence. To prove copying indirectly, the copyright owner must prove that the alleged infringer had access to the protected work, and that the infringing work is substantially similar to the copyrighted work.

The courts apply a number of tests to determine whether the works are substantially similar. The three main tests are generally referred to as the Copyright/Unlawful Appropriation Test, the Abstraction-Filtration Comparison Test, and the Extrinsic/Intrinsic or Objective/Subjective Test. Those tests objectively dissect the copyrighted work and filter out unprotectable elements. The remaining copyrighted elements are then compared to the corresponding elements of the accused work.

Aside from direct infringement, a copyright owner may allege that his exclusive rights have been infringed upon indirectly by vicarious infringement, contributory infringement, or an inducement to infringement. Defendants may be found liable as contributory infringers if they distribute a product intending for it to be used to infringe or as vicarious infringers if they fail to adequately supervise a direct infringer under their control.

a. Valid Copyright

To establish infringement the plaintiff must prove ownership of a valid copyright, and copying of constituent elements of the work that are original. Copyright registration or the denial of registration is generally a prerequisite to a suit for infringement. There is a split of authority among courts as to what stage of the registration process must be completed before bringing suit— ranging from requiring that the copyright owner first receive a paper certificate of registration or a denial or registration from the Copyright Office, to requiring only a deposit of the work, payment of the fee, and receipt of the application by the Copyright office (with issuance of a certificate of registration a condition to recovering statutory damages).

As discussed previously, in order for the copyright to be valid, the work must be "original" and "fixed in a tangible medium of expression." 17 U.S.C. § 102(a). A certificate of registration creates a rebuttable presumption that the copyright is valid. 17 U.S.C. § 401(c); *Fonar Corp. v. Domenick*, 105 F.3d 99 (2d Cir. 1997). The presumption can be rebutted, for example, by evidence that:

(1) the work is not sufficiently original, *see Durham Indus., Inc. v. Tomy Corp.*, 630 F.2d 905 (2d Cir.1980) (small, plastic wind up toys of Mickey Mouse, Donald Duck, and Pluto held not sufficiently original — the "figures are instantly identifiable as embodiments of the Disney characters in yet another form");

(2) the work has been copied from the public domain, *see Folio Impressions, Inc. v. Byer Cal.*, 937 F.2d 759, 763–64 (2d Cir.1991) (presumption rebutted by testimony that copyrighted fabric pattern was copied from a design that was part of the pubic domain, not protected by copyright);

(3) the work was utilitarian and not copyrightable, *see Carol Barnhart Inc. v. Economy Cover Corp.*, 773 F.2d 411, 414 (2d Cir.1985) (presumption rebutted where certificate issued to "mannequins of partial human torsos used to display articles of clothing"); or

(4) the copyright holder made deliberate misrepresentations in obtaining the certificate, *see Whimsicality, Inc. v. Rubie's Costume Co.*, 891 F.2d 452, 455 (2d Cir.1989) (presumption rebutted where copyright holder classified its animal character costumes as "soft sculptures" knowing the application would be denied if the works were described as costumes).

b. Copying

Once a plaintiff has established ownership of a valid copyright, the plaintiff must show the defendant copied original elements of the work. Copying may be proven by direct evidence, or, as is most often the case, copying may be inferred where the defendant had access to the copyrighted work and the accused work is substantially similar to the copyrighted work.

i. Access

Access means a reasonable opportunity to view, hear or experience the protected work. Access can be shown by evidence the defendant possessed the work or a copy of it. In *Susan Wakeen Doll Co., Inc. v. Ashton Drake Galleries*, 272 F.3d 441 (7th Cir. 2001), access was shown where the plaintiff testified and produced a UPS receipt showing she had sent defendant the "master skin" — a vinyl prototype head — of the doll at issue.

Access may also be inferred where the plaintiff and defendant both had dealings with a third party who had possession of the work, though the burden of proof with regard to access remains on the party alleging copying. For example, in *Ellis v. Diffie*, 177 F.3d 503 (6th Cir. 1999), the plaintiff alleged that defendant's song "Prop Me Up Beside the Jukebox (If I Die)" was copied from plaintiff's song "Lay Me Out By the Jukebox When I Die." Despite similarities between the songs and the dealings by both parties with the same publisher, that publisher denied having heard the song, and the court held that the complaint was properly dismissed because the plaintiff had not proven that the defendant had ever heard the song.

Reasonable opportunity to view or hear or experience the work can be established where the work has been widely disseminated or mass produced. For example, in *ABKCO Music, Inc. v. Harrisongs Music, Ltd.*, 722 F.2d 988 (2d Cir. 1983), the plaintiff alleged that former Beatle George Harrison's song "My Sweet Lord" infringed on the earlier composition "He's So Fine," which had achieved wide commercial success before Harrison's song was first written. Although Harrison denied consciously copying the plaintiff's work, and no direct proof of access was presented at trial, the court held that the wide dissemination of the plaintiff's song was sufficient evidence from which to infer Harrison's access.

Finally, access may sometimes be inferred if two works are so similar as to make it highly probable that the later one is a copy of the earlier one. In *Ty, Inc. v. GMA Accessories, Inc.*, 132 F.3d 1167, 1171 (7th Cir. 1997), the court held that access was inferred because GMA's bean bag pig was "strikingly similar" to Ty's "beanie baby" pig but was not similar to anything in the public domain.

ii. Substantial Similarity

Courts generally use a two step process to compare two works in order to determine if there is a substantial similarity. The first step involves an analytical dissection of the works and then a comparison of their components and details to determine if there is copying. The second step is a more subjective ordinary observer test to determine if an audience of reasonable people would perceive substantial similarities between the accused work and the protected expression in the copyrighted work. Different circuits use different tests, called variably the copying/unlawful appropriation test, the abstraction-filtration test (used primarily for computer programs), and the extrinsic and intrinsic test, but all accomplish the same evidentiary goal. Regardless of the name or version of the test being applied, it is important to keep in mind that protection is afforded only to a work's particular expression of an idea and not the idea itself.

A. Copying/Unlawful Appropriation Test

Some courts use variations of the copying/unlawful appropriation test to determine if there is a substantial similarity indicative of copying. Under this approach, "a copyright claim requires both proof of (1) actual copying, which a plaintiff may establish by demonstrating probative similarity, and of (2) improper use, which requires substantial similarity." To analyze the first element, the court inquires into the "probative" similarities between the works, considering the works as a whole. The aim is to determine whether there was any copying at all. The court then inquires into the "substantial" similarities between the works — that is, whether any *impermissible* copying has occurred. This second prong of the analysis allows the court to determine which aspects of the artist's work, if any, are protectable by copyright and whether those elements were unlawfully appropriated.

Usually this test is accomplished by first dissecting the work into its various details and elements, e.g., a song into its lyrics, melody, harmony, structure, beat, and key. For example, in *Boone v. Jackson*, 206 F. Appx. 30 (2d Cir. 2006), the court focused on the "hooks" of the songs "Young N" and the allegedly infringing song "Holla Back," in particular:

> (1) the position of the phrase "holla back" in the hook, or chorus, of the song; (2) the rhythmic construction of the phrase, specifically the eighth-note, eighth-note, quarter-note syncopation and its instrumentation; and (3) the nature and quality of the lyric's repetition in the hook, particularly the call and response element.

Courts then filter out the unprotectable elements, including utilitarian elements, items in the public domain, and ideas (rather than expression), from the protectable elements of the work. For example, in *Suntrust Bank v. Houghton Mifflin Co.*, 268 F.3d 1257 (11th Cir. 2001), the court compared Margaret Mitchell's *Gone With the Wind* and Alice Randall's satire *The Wind Done Gone.* The court distinguished between the scenes a faire — stock scenes and characters that naturally flow from a common theme — and the protected characters and scenes. The scenes a faire are merely ideas, such as the ante-bellum south and plantation life, and are unprotected by copyright and are free for any to use. The specifically developed characters and scenes, such as Scarlet and Terra, are protected, but in this instance the appropriation was allowed as a fair use for satire, at least in the context of preliminary injunction proceedings.

In *Leigh v. Warner Bros.*, Inc., 212 F.3d 1210 (11th Cir. 2000), the court held that the copyrighted photograph of a cemetery statute covered only the artistic elements, such as the selection of lighting, shading, timing, angle, and film. The copyright did not cover the appearance of the statue itself or the overall mood the photograph conveyed—the eerie, spiritual mood—because it was an expression commonly associated with cemeteries and thus non-original and unprotectable.

After extracting the unprotectable elements, the court considers whether the protectable elements are substantially similar. Substantial similarity exists where the accused work is so similar to the plaintiff's work that an ordinarily reasonable person would conclude that the defendant unlawfully appropriated the plaintiff's protectable expression by taking material of substance and value. The works' total concept and feel are subjectively examined as a question of fact rather than under some rigid standard.

In *Hamil America Inc. v. GFI*, 193 F.3d 92, 100 (2d Cir. 1999), the plaintiff's and defendant's fabric patterns were found to be substantially similar. Both patterns depicted small clusters of flowers and leaves with almost identical shapes in a similar "tossed" repeating pattern.

In *Gund, Inc. v. Applause, Inc.*, 809 F. Supp. 304, 308–09 (S.D.N.Y. 1993), the court held that two stuffed toy dogs were not substantially similar under the ordinary observer test.

> First and most significantly, an ordinary observer would be immediately struck by the different overall look of the two dogs. Muttsy's fur is made of a fine fiber, giving the dog a very smooth texture and finish. By contrast, Skippy has a mongrel-like appearance, with uneven and longer fur, resulting in a scruffy, rough look. More specifically, whereas Muttsy's plush material gives it an extremely smooth finish, Skippy looks as if he was sprayed with water by a passing car and left outside to dry. Second, as a result of being more softly stuffed, Muttsy is a skinny dog with a greater degree of floppiness. If an adult or child purchaser attempted to pick Muttsy up by the tail area it would flop downward, unable to be held in a horizontal position. On the other hand, Skippy is more firmly stuffed, giving it a chubby appearance. And although Skippy retains its floppy charm, it is a more rigid dog, able to maintain its form when held by the tail area.

The court noted "all floppy dogs may share certain characteristics inherent in the idea of a floppy dog, such as the fact that they flop on their stomach, have no set shape, and are extremely huggable." The court concluded "Skippy and Muttsy are not substantially similar, and that any similarity between the two dogs would appear to the ordinary observer to result solely from the fact that both are more or less nonnaturalistic, reclining, huggable, floppy dogs.

In *JCW Investments, Inc. v. Novelty, Inc.*, 482 F.3d 910, 916 (7th Cir. 2007), the court concluded that the ordinary observer would find the plaintiff's and defendant's flatulent plush dolls, "Pull My Finger Fred" and "Fartman," substantially similar.

> The pictures show that the similarities between Fred and Fartman go far beyond the fact that both are plush dolls of middle-aged men sitting in armchairs that fart and tell jokes. Both have crooked smiles that show their teeth, balding heads with a fringe of black hair, a rather large protruding nose, blue pants that are identical colors, and white tank tops. On the other hand, Fartman has his name emblazoned in red across his chest, his shoes are a different color from Fred's, as is his chair, and Fartman wears a hat. In the end, despite the small cosmetic differences, the two dolls give off more than a similar air.

The court rejected the defendant's argument that it merely made a similar doll based on the same comic archetype, that of "a typical man wearing jeans and a T-shirt in a chair doing the 'pull my finger' joke." The court stated:

> It is not the idea of a farting, crude man that is protected, but this particular embodiment of that concept. Novelty could have created another plush doll of a middle-aged farting man that would seem nothing like Fred. He could, for example, have a blond mullet and wear flannel, have a nose that is drawn on rather than protruding substantially from the rest of the head, be standing rather than ensconced in an armchair, and be wearing shorts rather than blue pants.

B. Abstraction-Filtration-Comparison Test

Some courts use the abstraction-filtration-comparison test to determine substantial similarity between works. The first step requires identifying the aspects of plaintiff's work that are protected by copyright, which means abstracting the works—separating the ideas and utilitarian elements from the expressive elements—and then filtering out the unprotectable elements. The next step is to compare the protectable elements for substantial similarity based on the perspective of the intended audience.

For example, in *Jacobsen v. Deseret Book Co.*, 287 F.3d 936 (10th Cir. 2002), both the plaintiff's memoir and the defendant's novel described the main character's imprisonment by the Japanese on the Bataan Peninsula during World War II. The court evaluated the substantial similarity of the works by applying the abstraction-filtration-comparison test as follows:

> At the abstraction step, we separate the ideas (and basic utilitarian functions), which are not protectable, from the particular expression of the work. Then, we filter out the nonprotectable components of the product from the original expression. Finally, we compare the remaining protected elements to the allegedly copied work to determine if the two works are substantially similar.

The *Jacobsen* court found "substantial similarity" present where "the accused work is so similar to the plaintiff's work that an ordinary reasonable person could conclude that the defendant unlawfully appropriated the plaintiff's protectable expression by taking material of substance and value." Applying the test, the court held that the works were substantially similar. Beyond the similarities in the bare facts of the two narratives, the particulars of the protagonists' experiences and their emotional reactions were consistently analogous, they relayed the same anecdotes, and the defendant occasionally reproduced the plaintiff's words exactly.

In *Kohus v. Mariol*, 328 F.3d 848 (6th Cir. 2003), the court compared patent drawings of latches used with portable children's playgrounds. Because the drawings were technical and not intended for the lay public, the court held that similarity should be considered from the standard of one with specialized expertise rather than an ordinary observer and that expert testimony was appropriate to determine substantial similarity.

C. Extrinsic/Intrinsic Test

Under the Extrinsic/Intrinsic Test substantial similarity may be found when the works share significant similarity in protected expression both on an objective, analytical level and a subjective, audience-response level.

In the first step, similarity of ideas is analyzed objectively using dissection and expert testimony, if helpful. For example, criteria such as the type of artwork involved, the subject matter, the setting and materials used might be analyzed. If there is substantial similarity of ideas, similarity of expression is evaluated using the subjective intrinsic test. This test is whether ordinary, reasonable observer would find the works, as a whole, to be substantially similar. The ordinary observer is to be a member of the work's intended audience.

Sid & Marty Krofft Television Productions, Inc. v. McDonald's Corp., 562 F.2d 1157 (9th Cir. 1977), was an infringement action involving plaintiffs' "H. R. Pufnstuf" children's TV show and "McDonaldland" TV commercials. The extrinsic test was met because the defendants copied the idea of plaintiffs' Pufnstuf television series, basically a fantasyland filled with diverse and fanciful characters in action. The court rejected the defendants' argument that in applying the intrinsic test the Pufnstuf series should be dissected into characters, setting, and plot and compared individually to those portions of defendants' commercials. The court held that this sort of dissection was appropriate in the first extrinsic step, but not the intrinsic step. Subjective similarity is determined by the observations and impressions of the average reasonable reader and spectator.

In *Dr. Seuss Enterprises, L.P. v. Penguin Books USA, Inc.*, 109 F.3d 1394 (9th Cir. 1997), the copyright holder of *The Cat in the Hat* sought an injunction against Penguin Books' publication of *The Cat NOT in the Hat! A Parody by Dr. Juice*, "a poetic account of the O.J. Simpson double murder trial." The court held that the supposed parody amounted to an infringement under both the objective/analytical and subjective tests because of the defendant's impermissible copying of "the back cover illustration and the Cat's Hat, [rather than] the typeface, poetic meter, whimsical style or visual style" of the original. The cover of the defendant's work featured the famous Hat worn by Cat in the Hat, which appeared 26 times in the original work and 13 times in the parody. (The court preferred the terms objective and subjective over extrinsic and intrinsic.)

In *Lyons Partnership, L.P. v. Morris Costumes, Inc.*, 243 F.3d 789 (4th Cir. 2001) the owner of "'Barney' the famous purple dinosaur who speaks in a distinctive baritone" brought an infringement action against the owners of "'Duffy the Dragon,' a purple reptilian costume." The district court concluded that Barney and Duffy were extrinsically similar, but not subjectively intrinsically similar based on the intended audience of "the average adult renter or purchaser of these costumes"

The Fourth Circuit reversed, holding the district court erred in disregarding the substantial evidence of confusion between Barney and Duffy among children. The court noted, for example:

> An elementary school administrator testified that her school rented the Duffy costume for a school rally called "Character Counts," because Barney exemplified the qualities that the rally intended to communicate. When the administrator appeared without advance notice

before 500 children in the Duffy costume, the children saw Barney. As she testified, "the kids just went wild. They went crazy and they were just going, 'Barney. Barney. Barney.'" Also, various parents testified that they rented Duffy knowing that it would be perceived by children as Barney.

The court held that while adults were the ones who rented or purchased the costumes, the intended audience was children.

D. Computer Programs

Most courts use the Abstraction-Filtration-Comparison process for comparing the similarities of computer programs. Computer programs invariably contain a combination of protectable and unprotectable components. In the abstraction step, the court breaks down the program to at least six levels in declining order of abstraction:

(1) the main purpose,

(2) the program structure or architecture,

(3) modules,

(4) algorithms and data structures,

(5) source code, and

(6) object code.

Then at each level of abstraction, the court filters out elements not protected by copyright, including:

(1) Ideas, e.g., the main purpose of the program is an idea and is not protectable;

(2) Processes—the actual methods of achieving a particular result as opposed to the expression of those methods;

(3) Facts;

(4) Material in the Public Domain; and

(5) Scenes a Faire—expressions that are standard, stock, or common to a particular topic, in the computer programs these are elements dictated by external factors such as hardware or software standards and compatibility requirements.

After filtering out the elements that are unprotectable, the protected elements can be compared to the alleged infringing program. Ultimately the court must decide whether those protectable portions of the original work that have been copied constitute a substantial part of the original work that is significant in the plaintiff's program.

For example, in *CyberMedia, Inc. v. Symantec Corp.*, 19 F. Supp. 2d 1070 (N.D. Cal. 1998), the court found a likelihood of infringement and issued a preliminary injunction where lines of code copied by defendant comprised a small percentage of plaintiff's program. The court noted "there is substantial evidence that the files in which these code lines appear are essential to the functioning of the program. Indeed, a page from the NUD project manager's notebook refers to one of the files containing copied code as the "[h]eart of product." On the other hand, in *Computer Associates Intern., Inc. v. Altai, Inc.*, 982 F.2d 693 (2d Cir. 1992), no infringement was found where "only a few of the [parameter] lists and macros were similar to protected elements in [the plaintiff's program]; the others were either in the public domain or dictated by the functional demands of the program."

c. Secondary Infringement

United States common law provides a right of action against "contributory" and "vicarious" infringers. In *Sony Corp. of America v. Universal City Studios*, 464 U.S. 417 (1984), the Supreme Court held that, though not explicitly mentioned, contributory infringement was encompassed by § 106's inclusion of a copyright owner's right to authorize others to copy or display a work. Under the doctrine of contributory infringement, a knowing participant who furthers a tort is joint and severally liable with the primary tortfeasor: "one who, with knowledge of the infringing activity, induces, causes, or materially contributes to the infringing conduct of another, may be liable as a 'contributory' infringer." For example, in *Gershwin Publishing Corp. v. Columbia Artists Management, Inc.*, 443 F.2d 1159, 1162 (2d Cir. 1971), a concert promoter had actively worked to gather audiences for a series of concerts featuring local musicians. Because the promoter knew before the series began that some of the performers intended to perform copyrighted music without first obtaining licenses, the court held he had "materially contributed" to their infringement, and become liable himself for contributory infringement. A party may also be vicariously liable based upon their ability and responsibility to supervise the direct infringer.

In *Fonovisa, Inc. v. Cherry Auction, Inc.*, 76 F.3d 259 (9th Cir. 1996), the court found grounds for both types of secondary infringement. The defendant, Cherry Auction, operated a flea market where counterfeit recordings of copyrighted works were routinely sold. Because the defendants could decide who participated in the flea market, the court concluded that the flea market operators had the ability to control the vendors' activities, specifically the selling of counterfeit recordings, and were therefore vicariously liable for the infringement. In addition, the court found contributory infringement because the defendants knew about past infringement and provided the facilities for future infringements.

Inducement liability for copyright infringement lies where the defendant distributes a product intending and encouraging the product to be used to infringe, resulting in infringement by third parties. In *Metro-Goldwyn-Mayer Studios Inc. v. Grokster, Ltd.*, 545 U.S. 913 (2005), the distributor peer-to-peer file sharing software (Morpheus) was found liable for infringement on an inducement theory where its business model "depended on massive infringement," and it targeted known infringers (former Napster users) resulting in "staggering infringement" of the plaintiff's copyrighted music and videos.

4. Defenses to Infringement

a. Miscellaneous Exceptions

Title 17 contains a variety of exceptions for uses that would otherwise be infringing. Some of the statutory exceptions apply to noncommercial users of copyrighted works. Section 108 supplies a defense to libraries and archives that make a limited number of copies of copyrighted works either on behalf of patrons or to preserve the works. Likewise, the adaptation or reproduction of "nondramatic" works for use by the blind or other disabled persons is permitted under §121.

Section 110 contains a long list of limitations on the scope of the author's rights in copyrighted material:

> §§110(1) and (2) allow for the use of copyrighted materials for educational purposes—to a nearly unlimited extent in a "face-to-face" classroom context, and a carefully circumscribed extent online;
> §110(3) allows the performance and display of copyrighted works in the course of worship;
> §110(4) forecloses a claim of infringement arising from free public concerts and truly charitable fundraising events;
> §110(5) allows stores and restaurants to play the radio or television on (under certain circumstances) without being held liable for infringement;

§ 110(6) insulates governmental entities and nonprofit agricultural or horticultural organizations from liability for both direct and vicarious infringement arising for allowing copyrighted works to be performed at fairs and similar events;

§ 110(7) permits record stores to play the records they sell;

§§ 110(8) and (9) permit very limited use of copyrighted works in broadcasts or publications designed for and directed toward blind or otherwise disabled persons;

§ 110(10) allows veterans organizations to turn a profit on fundraising events, provided that the proceeds are used for charitable purposes; and

§ 110(11) specifically allows the "making imperceptible" of objectionable portions of copyrighted materials "by or at the direction of a member of a private household."

Several sections of Title 17 afford licensees with an otherwise unauthorized right to reproduce copyrighted works. Private purchasers of audio recordings are justified in making copies of those recordings under § 109, so long as the copies are for purely personal use. Similarly, § 117 allows computer software licensees to back-up their software, and even to alter it if necessary to render the software functional for their needs. Section 112 provides a similar defense to licensees who make "ephemeral" backup recordings for archival or permitted rebroadcast purposes.

Several exceptions are also available in the form of a "statutory license" created under §§ 111, 119 and 122 in favor of those who rebroadcast, for commercial purposes, programming copyrighted by the original broadcaster. Each of those sections is very dense, and the several defenses afforded by each are narrowly drawn. Among the more significant is that provided in § 119 to satellite carriers that relay, for profit, copyrighted television programming to "unserved households" otherwise beyond the range of other broadcasters. Section 122 ensures that satellite rebroadcasters are also able to provide their unserved subscribers with local broadcast programming. Likewise, § 111 affords rebroadcasters with several statutory exceptions to the otherwise exclusive right of performance. Most clearly, § 111(a) allows hotel and apartment-house proprietors to relay the transmission of cable television signals into each of their rooms without paying royalties. Section 111(c) also allows cable networks to relay broadcast signals at the same time they are originally broadcast, while § 111(e) allows U.S. cable networks operating outside of the continental United States to record broadcast programming for a single later rebroadcast.

But the most important statutory defense to a charge of infringement is that the allegedly infringing use is in fact a "fair use," as provided in 17 U.S.C. § 107, discussed below after the discussion of the defense of independent creation.

b. Independent Creation

Independent creation — as opposed to copying — is also a defense to infringement. In *Ellis v. Diffie*, 177 F.3d 503 (6th Cir. 1999), the three writers of "Prop Me Up Beside the Jukebox (If I Die)," which allegedly infringed upon a song called "Lay Me Out By the Jukebox When I Die," testified about the song's development. They produced written notes and tapes of some of the work sessions, and presented their reasons for choosing various lines or turns of phrase. As a result, the court concluded that any inference of copying was rebutted by the showing of independent creation.

c. Fair Use

The fair use doctrine, codified at 17 U.S.C. § 107, is probably the most important exception to the exclusive rights inherent in copyright ownership. Although codified, fair use is an equitable doctrine, intended — like the idea/expression dichotomy — to ensure that the protection afforded to copyright owners remains firm enough to encourage the useful arts, but flexible enough to avoid chilling free speech. Each case of allegedly fair use must be decided on its own facts, and because the question of whether a particular use qualifies as a fair use is a mixed question of law and fact, an appellate court may, given a sufficient factual record, balance all relevant considerations without deference to the conclusions of the court below. With regard to the appropriate balance factors, the defendant bears the burden of proof that his use of copyrighted material was fair. Section 107 lists various purposes that may justify reproduction of a work without permission under the rubric of "fair use," such as criticism, comment, news reporting, teaching, scholarship, and research. Section 107 also sets out four factors to be considered in determining whether or not a particular use is fair:

(1) the purpose and character of the use, including whether such use is of commercial nature or is for nonprofit educational purposes;

(2) the nature of the copyrighted work;

(3) amount and substantiality of the portion used in relation to the copyrighted work as a whole; and

(4) the effect of the use upon the potential market for or value of the copy-
     righted work.

The distinction between "fair use" and infringement can be unclear and not
easily defined—it is best thought of as an affirmative defense to a claim of infringement rather than an independent right to publish. There is no specific
amount of material, number of words or lines of text that may be fairly used
without permission. Although acknowledgement of the source does weigh towards the fairness of a use, as opposed to unacknowledged appropriation, acknowledgement of a source is not a substitute for permission.

The fair use doctrine has a long history. *Folsom v. Marsh*, 9 F. Cas. 342
(C.C.D. Mass. 1841) is credited with being the first articulation of the fair use
doctrine's underlying principles. In *Folsom*, the plaintiff owned the copyright
to much of the correspondence of George Washington, and the defendants
used portions of the correspondence to produce a biography "in the form of
an autobiography." Judge Story explained that "[i]f so much is taken, that the
value of the original is sensibly diminished, or the labors of the original author
are substantially to an injurious extent appropriated by another, that is sufficient, in point of law, to constitute [infringement]." In making its decision,
the court "look[ed] to the nature and objects of the selections made, the quantity and value of the materials used, and the degree in which the use may prejudice the sale, or diminish the profits, or supersede the objects, of the original
work," and concluded that the use of the letters was fair and did not impede
upon the copyright owner's rights.

The 1976 House Report that accompanied the revised Copyright Act included
a number of examples of fair uses including: short quotations in reviews, short
quotations in scholarly works, use in a parody work, reproduction by a library to
replace a portion of a damaged work, reproduction of a small portion by a teacher
for use in a lesson, reproduction for legislative or judicial proceedings, and reproduction in a broadcast of an incident. All of these examples apply only to limited portions of works and give neither free reign nor assure that the uses or parties
described in the examples will always be protected. Although the House provided
these examples, it did not adopt a test or exact standard for determining whether
a use falls under the protection of the fair use doctrine. These determinations are
fact intensive and decided based on the facts of each particular case.

In *Harper & Row Publishers, Inc. v. Nation Enterprises*, 471 U.S. 539, 561
(1985), the Court explained that these statutory factors "give some idea of the
sort of activities the courts might regard as fair use under the circumstances,"
but the list of factors is neither exhaustive nor a basis for the presumption that
a particular use is always fair. As a practical matter, this means publishers and

others that exploit works for profit will normally require their authors to obtain releases or permissions for any outside work quoted or reproduced within a work; fair use is a defense in litigation, not a doctrine that is relied upon when structuring a transaction.

Works that may qualify as fair uses can be divided into two categories, transformative and non-transformative. In the first category are works that have borrowed from earlier copyrighted materials to produce a new work. A transformative work adds something new, a different character, altering the first work with new expression, meaning, or message. *Campbell v. Acuff-Rose Music, Inc.*, 510 U.S. 569, 579 (1994). Courts are cautious in enjoining transformative works because their creation generally furthers the goal of copyright, to promote science and the arts. For example, in *World Wrestling Federation Entertainment, Inc. v. Big Dog Holdings, Inc.*, 280 F. Supp. 2d 413, 422 (D.Pa. 2003), the World Wrestling Federation alleged that Big Dog clothing had infringed copyrighted material by, *inter alia*, printing t-shirts featuring "Hollywoof Hound Hogan," "Bone Cold Steve Pawstin," "Goldbark," "The Underdogger," and "The Rockweiler" posing under the logo " 'WBDF' [printed] in a lettering style identical to the WWF scratch logo." Big Dog countered that its work amounted to parody, in that "the heart of any parodist's claim to quote from existing material is the use of some elements of a prior author's composition to create a new one that, at least in part, comments on that author's works." The court agreed, and in dismissing the complaint noted that the similarities between the plaintiff's work and the defendant's were necessary "in order to conjure up thoughts of the original, while clearly not being the original." The defendant's works, the court concluded, were protected parodies on the seriousness and severity of the WWF's image, and to impose liability for the defendant's willingness to poke fun "would constitute a serious curtailment of a protected form of expression."

The second category—non-transformative works—includes instances where the defendant has simply made direct copies from the copyrighted work and distributed them. In these cases, injunctive relief against infringement is relatively easy to obtain.

In *Castle Rock Entertainment, Inc. v. Carol Publishing Group, Inc.*, 150 F.3d 132, 135–36 (2d Cir. 1998), the defendants produced a book entitled *The Seinfeld Aptitude Test*. The book was composed of multiple-choice and other trivia questions drawn from 84 of the 86 episodes of the *Seinfeld* sitcom that had been aired at that time. Castle Rock Entertainment, the company that owned the copyright to every episode of *Seinfeld*, filed an infringement action against Carol Publishing, who in turn claimed that they had made fair use of information from *Seinfeld*. The Court of Appeals made what it considered to be a "critical inquiry" into transformative qualities. The court explained that whether or not something is a fair use turns upon whether the allegedly infringing work merely supersedes the original work or instead adds something new, with a further purpose or different character, altering the first with new meaning or message. The court held that the purpose of *The Seinfeld Aptitude Test* was to repackage *Seinfeld* to entertain *Seinfeld* fans and viewers rather than to educate, criticize, parody, report upon, or research the sitcom, and as a result, the publication was not protected as fair use.

A work may qualify as fair use if its purpose is to criticize the copyrighted work. In *Chicago Board of Education v. Substance Inc.*, 354 F.3d 624 (7th Cir. 2003), the court addressed critical works as fair use. The editor of *Substance*, a magazine for teachers, published six secret, standardized tests that the plaintiff school board had developed. The magazine's editor, a teacher himself, published the tests to publicly criticize their quality. The court recognized that the editor was entitled to criticize the tests and that to do so he would have to draw quotes from them. However, the general rule is that the critic must copy no more from the copyrighted work than is reasonably necessary to carry out his lawful aim. The court found that by publishing the six tests in their entirety, he went far beyond what was reasonably necessary to convey his criticisms.

A number of non-transformative direct copying cases involve arguments that the defendant made fair use of the copyrighted work because the copies were used for educational purposes, but courts have been conservative in recognizing fair use defenses grounded in a supposed educational purpose. For example, in *Basic Books, Inc. v. Kinko's Graphics Corp.*, 758 F. Supp. 1522, 1526 (S.D.N.Y. 1991), the defendant had prepared materials packets consisting largely of copyrighted materials that were used by students at the New School for Social Research, New York University, and Columbia University, for which the defendant did not pay royalties. Despite the fact the materials packets were clearly put to educational use, the court held that Kinko's use did not qualify as a "fair use." Particularly relevant to the court's analysis were the profit motive underlying the duplication and lack of evidence that Kinko's had seriously pursued the licenses necessary to prepare the packets without infringing.

5. Remedies

The remedies for copyright infringement include:

a. Injunctions, 17 U.S.C. § 502;

b. Impoundment and disposition (destruction) of the infringing articles, 17 U.S.C. § 503;

   c.   Actual damages and any additional profits realized by the infringer, or statutory damages, at the election of the prevailing party, 17 U.S.C. §504; and

   d.   Attorney fees and costs, 17 U.S.C. §505.

Also, 17 U.S.C. §506 provides for criminal penalties of fines up to $250,000 and imprisonment of up to 10 years (for multiple subsequent offenses) for cases of willful infringement for commercial advantage or personal financial gain.

a. Injunctions — 17 U.S.C. § 502

A court may issue a permanent injunction to prevent or restrain infringement of a copyright. This may include enjoining the defendant from infringing the works at issue in the litigation, as well as any future copyrightable works created by the plaintiff.

To obtain an injunction the prevailing party must satisfy the traditional four-part test for obtaining equitable relief, that:

(1) it suffered irreparable harm;

(2) remedies available at law, such as money damages, are inadequate;

(3) considering the balance of hardships between the plaintiff and defendant, a remedy in equity is warranted; and

(4) the public interest would not be disserved by a permanent injunction.

eBay Inc. v. MercExchange, L.L.C., 547 U.S. 388 (2006). Courts vary in how strictly or intricately they apply this test. A permanent injunction will not automatically follow upon a showing of infringement, but is likely to be granted where a substantial likelihood of future infringement has been demonstrated.

In *Disney Enterprises, Inc. v. Merchant*, No. 6:05-CV-1489, 2007 U.S. Dist. Lexis 10365, 2007 WL 1101110 (N.D.N.Y.), the court found defendant infringed and continued to infringe Disney's copyrights to the movies "The Incredibles" and "Fever Pitch" by using an online media distribution center to download the movies and make them widely available to the public through a variety of peer-to-peer networks, and that there was no evidence defendant had or would cease their downloading and distribution activities. Thus, the court permanently enjoined the defendants from directly or indirectly infringing the copyrights to those two movies, "and any other copyrighted motion picture, whether now in existence or later created, that is owned or controlled by the plaintiffs."

The injunction should be limited to the part of the work that is protected by copyright. In *Lipton v. Nature Co.*, 71 F.3d 464 (2d Cir. 1995), the defendant used plaintiff's compilation of terms for identifying certain animal groups on posters and scarves and was found liable for copyright infringement. The court issued a permanent injunction that not only prohibited defendant from infringing plaintiff's compilation, but from producing and marketing shirts and mugs containing just one term taken from the compilation. The appellate court held this injunction was excessively broad because only the selection and arrangement of compilation were protectable, not the individual terms themselves.

The scope of the injunction should also relate to the particular infringing conduct at issue, although courts have still issued broad injunctions prohibiting a laundry list of infringing activities or "any and all violation of federal and state copyright laws." The court recognized this in *Metro-Goldwyn-Mayer Studios, Inc. v. Grokster, Ltd.*, 518 F. Supp. 2d 1197 (C.D. Cal. 2007), when it partially denied the prevailing plaintiff's motion for an expansive permanent injunction. There, the distributor of peer-to-peer file sharing software (Morpheus) whose business model "depended on massive infringement" of the plaintiff's copyrighted music and videos was found liable for inducing copyright infringement, but not direct infringement. The court granted an injunction that was limited to acts and words that would induce infringement, stating "it would be inappropriate to issue an injunction in which [defendant] would be barred from violating the Copyright Act in any other manner."

b. Impoundment and Disposition — 17 U.S.C. § 503

Once suit is filed, a court may order the impoundment of allegedly infringing articles, § 503(a), and then order the destruction or other disposition of articles found to be infringing, § 503(b). Articles affected include "all copies or phonorecords" as well as "all plates, molds, matrices, masters, tapes, film negatives, or other articles by means of which such copies or phonorecords may be reproduced."

Impoundment means the seizure and delivery of the allegedly infringing goods and articles that can be used to copy them. The purpose of impoundment is to safeguard such items during the pendency of litigation so that they can be destroyed or otherwise disposed of if found to violate the copyright laws. To obtain an impoundment order, the plaintiff must show a danger exists that the articles will be destroyed or transferred. Section 503 does not apply to innocent purchases of infringing articles. In *Societe Civile Succession Richard*

Guino v. International Foundation for Anticancer Drug Discovery, 460 F. Supp. 2d 1105 (D.Ariz. 2006), the court denied the prevailing plaintiff's request for impoundment against person who, unaware, bought an unauthorized replica of a Renoir sculpture at a charity ball.

If infringement is found, § 503(b) allows the court to order all infringing items, and all articles that may be used to reproduce such items, destroyed or turned over to the plaintiff. In *RSO Records, Inc. v. Peri*, 596 F. Supp. 849 (S.D.N.Y. 1984), the court ordered the destruction of records and audiotapes that infringed the copyrights of numerous sound recordings, as well as color separators — machinery used to duplicate record and audio-tape labels and packaging. In *National Broadcasting Co., Inc. v. Sonneborn*, 630 F. Supp. 524 (D.Conn. 1985), the court ordered the defendant to deliver to the plaintiff all unauthorized master recordings and copies of the plaintiff's 1960 broadcast of Peter Pan. However, the court denied plaintiff's request that the defendant turn over all catalogs, advertisements, and other materials related to the 1960 Peter Pan production because the plaintiff had not shown that these items infringed its copyright.

c. Actual Damages and Profits, Statutory Damages, 17 U.S.C. § 504

The prevailing plaintiff may recover its actual damages as well any profits realized by the infringer that were not taken into account in computing actual damages. Damages are awarded to compensate the plaintiff for losses it suffered as a result of the infringement, while profits are awarded to prevent the infringer from otherwise benefiting from its acts. If plaintiff's damages are measured by profits gained by the infringer, damages and profits will not be awarded cumulatively.

Any time before final judgment is rendered, the prevailing plaintiff may elect, instead, to recover statutory damages of $750 to $30,000 per work from each infringer, which the court may increase to $150,000 in cases of willful infringements, or reduce to $200 in cases of innocent infringement. In compilations and derivative works all the various parts are considered just one work for purposes of § 504. It is important to note that statutory damages are calculated based on the number of protected works that are infringed and are not multiplied based on the number of incidents infringement of each work. The purpose of statutory damages is to deter infringement where no actual damages were caused or profits realized, or where such are difficult to prove. Statutory damages are only available if the work is registered.

i. Actual Damages

Actual damages reflect the loss of fair market value of the plaintiff's copyright. This is generally measured, as a start, by the profits plaintiff would have realized but for the defendant's infringement. In *Mary Ellen Enterprises v. Camex, Inc.*, 68 F.3d 1065 (8th Cir. 1995), the defendant infringed plaintiff's copyright to the book "Mary Ellen's Best of Helpful Hints" by distributing 300,000 unauthorized copes to L'eggs hosiery for use in a promotional campaign. Plaintiff was awarded $202,000 representing lost profits on the sale of the book, as well as $300,000 for further damage to the value of the copyright. The court concluded the book's actual and endorsement value was "substantially diminished [by the infringement] because L'eggs used the book in an attempt to sell seconds or damaged hosiery, offered the book free with any purchase no matter how small, and identified the book with a $3.95 retail price rather than the $4.95 retail price then in effect."

In addition to lost sales, actual damages have been awarded for lost licensing fees and royalties, development costs, loss of market recognition, and loss of goodwill or reputation.

The plaintiff must demonstrate a causal connection between defendant's infringement and the damages claimed. In *Banff Ltd. v. Express, Inc.*, 921 F. Supp. 1065 (S.D.N.Y. 1995), a jury found the defendant retailer infringed plaintiff's copyright by selling a knockoff of plaintiff's high-end Aran fisherman's sweater. The jury awarded actual damages of $200,685 based on the plaintiff's claim that, as a result of defendant's infringement, it lost sales it would have made to defendant of its genuine sweaters. The court struck this award because the plaintiff did not demonstrate that it could have supplied the quantity of sweaters the defendant needed, or that defendant would have bought them if available.

ii. Profits

The prevailing plaintiff may also recover any profits of the infringer attributable to the infringement that were not taken into account in measuring actual damages. In other words, if the profits gained by the defendant as a result of the infringement are greater than the profits lost by the plaintiff and awarded as actual damages, the plaintiff may recover the difference. Or, even if the plaintiff did not suffer lost profits or other actual damages, it can still recover the infringer's profits. In both instances, the infringer is prevented from unfairly benefiting from the infringement. In *Banff Ltd. v. Express, Inc.*, 921 F. Supp. 1065 (S.D.N.Y. 1995), the court awarded $1,017,240 representing the defendant's profits from the sale of the infringing sweaters even though it found that the plaintiff itself had not suffered any lost profits as a result of the infringement.

The plaintiff must first make a prima facie showing of the defendant's gross revenue reasonably related to the infringement. In *On Davis v. The Gap, Inc.*, 246 F.3d 152, 160 (2d Cir. 2001), a prominent Gap advertisement featured a model wearing distinctive eyeglasses designed and copyrighted by the plaintiff. To demonstrate the Gap's gross profits, the plaintiff submitted evidence of an increase of $146 million in net sales realized by the Gap's corporate parent following the use of the advertisement, compared to the same period the previous year. The court held this evidence was not reasonably related to the infringement, explaining that the ad infringed only with respect to Gap label stores and eyewear so the evidence must be at least limited to the gross revenues of the Gap stores, and perhaps also limited to eyewear or accessories.

Once the plaintiff makes a prima facie showing of gross revenue, the burden shifts to the defendant to prove deductible expenses and any portion of profits attributable to factors other than the copyrighted work. Deductible expenses include direct costs of developing, producing, and selling the infringing article, as well as overhead expenses, such as rent, payroll, advertising, shipping, and storage, that are sufficiently related and properly apportioned to the production or sale of the infringing article. The other step, apportioning defendant's profits, involves an assessment of the importance of the copyrighted work in generating revenue. In *National Conference of Bar Examiners v. Multistate Legal Studies, Inc.*, 458 F. Supp. 2d 252 (E.D. Pa. 2006), the defendant was found liable for infringing plaintiff's multistate bar exam questions for use in defendant's PMBR bar review course. Defendant's gross revenues from the course during the period at issue were $35,708,361, which the court apportioned—awarding one-third or $11,902,787 to the plaintiff. The court noted the infringing questions made up close to 40% of the course, and the quality of the PMBR practice questions was a major draw; "on the other hand, students taking the 3-day course also receive workbooks containing 2000 other practice questions, substantive law outlines, and study aids."

iii. Statutory Damages

At any time before final judgment is rendered, the plaintiff may elect to recover statutory damages in lieu of actual damages or the infringer's profits. Statutory damages generally range from $750 to $30,000 per work against each infringer "as the court considers just." In addition, the court may increase these damages to $150,000 in cases of willful infringement, or reduce them to $200 in cases of innocent infringement (where the defendant was not aware that her acts constituted an infringement of copyright). Statutory damages cannot be awarded against teachers, librarians, archivists, or public broadcasters who reasonably believed that their use of a copyrighted work was a fair use under 17 U.S.C. §107. Statutory damages are available only if the copyright is registered.

The court has wide discretion in determining statutory damages within the statutory limits, and may consider a variety of factors, including expenses saved and profits made by the infringer, profits lost by the plaintiff as a result of the infringer, and the infringer's intent—whether willful, knowing, or innocent. The goal is to award an amount that ensures the costs of violating the copyright laws are sufficiently greater than the costs of obeying them. In *Broadcast Music, Inc. v. Entertainment Complex, Inc.*, 198 F. Supp. 2d 1291 (N.D. Ala. 2002), a night club operator and its principal officer were found liable for infringement based on the club's performance of 11 copyrighted songs without a license. The court awarded statutory damages of $43,000—approximately $3,909 for each of the 11 songs and three times the amount of licensing fees the defendants should have paid the plaintiffs. In *Knitwaves, Inc. v. Lollytogs Ltd.*, 71 F.3d 996 (2d Cir. 1995), the court awarded statutory damages of $50,000–$25,000 per work infringed, many thousands more than the plaintiff's actual damages and profits. The court concluded the defendant's admission that it set out to create designs having the same "look" and "feel" as the copyrighted sweaters and that it did not look for copyright notice on sweaters demonstrated willfulness. By contrast, in *D.C. Comics Inc. v. Mini Gift Shop*, 912 F.2d 29 (2d Cir. 1990), the court determined the owners of retail stores that sold unlicensed Batman merchandise were innocent infringers and assessed statutory damages of $200 against each. The court noted the defendants were all recent immigrants who spoke little or no English, lacked business sophistication, and the infringing goods did not have a copyright notice.

d. Attorneys' Fees — 17 U.S.C. § 505

The court, in its discretion, may award costs of suit as well as attorneys' fees to the prevailing party. In *Fogerty v. Fantasy, Inc.*, 510 U.S. 517 (1994), the Supreme Court held prevailing plaintiffs and prevailing defendants must be treated alike for purses of awarding attorney fees under § 505. Prior to that decision many courts awarded attorney fees to prevailing plaintiffs as a matter of course, but awarded attorney fees to prevailing defendants only if the suit was frivolous or brought in bad faith. Factors to be considered in awarding attorney fees include "frivolousness, motivation, objective unreasonableness (both in the factual and in the legal components of the case), and the need in particular circumstances to advance considerations of compensation and deterrence." The goal of attorney fee awards is to vindicate the purpose of the Copyright Act—encouraging the production of original literary, artistic, and musical expression.

Courts are likely to award the prevailing plaintiff attorney fees if the defendant's infringement was knowing or willful. In *Controversy Music v. Down Under Pub Tyler, Inc.*, 488 F. Supp. 2d 572 (E.D. Tex. 2007), the court granted plaintiff's request for attorney fees where the defendant publicly performed a series of copyrights songs without authorization. The court noted "ASCAP representatives tried on numerous occasions to secure a licensing agreement with the defendant and defendants were clearly aware of the necessity of obtaining permission to publicly perform protected musical compositions." On the other hand, in *Clark v. Hudson Bay Music, Inc.*, 104 F.3d 351 (2d Cir. 1996), the court denied attorney fees to the prevailing plaintiff where the plaintiff was awarded past royalties in an amount greater than its estimated attorney fees, was also awarded future royalties, and the defendants had held and exercised copyrights in the song at issue without contest for thirty years.

Courts have awarded attorney fees to the prevailing defendant where the plaintiff's infringement claims were frivolous, brought in bad faith, or merely weak. In *Matthews v. Freedman*, 157 F.3d 25 (1st Cir. 1998), an action involving makers of souvenir T-shirts, the court awarded attorney fees to the prevailing defendant, concluding that the plaintiff's suit was not frivolous or brought in bad faith but she "did try to extend her copyright protection far beyond what is allowed by law." The appellate court affirmed, stating that under *Fogerty v. Fantasy*, "[a] plaintiff's decision to bring a weak, if nonfrivolous, case and to argue for an unreasonable extension of copyright protection are relevant concerns."

Checkpoints

- Copyright protection of a work attaches upon the work's creation, but to enforce the copyright against infringers and to recover statutory damages or attorneys' fees the copyright must be registered.

- Under the 1909 Copyright Act, the failure to place notice precluded protection, but under the 1976 Act, the lack of notice only limited remedies and reduced damages. After the revisions in the wake of the Berne Convention, notice is irrelevant to copyright protections and remedies for works created after 1989, except as it relates to the innocent infringer defense.

- The exclusive rights under the copyright act include the right to reproduce the work; prepare derivative works; distribute copies through sale, rental, lease, or lending of the work; perform the work publicly; display the work publicly; and perform the work publicly via digital audio transmission.

- The right to reproduction allows the copyright holder to prevent others from making an unauthorized copy or phonorecord.

- The right to derivative works allows the copyright holder to prevent others from making unauthorized translations, dramatizations, fictionalizations, motion picture adaptations, abridgments, and other transformative works.

- The right to distribution allows the copyright holder to prevent others from selling, renting, leasing, or lending the work.

- The "first sale doctrine" limits the copyright holder's right of distribution by providing an exception so that once a copyrighted article is sold without restriction, the distribution rights no longer prevent further distributions of that same article.

- The right to performance allows the copyright holder to prevent others from publicly performing the work, but there are exceptions for non-profit groups, religious services, and charity fundraisers.

- The right to display allows the copyright holder to prevent others from publicly displaying the copyrighted work, but the face-to-face exception allows the public display of the work at the place where the work is located.

- Copyright infringement occurs whenever another engages in activities otherwise reserved for the copyright owner without permission.

- To prevail in a copyright infringement suit, the plaintiff must show that there is a valid copyright, one that is original and fixed in a tangible medium of expression. Also, the mark must be registered (or denied registration) in order to bring suit.

- Copying can be proven directly if possible, or through circumstantial evidence. To indirectly prove copying, one must show that the alleged infringer had access to the protected work and that the accused work is substantially similar to the protected work.

- Access is the reasonable opportunity to view, hear, or experience the protected work. Access can be shown by possession of a copy of the work, inferred based on interaction with those in possession of the work, presumed when the work has been widely disseminated or mass produced, or inferred when the two works are strikingly similar when considered against the diversity in the marketplace.

- Substantial similarity is determined through tests that objectively and subjectively compare the copyrighted work with the alleged infringing work.

- Secondary infringement liability exists for those who induce, cause, or materially contribute to the infringement of another.

- Defenses to infringement include fair use; independent creation; uses for educational purposes, in the course of worship, or for free public concerts and charitable fundraisers; and copies for personal use and software backups, among others.

- Fair use is an equitable doctrine that acts as an affirmative defense. Fair use is determined by balancing four factors: the purpose and character of the use, including if it is a commercial or non-profit use; the nature of the copyrighted work; the amount and substantiality of the portion used in relation to the work as a whole; and the effect of the use upon the market for or value of the copyrighted work.

- The types of fair use are transformative works, which borrow from the earlier work to produce a new work and includes parody, and non-transformative works, those that are direct copies of the original work, such as works reproduced for criticism or educational purposes.

- Copyright infringement remedies include injunctions, impoundment, monetary damages, and attorneys' fees. Criminal penalies are also available in cases of willful infringement for commercial advantage or personal financial gain.

- Injunctions issue after meeting the traditional four part test: a showing of irreparable harm; that money damages are inadequate; a balancing of the hardships; and that the public interest is not disserved.

- Courts can order the impoundment and destruction of infringing articles as an additional non-monetary remedy.

- Monetary damages are available for lost profits, lost royalties, loss of goodwill, and the like.

- Infringers profits may be ordered if the profits are greater than the actual damages, but double recovery is not allowed.

- Statutory damages are available in lieu of actual damages/infringers profits, and may be awarded in an amount of $750–$30,000 per infringement (as low as $200 for innocent infringement and up to $150,000 if willful infringement), as set by the court.

- Attorneys' fees and costs are awardable to the prevailing party if the infringement was willful or if the suit was frivolous or brought in bad faith.

Chapter Seven

Moral Rights

Roadmap

After reading this chapter, you should understand:

- Moral rights — a set of protections for authors and their works that secure artists control over their work and allow them some control over their reputations. Traditionally they have not been widely recognized in the United States.

- Moral rights — rights retained by the author, even if the copyright in the work is assigned, which last as long as the work exists.

- The right of integrity — allows artists to prevent changes to their work.

- The right of attribution — allows artists to identify their work as their own.

- The right of disclosure — allows artists to control over whether and how their work is shared with the public.

- The right of withdrawal — allows artists to remove their previously disclosed work from the public if the work truly misrepresents their convictions or is obsolete and would thereby damage their reputations.

- *Droit de suite* — additional artists' rights beyond the core moral rights described above, which include the right to collect a fee upon resale of their work.

- The Visual Artists Rights Act (VARA) — the primary United States protection of moral rights, but it is strictly limited to works of visual art. VARA protects the rights of attribution and integrity, and even allows visual artists to prevent the destruction of their work if the work is of a "recognized stature."

- Copyright law's indirect protection of moral rights — artists that still hold the copyright to their work can use copyright protections to enforce some moral rights, such as by using the copyright prohibition on derivative works to enforce the moral right of integrity and the copyright protections of performance and display to protect the moral right of disclosure.

---

1. Introduction

When artists make their work public, the economic benefit of that work is often only one of several considerations. The work represents a projection of the artist's personality into the public domain. In order to protect the relationship between authors and their work, 19th century continental European countries developed a series of rights called the *droit moral*—translated in English as "moral rights." Moral rights secure artists' control over their work and allow them some control over their reputations. Theoretically, moral rights may be infinite in duration, lasting as long as the work exists. The United States has historically overlooked recognition of moral rights and now offers only limited moral rights protection through the Visual Artists Rights Act of 1990.

Moral rights have traditionally included four separate rights:

(1) the right of *integrity*—involving artists' right to prevent changes to or the mutilation of their work;

(2) the right of *attribution*—involving artists' right to have their name associated with their work;

(3) the right of *disclosure*—involving artists' right to determine whether and how to share their work with the public; and

(4) the right of *withdrawal*—involving artists' right to withdraw their previously disclosed work from the public.

Additional rights not considered to be within the core group of *droit moral* are recognized in some European jurisdictions. These rights are often collectively referred to as the "*droit de suite*"—the "right to follow"—though the term also refers more specifically to artists' right to collect a portion of the fee paid upon the resale of their work of art. Another example of a *droit de suite* recognized in several countries is authors' right to access their work under certain circumstances, even after economic or property rights in the work have been relinquished to another person. Additionally, in many countries and in several jurisdictions within the United States, authors, musicians, and visual artists may be entitled to receive royalties for the resale of their works of art.

American state statutes sometimes vest artists with moral rights, even *droit de suite*, which VARA does not. For example, under Cal. Civ. Code § 986, any person who sells a piece of fine art—defined as "an original painting, sculpture, or drawing or an original work of art in glass"—must pay five percent to the artist upon the sale of the art if the seller lives in California, or the sale occurs in California.

2. Scope & Character of the Moral Rights

a. The Right of Integrity

The right of integrity was the earliest moral right to be recognized, and is often considered the most important. The traditional purpose of the right of integrity is to give artists more control over their creative output—even after they first determine that it is finished. In traditional continental European law, the right of integrity protects artists' rights to augment or modify their work, and is sometimes specifically referred to as the "right of modification." Should artists' convictions change over time, they are entitled to amend previous work to make it conform to their present intent.

The right of integrity also prevents others from modifying or adding to an author's work without permission. In countries most amenable to the protection of moral rights, it protects the author against modifications or additions regardless of whether they would negatively or positively affect the work. In other countries, and under Article *6bis* of the Berne Convention, this right applies only to modifications that would cause damage to the artist's reputation.

The right of integrity has great potential to cause problems between artists and those who have acquired the copyrights or property rights in their work. For example, there may be conflicts between an architect who has designed a building and the owners of that building who wish to modify it in order to better suit their own needs. As with other moral rights, the solution may lie in contract law: providing or requiring a modification of this or another moral right at the time of contracting for the architect's services.

The traditional right of integrity does not protect artists against another person's *destruction* of their work. This is because the right has a limited scope; it is intended only to protect authors' control over the personal vision they convey to the world. The rational is that where a work no longer exists, there is no vision conveyed—and thus, under the traditional view, there is no potential for the misconception of the artist's ideals.

The right of integrity is a right, not an obligation; authors may authorize others to modify their work. This authorization may be express or implied, but in either case is never an absolute. A certain amount of latitude is afforded to editors of a work, but those editors are not given the authority to attribute ideas to authors that they do not hold and did not originally express or to change the intrinsic aesthetic quality of the work.

An example of a violation of the right of integrity occurred in Belgium, as reported in the case of *Herscovici v. Loterie Nationale*, (Sept. 9, 1994, RIDA, n° 163, p. 190, confirmed by Court of Appeals of Brussels, Apr. 18, 1997, *SABAM*

& C. Herscovici v. Loterie Nationale, RIDA, n° 174, 1997, p. 201). There, the defendant Lottery Office, an agency of the Belgian Ministry of Finance, reproduced "elements" of three masterpieces by artist Rene Magritte on state-issued lottery tickets. Although the defendants had intended to honor the surrealist painter, the Society of Authors, Magritte's successors in interest, sued claiming damages for violation of the artist's right of integrity. The court balanced the defendant's good intentions against the plaintiff's right to prevent injury to the works, and awarded 1,000,000 Belgian Francs in damages.

In another example of a violation of this right of integrity, the descendants of the Irish playwright Samuel Beckett filed suit when a French director had cast women in a production of Beckett's play *Waiting for Godot*. During his lifetime, Beckett had expressed his wish that only men play these characters. On this basis, a Paris district court enjoined the production. T.G.I. Paris, 3e ch., Oct. 15, 1992, 155 RIDA 225 (1993).

b. The Right of Attribution

The right of attribution protects authors' right to correctly identify a work as their own. This right arose from a general recognition that the process of artistic creation causes a special, personal relationship between authors and their work. Countries that recognize the right of attribution do so to protect vulnerable authors from the non-economic harms that may result from misattribution of work, including loss of respect within the community and even emotional distress.

Traditionally, artists have a cause of action against a person who removes the artist's name from the work, against another person who falsely claims authorship in the work, or against a person that incorrectly attributes the work to a third party. For example, in *Clark v. Associated Newspapers Ltd*, 1998 E.C.C. 185, a British court enjoined the defendant from publishing the plaintiff conservative Member of Parliament's name and photograph in conjunction with a satirical article under the anti-misattribution provisions of United Kingdom Statute 1988 c 48 Pt I c IV s 84. The article, which purported to excerpt the MP's diary from the period immediately surrounding his election, was salacious enough that, if readers did not realize that the false attribution of authorship was part of the satire, the plaintiff's reputation would be harmed.

By contrast, in 1987 E.C.C. 322 *Daniel Robert v. Societe Crehallet-Folliot-Recherche et Publicite* before the French Cour de Cassation 15 April 1986, the former creative director of an advertising firm represented to prospective clients that he had been responsible for substantial portions of the work performed on successful campaigns, of which his former employer owned the copyright and was considered the author under French law. The creative director was found liable for unfair competition in the lower courts and appealed. The Cour de Cassation held that, as his representations were plainly true, his moral rights included the right to identify himself as a creative force behind ad campaigns in which the plaintiff held an economic copyright.

The right of attribution protects the identity of source and encompasses authors' rights to attach their name to a work or to prevent the attachment of his name to a work. Notably, however, artists cannot use the right of attribution to prevent disclosure of their real name while using a pseudonym and traditionally have no legal redress against a person who correctly identifies them with their work, regardless of the desire to remain anonymous.

c. The Right of Disclosure

The right of disclosure recognizes artists' exclusive rights to exert control over their own work by ensuring that the author alone can determine when their work is finished, ready for public exposure, and the mode in which the work will be revealed to the public. A consequence of the right of disclosure is that creditors and bankruptcy trustees may not force artists to publish a work in order to repay their debts.

An example of the right of disclosure is found in the 1900 French case involving the American painter James McNeill Whistler, who was living in Paris at the time. Whistler had painted a commissioned portrait of the British aristocrat Lady Eden, and had even permitted its public exhibition. However, he later refused to deliver the painting to Lord Eden, who filed suit on the contract. Because the artist alone may determine whether to divulge his work, the French *Cour de Cassation*—the highest court in the French judiciary—refused to order Whistler to deliver the painting, but required him to refund the prepaid commission and prohibited any future public exhibition of the portrait in recognizable form. *Eden c. Whistler*, CA Paris, 1898 D.P. II 465, aff'd 1900 D.P. I 497.

d. The Right of Withdrawal

The right of withdrawal allows authors to withdraw a previously released work when that work no longer reflects their convictions or artistic vision. The right of withdrawal generally may only be exercised when:

(1) the work truly misrepresents the author's convictions and its publication would present the author with "serious moral" issues, or

(2) new discoveries have made the author's work obsolete and its publication would damage the author's reputation.

The author's economic interests do not provide a valid excuse to exercise this right.

The right of withdrawal includes the right to rescind assignments or licenses of economic rights in the work to other parties, but the author will be held responsible for, at a minimum, reimbursing the other party for its investment in the work. In some countries, authors will only be able to exercise this right if they indemnify the other party for damages to themselves and third parties in advance.

For example, it is possible that an author who published a book advancing the theory of creationism, but later became convinced that the development of human life is best described by the theory of evolution, could assert the right of withdrawal with regard to his earlier book.

3. The Visual Artists Rights Act of 1990

The United States' copyright system was created primarily to protect the economic interests of copyright holders and was not concerned with the personal interests of authors. As a result, moral rights have had a somewhat tepid recognition in the United States. The U.S. participated in many international conferences related to authors' rights, but did not ratify any uniform moral right's protections until 1989 in response to objections by American authors, whose rights were disadvantaged abroad by the lack of United States membership in the Berne Convention. The United States' adoption of the Berne Convention makes it subject to its Article 6*bis* requirements, which provide for the moral rights of authors.

After ratifying the Berne Convention, the United States at first took the position that it was already in compliance and could reinterpret its pre-existing laws to comply with Article 6*bis*'s requirements rather than create an entirely new set of laws. However, in 1990, the United States passed the Visual Artists Rights Act (VARA), which specifically addressed the moral rights of visual artists.

VARA offers the most explicit protection of moral rights in the United States, but it applies only to works of visual art, narrowly defined in 17 U.S.C. § 101 to encompass just paintings, drawings, prints, sculptures, and photographic images (still photos only, not motion pictures) that are produced solely for the purpose of exhibition. Additionally, to qualify as a "work of visual art," the work must consist of either a single, signed copy or an edition of 200 or fewer copies that are signed and consecutively numbered by the artist.

Only visual art as defined by § 101 is within the scope of VARA's protections — other art forms, no matter how worthy, are simply ineligible. Works of visual art do *not* include posters, maps, globes, charts, technical drawings, diagrams, models, applied art, motion pictures or other audiovisual works, books, magazines, newspapers, periodicals, databases, electronic information services, electronic publication or similar publication, or marketing, advertising, or product packaging materials. Also, works made for hire are not considered works of visual art. In essence, VARA does not protect the creators of most mass produced and commercial art but instead protects the work of the iconic, individual artist working in a garret apartment to create a masterpiece.

In *Kettenburg v. University of Louisville*, Slip Op. No. CVA 3:06 CV 79 H, 2005 U.S. Dist. Lexis 12170, 2005 WL 4444092 (W.D. Ky.), the plaintiff brought a VARA claim against his alma mater after recognizing similarities between a short story he had written for class and the David Hasselhoff movie "One True Love," which led him to believe that the University had "obviously submitted this story to someone in Hollywood and made a movie out of it." Without reaching the merits of the claim, the court dismissed the complaint because neither a short story nor a motion picture qualifies as a work of visual art under VARA.

Courts have strictly construed VARA's narrow definition of "works of visual art." For example, in *Lilley v. Stout*, 384 F. Supp. 2d 83 (D.D.C. 2005), the plaintiff, a photographer, had produced a series of photographs for use as studies by the defendant, a painter. The photographs were never themselves intended for exhibition, but when the painter incorporated some of the actual photographic prints into final compositions without crediting the photographer, the plaintiff sued under VARA. The court dismissed, holding that because the plaintiff had failed to demonstrate his "intent to exhibit, uniqueness [of the works], and signing" of the works, they did not qualify as works of visual art within the definition in 17 U.S.C. § 101.

Moreover, where an otherwise protected work of visual art is used in a manner excluded from VARA's scope, the artist does not have a claim under VARA. In *Berrios Nogueras v. Home Depot*, 330 F. Supp. 2d 48 (D.P.R. 2004), the plaintiff brought a VARA claim against Home Depot for having reproduced his painting in brochures and other promotional materials "without his knowledge, compensation, or consent," and without attribution. The court dismissed the plaintiff's VARA claim because the definition of "work of visual art" in 17 U.S.C. § 101 specifically excludes "any merchandising item or advertising [or] promotional" materials.

VARA provides for the right of attribution by giving visual artists the right to "claim authorship of [their] work" and to "prevent the use of his or her name as the author of any work of visual art which he or she did not create." 17 U.S.C. § 106A(a)(1). In addition, VARA protects visual artists' right of integrity by allowing artists to prevent the use of their name on works that have been modified or mutilated, if the modified work would be prejudicial to their honor or reputation. 17 U.S.C. § 106A(a)(2). VARA gives artists preemptive rights with regard to modifications of their work. Under 17 U.S.C. § 106A(a)(3), artists can prevent intentional modifications that would prejudice their reputation. Because VARA is a federal law that preempts "equivalent" common law causes of action and state statutes, it is arguably the only means of redress in the United States for a violation of the rights of attribution or integrity in a qualifying work of visual art.

The traditional right of integrity generally extends only to modifications of the work. However, the U.S. expands upon the traditional right of integrity by allowing some visual artists the right to prevent destruction of their work if it is of a "recognized stature." In order to qualify as a work of "recognized stature," there must be objective evidence of its artistic merit and that merit must be "recognized" by either the artistic or broader community. For example, in *Martin v. City of Indianapolis*, 192 F.3d 608 (7th Cir. 1999), the plaintiff had erected a metal sculpture on a tract of land then owned by his employer. That landowner later transferred the parcel to the city of Indianapolis to aid the city government in an urban renewal project, during which the city demolished the sculpture without notice to the artist. The court held that the plaintiff's sculpture was of a "recognized stature" in view of an award that a maquette of the sculpture had won at an art exhibition, favorable coverage in the arts section of the Indianapolis Star, and favorable written statements made regarding the sculpture by the director of the Herron School of Art in Indianapolis. The court therefore found that the artist was entitled to damages under 17 U.S.C. § 106A because he had never waived his rights.

However, 17 U.S.C. § 113(d) provides an exception with regard to works that have been incorporated into buildings. If the work cannot be removed without modification, and the artist consented to the incorporation of the work into the structure before 1990, or waived their right to object to the modification, then the protections in 17 U.S.C. § 106A(a)(2)–(3) do not apply. Other exceptions to the right of integrity granted by 17 U.S.C. § 106A include modifications that are merely a result of the passage of time or the limitations of the materials used in creating the work. Also, modifications made in order to preserve or publicly display the work are excepted so long as the preservation techniques fall short of "gross negligence." In *Flack v. Friends of Queen*

Catherine Inc., 139 F. Supp. 2d 526 (S.D.N.Y. 2001), the district court held that a sculptor had stated a claim under VARA where she had alleged that a botched restoration of her sculpture by a person untrained in sculpture conservation amounted to mutilation of the work through gross negligence. However, the court dismissed the plaintiff's claim that the defendants violated VARA by placing the sculpture outside in a "garbage dump."

VARA emphasizes that the rights set out in 17 U.S.C. § 106A apply exclusively to the author of the visual work, whether or not the author is the copyright owner. The section notes that the moral rights conferred are distinct from ownership of a copy of the work or ownership of a copyright and are not waived by transfer of ownership of a copy of the work or copyright or any right conferred by a copyright. Joint authors of a work are considered co-owners of the rights secured by VARA. Because works made for hire do not constitute works of visual art under VARA, the authors of works for hire are not granted moral rights through § 106A and neither are the hiring parties.

An example of a case arising under VARA is *Carter v. Helmsley-Spear, Inc.*, 71 F.3d 77 (2d Cir. 1995). In *Carter*, the district court granted the artists' request for an injunction prohibiting the building's new owner from renovating a large, walk-through sculpture made out of recycled materials from its lobby. However, the Second Circuit reversed, holding that the sculpture was a work-for-hire and therefore did not fall within VARA's reach.

VARA allows artists to expressly waive the rights secured by § 106A in a written document. 17 U.S.C. § 106A(e)(1). However, they may not transfer those rights to another party. The section provides specific instructions for what must be included in such a waiver, and notes that a transfer of ownership in a copy or a copyright of the work does not constitute a waiver. It also specifies that, for joint works, a valid waiver of rights in a particular work by one author constitutes a waiver of the rights held by every author of that work, although case law has, in at least one instance, limited the effect of this provision. In *Grauer v. Deutsch*, 2002 U.S. Dist. Lexis 19233, 2002 WL 31288937 (S.D.N.Y. 2002), one of two photographers who had collaborated on a series of photographs exhibited them without attributing coauthorship to the plaintiff. The court held that although a waiver executed by only one coauthor may be effective to waive both author's attribution rights with regard to a nonexclusive license of the work to a third party, one coauthor may not waive the other's attribution rights in order to exhibit the works solely under his own name.

17 U.S.C. § 106 governs the duration of moral rights protection in works of visual art under VARA, and this protection depends on when the work was created. For works created on or after June 1, 1991, the artists hold these rights for their lifetimes. For works created prior to June 1, 1991, to which the artist

has retained title, moral rights exist for the same duration as the copyright would (under the current scheme, this would mean the artist's lifetime plus seventy years). If the artist created the work prior to June 1, 1991, but did not retain title to it, there is no protection under VARA. In keeping with copyright laws, the duration of protection for joint works ends with the death of the last surviving author.

4. Options for Enforcing Moral Rights in Works Not Covered by VARA

a. Other Copyright Act Options

The U.S. Copyright Act is inherently different from moral rights law in that it confers rights on the holder of a copyright rather than the author of a work. However, where authors hold the copyright to their work, they may be able to use those rights to enforce rights similar to those guarded by moral rights laws in other countries. For example, the right to prohibit derivative works may encompass the moral right of integrity because a modification often creates an unauthorized derivative work, and the rights of performance and display seem to encompass the right of disclosure. Again, however, artists can only use copyright law to protect their moral rights if they hold the copyright. This is a significant limitation because the modern commercial art world runs on assignments, licenses, and sales of copyrights.

Additionally, the termination rights conferred on authors by 17 U.S.C. §§ 203 and 304(c), applicable to post-1978 and pre-1978 copyrights respectively, seem to follow moral rights doctrine in spirit. Those sections give authors the right to terminate an assignment or license of any copyright upon notice given during a five-year period beginning 35 years after the license is granted or the assignment is made. Moreover, 17 U.S.C. § 203(5) guarantees an author's termination right "notwithstanding any agreement to the contrary," which the Supreme Court has construed to mean that "[t]he 1976 Copyright Act provides a single, fixed term, but provides an inalienable termination right." *Stewart v. Abend*, 495 U.S. 207, 110 (1990).

b. The Lanham Act

When the United States joined the Berne Convention, lawmakers insisted that currently existing laws provided the protections of moral rights required by Article *6bis*. Among the existing laws claimed to protect moral rights — specifically, the right of attribution—was §43(a) of the Lanham Act. That section protects against "any false designation of origin [used in commerce] … which is likely to cause confusion, or to cause mistake, or to deceive." Lanham Act §43(a), 15 U.S.C. §1125. The Lanham Act is the foundation of trademark law in the United States and is discussed in depth in chapters eight and nine below.

In *Dastar Corp. v. Twentieth Century Fox Film Corp.*, 539 U.S. 23 (2003), the Supreme Court may have halted—or at least severely limited—use of the Lanham Act to protect moral rights. In *Dastar*, Time, Inc. produced a set of documentary videos on General Dwight D. Eisenhower's experiences in World War II under an agreement with a Twentieth Century Fox affiliate. After the copyright in the series lapsed, Dastar bought copies of the original show, re-edited and modified the series, and sold it as its own creation. Because the work had fallen into the public domain, Twentieth Century Fox could not seek redress under the copyright statute, and instead sought to recover under §43(a) of the Lanham Act for Dastar's distribution of the documentary videos under its own name, rather than that of the original producer. The Court held that the term "origin," as used in the Lanham Act, does not refer "to the author of any idea, concept, or communication embodied in [tangible] goods," but rather to the producer of the goods themselves.

The *Dastar* holding has been applied in later cases as forbidding the use of Lanham Act §43(a) to protect an author's moral right of attribution. For example, in *Williams v. UMG Recordings, Inc.*, 281 F. Supp. 2d 1177 (C.D. Cal. 2003), the plaintiff brought a Lanham Act claim against film producers who had omitted his name from the credits of a film on which he had worked, allegedly misattributing his work to other directors. Following the *Dastar* decision, the court held that misattribution is actionable "only where the defendant literally repackages the plaintiff's goods and sells them as the defendant's own [but not where] the defendants are accused only of failing to identify someone who contributed not goods, but ideas or communications (or, for that matter, "services") to defendants' product." Similarly, in *Zyla v. Wadsworth*, 360 F.3d 243 (1st Cir. 2004), one of two coauthor's of a college textbook withdrew her authorship, and permission for her contributions to be used, from the book's fourth edition. When the book was published with Zyla's work but without mention of her as coauthor, she brought a claim under §43(a) of the Lanham Act. The court dismissed Zyla's claim, holding that although §43(a) can protect more than just trademarks, it does not protect the ideas that an author contributes to a work, which is protected by contract or copyright.

Dastar has also been held to bar the use of state law claims for unfair competition as a means of enforcing authors' moral rights. For example, in *Freeplay Music, Inc. v. Cox Radio, Inc.*, 409 F. Supp. 2d 259 (S.D.N.Y. 2005), Freeplay alleged that the defendant had engaged in unfair competition under New York law by incorporating Freeplay's copyrighted sound recordings into their own radio programming without attributing the works to Freeplay. The court, however, concluded that the heart of Freeplay's complaint concerned the unauthorized copying, which under *Dastar* is "the domain of copyright, not of trademark or unfair competition." The court then dismissed Freeplay's state law unfair competition claim as "essentially redundant" of claims properly pled under the Copyright Act.

c. State Statutory and Common Law

Although the U.S. Copyright Act preempts state legal and equitable rights that are "equivalent" to those conferred by the federal statute, state protections of moral rights that extend beyond the protections offered by VARA are explicitly allowed under 17 U.S.C. § 301(f)(2). States such as California and New York have legislation that provide for the attribution and integrity rights of artists. These are found in California's Art Preservation Act, Cal. Civ. Code § 987 (1980), and New York's Artists' Authorship Rights Act, New York Arts and Cultural Affairs Law § 14.03 (1984). However, courts may or may not view state statutes as preempted by federal law because of uncertainty as to the meaning of "equivalent" in § 301(f)(2)

In *Botello v. Shell Oil Co.*, 280 Cal. Rptr. 535 (Cal. Ct. App. 1991), the plaintiff's mural was destroyed—along with the wall on which it was mounted—to make room for an extension of defendant's parking lot. The court held that the term "painting" as defined by § 987(b) includes murals, and that the plaintiff had stated a claim for relief under California law.

Other state laws also extend protections beyond those available under VARA. For example, in *Phillips v. Pembroke Real Estate, Inc.*, 288 F. Supp. 2d 89 (D.Mass. 2003), a sculptor sought to enjoin a local park from moving a series of sculptures that had been commissioned for placement in the park. The court found that the sculptures together constituted an integrated work of art, the environment and location of which the artist claimed was crucial to his artistic intent. When the sculptor sought relief under both VARA and the Massachusetts Art Preservation Act (Mass. Gen. Laws ch. 231, § 85S (1984)), the court held that VARA did not protect artist's choice of the works location within the park, but that MAPA did.

American authors have also sought and won moral rights protection through state and federal common law causes of action—for instance, authors may protect attribution rights through such causes of action as invasion of privacy or defamation. In *Gilliam v. American Broadcasting Companies, Inc.*, 538 F.2d

14 (2d Cir. 1976), the members of Monty Python's Flying Circus sued ABC alleging that the edited versions of their programs were so altered as to effectively defame the creators. The court agreed, holding that the cuts made by ABC probably constituted an "actionable mutilation," justifying an injunction against further broadcasts. By contrast, in *Geisel v. Poynter Products, Inc.*, 295 F. Supp. 331 (S.D.N.Y. 1968), Dr. Seuss sued the manufacturers of dolls based on his characters, alleging that the defendant's association of his name with dolls that were "tasteless, unattractive and of an inferior quality" amounted to defamation. The court dismissed the claim of defamation, holding that there was no defamation because the court, found the dolls to be "attractive and of good quality."

Checkpoints

- Moral rights are a set of protections for authors and their works that secure artists control over their works and allow them some control over their reputations. Traditionally they have not been widely recognized in the United States.

- Moral rights remain with the author, even if the copyright in the work is assigned, and last as long as the work exists.

- The right of integrity allows artists to prevent changes to their work.

- The right of attribution allows artists to identify their work as their own.

- The right of disclosure allows artists control over whether and how their work is shared with the public.

- The right of withdrawal allows artists to remove their previously disclosed work from the public if the work truly misrepresents their convictions or is obsolete and would thereby damage their reputations.

- Some jurisdictions also recognize additional artists' rights beyond the core moral rights, described above, called the *droit de suite*, which include the right to collect a fee upon resale of their work.

- The Visual Artists Rights Act (VARA) is the primary United States protection of moral rights, but it is strictly limited to works of visual art.

- VARA protects the rights of attribution and integrity, and even allows visual artists to prevent the destruction of their work if the work is of a "recognized stature."

- Artists that still hold the copyright to their work can use copyright protections to enforce some moral rights, such as by using the copyright prohibition on derivative works to enforce the moral right of integrity and the copyright protections of performance and display to protect the moral right of disclosure.

- Some states have enacted laws that provide moral rights protections beyond the scope of VARA.

Chapter Eight

Trademark Law

Roadmap

After reading this chapter, you should understand:

- Trademarks — any distinctive mark, symbol, device, or emblem used by a business to identify and distinguish its goods from those of others and that enables consumers to identify products and their source.

- Sources of United States trademark law — state and federal law.

- Other trademark protections —

  - Service marks, which are used by a company to identify and accumulate goodwill toward specific intangibles such as services.

  - Collective marks, which distinguish membership in an association, union, or other group.

  - Certification marks, which are used by third parties to guarantee that certified goods or services meet certain criteria.

  - Trade dress, which is the nonfunctional overall appearance of a product's design as presented in the marketplace, including the decor, packaging, wrappers, and labels.

- *De facto* functionality — where the elements of the design are arbitrary or superfluous. Trade dress that is *de facto* functional is eligible for protection.

- *De jure* functionality — where the overall appearance is the consequence of entirely and necessarily utilitarian considerations. Trade dress that is *de jure* is not eligible for protection.

- The four categories of trademarks — (1) generic, (2) descriptive (including deceptively misdescriptive), (3) suggestive, and (4) arbitrary or fanciful.

  - Generic marks — never distinctive and not eligible for protection.

  - Descriptive and deceptively misdescriptive marks — eligible for protection only if they acquire secondary meaning, but primarily geographically deceptively misdescriptive marks adopted after 1992 are ineligible for trademark protection.

  - Suggestive marks — inherently distinctive and eligible for protection.

  - Arbitrary and fanciful marks — inherently distinctive, eligible for protection, and considered the strongest type of mark.

197

- Trademark protection — requires distinctiveness and use.

  - Distinctiveness — trademarks must identify the origin of goods or services to be eligible for protection. Distinctiveness may be inherent (as with suggestive, arbitrary, and fanciful marks) or through use once the mark has obtained secondary meaning, as with some descriptive marks.

  - Use — a mark must actually be used or there must be a bona fide intention to use the mark in commerce. The standard of use is minimal, but must be continuous from its first instance until ownership is asserted in order to preserve the user's priority.

- Priority — the first party to use a mark in commerce is typically given priority in the mark and is often referred to as the "senior user."

- Trademark registration — registration does not create rights in a trademark, but federal registration is prima facie evidence of the mark's validity, the registrant's ownership of the mark, and its exclusive right to use the mark in commerce. Registration also provides constructive notice of the registrant's claim to the mark, thereby foreclosing any claims of innocence or good faith by later or "junior" users.

- Marks barred from registration — marks that are generic, deceptive, primarily geographically deceptively misdescriptive, immoral, scandalous, or disparaging are barred from registration. Marks that are confusingly similar with a prior mark or marks comprised of government insignia are also barred.

- Incontestable marks — after a mark is registered and in continuous use without challenge for five years, the mark becomes "incontestable." Incontestable status provides conclusive evidence of the validity of the mark and the registrant's ownership and exclusive right to use the mark.

- The Supplemental Register — a mark that does not meet all of the requirements for registration on the Principal Register, but that is capable of distinguishing the applicant's goods or services, may be registered on the PTO's Supplemental Register. Registration on the Supplemental Register is not evidence of the mark's validity, but it enables the registrant to satisfy some foreign home registration requirements, creates federal jurisdiction for disputes involving the mark, and will establish priority if the mark ever becomes eligible for registration on the Principal Register.

- Trademark owners can cancel their trademark registration on their own accord or can loose their rights to the mark if it becomes generic or is abandoned.

- Abandonment — non-use of a trademark with intent to not resume use. Non-use within the United States for three consecutive years is prima facie evidence of abandonment, but this may be rebutted by showing that the non-use was excusable and that the owner intended to resume use within a reasonable time. Additionally, assignments in gross and naked licensing may lead to a finding of abandonment.

- Assignments of a mark — permitted only if transferred with the associated goodwill; otherwise it is invalid as an assignment in gross (and may lead to a finding of abandonment).

- Licensing of a mark — permitted only if the owner of the mark retained suffi-cient control over the quality and consistency of the goods or services pro-vided, otherwise the owner may be found to have abandoned the mark by granting a "naked" license.

- The basics of trademarks used in secured transactions — trademark owners may use their marks as valuable collateral in secured transactions. But it is important that creditors perfect an interest in both the mark and the associated goodwill.

1. Introduction

Trademark law allows providers of goods and services to distinguish their products from those of their competitors. Trademarks play an important role in all commercial transactions by providing a way for consumers to distinguish products and identify their sources. The goodwill corresponding to a trade-mark can be among a business's most important assets. Assuring the integrity of trademarks is the chief aim of trademark law. In the United States, both state and federal law apply to trademarks.

A trademark is a distinctive mark, symbol, or emblem used by a business to identify and distinguish its goods from those of others. A trademark en-ables a consumer to identify a product and its source. In the Lanham Act, the principal federal trademark law, Congress has further defined a trade-mark as

> [A]ny word, name, symbol, or device, or any combination thereof,
> (1) used by a person, or (2) which a person has a bona fide intention
> to use in commerce and applies to register on the principal register es-tablished by this Act, to identify and distinguish his or her goods, in-cluding a unique product, from those manufactured or sold by others
> and to indicate the source of the goods, even if that source is unknown.

15 U.S.C. § 1127. In essence, trademark law is based on the traditional prop-erty law notion that a right in property is a legally enforceable power to ex-clude others from using a resource.

The character of trademark has changed over time. Originally, trademarks indicated ownership of a particular item. As commercial trade grew more so-phisticated and extensive, the marks shifted to a purpose of identifying the source of goods offered for sale in a marketplace. Historically, the Romans and medieval English guilds used trademarks to identify their products. Guilds used trademarks to fix responsibility for defective goods and protect their man-ufacturing monopolies, a system that eventually developed into the modern trademark system. As distribution networks extended into expanding markets, manufacturers began to adopt marks solely to allow consumers to identify their goods and purchase them with confidence based on the reputation of the manufacturer. The United States adopted the English trademark law to prevent unfair competition through the misappropriation of marks.

Trademark law protects manufacturers against free riding, and ensures that consumers can confidently identify the origin of, and anticipate the quality and uniformity of, the goods they purchase. As stated in 15 U.S.C.A. § 1127, the express purpose of the Lanham Act is to protect the owner's rights as well as those of the public.

For example, Nike relies heavily on trademarks in its business practices. Both the name "Nike" and the ubiquitous Nike "swoosh" are trademarks that allow consumers to easily recognize the Nike brand and rely on the associated product quality. Because those trademarks consistently correspond to a predictable quality, they reduce consumers' cost of searching. Without Nike's trademarks and adequate protection of those trademarks, it would be difficult for consumers to distinguish Nike shoes from those made by other companies.

The trademark system also protects service marks, collective marks, and certification marks. A *service mark* is a mark used by a company to identify and accumulate goodwill toward specific intangibles such as services. 15 U.S.C. § 1127. "Merry Maids" is a service mark used by a cleaning services company. A *collective mark* is a mark that distinguishes membership in an association, union, or other group. "Girl Scouts of America" and "Realtor" are collective marks. A *certification mark* is used by third parties to guarantee that certified goods or services meet certain criteria. The "Good Housekeeping Seal of Approval" and Underwriters Laboratory's "UL" are certification marks. The Lanham Act extends these three other types of marks the same protections as a traditional trademarks if the owner has a bona fide intent to use the mark in commerce. (See chart on the following page.)

2. Sources of U.S. Trademark Jurisprudence

In the United States, trademarks are protected by federal law and by state statutory and common law. Federal rights and registration requirements are governed by the Lanham Trademark Act of 1946, codified in Title 15, of the United States Code. The Lanham Act is rooted in the Commerce clause of the U.S. Constitution. 15 U.S.C. § 1127 states that "... it is the intent of this chapter to regulate commerce within the controls of Congress by making actionable the

---

Trademark Basics

- Anyone has the right to place a mark not used by another on products she manufactures or distributes to distinguish them from other products in the market.

- This allows her to inform the public of the origin of the product and thus develop a reputation in the market.

- A trademark is both a sign of the quality of the article and an assurance to the public that it is the genuine product of the manufacturer.

- A trademark owner may petition the court to protect her right to the mark's exclusive use and to prevent others from using the mark.

- This protection benefits the trademark holder, the market, and the public.

---

deceptive and misleading use of such marks in such commerce." In the *Trade-Mark Cases*, 100 U.S. 82 (1879), the Supreme Court held that, because the common law property interest in a trademark arose from use rather than originality, trademarks are not among those property interests protected by the Copyright clause. Therefore, state trademark law is not preempted by the Lanham Act, are state copyright and patent law, and, so, a dual system of state and federal trademark law exists. The federal system has developed primarily to register and establish the priority of trademarks.

Every state has enacted legislation to protect trademarks, usually derived from the Model State Trademark Bill, which is very similar to the Lanham Act. Despite their differences, there is seldom conflict between the various state and federal approaches to trademark law and often courts do not even specify in their decisions and orders which particular scheme applies absent an obvious conflict.

Alabama	ALA. CODE § 8-12-6 et seq.
Alaska	ALASKA STAT. § 45.50.010 et seq.
Arizona	ARIZ. REV. STAT. ANN. § 44-1441 et seq.
Arkansas	ARK. CODE ANN. § 4-71-201 et seq.
California	CAL. BUS. & PROF. CODE § 14200 et seq.
Colorado	COLO. REV. STAT. § 7-70-102 et seq.
Connecticut	CONN. GEN. STAT. § 35-11a et seq.
Delaware	DEL. CODE ANN. tit. 6, § 3301 et seq.
Florida	FLA. STAT. § 495.011 et seq.
Georgia	GA. CODE ANN. § 10-1-440 et seq.

Hawaii	HAW. REV. STAT. § 482-1 et seq.
Idaho	IDAHO CODE ANN. § 48-501 et seq.
Illinois	765 ILL. COMP. STAT. 1036/5 et seq.
Indiana	IND. CODE § 24-2-1-0.5 et seq.
Iowa	IOWA CODE § 548.101 et seq.
Kansas	KAN. STAT. ANN. § 81-202 et seq.
Kentucky	KY. REV. STAT. ANN. § 365.561 et seq.
Louisiana	LA. REV. STAT. ANN. § 51:211 et seq.
Maine	ME. REV. STAT. ANN. tit. 10, § 1521 et seq.
Maryland	MD. CODE ANN., BUS. REG. § 1-401 et seq.
Massachusetts	MASS. GEN. LAWS. ch. 110H, § 1 et seq.
Michigan	MICH. COMP. LAWS § 429.31 et seq.
Minnesota	MINN. STAT. § 333.001 et seq.
Mississippi	MISS. CODE ANN. § 75-25-1 et seq.
Missouri	MO. REV. STAT. § 417.005 et seq.
Montana	MONT. CODE ANN. § 30-13-301 et seq.
Nebraska	NEB. REV. STAT. § 87-127 et seq.
Nevada	NEV. REV. STAT. § 600.240 et seq.
New Hampshire	N.H. REV. STAT. ANN. § 350-A:1 et seq.
New Jersey	N.J. STAT. ANN. §§ 17:16Y-1 et seq., 56:3-13a et seq.
New Mexico	N.M. STAT. § 57-3B-2 et seq.
New York	N.Y. GEN. BUS. LAW § 360 et seq.
North Carolina	N.C. GEN. STAT. § 80-1 et seq.
North Dakota	N.D. CENT. CODE § 47-22-01 et seq.
Ohio	OHIO REV. CODE ANN. § 1329.54 et seq.
Oklahoma	OKLA. STAT. tit. 78, § 21 et seq.
Oregon	OR. REV. STAT. § 647.005 et seq.
Pennsylvania	54 PA. CONS. STAT. § 1101 et seq.
Puerto Rico	P.R. LAWS ANN. tit. 10, § 171 et seq.
Rhode Island	R.I. GEN. LAWS § 6-2-1 et seq.
South Carolina	S.C. CODE ANN. § 39-15-1105 et seq.
South Dakota	S.D. CODIFIED LAWS § 37-6-4 et seq.
Tennessee	TENN. CODE ANN. § 47-25-501 et seq.
Texas	TEX. BUS. & COM. CODE ANN. § 16.01 et seq.
Utah	UTAH CODE ANN. § 70-3a-102 et seq.
Vermont	VT. STAT. ANN. tit. 9, § 2521 et seq.
Virginia	VA. CODE ANN. § 59.1-92.2 et seq.
Washington	WASH. REV. CODE § 19.77.010 et seq.

West Virginia	W. Va. Code § 47-2-1 et seq.
West Virginia	W. Va. Code § 47-2-1 et seq.
Wisconsin	Wis. Stat. § 132.01 et seq.
Wyoming	Wyo. Stat. Ann. § 40-1-101 et seq.

3. Types of Trademarks

Courts and commentators have traditionally divided potential trademarks into four different categories:

(1) generic,

(2) descriptive (including deceptively misdescriptive),

(3) suggestive, and

(4) arbitrary or fanciful.

The categories tend to bleed together at the edges, but courts use them as guidelines when determining whether a mark deserves trademark protection. The ultimate question, however, is whether the mark is distinctive.

- Generic marks are never distinctive and are not eligible for protection.

- Descriptive and deceptively misdescriptive marks are eligible for protection only if they acquire secondary meaning.

- Deceptive marks and geographically deceptively misdescriptive marks adopted after 1993 are ineligible for trademark protection.

- Suggestive, arbitrary, and fanciful marks are considered inherently distinctive and if otherwise valid, are eligible for protection when used.

Trademark Types and Protections	
Type of Mark	**Whether Protected**
Generic	Never
Descriptive	With Secondary Meaning
Misdescriptive	With Secondary Meaning
Deceptive	Never
Primarily Geographically Misdescriptive	Never (if adopted after 12/93)
Suggestive	When Used
Arbitrary	When Used
Fanciful	When Used

a. Generic Marks

A generic mark is the common name of an article or service. A generic term merely describes the character of a product as opposed to identifying its source. For example, "apple" is a generic mark when used in connection with the actual piece of fruit (rather than a computer). "A generic term answers the question 'What are you?' while a mark answers the question 'Where do you come from?'" *Colt Defense LLC v. Bushmaster Firearms, Inc.*, 486 F. 3d 701 (1st Cir. 2007). In *Colt Defense*, the court held the term "M4" used in conjunction with the sale of firearms was generic because consumers associated it with a type of carbine rather than the source of the products. *See also Schwan's IP, LLC v. Kraft Pizza, Co.*, 460 F. 3d 971 (8th Cir. 2006) (holding the term "brick oven pizza" is generic).

Because generic marks do not distinguish between different equivalent products, generic marks are ineligible for trademark protection. Many companies that enjoy trademark protection for their products would lose it if the trademarked term became generic. 15 U.S.C. § 1064(3). The makers of Band-Aids, Kleenex, and Xerox machines fight to prevent this from happening. At one time marks such as "cellophane" and "aspirin" had secondary meaning and were protected, but they have become generic terms—describing the good rather than its source—and consequently lost their former status as protected trademarks. *See DuPont Cellophane Co. v. Waxed Products Co.*, 85 F.2d 75 (2d Cir. 1936) (cellophane); *Bayer Co. v. United Drug Co.*, 272 F. 505 (S.D.N.Y. 1921) (aspirin).

b. Descriptive and Deceptively Misdescriptive Marks

Merely descriptive and deceptively misdescriptive marks are ordinarily not protected by trademark law. 15 U.S.C. § 1052(e)(1). Descriptive marks identify a product based on a characteristic or quality, such as color, smell, function, or ingredient. Deceptively misdescriptive marks do the same thing—only the description is inaccurate. However, if the marks have acquired a secondary meaning in the minds of the consuming public, then they can receive trademark protection. The secondary meaning shows that the descriptive term is not merely a description of the good, but is also an indication of the producer of the good. In other words, if consumers recognize it as signifying the good's origin, it has acquired secondary meaning.

i. Descriptive

In *In re Bayer Aktiengesellschaft*, 488 F.3d 960 (Fed. Cir. 2007), the applicant sought to register "Aspirina" for use on analgesic pain relievers chemically similar to generic aspirin. On appeal, the Federal Circuit concluded that, given the character of the substance to be sold under the mark, the mark was merely descriptive and therefore ineligible for trademark protection. Similarly, an aloe vera derivative product called "Alo" and an optometry center called the "Vision Center" both use descriptive terms to identify goods or services and, absent secondary meaning, are not eligible for trademark protection. *See Aloe Crème Laboratories, Inc. v. Milsan, Inc,* 423 F.2d 845 (5th Cir. 1970) (alo); *The Vision Center v. Opticks, Inc.,* 596 F.2d 111 (5th Cir. 1979) (Vision Center).

However, a merely descriptive term may become distinctive and therefore protectable if it develops a "secondary meaning" that indicates the origin of goods rather than simply describing their character. For example, in *Schmidt v. Honeysweet Hams, Inc.,* 656 F. Supp. 92 (N.D. Ga. 1986), the court held that although "Honey Baked Ham" is plainly a descriptive mark, it had gained a secondary meaning sufficient to justify federal registration and trademark protection. Particularly persuasive were surveys showing that 53% of participants volunteered "Honey Baked" as a distinct brand, "nearly double the percentage of brand name recall for any other major brand name of pre-cooked sliced hams," 96% recognized the brand, and when shown a picture of defendant's store, 29% believed the defendant sold "Honey Baked" brand hams.

A "merely descriptive" mark that has become incontestable is a valid trademark, regardless of whether it should have been registered in the first place, because 15 U.S.C. §§ 1064 and 1065 do not include descriptiveness as a reason to cancel a mark. For example, in *Park 'N Fly, Inc. v. Dollar Park and Fly, Inc.,* 469 U.S. 189 (1985), the plaintiff used the mark "Park 'N Fly" in its airport pay-to-park business. The Court held that although the mark was purely descriptive for that purpose, its incontestable status was conclusive as to the mark's validity and plaintiff's exclusive right to the mark.

Under 15 U.S.C. § 1052(e)(2), unless the applicant shows its mark has a secondary meaning, a mark that is primarily geographically descriptive of the goods is unregisterable, except as an indication of regional origin specifically registerable as a certification mark under § 1054.

A mark is primarily geographically descriptive if consumers would understand it to describe the actual geographic origin of the goods or services bearing the mark. If the place is obscure, or otherwise has meaning beyond the merely geographical, the term may not be primarily geographically descriptive. For example, in *In re International Taste Inc.,* 53 U.S.P.Q.2d 1604 (T.T.A.B. 2000), the examiner refused to register the applicant's "Hollywood Fries" mark on the grounds that "Hollywood" is the name of a famous small town in California. The TTAB reversed the examiner, holding that to most consumers the term "Hollywood" means the entertainment industry in general rather than any particular neighborhood.

Even if a registrant can prove secondary meaning, if a particular product or service is associated with a particular place, the strength of a mark incorporating that place-name is likely diminished. The consumer is likely to associate the place-name with products or services other than those sold under the registrant's particular mark. For example, in *Vail Associates, Inc. v. Vend-Tel-Co., Ltd.*, 516 F.3d 853 (10th Cir. 2008), the plaintiff, which operated a Vail, Colorado ski resort, claimed that its incontestable service mark "Vail Ski Resort" was infringed by the defendant ski-resource hotline's "1-800-SKI-VAIL" mark. Although the plaintiff's mark was incontestable—which is conclusive proof of its secondary meaning—the court held that the mark was exceptionally weak given that it contained no inherently distinctive elements, and that "[t]he presence of secondary meaning ... does not provide the mark holder with an exclusive right to use the mark in its original descriptive sense." In view of the mark's weakness and with no evidence of actual confusion, the court held that confusion was unlikely, concluding that "[i]f some confusion exists, such is the risk [the plaintiff] accepted when it decided to identify its services with a *single word* that is primarily descriptive of a geographic location." Both users in *Vail Associates, Inc. v. Vend-Tel-Co., Ltd.*, 516 F.3d 853 (10th Cir. 2008), used their marks in relation to the provision of services actually provided in Vail, Colorado. Thus any bar to registration arose under § 1052(e)(2).

ii. Deceptively Misdescriptive

A mark is deceptively misdescriptive if it misdescribes a product in a way that is plausible but inaccurate. Deceptively misdescriptive marks are a subset of descriptive marks for which § 1052(e)(1) raises an impediment to registration. Deceptively misdescriptive marks are only eligible for trademark protection if they have obtained secondary meaning. A deceptively misdescriptive mark is distinct from a deceptive mark only in that any misdescription is *not* likely to be a material factor in the consumer's purchasing decision.

For example, in *Glendale International Corp. v. U.S. Patent & Trademark Office*, 374 F. Supp. 2d 479 (E.D. Va. 2005), the court affirmed the PTO's determination that the plaintiff's use of the mark "Titanium" for recreational vehicles was deceptively misdescriptive given that titanium is a lightweight metal commonly used in the automotive industry. Thus, the mark plausibly but inaccurately described the vehicles, but, because consumers were not likely to purchase the RV because of their confusion as to its titanium content, the mark was not deceptive.

Likewise, in *In re Woodward & Lothrop Inc.*, 4 U.S.P.Q.2d 1412 (T.T.A.B. 1987), the Trademark Trial and Appeal Board found the mark "Cameo" to be deceptively misdescriptive of jewelry because none of the jewelry to be sold under the mark included or incorporated any actual cameos—a type of jewelry in which the stone around a design is cut away leaving the design in relief, typically against a contrasting backround— although a mistaken belief that it did was unlikely to induce consumers to make a purchase.

Hence, a misdescriptive mark is not necessarily invalid provided that it will not cause confusion among consumers as to the character of the goods. For example, in *Steinberg Bros., Inc. v. New England Overall Co.*, 377 F.2d 1004 (C.C.P.A. 1967), the plaintiff challenged the registrant's use of the mark "Nuhide" in connection with dungarees made from heavy cotton fabric. The court held that although the mark was misdescriptive insofar as the term "hide" is a synonym for leather, it was not ineligible for that reason because consumers are unlikely to confuse cotton cloth for leather, regardless of what it is called.

As with descriptive marks, even clearly misdescriptive marks that have become incontestable cannot be challenged on the grounds of being misdescriptive. For example, in *DS Waters of America, Inc. v. Princess Abita Water, L.L.C.*, 539 F. Supp. 2d 853, (E.D. La. 2008), the court held that DS Waters' incontestable "Abita Springs" mark was not open to challenge by Princess Abita Water's allegations that it was neither spring water nor water produced in Abita, Louisiana, although both facts caused the mark to be misdescriptive. Note, however, the "Abita Springs" mark was adopted before the post-NAFTA amendments to the Lanham Act made primarily geographically deceptively misdescriptive marks ineligible for trademark protection, as discussed below.

iii. Deceptive

Unlike deceptively misdescriptive marks, which merely inaccurately state a fact, "deceptive" marks that induce the purchase because of that inaccurate fact are not eligible for trademark protection. 15 U.S.C. § 1052(a). A mark is deceptive if the inaccurate information conveyed by a misdescriptive designation is likely to influence the purchasing decisions of a significant amount of prospective consumers. These marks are not eligible for protection because of policy concerns about inducing reliance on an intentionally inaccurate fact. See, e.g., *In re Budge Manufacturing Co.*, 857 F.2d 773 (Fed. Cir. 1988) (Lovee Lamb on synthetic seat covers held deceptive); *Neuman & Co. v. Overseas Shipments, Inc.*, 326 F. 2d 786 (C.C.P.A. 1969) (Dura-Hyde for plastic material with the appearance of leather held deceptive).

15 U.S.C. § 1052(e)(3) raises an independent bar to the registrability of "primarily geographically deceptively misdescriptive" marks. Unlike the bar imposed by § 1052 (e)(2), the prohibition on registration of primarily geographically deceptively misdescriptive marks is absolute, regardless of any secondary meaning the mark may have acquired. These marks are not protected under the Lanham Act. Section 1052(f) provides a limited exception to that prohibition with regard to primarily geographically deceptively misdescriptive marks that "became distinctive" by acquiring secondary meaning prior to December 8, 1993, the date that the North American Free Trade Agreement (NAFTA) was passed into law.

After the passage of NAFTA and revision of § 1052(e) to bar primarily geographically deceptively misdescriptive marks, the Federal Circuit applied a two-part test to determine whether a mark was barred. As described by the court in *In re Save Venice New York, Inc.*, 259 F.3d 1346 (Fed. Cir. 2001), in order to deny registration to a mark as primarily geographically deceptively misdescriptive,

> [T]he examiner has the initial burden of proving that: (1) the mark's primary significance is a generally known geographic location; and (2) consumers would reasonably believe the applicant's goods are connected with the geographic location in the mark, when in fact they are not.

The court held that the word "Venice," and the image of St. Mark's lion were primarily significant of Venice, because St. Mark is that city's patron saint, and the lion associated with St. Mark is a common theme in Venetian public art and iconography, including the city's flag. Moreover, the court held that consumers were likely to believe that the typically-Venetian goods to be sold under the mark were actually made in Venice, though they were in fact made elsewhere. Both prongs having been satisfied, the court affirmed the PTO's refusal to register the mark.

In 2003, the Federal Circuit added a third prong to the analysis. In *In re California Innovations, Inc.*, 329 F.3d 1334 (Fed. Cir. 2003), the PTO refused to register the applicant's "California Innovations" mark for use on a range of "sewn goods" including backpacks and thermal insulated bags and wraps — koozies — for cans to keep the containers cold or hot. The basis of the PTO's decision was that the word "California" is primarily geographically descriptive, and consumers might mistakenly believe that the goods sold under the mark were manufactured in California. The court found the PTO's analysis entirely lacking, holding that "the relatively easy burden of showing a naked goods-place association without proof that the association is material to the consumer's decision is no longer justified." Under the court's reformulated test, the PTO may not refuse registration of a mark under § 1052(e)(3) unless the examiner can show that:

(1) the primary significance of the mark is a generally known geographic location,

(2) the consuming public is likely to believe the place identified by the mark indicates the origin of the goods bearing the mark, when in fact the goods do not come from that place, and

(3) the misrepresentation was a material factor in the consumer's decision.

c. Suggestive Marks

Suggestive marks are inherently distinctive and are protectable without any proof of a secondary meaning. A suggestive mark simply suggests a particular characteristic of the goods or services and the consumer must exercise imagination in order to draw a conclusion as to the nature of the goods and services. For example, "Golden Bake" pancakes, "Mouse Seed" mouse poison, and "CopperTone" suntan lotion are suggestive trademarks as each requires that consumers exercise some degree of imagination to discern the nature of the item being sold.

In *Renaissance Greeting Cards, Inc. v. Dollar Tree Stores, Inc.*, 227 Fed. Appx. 239 (4th Cir. 2007), the court affirmed a district court's conclusion that the mark "Renaissance" was suggestive because rather than actually describing the greeting cards sold under the mark, it "require[d] some imagination to connect it with the goods."

Similarly, in *Blendco, Inc. v. Conagra Foods, Inc.*, 132 Fed. Appx. 520 (5th Cir. 2005), ConAgra claimed that a competitor's use of the mark "Better 'N Butter" was merely descriptive when used to sell an oil-based butter substitute. The court disagreed, holding that the mark was suggestive because none of the terms used in the mark were necessary to describe the product, and the mark itself required some imagination to tie it to the goods. The court found Con Agra's own expert testimony particularly persuasive: only 22% of survey respondents thought of a butter substitute when they were shown the mark, and only 1% guessed that the substitute was oil-based.

Where a question exists as to whether a mark is merely descriptive or suggestive, the PTO's prior determination serves as is prima facie evidence of the strength of the mark and raises a rebuttable presumption as to the mark's strength. For example, in *Synergistic Intern., LLC v. Korman*, 470 F.3d 162 (4th Cir. 2006), the PTO found the mark "Glass Doctor®," a product used for marketing window and auto-glass installation, was suggestive. This created a presumption against the defendant's claim the mark was merely descriptive that it did not successfully rebut at trial.

d. Arbitrary or Fanciful Marks

Arbitrary or fanciful marks are those that bear no relationship to the products or services to which they are applied. A fanciful trademark is essentially a made up word created solely for use as a trademark. For example, "Kodak" is a fanciful term developed to mark photographic supplies. An arbitrary mark, although a real word, has no real relation to the product it is identifying and is used in an unfamiliar way to mark a product. "Ivory" is an arbitrary term to mark soap. Like suggestive terms, arbitrary or fanciful terms do not need a secondary meaning to receive trademark protection. Arbitrary and fanciful marks are generally considered the strongest types of trademarks and, as such, receive the highest trademark protection.

4. Trade Dress

a. Trade Dress Generally

Trademark protection may be extended to "trade dress," which encompasses the overall appearance of a product's design as presented in the marketplace. Trade dress typically includes decor, packaging, wrappers, labels, and all other materials used in presenting the product to the consumer. When the design or packaging of a product is distinctive enough to identify the manufacturer of a product, and meets the other requirements of a trademark, it may be protected as trade dress. However, the distinctive qualities of the design must be nonfunctional for trademark protection to apply.

In *Two Pesos, Inc. v. Taco Cabana, Inc.*, 505 U.S. 763 (1992), Taco Cabana claimed that a Two Pesos restaurant had infringed upon its trade-dress by copying the overall combination of decorative elements that comprise the "Mexican" theme of Tac Cabana's restaurants. Although the decorative features were each either entirely descriptive or functional by themselves, the court held that in combination, they constituted trade dress. Because Taco Cabana's trade dress had developed a secondary meaning for local diners, protection was therefore warranted.

b. Functionality

Under 15 U.S.C. §§ 1052(e)(5) and 1064, a mark is ineligible for registration and can be cancelled at any time if it "comprises any matter that, as a whole, is functional." As a general rule, trademark rights cannot be claimed in a product's functional shapes or features. This rule serves two purposes:

(1) it prevents trademark law from becoming unduly anti-competitive by ensuring that competitors remain free to copy useful product features; and

(2) the functionality doctrine addresses the conflict with patent law by preventing a trademark monopoly of possibly unlimited duration on utilitarian features.

This limitation is particularly relevant with regard to trade dress. A product feature is "functional" when it is essential to the device's use or purpose or when it affects the device's cost or quality. Functionality is fact dependent, and what is functional in one instance might not be functional in another context.

In deciding whether to apply trademark protections to a product's trade dress, courts distinguish between functional and non-functional trade dress. The common law distinguishes between *de jure* and *de facto* trade dress functionality.

i. De Facto Functionality

A design is functional in the *de facto* sense when, despite the fact that the product is capable of performing its intended function, elements of the design are arbitrary or superfluous. Both nonfunctional ornamentation and arbitrary combinations of entirely functional elements can qualify for protection as trade dress, though in either case they must also carry a secondary meaning to indicate a product's origin.

For example, in *In re Morton-Norwich Products, Inc.*, 671 F.2d 1332 (C.C.P.A. 1982), the applicant sought trade dress protection for the design of spray bottles used for its family of spray-cleaners, including "Glass Plus" and "Spray 'N Wash," in a spray bottle the design for which it sought trade-dress protection. The court found that certain aspects of the design — particularly its arbitrary contours — were not essential to its utility, but only functional in the *de facto* sense. Moreover, competitors successfully used a variety of alternative bottle shapes. The court therefore held that the design was protectable with regard to the overall impression created by its arbitrary elements, provided that the overall impression in fact carried a secondary meaning for consumers.

ii. De Jure Functionality

De jure functionality is the legal conclusion that a particular trade dress is unfit for trademark protection, either because the product's overall appearance is the consequence of entirely and necessarily utilitarian considerations, or because the design does not serve to indicate the product's source. A design is *de jure* functional if "it is one of a limited number of equally efficient options available to competitors, and free competition would be unduly hindered by according the design trademark protection." For example, in *Sportvision, Inc. v. Sportsmedia Technology Corp.*, No. C04-03115 JW, 2005 U.S. Dist. Lexis 22682, 2005 WL 1869350 (N.D. Cal.), the plaintiff had trademarked the use of a yellow line projected on a television to mark the first down line in televised football games. The court held that the color yellow was *de jure* functional because the plaintiff had proved that networks specifically preferred vendors that were able to mark first down with a *yellow* line, putting plaintiff's competitors at "a significant non-reputation-related disadvantage."

A further example is found in *Tie Tech, Inc. v. Kinedyne Corp.*, 296 F.3d 778 (9th Cir. 2002). In that case the plaintiff alleged an infringement of its registered trade dress, the design for its emergency restraining-strap cutting tool which featured an oval grip and a guide-bar with a rounded tip running parallel to that grip to safely guide straps—such as seat belts—toward a recessed blade. The court held that because every feature of the tool's design was necessary for it to be used to safely free injured persons from restraints in emergency situations, the design was functional as a matter of law, and the plaintiff's registration should be cancelled.

c. Trade Dress and Patents

Trademark protection of trade dress may overlap with patent law since design patents may be granted to protect a "new, original, and ornamental design" for a manufactured article. This distinction is important because patent protection is only granted for a limited amount of time, while trademark protection typically extends as long as a valid trademark continues to be used in commerce. Because a design patent cannot be issued for a design that is essential to the utility of an article, a design patent is presumptive evidence of nonfunctionality, which may support a similar trademark claim for the design.

The party asserting trade dress protection bears the burden of proving that the allegedly protected design is nonfunctional, and the existence of any other protections based on functionality weigh heavily against them. For example, in *TrafFix Devices, Inc. v. Marketing Displays, Inc.*, 532 U.S. 23 (2001), the plaintiff alleged that its design for road-sign stands—particularly their exposed "dual spring" supports—was so unique that it had become significant as an identifier of the manufacturer. However, the Supreme Court held that the existence of expired utility patents that had previously protected the dual-spring system constituted almost insurmountable proof of the design's functionality. The Court refused to allow the plaintiff to have the exclusive right to produce road-signs with the dual-spring design simply by asserting that consumers associate it with the look of the invention itself. As the Court noted "The dual-spring design is not an arbitrary flourish in the configuration of MDI's product; it is the reason the device works."

5. Trademark Requirements

A trademark can be virtually anything used to identify the source or origin of goods or services provided it is distinctive and is in use or there is a bona fide intent to use the mark at the time of registration.

a. Subject Matter

Almost any objective signifier that helps consumers identify a product can be protected as a trademark. Words or symbols are most typical. Trademarks are *any* word, name, symbol, or device or any combination thereof used to identify and distinguish particular goods and to indicate the source of the goods. 15 U.S.C. § 1127.

Words can be protected as trademarks against their phonetic equivalents. In *Coca-Cola Co. v. Koke Co. of America*, 254 U.S. 143, 145 (1920), the Supreme Court held that the name "Coca-Cola" is protected as a trademark, and that the name "Koke Cola" was obviously "chosen for the purpose of reaping the benefit of the advertising done" by Coca-Cola.

Symbols, such as the Nike swoosh, are also commonly entitled to trademark protection. For example, in *Au-Tomotive Gold, Inc. v. Volkswagen of America, Inc.*, 457 F.3d 1062 (9th Cir. 2006), a manufacturer of key-chains and other automotive accessories featuring trademarked insignia sought a declaratory judgment approving its use of insignia owned by Volkswagen and Audi. The plaintiff argued that the aesthetics of the insignia made them desirable even ignoring their meaning as designations of origin. The plaintiff further claimed to have used the symbols in a purely, aesthetically functional manner. The court noted that the plaintiff had not produced any evidence that its customers were interested in the marks solely for aesthetic reasons, and demand for goods bearing the mark likely arose directly from the marks' value as designations of origin. Without denying the possibility of legitimate aesthetic functionality in the appropriate case, the court held that the symbols were protected trademarks and dismissed the plaintiff's case.

In *Ride the Ducks, LLC v. Duck Boat Tours, Inc.*, No. 04-CV-5595, 2005 U.S. Dist. LEXIS 4422, *22 (E.D. Pa. Mar. 21, 2005), *aff'd* 2005 U.S. App. Lexis 13554 (3d Cir. July 6, 2005), the court held that sounds may be protected as trademarks, but the quacking noise used by a boat tour company in that case was not inherently distinctive and lacked secondary meaning. Similary Harley-Davidson ventured to apply for trademark protection for its bikes' distinctive engine sound. Facing opposition, it withdrew its application without litigating the issue.

Even a unique color may be afforded trademark protection. For example, in *In re Owens-Corning Fiberglas Corp.*, 774 F.2d 1116 (Fed. Cir. 1985), the court held that the bubblegum pink color of Corning's fiberglass insulation served no function but as an indication of origin, and should be afforded trademark protection. Likewise, in *Qualitex Co. v. Jacobson Products, Inc.*, 514 U.S. 159 (1995), the Court held that the green-gold color of the plaintiff's dry-cleaning press pad was a non-functional indication of origin, and that the color was therefore eligible for trademark protection. Regardless its form, any characteristic that serves to unambiguously distinguish one product or service from its competition can qualify for trademark protection.

b. Distinctiveness

To be eligible for trademark protection the mark must be distinctive — it must serve the purpose of identifying the origin of the goods or services. As detailed earlier, the categories of distinctiveness are generic, descriptive, suggestive, arbitrary or fanciful. The further along this spectrum a term or mark fall, the more likely it is to be distinctive.

In *Nutro Prods. v. Cole Grain Co.*, 5 Cal. Rptr. 2d 41 (Cal. Ct. App. 1992), the makers of "Nutro" and "Nutro Max" brand dog food sought injunctive relief against the makers of "Nutrix" brand dog food. In evaluating the strength of the plaintiff's mark, the court held that "distinctiveness" implies three characteristics:

(1) the mark is sufficiently different from others associated with equivalent goods to distinguish one from the other,

(2) the mark does not simply describe or signify characteristics common to the class of goods, and

(3) the mark serves to indicate the product's source rather than decorative or other purposes.

Applying that analytical framework to the "Nutro" and "Nutro Max" marks, the court concluded that they were in fact distinctive, classifying them as suggestive marks and granting the requested injunction.

The distinctive quality of a trademark can be either inherent or acquired. For example, in *Playtex Prods. v. Georgia-Pacific Corp.*, 390 F.3d 158 (2d Cir. 2004), the court considered plaintiff Playtex's trademark "Wet Ones" for its pre-moistened towlettes and whether the defendant's mark "Quilted Northern Moist-Ones" was confusingly similar. The court held that the marks were not confusingly similar because the "Wet Ones" mark was a well established mark that had acquired distinctiveness in the marketplace.

Suggestive, arbitrary, and fanciful marks are inherently distinctive. In contrast, a descriptive mark is distinctively only to the extent that the mark has acquired a secondary meaning and is recognized in the market. A mark acquires distinctiveness as consumers begin to recognize the mark as denoting the source of particular goods and disassociate the mark from any prior connotations. The question is whether distinctiveness outweighs descriptiveness. For example, in *Virgin Enterprises Ltd. v. Nawab*, 335 F.3d 141 (2d Cir. 2003), Virgin Entertainment brought a claim of infringement against a cell phone company that operated retail stores under the name "Virgin Wireless." The court noted that although the "Virgin" mark was not an invented term, Virgin Enterprises' enduring and conspicuous association with consumer electronics had imbued the mark with distinctiveness as a designation of origin for goods unassociated with the word's dictionary definition. Because of the mark's distinctiveness, the court concluded that its use by another, even in a somewhat different commercial context, was likely to cause consumer confusion as to the origin of goods or services sold under the mark.

c. Use of a Trademark

Historically, United States trademark protection was not available to marks not actually in use. That changed in 1988, when the Lanham Act was amended to allow registration of a trade, service, certification, or collective mark where the registrant has a bona fide intention to use the mark in commerce. 15 U.S.C. §§ 1127, 1051–54.

The Lanham Act defines a trademark as "used in commerce" when:

1. It is placed in any manner on the goods or their containers or the displays associated therewith or on the tags or labels affixed thereto, or if the nature of the goods makes such placement impracticable, then on documents associated with the goods or their sale, and the goods are sold or transported in commerce, or

2. When it is used or displayed in the sale or advertising of services and the services are rendered in commerce, or the services are rendered in more than one State or in the United States and a foreign country and the person rendering the services is engaged in commerce in connection with the services.

15 U.S.C. § 1127. The "commerce" to which § 1127 refers is "interstate commerce" subject to Congressional regulation, rather than simply for-profit activity. For example, *Planetary Motion, Inc. v. Techsplosion, Inc.*, 261 F.3d 1188 (11th Cir. 2001), involved claims related to a free email management software called "Coolmail" distributed over the internet. The court ruled this activity to be within the scope of commerce, and thus the Lanham Act, despite the non-profit nature of the activity because the software was downloaded by users across the country.

The standard of "use" necessary to establish priority is minimal. All that is required is that the mark be adopted and thereafter used in a way sufficiently public to identify the marked goods or services to the appropriate segment of the public, regardless of any actual sales. For example, in *New West Corp. v. NYM Co. of California, Inc.*, 595 F.2d 1194 (9th Cir. 1979), the court held that the plaintiff had used its "New West" mark "in a way sufficiently public to identify or distinguish the marked goods in an appropriate segment of the public mind" where, though it had not sold a single issue of it's planned "New West" magazine:

> 430,000 individuals received a subscription mailing which contained the "New West" mark on exemplar covers of appellee's new magazine. Countless others saw the "New West" supplement in the February 23, 1976, issue of New York magazine with the mark prominently displayed thereon. Over 13,500 people subscribed to appellee's "New West" magazine prior to the printing of appellant's preview edition.

A person or organization that applies for a mark with a bona fide intention to use the mark in commerce will be issued a notice of allowance, assuming the mark otherwise qualified for protection. 15 U.S.C. § 1063(b)(2). Within six months of the date of issuance of the notice of allowance, the trademark holder must file a verified statement with the PTO that the trademark has been used in commerce. 15 U.S.C. 1051(d)(1). Subject to examination and acceptance of the statement, the PTO will issue a certificate of registration of the mark. The six month period will be extended another six months upon written request of the applicant, and up to a total of 24 months upon a showing of good cause. 15 U.S.C. 1051(d)(1)(2). In essence the Act allows temporary or provisional protection to an applicant with a bona fide intention to use the mark in commerce.

d. Priority

Use of a mark in commerce is essential to establishing priority, because the right to a given trademark typically belongs to the first party that uses the mark in connection with the sale of goods or services. That person is the "senior user" and persons who later use the same or allegedly similar marks are "junior users."

However, what constitutes "use" is somewhat ambiguous, where, for instance, a mark is contested as between the manufacturer of goods sold under that mark and the goods' exclusive distributor, because both parties played an integral role in bringing the marked goods to market. For example, in *Sengoku Works Ltd. v. RMC Intern., Ltd.*, 96 F.3d 1217 (9th Cir. 1996), the trademark in "Keroheat" brand kerosene heaters was claimed by both the manufacturer and the exclusive distributor of the goods. At trial, the jury found that the manufacture, Sengoku, was the first to use the mark, and therefore its owner. Although the distributor, RMC, had registered "Keroheat" in 1992, claiming first use in 1985, Sengoku had begun manufacturing "Keroheat" heaters in 1982. On appeal, the Ninth Circuit noted that, all else being equal, in a dispute between manufacture and exclusive distributor, the manufacturer is presumed to own the trademark. However, that presumption is rebuttable, and in order to discern whether it has been rebutted a court must consider:

(1) which party invented and first affixed the mark onto the product;

(2) which party's name appeared with the trademark;

(3) which party maintained the quality and uniformity of the product; and

(4) with which party the public identified the product and to whom purchasers made complaints.

In applying these factors, the *Sengoku* court noted that the balance was relatively even because:

> Only RMC's name appears on the product and packaging, and RMC handles all customer complaints and returns. However, Sengoku exercises control over the product quality and uniformity, and Sengoku apparently first affixed the trademark to its heaters. Also, other dealers in the business testified that they attribute the heaters bearing the Keroheat mark to Sengoku.

In view of the evidentiary balance between the parties, the court affirmed as reasonable the jury's conclusion that Sengoku was the first to use the mark in commerce, and therefore was its owner.

A registered mark confers a nationwide right of priority against any other person except for a person who used the mark prior to the filing. 15 U.S.C § 1057(c)(1). Thus a nonregistrant may rebut the presumption of validity and ownership if it can show that it used the mark in commerce first. To satisfy this burden a registrant user must prove:

(1) that it actually adopted and used the mark in commerce prior to the other party's registration in such a manner that sufficiently associated the mark with the prior user, and

(2) that its use of the marks has been continuous and not interrupted.

Department of Parks and Recreation for the State of Calif. v. Bazaar Del Mundo, 448 F.3d, 1118, 1125–26 (9th Cir. 2006). *Bazaar Del Mundo* involved trademark rights to the names "Casa del Pico" and "Casa Bandini," two popular restaurants located in historic buildings and operated by the defendant in San Diego's Old Town State Historic Park. Although the defendant registered the trademarks in 1985, the state claimed priority based on its use of these names in historical documents, in a 1969 brochure advertising San Diego's bicentennial celebration, and another brochure entitled "Old Town Sand Diego State Historic Park." The court held that these documents failed to establish a prior commercial use by the state, and that even if the state had acquired seniority of use at one time, its failure to continue to use the marks in commerce allowed Bazaar Del Mundo to acquire priority.

If a trademark has not been registered, an entity asserting priority in ownership can prevail only if it shows prior use of the mark in a way sufficiently public to identify or distinguish the marked goods in an appropriate segment of the public mind as those of the adopter of the mark. For example, in *Lucent Information Management, Inc. v. Lucent Technologies, Inc.*, 186 F.3d 311 (3d Cir. 1999), the plaintiff claimed priority based on a single sale under its unregistered mark "Lucent" about three months before Lucent Technologies filed its intent to use application with the PTO. Noting that the unregistered claimant of a mark "can prevail only if it shows prior use of the mark in a way sufficiently public to identify [itself as owner of the mark] in an appropriate segment of the public mind," the court held that the few private "sales presentations" given by plaintiff before the defendant's application did not suffice.

Although the standard of "use" is minimal, the use must be continuous from its first instance until ownership is asserted in order to preserve the user's priority.

6. Trademark Registration

a. Introduction

The federal government, as well as every state, maintains trademark registration services. On the federal level, the Patent and Trademark Office or PTO is in charge of receiving, reviewing, and registering all federal trademarks in the United States. Each state employs a trademark registration system that is separate from the federal system. The state systems aim to determine whether an identical trademark already exists and issue a state registration if it does not. The federal PTO, however, reviews each trademark application and analyzes the proposed mark for "registerability."

b. What Registration Gives the Holder

Rights in a trademark are acquired by *use*, not registration. However, registration of a mark on the Principal Register is prima facie evidence of its validity and the owner's exclusive right to use the registered mark in commerce on the goods or services described in the registration. 15 U.S.C. § 1115(a). Registration provides constructive notice of the registrant's ownership in the mark and forecloses a later user of the same or confusingly similar mark from claiming innocence, good faith, or lack of knowledge. 15 U.S.C. § 1072. Thus, once a mark is registered with the PTO, it is afforded national protection regardless of where it is used. 15 U.S.C. § 1072 provides for constructive notice of registration and modifies the common-law rule that allowed acquisition of concurrent rights by user in distinct geographic areas if the subsequent user adopted the mark without knowledge of the prior use. *In Geoffrey, Inc. v. Toys R Us, Inc.*, 756 F. Supp. 661 (D.P.R. 1991), the court held that the plaintiffs' registration of the mark "Toys R Us," provided nationwide protection and constructive notice of the plaintiffs' ownership of the mark to defendants in Puerto Rico. Similarly, in most state systems a registered mark is afforded a presumption that the mark is not merely descriptive.

In general, the duration of a registered mark is ten years. 15 U.S.C. § 1068(a). However, a mark will be automatically cancelled six years after its registration date unless the registrant files an affidavit or declaration that the mark is in use in commerce or an affidavit showing that the non-use is excusable, due to special circumstances and not due to any intention to abandon the mark. 15 U.S.C. § 1068(b). Registration may be perpetually renewed for periods of 10 years within one year of the end of each successive 10 year period. Marks registered or renewed prior to November 16, 1989, remain in force for 20 years, provided an affidavit of use or excusable non-use was filed within the sixth year after registration. Registration of these marks may also be renewed every ten years. 37 C.F.R. 2.181(a)(1).

c. What Cannot Be Registered

15 U.S.C. § 1052 sets forth the various grounds for refusal to register a mark. As discussed previously in Section 3 "Types of Trademarks," marks that are merely descriptive without obtaining secondary meaning, are deceptive, or are primarily geographically deceptively misdescriptive are barred from registration. Also barred are marks that are confusingly similar to a prior mark, and marks that are misdescriptive geographic indications of wine or liquor where the marks were first used on or after January 1, 1996 (e.g., a mark that includes the "Bordeaux" for a wine that does not come from that region in France). Although § 1052 does not bar the registration of generic marks specifically, the Federal Circuit in *BellSouth Corp. v. Data National Corp.*, 60 F.3d 1565 (Fed. Cir. 1995), stated that a generic term is "the ultimate in descriptiveness" and thus should be barred. Section 1052 specifically bars registration of marks that are immoral or scandalous, disparaging, or consist of or comprise insignia of the United States or of any state, municipality or foreign nation. These categories are discussed in more detail below.

i. Immoral or Scandalous

In determining whether a mark is immoral or scandalous under 15 U.S.C. § 1052, a showing by the PTO that the mark is "vulgar" is generally sufficient. For example, in *In re Boulevard Entertainment, Inc.*, 334 F.3d 1336, 1340 (Fed. Cir. 2003), the court affirmed the PTO's refusal to register the marks "1-800-JACK-OFF" and "JACK-OFF" on the grounds the marks were immoral or scandalous. The mark must be considered in the context of the marketplace for the goods or services as described in the registration application. The issue must be determined from the standpoint of a substantial composite of the general public—although not necessarily a majority—and in the context of prevailing attitudes. Thus, for example, the *Boulevard Entertainment* court turned to multiple dictionaries uniformly characterized the term "jack-off" as a vulgar reference to masturbation. On the other hand, in *In re Mavety Media Group*,

Ltd., 33 F.3d 1367 (Fed. Cir. 1994), the court reversed the PTO refusal to register the term "Black-tail" for a men's magazine featuring African-American women, finding the use was not scandalous; the court noted the dictionaries cited provided both a "non-vulgar" definition of tail such as "buttocks or the hindmost or rear end" and vulgar definition of tail "as a female sex partner."

If there is any doubt as to whether a mark is immoral or scandalous under § 1052(a), the Federal Circuit has encouraged the PTO resolve the issue in favor of the applicant and to pass the mark for registration. If a group finds the mark to be immoral scandalous, an opposition proceeding can be brought and a more complete record can be developed. In resolving doubts in favor of the applicant, the PTO or the Trademark Trial and Appeal Board has allowed registration of "Big Pecker Brand" for t-shirts; "Old Glory Condom Corp." with a picture of a condom decorated with stars and stripes, and "Moonies" with the o's in the mark resembling two buttocks in connection with a doll that drops its pants. However, registration of the term "Bull-Shit" has been rejected at least twice. *In re Tenseltown, Inc.*, 212 U.S.P.Q. 863 (T.T.A.B. 1981); *see also In re Wilcher Corp.*, 40 U.S.P.Q. 2d 1929 (T.T.A.B. 1996) (registration refused for the mark "Dick-Heads" with a picture of male genitalia).

ii. Disparaging

The guidelines for determining whether a mark should be barred as "disparaging" under § 1052(a) are vague and the inquiry is highly subjective. In *In re In Over Our Heads, Inc.*, 16 U.S.P.Q. 2d 1653 (T.T.A.B. 1999), the court considered whether the "Moonies" mark (discussed previously) was disparaging to members of the Unification Church. In approving the application for trademark registration, the Board stated that "if a group does find the mark to be scandalous or disparaging, an opposition proceeding can be brought and a more complete record can be established." Similarly in *In re Hines*, 32 U.S.P.Q. 2d 1376 (T.T.A.B. 1994), the Board reconsidered its earlier decision to deny registration to the mark "Budda Beach Wear" on the ground it was disparaging, noting that "it is imperative that the Board be careful to avoid "interposing it's own judgment for that of Buddhists."

A mark may also be refused registration under § 1052(a) if it disparages, brings into contempt or disrepute, or falsely suggest a connection with persons living or dead, institutions, beliefs, or national symbols. This rule is designed primarily to protect persons and institutions from exploitation of their persona by others. Hence, it embraces the concepts of both the right to privacy and the right to publicity. To bar registration on this ground,

(1) the mark must be "unmistakenly" associated with a person or institution—in other words the same or a close approximation or their name or identity;

(2) it must be clear that the person or institution identified by the mark is not connected to the goods or services associated with the mark; and

(3) the fame or reputation of the person or institution is such that a connection would be presumed.

In *In re North American Free Trade Association*, 43 U.S.P.Q. 2d 1282 (T.T.A.B. 1996), the Appeals Board affirmed the PTO's refusal to register the mark "NAFTA" as a service mark for the applicant, concluding it suggested a false connection with the "NAFTA" treaty. On the other hand, in *Lucien Piccard Watch Corp. v. Since 1868 Crescent Corp.*, 314 F. Supp. 329 (S.D.N.Y. 1970), the court held that the mark "Da Vinci" on plaintiff's jewelry products did not falsely suggest a connection with Leonardo Da Vinci since no one was likely to believe he was connected with the goods.

15 U.S.C. § 1052(c) bars registration of a mark that "[c]onsists of or comprises a name, portrait, a signature identifying a particular living person except by his written consent" or "the name, signature or portrait of a deceased President of the United States during the life of his widow, if any, except by the written consent of the widow." (It is unclear whether this statute would require the consent of the widower if the president at issue was female). The written consent requirement under § 1052(c) also applies to a nickname if it identifies a particular living individual.

Written consent to use a name does not suffice as consent to register the mark. In *Hot Stuff Foods, LLC v. Mean Gene Enterprises, Inc.*, 468 F. Supp. 2d 1078, 1088 (D.S.D. 2006), wrestling personality and announcer Gene Okerlund, known as "Mean Gene," entered into a Personal Endorsement Agreement with Hot Stuff Foods and promoted their products "Mean Gene Pizza" and "Mean Gene Burgers." Hot Stuff Foods registered Mean Gene Burgers as a service mark in 1998. After a falling out, Okerlund started his own food product company, "Mean Gene Enterprises" and solicited Hot Stuff licensees. Hot Stuff sued for infringement and Okerlund sought cancellation of the mark. The court ordered the Mean Gene Burgers mark cancelled because Okerlund had only given his consent under the Personal Endorsement Agreement at issue to use of his nick-name, not to register it as a trademark.

On the other hand, in *In re D.B. Kaplan Delicatessen*, 225 U.S.P.Q. 342 (T.T.A.B. 1985), the court held the written consent requirement was met where the buy-out agreement provided that the trade name and service mark of D.B.

Kaplan Delicatessen was the property of D.B. Kaplan Delicatessen or any assignee, and that Kaplan could not use the trade name or service mark in any subsequent business. Thus, the form and context of the transactional documents underlying use of another's name as a trademark can be critical.

iii. Insignia

15 U.S.C. § 1052(b) bars registration of any mark that "[c]onsists of or compromises the flag or coat of arms or any other insignia of the United States, or of any State or municipality or of any foreign nation or any simulation thereof." This category is relatively narrow and includes only those emblems and devices that represent authority and are of the same class and character as flags and coats of arms. Such insignia include the Great Seal of the United States, the Presidential Seal, and the seals of government departments.

In *Heroes, Inc. v. Boomer Esiason Hero's Foundation, Inc.*, 1997 U.S. Dist. Lexis 12192, 1997 WL 335807 (D.D.C.), the court held that a mark containing a depiction of the United States Capitol was protectable, noting there was no evidence that the Building was formally adopted as an emblem of governmental authority. Similarly, in *Liberty Mutual Insurance Co. v. Liberty Insurance Co. of Texas*, 185 F. Supp. 895 (D.Ark. 1960), the court held that the statute of Liberty was not an insignia of the United States. In *In re United States Department of the Interior*, 142 U.S.P.Q. 506 (T.T.A.B. 1964), the Department of Interior was permitted to register an insignia for the National Park Service because it was not otherwise an insignia of the United States. In *United States Navy v. United States Manufacturing Co.*, 2 U.S.P.Q. 2d 1254 (T.T.A.B. 1987), the court held that §1052(b) did not bar registration of the mark "USMC" for orthopedic braces made by defendant.

The term "simulation" in § 1052(b) refers to something that gives the appearance or effect or has the characteristics of the original item. In *In re Advance Industrial Security, Inc.*, 194 U.S.P.Q. 344 (T.T.A.B., 1977), the Board concluded that a mark containing the word "Advanced Security" in the upper third portion along with an eagle that was similar to the United States Coat of Arms was not a simulation of the United States Coat of Arms or Great Seal. The Board noted that the mark created an overall commercial impression distinctly different from the Great Seal.

d. Incontestable Marks

After a mark is registered and in continuous use without challenge for five years, and the filing of an affidavit to that effect with the PTO, a mark becomes "incontestable" and is further insulated and protected from attacks by later users or infringers. 15 U.S.C. § 1065; 1115. Section 1115(a) provides that "incontestable" status is conclusive evidence of registration and validity of the mark, and the registrant's ownership and exclusive right to use the mark. If a mark has become incontestable it cannot be challenged on the ground that it is merely descriptive and has not acquired secondary meaning.

For example, in *Park 'N Fly, Inc. v. Dollar Park and Fly, Inc.*, 469 U.S. 189 (1985), the court held that the use of the mark "Park N' Fly" by a company operating airport pay-parking lots was descriptive, which could be grounds for cancellation within 5 years of registration. However, the Court held that because the mark had become incontestable, it descriptiveness was neither a defense for infringement under 15 U.S.C. § 1115, nor a grounds for cancellation under 15 U.S.C. § 1064. Section 1115 sets forth myriad other defenses available in the case of an incontestable mark, which are detailed in Chapter Nine, section 5, Defenses to Infringement Actions.

A mark cannot acquire incontestable status if it is or has become generic. 11 U.S.C. § 1065(4). Also, under § 1064(3), registration of a mark may be cancelled at any time—even after becoming incontestable—for a limited number of reasons. The most important reasons for cancellation of registration include that:

> [T]he registered mark becomes the generic name for the goods or services, or a portion thereof, for which it is registered, or is functional, or has been abandoned, or its registration was obtained fraudulently....

e. Supplemental Register

A mark that does not meet all the requirements for registration on the PTO's Principal Register, but that is capable of distinguishing the applicant's goods or services, may be registered on the PTO's Supplemental Register. Thus, a mark that is merely descriptive may be registered on the Supplemental Register if it is capable of later becoming distinctive of acquiring secondary meaning. If the mark later acquires distinctiveness through use in commerce it will become eligible for registration on the Principle Register. In *In re Bush Bros. & Co.*, 884 F.2d 569, 570 (Fed. Cir. 1989), the court held that the term "Deluxe" was capable of distinguishing the applicant's pork and beans and thus reversed the PTO's refusal to register the mark on the Supplemental Register.

Supplemental registration confers significantly fewer advantages than principal registration. Registration on the supplemental register is not evidence of the mark's validity, or the registrant's ownership of or exclusive right to use the mark. However it enables the registrant to satisfy the home registration requirement of some foreign countries and creates jurisdiction in a federal forum for disputes involving the mark.

7. Loss of Trademark Rights

Trademark owners can lose their rights to the mark if the mark becomes generic or if they abandon the mark. 15 U.S.C. § 1064 (3). Marks are considered abandoned if (1) use of the mark is discontinued with the intent not to resume use, or (2) there is a course of conduct by the owner that "allows the mark to become generic"). 15 U.S.C. § 1127. Owners may also cancel their trademark registration on their own accord.

a. "Genericide"

A trademark may lose protection if it becomes generic. Terms like aspirin, cellophane, nylon, thermos, and escalator, at one point, were all trademarks protected under United States trademark law. Lifelong protection of a trademark is not a certainty. If consumers come to associate a trademark with the class of product instead of a particular brand, the mark will become generic and its owner will loose rights to it.

Generic terms are not registerable, and a registered term may be cancelled at any time on the grounds it has become generic. 15 U.S.C. § 1064(3). A registered mark will not be deemed to be the generic name of goods or services solely because the mark is also used as a name of or to identify a unique product or service. 15 U.S.C. § 1064(3). Congress added this language in 1984 to clarify "that it is not destructive of the trademark function to identify a product by the name coined by its purveyor." In *In re Montrachet S.A.*, 878 F.2d 375, 377 (Fed. Cir. 1989), the court held that the fact that the trademark term "montrachet" was used to identify a type of French cheese as well as the source of the cheese did not make the term generic. Thus, a name may be used to indicate both a product and its source.

In determining whether a mark has become generic, the issue is whether the trademarked term has become synonymous with the nature or class of products of which it is a part. In *Bayer Co. v. United Drug Co.*, 272 F. 505, 509 (S.D.N.Y. 1921), the case in which "aspirin" was found to be generic, Judge Learned Hand stated: "The single question as I view it, in all these cases is merely one of fact: What do buyers understand by the word for whose use the parties are contending?" Similarly, in *King-Seeley Thermos Co. v. Aladdin Industries,*

Inc., 321 F.2d 577, (2d Cir. 1963), the court determined that the trademark "thermos" had become generic, holding that once the public expropriates a trademark as its own, it is unfair to restrict the rights of competitors to use the word. In other words, "thermos bottle" and "vacuum bottle" had become "virtually synonymous."

Not surprisingly, owners of popular marks often engage in extensive policing efforts to prevent them from becoming generic and falling into the public domain. For example, in *E. I. duPont de Nemours & Co. v. Yoshida Intern., Inc.*, 393 F. Supp. 502 (E.D.N.Y. 1975), the continued viability of DuPont's mark "Teflon" was at issue. The court held that the term had not become generic, largely because of DuPont's trademark protection program, including extensive efforts by its legal and advertising departments to ensure that "whenever a misuse of the mark is detected, it is promptly called to the misuser's attention." Another technique used to prevent a term from becoming generic is to accompany the term with the word "brand" and a generic description of the product, e.g., Scotch Brand Cellophane Tape, Xerox Brand Photocopier. This supplies consumers with a word for the goods sold under the mark other than the mark itself. The actual primary significance of the mark to purchasers is controlling, however. In other words, even the best efforts of the trademark owner to prevent public appropriation of the mark as a generic description can be unsuccessful.

b. Abandonment

A trademark owner forfeits all right in any mark they have abandoned under 15 U.S.C. § 1064(3), and abandonment is a defense to infringement under § 1115(b)(2). Trademarks may be found to have been abandoned because of non-use, assignments in gross or naked licensing. (The later two are discussed below in Section 8.)

Under 15 U.S.C. §1127, a mark is abandoned because of non-use when its owner has ceased using the mark with an intent not to resume its use. At common law, a party alleging abandonment had to prove "intent to abandon," but because trademark owners could overcome any circumstantial proof of their intent to abandon simply by testifying that they did *not* intend to abandon their marks, the Lanham act reformulated the test. Under § 1127, proof of three consecutive years of non-use establishes a *prima facie* case of intent not to resume use, which the trademark owner must then rebut with objective proof of its intent to resume use of the mark. Thus, "an affirmative desire not to relinquish a mark" is no longer the determinative factor. This change helps ensure that the Lanham Act does not allow the "warehousing" of unused trademarks by their owners.

Whether a mark has been abandoned through non-use is a question of fact, and the owner's intent is inferred from the circumstances, aided by the statutory presumption. Because a finding of abandonment results in the forfeiture of a property interest by the trademark owner, the party alleging abandonment bears the burden of proof on their claim, and abandonment must be proven by clear and convincing evidence.

i. Non-use

To trigger the presumption raised by three consecutive years of non-use, the party alleging an abandonment must show that during those three consecutive years the trademark owner did not employ its mark for any purpose that qualifies as "use" within the meaning of Title 15. Under § 1127:

> The term "use in commerce" means the bona fide use of a mark in the ordinary course of trade, and not a use made merely to reserve a right in a mark. For purposes of this chapter, a mark shall be deemed to be in use in commerce —
>
> (1) on goods when —
>> (A) it is placed in any manner on the goods or their containers or the displays associated therewith or on the tags or labels affixed thereto, or if the nature of the goods makes such placement impracticable, then on documents associated with the goods or their sale, and
>> (B) the goods are sold or transported in commerce, and
>
> (2) on services when it is used or displayed in the sale or advertising of services and the services are rendered in commerce, or the services are rendered in more than one State or in the United States and a foreign country and the person rendering the services is engaged in commerce in connection with the services.

So in order to be "used" within the meaning of § 1127, the mark must be affixed to goods, and the goods must be either sold or transported in commerce, all in the ordinary course of trade. Token use for the purpose of establishing and reserving a right in the mark is insufficient. For example, in *La Societe Anonyme des Parfums le Galion v. Jean Patou, Inc.*, 495 F.2d 1265 (2d Cir. 1974), the defendant had registered the trademark "Snob" in 1951 for use on perfumes, but over the following twenty years sold only 89 bottles of perfume bearing the mark for a profit of about $100. Meanwhile, the plaintiff—a French manufacturer of perfume sold abroad as "Snob"—was consistently denied a right to import its product because of conflict with the defendant's registered trademark. When the plaintiff alleged invalidity of the defendant's mark for non-use, the court agreed. The defendant's extraordinarily limited use of the mark amounted "a relatively painless way to keep a potential competitor at bay" rather than a bona fide attempt to build goodwill in the mark through use in the ordinary course of trade. The court ordered that the defendant's registration be cancelled, holding that the defendant's use of the mark was not bona fide use of the mark in the ordinary course of trade and therefore not "use" within the meaning of § 1127.

On the other hand, in *Electro Source, LLC v. Brandess-Kalt-Aetna Group, Inc.*, 458 F.3d 931 (9th Cir. 2006), the defendant alleged the plaintiff's mark registered in 1995 "Pelican" for backpacks and luggage, had been abandoned by plaintiff's predecessor in interest. That predecessor, a sole proprietor, had between 1998 and 2001 sold fewer than one thousand branded items, entirely from a dwindling overstock, and largely from the trunk of his car. The court rejected the defendant's argument that such use was not "bona fide" and therefore a non-use under § 1127. Despite the limited and sporadic sales of goods bearing the mark, the court held that they were evidence of "a small, troubled business[es]" best efforts to continue in the ordinary course of trade, rather than simply an attempt to liquidate remaining stock or reserve a right in the mark.

In order to qualify as use, any bona fide use in the ordinary course of trade must also be "in commerce," defined by § 1127 as "all commerce which may lawfully be regulated by Congress." Therefore, only use within the United States, and therefore subject to Congressional authority, is relevant for trademark purposes. For example, in *Imperial Tobacco, Ltd. v. Philip Morris, Inc.*, 899 F.2d 1575, (Fed. Cir. 1990), in 1981 the defendant registered "JPS" for use on cigarettes. Between 1981 and 1987 the defendant did a heavy foreign business in cigarette sales under the mark, its use of the mark in the United States was limited entirely to promotional goods such as whiskey, watches, pens, and sunglasses. The court ordered cancellation of the mark, but held that because sales of cigarettes under the mark were made only outside the U.S., they could not qualify as use within the meaning of § 1127. Likewise, in *Rivard v. Linville*, 133 F.3d 1446 (Fed. Cir. 1998), the defendant's registration for the mark "Ultracuts" was challenged for non-use. The court agreed, and ordered the registration be cancelled. Although the defendant had used the name "Ultracuts" for his chain of hair salons in Canada, he had never used the mark in the United States. Moreover, the defendant was unable to demonstrate a legitimate intent to use the mark in the United States where only evidence of a plan to open salons in the United States was the registrant's own self-serving testimony. Indeed, a registrant's proclamations of intent have little, if any, weight.

ii. Rebuttal

Under § 1127, "[n]onuse for 3 consecutive years shall be prima facie evidence of abandonment." Therefore, once the party alleging abandonment has established that the trademark owner either did not use the mark at all, or did not put the mark to bona fide use in the ordinary course of trade for three consecutive years, a presumption arises that the mark has been abandoned. Thereafter, the trademark owner bears the burden of production to show that despite the non-use it intended to resume use of the mark.

The presumption of abandonment can is generally rebutted by showing efforts by the registrant to resume use or by showing that the non-use was excusable, both of which indicate that the non-use was not coupled with an intent not to resume use, or an intent to abandon.

Proof of active efforts by the trademark owner to resume use of the mark during the period of non-use will usually over come the presumption of abandonment. For example, in *Sands, Taylor & Wood v. Quaker Oats Co.*, 18 U.S.P.Q.2d 1457 (N.D. Ill. 1990), the plaintiff had not used its registered trademark "Thirst-Aid" for use on fountain drinks in 25 years, but the court held that proof of active efforts to license the mark for that purpose during prolonged period of non-use was sufficient to rebut the presumption of abandonment.

A trademark owner may also rebut a prima facie case of abandonment by showing that the non-use was not the result of an intent to abandon or lack of intent to resume use of the mark, but rather that it was provoked by some excusable external pressure—e.g. labor strikes, litigation, war, bankruptcy, or government restrictions. For example, in *Miller Brewing Co. v. Oland's Breweries (1971) Ltd.*, 548 F.2d 349 (C.C.P.A. 1976), the trademark owner, a Canadian brewery, had not imported its "Oland's Schooner" brand beer to the United States for several years, raising a presumption of abandonment under § 1127. However, the court held that presumption of abandonment to have been rebutted by proof that the non-use was caused by financial problems that forced the trademark owner to reduce production and limit sales of its beer to the Canadian market. In *Sterling Brewers, Inc. v. Schenley Industries, Inc.*, 441 F.2d 675 (C.C.P.A. 1971), the trademark owner had stopped manufacturing it's "Cook's Goldblume" beer when it shuttered its factory in the midst of a labor dispute. The court held that the prima facie case of abandonment was adequately rebutted by proof of trouble meeting increased costs in the face of the strike, rather than an intent not to resume use of the mark, caused the period of non-use.

In most cases rebuttal requires proof of an intent to resume use in the reasonably foreseeable future. For example, in *Emmpresa Cubana Del To-*

bacco v. Cohiba Corp., 213 F. Supp. 2d 247 (S.D.N.Y. 2002.), the court held the registrant, General Cigar, abandoned the mark "Cohiba" when it did not use it commercially in the U.S. from 1987 to 1992. General Cigar contended that it withdrew the mark because of a slump in the market and used the time to plan for a new Cohiba cigar that would have constituted a reasonable business explanation or excuse to avoid a finding of abandonment. However, the court noted this contention was belied by the record, because the "new" cigar introduced in 1992 was simply an existing General Cigar product with an old Cohiba label on it. The court also noted that a reasonable business explanation for discontinuing use of the mark was insufficient absent evidence that it intended to resume use of the mark in the foreseeable future; evidence that General Cigar did not intend to abandon the mark was not enough. It had to have intended to do more than merely "warehouse" the mark until it was useful again. This meant producing "concrete plans" to resume its use.

Changing the use of a mark from one product to another generally will not result in abandonment if the products are similar. So, for example, in *Lucien Piccard Watch Corp. v. 1868 Crescent Corp.*, 314 F. Supp. 329, (S.D.N.Y. 1970) the court found no abandonment where a mark first used for leather gift items and jewelry was later used on luggage. Minor changes or modernization in the format of the mark will also not result in abandonment as long as both marks make the same commercial impression. Likewise, in *Sands, Taylor & Wood v. Quaker Oats, Co.*, 978 F.2d 947 (7th Cir. 1992) the change of a mark from "Thirst-Aid First Aid for Your Thirst" to "Thirst Aid" was not an abandonment, because it was unlikely to cause confusion. Moreover, nonuse must be nationwide to amount to abandonment; any lingering interstate activity will defeat a claim of abandonment, though proof of intrastate activity will not.

If a trademark owner cannot rebut the presumption of abandonment raised by the prima facie case described in § 1127, the resulting cancellation of its federal registration will leave the trademark owner with only those rights arising under state and common law from their actual use of the mark. In most cases, the non-use proved to establish the prima facie case of abandonment was a total non-use, and so the trademark owner will be left without any rights in the mark. Thereafter, the mark will be equally available to all prospective users, including the former owner, and the first to meet the statutory preconditions after the date on which the court has deemed the mark abandoned may register the mark anew.

Assignments in gross and naked licensing, both discussed below, may also result in abandonment and strip the owner of trademark rights. This is consistent with the purposes of a trademark: to identify goods or services of a particular quality or point of origin. Stripped of these purposes, the trademark may be deemed abandoned.

8. Property Interests in Trademarks

The property interest in a trademark can be characterized as a right to exclude or the right of exclusive use. As the court noted in *College Savings Bank v. Florida Prepaid Postsecondary Education Expense Board*, 527 U.S. 666, 673 (1999), trademarks "are the property of the owner because he can exclude others from using them." However, it bears emphasizing that, unlike other types of intellectual property, property rights in trademarks are shaped by consumer perception. In order for the right to be created, a mark must be used in commerce and must distinguish the goods or services from those of others in the minds of current or potential consumers. 15 U.S.C. §§ 1052, 1127. Similarly, violation of trademark rights depends on consumer perception—are they confused or deceived by use of a similar mark or has such use made the mark distinctive to consumers. *See* 15 U.S.C. § 1125.

As property rights, trademarks can be sold (assigned) and licensed (allowing a limited right to use). Unique rules apply, however: The property interest in a trademark, trade name, service mark, collective mark, or certification mark rests in the goodwill associated with the mark. Property rights in a trademark exist soley as a right appurtenant to an established business or trade in connection with which the mark is employed. In other words, there is no right in a trademark "in gross"; the right to a trademark is connected with the trademarked product or service and associated goodwill.

a. Assignments

15 U.S.C. § 1060(a)(1) addresses to trademark assignments and provides that a mark "shall be assignable with the goodwill of the business in which the mark is used, or with that part of the goodwill of the business connected with the use of and symbolized by the mark." Assignments of a mark without the goodwill of the business associated with the mark are often referred to as "assignments in gross" or "naked assignments" and will be invalidated (and may also lead to a finding of abandonment).

The requirement of "substantially the same characteristics" is construed liberally today, but was much more strict in the past. For example, in *Independent Baking Powder Co. v. Boorman*, 175 F. 448 (C.C.N.J. 1910), the court held that the trademark "Solar" was forfeited where the assignee sold phosphate-based baking powder rather than alum-based baking powder that the assignor had sold. The court stated: "The trademark in question was not acquired in connection with baking powder in general, but with baking powder of a specific kind, apart from which its use is unjustifiable." Also, in *PepsiCo, Inc. v. Grapelce*, 416 F. 2d 285 (8th Cir. 1969), the court held an assignment of the mark "Peppy" was an invalid assignment in gross because the assignor's cola flavored soft drink and the assignee's pepper flavored soft drink were not substantially similar.

The prohibition on assignments in gross is intended to prevent consumer confusion or deception. Where a mark has accumulated consumer goodwill as an indication of the origin of a particular good or service, the mark is at best of no assistance to consumers attempting to discern between the quality or origin of goods or services that are different. At worst, an assignment in gross can result in genuine confusion amongst consumers, or even "in a fraud on the purchasing public who reasonably assume that the mark signifies the same thing, whether used by one person or another." *Marshak v. Green*, 746 F.2d 927 (2d Cir.1984). For that reason, the *Marshak* court refused to allow the defendant's trade name "Vito and the Salutations" to be seized and sold by his creditors, holding that because the trademark could not be sold with its good will intact, it could not be sold at all.

The possibility of invalid assignment in gross poses a risk of abandonment, as an assignor may cease its use of the ostensibly but ineffectually assigned mark, which after time may result in an abandonment. Once the trademark has been abandoned, it cannot be re-assigned because there is no property right to be transferred from another. For example, in *interState Net Bank v. NetB@nk, Inc.*, 348 F. Supp. 2d 340 (D.N.J. 2004), the operator's of a point-of-sale electronic debit service had assigned their registered trademark, "NetBank," to the defendant NetB@ank, which operated a full-service online bank under the mark. Years later, *inter*State Net Bank challenged NetB@nk's registration of the mark, alleging that original assignment had been in gross and therefore invalid. The court agreed, holding that because the assignor had used the mark to identify a substantially different sort of business from that operated by NetB@nk, no good will could have been assigned along with the mark. Moreover, because the assignment had been invalid, rights in the mark had reverted immediately to the assignor and, in the intervening years, been abandoned for lack of use. Holding the mark had been abandoned, the court ordered that its registration be cancelled.

Several brand names have been purchased in bankruptcy auctions, however, without resulting abandonment. These include "Polaroid" for use with products like digital cameras, televisions, and global positioning systems, and "Bombay Co." for use with housewares, paint, wallpaper, and window treatments.

b. Licenses

Prior to enactment of the Lanham Act, many courts held that a trademark represented to the consumer the physical source or origin of the goods and services. By that reasoning, licensing of a trademark was held to effect an abandonment of the mark. As the use of trademarks shifted to identify a standard of quality to consumers rather than a geographical source, courts held that licensing was permitted, provided the owner of the mark retained sufficient control over the quality of the goods or services provided. Under 15 U.S.C. § 1055, the Lanham Act specifically recognizes that the use of a mark by a licensee inures to the benefit of the trademark owner. This is the basis for modern franchising in the United States.

For example, in *Financial Matters, Inc. v. PepsiCo, Inc.*, 806 F. Supp. 480 (S.D.N.Y. 1992), the plaintiff contested Pepsi's rights in the trademark "Stolichnaya," alleging that by failing to use the mark itself, Pepsi had abandoned the mark. The court, however, concluded "that plaintiffs fundamentally misperceive U.S. trademark law." Pepsi had properly registered the mark, and since the date of registration had kept "Stolichnaya" in continual use under license to importers and distributors of Stolichnaya vodka. The court concluded that a trademark owner "need not be the manufacturer, importer or distributor of the goods sold under its mark," but rather may "delegate the responsibility of daily control over the quality of the product to a reliable party if it wishes, without relinquishing a mark."

A trademark licensor must take precautions to ensure that the quality of goods sold under its mark remains consistent over time and between licensees. Thus § 1055 provides that only use by a *related* company will inure to the benefit of a trademark owner. Section 1127, in turn, defines a "related company" as "any person whose use of a mark is controlled by the owner of the mark with respect to the nature and quality of the goods or services on or in connection with which the mark is used." If a court determines that a trademark owner has not exercised sufficient control over its licensees, the owner will be held to have abandoned its mark by granting a "naked license."

The Second Circuit explained the important of sufficient control in *Dawn Donut v. Hart's Food Stores, Inc.*, 267 F.2d 358 (2d Cir. 1959):

> Without the requirement of control, the right of a trademark owner to license his mark separately from the business in connection with which it has been used would create the danger that products bearing the same trademark might be of diverse qualities. . . . If the licensor is not compelled to take some reasonable steps to prevent misuses of his trademark

in the hands of others the public will be deprived of its most effective protection against misleading uses of a trademark. The public is hardly in a position to uncover deceptive uses of a trademark before they occur and will be at best slow to detect them after they happen. Thus, unless the licensor exercises supervision and control over the operations of its licensees the risk that the public will be unwittingly deceived will be increased and this is precisely what the Act is in part designed to prevent....Clearly the only effective way to protect the public where a trademark is used by licensees is to place on the licensor the affirmative duty of policing in a reasonable manner the activities of his licensees.

In *Dawn Donut*, the plaintiff had registered "Dawn" and "Dawn Donut" for use on cake and donut mixes which it sold to retail bakeries. Some of those bakeries were permitted under license to use the plaintiff's registered marks in connection with the sale of baked good prepared from the mixes. When the plaintiff sued the defendant for using "Dawn" in connection with baked goods, the defendant brought an affirmative defense of abandonment by naked licensing. The court noted that it was unclear from the record whether the registrant subjected licensees to inspections by trained personnel or only casual examinations by untrained salesmen. Holding that "[t]he latter system of inspection hardly constitutes a sufficient program of supervision to satisfy the requirements of the act," the court remanded for further fact-finding, instructing the district court that the plaintiff's trademarks should be cancelled unless it could demonstrate adequate supervision of its licensees.

The exercise of actual control over licensees—rather than the mere reservation of a right to control through the license agreement—is key to avoiding a naked license. This typically requires a showing of more than casual control. For example, in *Barcamerica International USA Trust v. Tyfield Importers, Inc.*, 289 F.3d 589 (9th Cir. 2002), the plaintiff sought to enjoin defendant's from using his registered "Leonardo Da Vinci" mark on imported wine, and the defendant's counterclaimed that the plaintiff had abandoned the mark through a "naked license" to another vintner. The court agreed, holding that the plaintiffs own random tastings and reliance on its exclusive licensee's good reputation were insufficient to ensure the quality of its licensee's wine where the plaintiff had not undertaken some minimally organized program of quality control. In its ruling, the court rejected the plaintiff's argument that because the licensee made "good wine," the public was not deceived by the mark. The court held that whether the wine was objectively good or bad was irrelevant; rather, the quality control requirement is intended to ensure that the licensed goods or services are of equal quality to goods formerly associated with the mark.

The amount of control that a licensor must exercise over its licensee varies with the circumstances, and the critical inquiry regards whether the amount of control exercised by a licensor is sufficient to ensure that goods manufactured, or services provided by, a licensee under the will remain of a consistent predictable quality expected by consumers. Under some circumstances the licensor need not exercise any actual quality control over its licensee. In *Syntex Laboratories, Inc. v. Norwich Pharmaceutical Co.*, 315 F. Supp. 45 (S.D.N.Y. 1970), the plaintiff pharmaceutical company had purchased both the trademark and formula for the medicated cream "Vagitrol," and while ramping up its own production facilities, a very long process, licensed both back to the assignor, itself a pharmaceutical company. The plaintiff never exercised any control over its licensee, and when it sued the defendant for use of the mark "Vagestrol" for a competing product, the defendant mounted an affirmative defense of abandonment by naked license. The court held that the licensor was justified in believing the quality of the goods would be maintained without oversight given both the licensee's proven competence in the manufacture of Vagitrol and the comprehensive quality control program imposed on pharmaceutical manufacture by federal regulation.

However, in most instances an unsupervised license will be held valid only where there was a familial or close working relationship between the licensor and licensee. For example, in *Taco Cabana International, Inc. v. Two Pesos*, 932 F.2d 1113, 1121 (5th Cir. 1991), two brothers operated separate restaurants under an unsupervised trade-dress cross-license. The court held that given their 8-year close business relationship prior to the license, they could "justifiably rely on [each other's] intimacy with standards and procedures to ensure consistent quality." Likewise, in *Doeblers' Pennsylvania Hybrids, Inc. v. Doebler*, 442 F.3d 812 (3d Cir. 2006), the court held that an implied, unsupervised, license granted by one family seed business to another controlled by the same family was valid where the two companies "were closely-held business entities owned and managed by family members and which included a high degree of interlocking ownership and control." In *Transgo, Inc. v. Ajac Transmission Parts Corp.*, 768 F.2d 1004 (9th Cir. 1985), the court upheld an unsupervised oral license of a mark used on transmission parts because 90% of the products sold by the licensee were manufactured by the licensor and the parties had worked together for ten years.

9. Security Interests in Trademarks

Trademarks, along with other intellectual property such as Copyrights and Patents, often represent a significant portion of a corporation's value and can be useful source of collateral for secured transactions. Failure to take a security interest in trademarks can actually devalue a secured party's collateral. For example, consider the foreclosure value of a fast-food franchise's business assets without its trademarks.

To maintain the priority of their security interests, lenders must know how to properly create and perfect their security interests in intellectual property. Security interests in intellectual property are governed by both the federal law and Article 9 of the Uniform Commercial Code.

Article 9 of the U.C.C. which has been adopted by all fifty states, governs the creation and perfection of security interest in intellectual property, which is categorized as a "general intangible." A security interest is defined as "an interest in personal property or fixtures which secures payment or performance of an obligation." U.C.C. § 1-201(b)(35). A security interest is not enforceable against either a debtor or third parties, and does not attach to the collateral, unless

(1) the secured party has given value in exchange for the collateral,

(2) the debtor has rights in the collateral, and

(3) the debtor has signed a security agreement that provides a description of the collateral.

U.C.C. § 9-203(b). Lenders must therefore ensure that the debtor has rights in the intellectual property collateral prior to obtaining the security interest.

Perfection is the method by which a secured party achieves and maintains the highest available priority for its security interest in collateral. An unperfected security interest may be effective against the debtor, but it is of little value against third parties. In bankruptcy, the difference between a perfected security interest and an unperfected security interest often means the difference between a full recovery as a secured creditor and little or no recovery as an unsecured creditor. 11 U.S.C. § 544.

A security interest is perfected when it attaches if the applicable requirements are satisfied before attachment. The process of perfecting a security interest in most types of personal property is accomplished when a properly completed UCC-1 financing statement is filed with the appropriate state office, usually the office of the secretary of state. The financing statement must name both the debtor and the secured party, and must describe the collateral covered by the financing statement. The U.C.C. no longer requires the debtor to sign an electronically filed financial statement, although the debtor must authorize the filing.

The relative priorities of creditors who hold conflicting security interests are straightforward. Under the U.C.C. (1) if the conflicting security interests are perfected, they rank according to priority in time of filing or perfection; (2) a perfected security interest has priority over a conflicting unperfected security interest; and (3) if conflicting security interests are unperfected, the first security interest to attach has priority. However, under §9-109(c)(1), Article 9 does not apply to the extent that it is preempted by federal law.

Filing a financing statement is neither necessary nor effective to perfect a security interest in collateral that is subject to a separate federal filing requirement. In such cases, compliance with such a federal requirement is equivalent to filing a properly completed UCC-1 financing statement, and compliance with federal law is the only means of perfection. U.C.C. §9-311(b). However, even in cases where federal law governs the perfection of security interests, Article 9 governs the relative priorities of conflicting security interests unless federal law also establishes separate priority rules. Sections 9-109 and 9-311 of the U.C.C. raise distinct issues: under §9-109, federal law preempts Article 9 where the former governs ownership rights in the property secured as collateral, while under §9-311, the U.C.C. defers to federal law regarding perfection if federal law has defined a filing requirement. The distinction between these sections is unclear, and it is equally unclear whether security interests in intellectual property rights governed by federal law must be perfected in accordance with federal law or the U.C.C. Because of this uncertainty, financing statements in patents, trademarks, or copyrights should be filed with both state and federal offices.

Security interests in both common law trademarks and state-registered trademarks are perfected by filing a UCC-1 financing statement with the appropriate state office. The steps to properly perfect a security interest in a federally registered trademark are less clear. Under the Lanham Act:

> A registered mark or a mark for which an application to register has been filed shall be assignable with the goodwill of the business in which the mark is used.... An assignment shall be void against any subsequent purchaser for valuable consideration without notice, unless the prescribed information reporting the assignment is recorded in the United States Patent and Trademark Office within 3 months after the date of the assignment or prior to the subsequent purchase.

15 U.S.C. §1060(a)(1) and (4). Thus, the Lanham Act provides for a recordation of "assignments" and contains a limited priority rule.

The Lanham Act does not define "assignment," and it is unclear whether security interests must be recorded with the PTO. Nevertheless, to give third parties notification of legal ownership or other equitable interests, the PTO does accept and file documents that create security interests in trademarks.

The courts have narrowly interpreted the Lanham Act, holding that—despite the PTO's acceptance of filings creating security interests—it was not intended to govern security interests in trademarks and does not preempt Article 9. In *In re Roman Cleanser Co.*, 43 B.R. 940 (Bankr. E.D. Mich. 1984), *aff'd*, 802 F.2d 207 (6th Cir. 1986), the bankruptcy court held that the federal provision for recordation of an assignment does not trigger an exception to the U.C.C. because a security interest is not a presently operative "assignment," but rather an agreement to assign in the event of a default. Also, in *In re Together Development Corp.*, 227 B.R. 439, 441 (Bankr. D.Mass. 1998), the bankruptcy court held that the reference to the term "assignment" in 15 U.S.C. § 1060 denoted an absolute assignment, not a security interest, and that filing a financing statement with the PTO is not sufficient to perfect a security interest in a trademark.

Furthermore, courts have consistently held that a security interest in a trademark must be perfected according to the U.C.C. requirements. For example, in *In re 199Z*, 137 B.R. 778 (Bankr. C.D. Cal. 1992), a lender's U.C.C. financing statement was held to be deficient because it did not describe the property of the debtor in which the secured party claimed an interest. Although the lender had filed its security interest with the PTO, the bankruptcy court held that recordation of a security interest in a trademark at the PTO is ineffective for perfection under the U.C.C. Likewise, in *In re TR-3 Industries*, 41 B.R. 128 (Bankr. C.D. Cal. 1984), the bankruptcy court held that the Lanham Act did prescribe a separate filing requirement for the perfection of security interests in trademarks and that the secured party had therefore validly perfected its interest by a U.C.C. filing. Finally, in *In re Chattanooga Choo-Choo Co.*, 98 B.R. 792 (Bankr. E.D. Tenn. 1989), the bankruptcy court held that Article 9 of the U.C.C. governs security interests in trademarks because the Lanham Act provides only for registration of ownership and was not designed to give notice of security interests.

Although the courts have consistently held that the U.C.C.—not federal law— governs the perfection of security interests in trademarks, the prudent approach to perfecting any security interest in a trademark is to both file a UCC-1 financing statement with the appropriate state office and to record that security interest with the PTO. Dual filing avoids any confusion regarding the term "assignment" under the Lanham Act and forecloses any risk that a security interest will be lost to a bona fide purchaser. The Lanham Act's limited priority rule addresses only the validity of an assignment "as against any subsequent purchaser for a valuable consideration without notice." 15 U.S.C. § 1060(a)(4). Subsequent lien creditors are not mentioned. However, because registering a trademark with the PTO serves as constructive notice of trademark ownership, 15 U.S.C. § 1072, filing the security interest with the PTO may also provide constructive notice of the secured party's interest to any prospective bona fide purchaser of the trademark.

Regardless of the method of registration, a security interest in a trademark is always at risk of being invalidated as an "assignment in gross." Trademarks, unlike patents and copyrights, cannot be freely bought and sold, but may only be assigned along with the associated goodwill. 15 U.S.C. § 1060. Any transfer of a trademark unaccompanied by the underlying goodwill will be invalid as an "assignment in gross." Because a security interest in a trademark may ripen into an assignment, unless the foreclosing creditor also holds a security interest in the goodwill associated with the trademark, the trademark assignment will be unenforceable. A secured party should therefore specifically identify the debtor's trademarks and the associated goodwill of the business in both the security agreement and the financing statement. This is generally the case when a secured party also has a blanket lien or security interest in the business assets associated with the use of the mark.

Finally, because the U.C.C. definition of "general intangibles" includes both rights in a trademark and the associated goodwill, U.C.C. § 9-102, cmt 5(d), a reference in the security agreement to "general intangibles" may be sufficient to cover trademarks. However, it is better practice to include a specific list of existing marks, registration numbers, and references to the goods, products, or services with which the trademarks are associated.

Checkpoints

- A trademark is any distinctive mark, symbol, device, or emblem used by a business to identify and distinguish its goods from those of others and that enables consumers to identify products and their source.

- Trademarks are protected by both state and federal law.

- Trademark protection is also available for service marks, collective marks, certification marks, and trade dress.

  - A service mark is used by a company to identify and accumulate goodwill toward specific intangibles such as services.

  - A collective mark distinguishes membership in an association, union, or other group.

  - A certification mark is used by third parties to guarantee that certified goods or services meet certain criteria.

  - Trade dress is the nonfunctional that encompasses the overall appearance of a product's design as presented in the marketplace, including the decor, packaging, wrappers, and labels.

    - *De facto* functionality exists where the elements of the design are arbitrary or superfluous. *De facto* functional marks and trade dress are eligible for protection.

    - *De jure* functionality exists where the overall appearance is the consequence of entirely and necessarily utilitarian considerations. *De jure* marks or trade dress are not eligible for protection.

- There are four categories of trademarks arranged in ascending order according to their strength: (1) generic, (2) descriptive (including deceptively misdescriptive), (3) suggestive, and (4) arbitrary or fanciful.

  - Generic marks are never distinctive and are not eligible for protection.

  - Descriptive and deceptively misdescriptive marks are eligible for protection only if they acquire secondary meaning, but primarily geographically deceptively misdescriptive marks adopted after 1992 are ineligible for trademark protection.

  - Suggestive marks are inherently distinctive and are eligible for protection.

  - Arbitrary and fanciful marks are inherently distinctive, eligible for protection, and considered the strongest type of mark.

- Trademarks must be distinctive — they must serve the purpose of identifying the origin of the goods or services — in order to be eligible for protection.

- Distinctiveness may be obtained inherently, as with suggestive, arbitrary, or fanciful marks, or through use once the mark has obtained secondary meaning, as with some descriptive marks.

- A mark must actually be in use or the mark holder must have a bona fide intention to use the mark in commerce in order to be protected.

- Priority in a mark is typically given to the first party to use the mark in commerce (the "senior user"). The standard of use is minimal, but must be continuous from its first instance until ownership is asserted in order to preserve the user's priority.

- Rights in a trademark are acquired by use, not registration, but federal registration is prima facie evidence of validity, the registrant's ownership of the mark, and the registrant's exclusive right to use the mark in commerce. Registration also provides constructive notice of the registrant's claim to the mark thereby foreclosing any claims of innocence or good faith by later or "junior users."

- Certain marks are barred from registration, including those that are generic, deceptive, primarily geographically deceptively misdescriptive, immoral, scandalous, or disparaging. Marks that are confusingly similar with a prior mark or marks comprised of government insignia are also barred.

- A registered mark confers a nationwide right of priority against any subsequent users.

- After being registered and in continuous use without challenge for five years and the filing of an affidavit to that effect, the mark becomes "incontestable." Incontestable status provides conclusive evidence of the mark's validity and the registrant's ownership and exclusive right to use the mark.

- Registration of a mark can be cancelled at any time, even if it is incontestable, if the mark has become generic, or if registration was procured by fraud.

- A mark that does not meet all of the requirements for registration on the Principal Register, but that is capable of distinguishing the applicant's goods or services, may be registered on the PTO's Supplemental Register.

- Registration on the Supplemental Register is not evidence of the mark's validity, but it enables the registrant to satisfy some foreign home registration requirements, creates federal jurisdiction for disputes involving the mark, and will establish priority if the mark ever becomes eligible for registration on the Principal Register.

- Trademark owners can cancel their trademark registration on their own accord or can loose their rights to the mark if it becomes generic or is abandoned.

- Abandonment is non-use with intent to not resume use. Non-use within the United States for three consecutive years is prima facie evidence of abandonment, but it may be rebutted by showing that the non-use was excusable and that the owner intended to resume the use within a reasonable time. Additionally, assignments in gross and naked licensing may lead to a finding of abandonment.

- Trademarks can be sold (assigned) and licensed, but both are subject to special rules because the mark also represents the goodwill associated with the mark.

- An assignment of the mark without the associated goodwill is an assignment in gross and is invalid (and may also lead to a finding of abandonment).

- Licensing of a mark is permitted only if the owner of the mark retains sufficient control over the quality and consistency of the goods or services provided. Otherwise the trademark owner may be found to have abandoned the mark through a naked license.

- Trademarks can provide valuable collateral for secured transactions, but perfecting a security interest in the mark without also perfecting an interest in the goodwill could lead to an invalid assignment in gross. Failure to also perfect an interest in a business's trademarks can greatly decrease the value of a secured party's collateral package.

Chapter Nine

Trademark Infringement and Dilution

Roadmap

After reading this chapter, you should understand:

- The elements of a trademark infringement action — (1) proof of a valid mark entitled to protection and (2) the defendant's use is likely to cause confusion.

- Proof of a valid mark — showing that (1) the owner of the mark used it commercially, (2) the owner is the senior user(i.e. has priority in the mark), and (3) the mark has distinctiveness (either inherent or acquired).

- Likelihood of confusion —

  - Junior marks and uses that are likely to cause confusion as to the source of goods or services will be found to infringe.

  - Junior marks and uses that are likely to deceive as to the affiliation with or sponsorship by the senior user will be found to infringe.

- Factors considered in determining confusion —

  - Similarity of the appearance, sound, and meaning of the marks;

  - Similarity in marketing and distribution of the products or services;

  - The sophistication of the relevant consumers;

  - The strength of the mark;

  - Similarity of relatedness of the goods or services;

  - Likelihood the owners will "bridge the gap" by expanding into the other user's market;

  - Recognition of the mark in the other user's geographic territory;

  - Intent to deceive or cause confusion;

  - Proof of actual confusion.

- The strength of the mark — both conceptual strength (in order of weakest to strongest: descriptive, suggestive, arbitrary, or fanciful) and commercial strength (market recognition and how strongly the goods or services are associated with the mark — *i.e.* the secondary meaning).

- Relatedness—similarity of the goods or services and their competitive proximity. The more similar the goods or services, the less similar the marks must be to support a finding of infringement.

- Reverse confusion—where goods bearing a weak senior mark are confused as originating from the owner of a stronger junior mark.

- General defenses—in addition to the defenses available to incontestable marks, defenses to infringement of unregistered and contestable marks include—showing that the plaintiff's mark is invalid because it is not used commercially, has subordinate priority to the defendant's, or is not distinctive.

- Defenses to infringement of incontestable marks—incontestable status provides conclusive evidence of the mark's validity and the registrant's ownership and exclusive right to use the mark. However, 15 U.S.C. § 1115 provides a list of defenses to infringement of incontestable (and other) marks including fraud in obtaining the registration, abandonment, misrepresentation of source, fair use, limited area and prior use defenses, violation of antitrust laws, functionality of the mark, and equitable defenses such as estoppel and unclean hands.

- Generic mark defense—a defendant may also show that an incontestable, contestable, or unregistered mark has become generic and is not entitled to protection because it has ceased to be a trademark.

- Remedies for trademark infringement—include injunctions, profits, damages, attorneys' fees, and destruction of the infringing articles.

- Injunctions—the most common remedy for trademark infringement. To receive an injunction, trademark owners must show (1) that they have suffered irreparable injury, (2) that money damages are inadequate, (3) a balance of the hardships favors granting the injunction, and (4) that the public interest would not be disserved.

- Monetary recovery—the plaintiff may be able to recover the infringer's profits, the plaintiff's actual damages—which may be increased up to threefold in the court's discretion. In exceptional cases the prevailing party is entitled to attorneys' fees.

- Additional damages—treble damages are awarded for intentional counterfeit marks or the plaintiff may choose to receive statutory damages in lieu of actual damages.

- Trademark dilution—occurs when a famous mark's distinctiveness (dilution by blurring) or reputation (dilution by tarnishment) is impaired by a junior mark even though there is no likelihood of confusion.

- Proving dilution—the plaintiff must show that (1) the mark is famous (widely recognized) and (2) the defendant's use caused a likelihood of dilution by blurring or tarnishment.

- Dilution defenses—fair use, including comparative advertising, criticism, and parody; news reporting and commentary; and other basic defenses such as statute of limitations and equitable defenses.

- Dilution remedies — the same as for trademark infringement. Injunctions are the most commonly awarded remedy.
- Cybersquatting — registering, using, or trafficking in domain names that are confusingly similar to or dilute a famous mark with the bad faith intent to profit.
- Gray market goods — foreign manufactured goods bearing a valid United States trademark that are imported without the consent of the trademark owner. Gray market goods give rise to claims for infringement and, if the goods are lower quality and the mark is famous, also for dilution.

Infringement is the unauthorized use of a mark that is likely to cause confusion among customers. Dilution is the impairment of a mark's distinctiveness or reputation where there is no likelihood of confusion.

1. Infringement

To prevail in an infringement action, the plaintiff must prove (1) that it has a valid mark entitled to protection and (2) that the defendant's use is likely to cause confusion.

2. Valid Trademark Entitled to Protection

In order to satisfy the first element of an infringement action, the plaintiff must show it has satisfied all the requirements for acquiring and maintaining a protectable mark or trade dress. Thus, the plaintiff must establish that it has used the mark commercially, prior to the defendant's use (i.e., that the plaintiff is the "senior user"), and that the mark is distinctive, either inherently or because it has acquired secondary meaning. Some cases turn on whether the senior user has abandoned the mark through non-use, an assignment in gross, or a "naked" license without adequate quality control. In other cases the issue is whether the mark has become generic.

Acquiring and maintaining a valid trademark is discussed in chapter 8.

3. Likelihood of Confusion

Once the plaintiff has established that his mark is valid and entitled to protection, it must also prove that the defendant's mark is likely to cause confusion among consumers. Likelihood of confusion is the basic test of infringement for both registered and unregistered marks under the Lanham Act, state trademark law, and common law.

15 U.S.C. § 1114(1), regarding infringement of registered marks, prohibits use that is "likely to cause confusion, or to cause mistake, or to deceive as to the affiliation, connection or association." Similarly, under 15 U.S.C. § 1125(a), regarding infringement of unregistered marks or trade dress, an action arises where a use is likely to cause confusion, mistake, or deception about the affiliation, connection, or association of people with another person, or as to the origin, sponsorship, or approval of goods, services, or commercial activities. Section 1052 prohibits registration of marks that so resemble an existing, registered mark, that its use is likely to cause confusion, mistake, or deception.

Most infringement cases concern whether consumers regarding the source or origin of goods or services. Generally, the test for likelihood of confusion is whether a reasonably prudent consumer in the marketplace is likely to be confused as to the origin of the good or service bearing one of the marks. As stated in *Estee Lauder v. The Gap*, 108 F.3d 1503, 1510 (2d Cir. 1997), "The issue of likelihood of confusion turns on whether numerous ordinary prudent purchasers are likely to be misled or confused as to the source of the product in question because of the entrance in the marketplace of defendant's mark." In *Estee Lauder*, the court held that Estee Lauder's mark "100%" for its skin moisturizer was not infringed by the Gap's "100% Body Care" mark because the marks and packaging were distinct, the companies' products were sold in different stores, and the price of one ounce the Gap's body products was about 5% of the cost of an ounce of Estee Lauder's products.

In most infringement cases, the issue is whether the junior user is "palming off" or passing off its products or services as those of the senior user. In *Beer Nuts, Inc. v. King Nut Co.*, 477 F.2d 326 (6th Cir. 1973), the court held that the defendant junior user had infringed on the senior user's mark "Beer Nuts" by using the name "Brew Nuts" along with a picture of a stein of beer on it's packaging. Pictures are treated just like words when examining likelihood of confusion. In that case, the picture of a stein of beer was equivalent to the word "beer."

Likelihood of confusion supporting an action for infringement also includes confusion regarding affiliation, connection, or sponsorship. "In order to be confused, a consumer need not believe that the owner of the mark actually produced the item and placed it on the market. The public's belief that the mark's owner sponsored or otherwise approved the use of the trademark satisfies the confusion requirement." In *Dallas Cowboys Cheerleaders, Inc. v. Pussycat Cinema, Ltd.*, 604 F.2d 200 (2d Cir. 1979), the plaintiffs, Dallas Cowboys' Cheerleaders, alleged their trademarked uniforms were infringed by the producers of the adult film Debbie Does Dallas, in which the "protagonist" was a Cheerleader for a Dallas-area football team, and wore an outfit similar to that used by the plaintiffs. The court held that although consumers were not likely to believe the plaintiff produced the film, they could be confused as to whether it sponsored or otherwise approved of it.

In *Champions Golf Club, Inc. v. The Champions Golf Club, Inc.*, 78 F.3d 1111 (6th Cir. 1996), the court noted the issue was not whether golfers would be confused regarding which course they were playing, but whether they would be confused about whether there was any affiliation between the two clubs. The issue in *Dreamwerks Prod. Group, Inc. v. SKG Studio*, 142 F.3d 1127, 1129 (9th Cir. 1998), was whether consumers would be confused that Dreamwerks' Star Trek conventions were sponsored by the movie studio DreamWorks. The court held that this confusion was possible.

Likelihood of confusion is not limited to confusion on the part of customers or potential customers; the issue is whether the confusion threatens the mark's goodwill—its commercial value. In *Beacon Mutual Insurance Co. v. OneBeacon Ins. Group*, 376 F.3d 8 (1st Cir. 2004) the parties had similar names and both companies sold worker's compensation insurance. The purchasers were not confused regarding the source of the products, but there was evidence of confusion among employers, employees, health care providers, attorneys for claimants, and courts that caused delays in processing claims and reimbursing providers, mistaken cancellations of policies, and violations of privacy rights. The court held that "the likelihood of confusion inquiry is not limited to actual or potential purchasers, but also includes others whose confusion threatens the trademark owner's commercial interest in its mark." In doing so it joined the courts holding that actual confusion is commercially relevant if the alleged infringer's use of the mark could inflict commercial injury by diverting sales, damaging goodwill, or causing the trademark holder to lose control over its reputation.

In extraordinary circumstances, the infringed party will be deemed responsible for the resulting confusion. For example, in *Sega Enterprises, Ltd. v. Accolade, Inc.*, 977 F.2d 1510 (9th Cir. 1992), the court held Sega responsible for another party's use of their trademark and reversed the preliminary injunction prohibiting its use. Sega designed its game system in such a manner that the console would not play any game without certain computer code that displayed Sega's trademark but served no other purpose. Accolade legally reverse engineered Sega's system and, in order to make their games compatible with the Sega console, included the required coding that displayed the Sega trademark. The court held that Sega, by knowingly including this non-functional limitation, was responsible for any confusion as to the producer of the games.

4. Likelihood of Confusion — Factors

"Likelihood of confusion" means confusion must be probable, not merely possible. Multiple factors are considered in making this determination:

(1) the similarity of the marks or trade dress;

(2) similarity in marketing methods and channels of distribution;

(3) characteristics of prospective purchasers and the degree of care they are likely to exercise in making purchasing decisions;

(4) strength of the senior user's mark or trade dress;

(5) competitive proximity, similarity or relatedness of the goods or services,

(6) where the goods or services are not competitive, the likelihood prospective purchasers would expect the senior or junior user to "bridge the gap" and expand into the other's market;

(7) where the goods or services are sold or provided in different geographic markets, the extent to which the senior user's mark is recognized in the junior user's territory;

(8) whether the junior user intended to deceive or cause confusion; and

(9) evidence of actual confusion.

See Restatement 3d. Unfair Competition §§ 21–23. The enumerated factors are guidelines to aid in evaluating of consumers' likely beliefs when facing competing designations in the market place. No single factor is determinative and not all enumerated factors are relevant in every case, although best practice is to address all of them in every case. In *Jada Toys, Inc. v. Mattell, Inc.*, 518 F.3d 628 (9th Cir. 2008), the court reversed summary judgment, holding that a reasonable tier of fact could conclude that the Jada Toys mark "Hot Rigs" for miniature toy vehicles was similar to Mattel's mark "Hot Wheels" for similar products. Even though the marks were subjectively dissimilar, the court found that evidence of actual confusion and the context in which the goods were sold was particularly relevant.

Thus, although courts may refer to the multi factor test as flexible or "pliant" and countenance against mechanical or rigid application, it is important to be thorough in applying it, examining each factor in turn, no matter what impression one has of the dispositive nature of any one factor in a particular case. The alternative is to invite award on appeal.

a. Similarity of the Marks

The multiple factor test was originally developed for use in cases where goods or services were not competing; in competitive good cases, the similarity of marks alone was dispositive. Now, most courts apply the multi factor test in all cases. Still, when the good or services of the defendant compete with those of the plaintiff, the similarity of the marks or trade dress is usually the most important factor in determining likelihood of confusion. In *Kos Pharms., Inc. v. Andrx Corp.*, 369 F.3d 700 (3d Cir. 2004), the owner of the mark "Advicor" for an anticholesterol drug brought an action for infringement against a competitor that used the mark "Altocor" on a different anticholesterol drug. The district court denied plaintiff's motion for a preliminary injunction, and the Third Circuit reversed. The appellate court found that the similarity of the marks was apparent "on their face." Both were seven-letter, three-syllable words that begin and end with the same letters and the same sounds." The court noted that similarity was the most important factor, but examined all of the likelihood of confusion factors in rendering its decision and did not rely upon this single factor.

Similarity is determined by appearance, sound and meaning of the marks or trade dress when considered in their entirety as they appear in the marketplace. This test is also known as the "sight, sound, and meaning trilogy." Under this test, the inquiry is whether the two marks are "sufficiently similar" that potential purchasers or other relevant persons are likely to be confused as to their source, origin, association or sponsorship. Thus, the determination should be made based on the overall impressions created by the mark, and not on a comparison of individual features. As the court stated in *Sun-Fun Products, Inc. v. Suntan Research & Development Inc.*, 656 F.2d 186, 189 (5th Cir. 1981), the "analysis begins with the well-established proposition that similarity of design stems from the overall impression conveyed by the mark and not a dissection of individual features." Also, the comparison of the marks should not be in the abstract but should be based on how they are encountered in the marketplace. In *Abercrombie & Fitch Co. v. Moose Creek, Inc.*, 486 F.3d 629, 636 (9th Cir. 2007), the district court compared the plaintiff's and the defendant's moose shaped logos used with apparel and determined that the differences outweighed the similarities and denied the plaintiff's motion for summary judgment. The Ninth Circuit reversed. It noted the lower court had compared catalog renderings and photographs of the logos, rather than viewing the marks as they appeared in the market place, which was embroidered on clothing. When the embroidered logos were compared in this context, many dissimilarities cited by the district court were nonexistent, and others were not noticeable, or did not affect the overall impression created by the marks.

i. Appearance

Determining similarity of appearance is essentially a "subjective eyeball test." In *Exxon Corp. v. Texas Motor Exchange of Houston, Inc.*, 628 F.2d 500 (5th Cir. 1980), the court applied the "eyeball test" to plaintiff's mark "Exxon" and the defendant's "Tex-On" mark, observing that "Defendant's mark Tex-On ... is quite different from plaintiff's use of the trademark EXXON." With regard to the defendant's other mark, "Texon," the court found that visual inspection revealed a likely confusing similarity to the plaintiff's mark where "Texon is printed in red with all block letters on a white background. The street address is printed in blue. EXXON is printed in red with all block letters on a white background. It is underlined with a blue bar."

ii. Sound

Marks may sound similar even though they look different or are spelled differently. Similarity in the way two marks sound is an especially significant factor with regard to goods that consumers must commonly ask to purchase, such as pharmaceuticals or goods purchased over the phone, as opposed to goods they purchase off the shelf. For example,, in *Aveda Corp. v. Evita Marketing, Inc.*, 706 F. Supp. 1419 (D.Minn. 1989) the court found the terms "Aveda" and "Avita," both used for hair care products, were phonetically similar based on the affidavit of an English and linguistics professor discussing principles of English pronunciation of the letters "t" "d" "e" and "i", as well as a market research survey.

By contrast, in *W.L. Gore & Associates v. Johnson & Johnson*, 882 F. Supp. 1454, 1458 (D.Del. 1995), the court determined the marks "Glide" and "Easy Slide," both used for dental floss, were not phonetically similar ... Easy Slide creates a different sound. Easy Slide has three syllables or pauses and Glide has only one syllable—one pause. The sound of the first letter in the rhyming words enhances the aural difference: Slide has a soft "s" sound and Glide has a hard "g" sound. The aural similarities are further attenuated when J & J's product is called by its complete name, "Johnson & Johnson 'Easy Slide.'"

iii. Meaning

Marks may also create such a similar mental impression that consumer confusion is likely. For example, in *Beer Nuts, Inc. v. King Nut Co.*, 477 F.2d 326, 329 (6th Cir. 1973), the court held "Brew Nuts" was confusingly similar to "Beer Nuts" particularly where the Brew Nuts package featured a stein of beer. On the other hand, in *Champagne Louis Roederer, S.A. v. Delicato Vineyards*, 148 F.3d 1373, 1375 (Fed. Cir. 1998), the court determined that the term "Cristal" for champagne and "Cristal Creek" for wine were not similar, because "that the word marks 'CRISTAL' and 'CRISTAL CREEK' evoked very different images in the minds of relevant consumers: while the former suggested the clarity of the wine within the bottle or the glass of which the bottle itself was made, the latter suggested 'a very clear (and hence probably remote from civilization) creek or stream.'"

b. Similarity in Marketing Methods and Channels of Distribution

Similarities in how goods or services are marketed and sold will also contribute to likelihood of confusion. This is a fact intensive inquiry that requires courts to examine the parties' marketing and sales methods. In *Checkpoint Systems, Inc. v. Check Point Software Technologies, Inc.*, 269 F.3d 270, 289 (3d Cir. 2001), a provider of security products and services for businesses to prevent shoplifting under trademark "Checkpoint," brought a trademark infringement action against a provider of computer network security products and services under trademarks "CHECKPOINT" "CheckPoint" and "Check Point." In holding there was not likelihood of confusion among prospective purchases, the court noted, inter alia, that the products were not marketed or sold through the same channels: "Checkpoint Systems advertises in trade shows and trade publications that are marketed to physical and retail security specialists. Check Point Software advertises in publications and at trade shows that are marketed to computer information specialists. [Also] Check Point Software's products are only sold to consumers through its 'specialized value added resellers.' These 'resellers' do not sell physical article security systems."

In *Estee Lauder Inc. v. The Gap, Inc.*, 108 F.3d 1503, 1507–08 (2d Cir. 1997), the district court noted the parties marketed their skin care products very differently:

- Gap's products were sold only in Gap's Old Navy stores which, with rare exceptions, sell nothing other than merchandise sold under the Old Navy name.

- Lauder sold only through the prestige retail channel: upscale department stores and the like.

- The difference in the ambiance between the stores that handle Lauder's product and Old Navy stores was dramatic.

- Lauder limited in distribution to outlets offering upscale images with a "polished" ambiance, Old Navy pursued a very different look and feel, featuring merchandise on industrial shelving and in other "funky" ways in stores where "loud modern rock music" is played, the floors are uncarpeted, and sales personnel dress informally—many in the New York store even wear headsets.

- No one knowledgeable about the sort of places in which Lauder sells its upscale products would be likely to think that the very same products would be available in an Old Navy store.

Nevertheless the district court held the Gap's mark "100% Body Care" infringed on Estee Lauder's mark "100%" for skin care products based on the prominent use of 100% by both parties in connection with similar products. The Second Circuit reversed, noting that although the products were similar, the remaining factors, specifically the disparity in the channels of distribution demonstrated that confusion among prospective purchasers was not probable.

In contrast, in *Boston Athletic Association v. Sullivan*, 867 F.2d 22, 30 (1st Cir. 1989), the court held the manufacturer of T-shirts with a Boston Marathon logo was liable for infringement, noting that "[t]he parties sell their shirts predominantly in Boston-area retail shops, at the exposition, and along the race course. Sales are largely seasonal, centering on the race date. The parties use the same general method of advertising: displays in store windows, in booths at the exposition, and along the race course."

c. Characteristics of Prospective Purchasers and the Degree of Care They Are Likely to Exercise in Making Purchasing Decisions

"Sophisticated" consumers are presumed to exercise greater care in making purchases than are "ordinary" consumers. Thus, a finding that the target consumers are particularly sophisticated will compel greater judicial tolerance of similarities between two marks. Consumer sophistication (or lack thereof) may be established by direct evidence, expert opinions, or survey evidence. In some cases, the court will emphasize the type of product at issue, and its price.

In *Star Industries, Inc. v. Bacardi & Co. Ltd.*, 412 F.3d 373 (2d Cir. 2005), the plaintiff Star Industries, maker of "Georgi" brand vodka, had developed an orange-flavored vodka marked "Ge0rgi," with an elongated, stylized "O." Star alleged that the stylized "O" on the label of Bacardi's "Bacardi O" line of orange-flavored rum infringed upon its mark, but the court disagreed. Given the relative weakness of the plaintiff's mark, the court concluded that "[u]nhurried consumers in a relaxed environment of the liquor store, making decisions about $12 to $24 purchases, may be expected to exhibit sufficient sophistication to distinguish between Star's and Bacardi's products, which are differently labeled." By contrast, in *Patsy's Brand, Inc. v. I.O.B. Realty, Inc.*, 317 F.3d 209, 219 (2d Cir. 2003), the issue was likelihood of confusion among purchasers of prepared pasta sauces with similar marks sold in and around New York City. The defendant introduced expert testimony that New Yorkers are "savvy and knowledgeable about restaurants and food." However, the Second Circuit held this did not outweigh the district court's "common sense assessment" that "pasta shoppers are ordinary consumers of inexpensive retail products, and would likely be confused by similar labels bearing similar marks."

Professional purchasers and purchasers of expensive products or services are often thought to be more discerning and less easily confused than retail purchasers of lower priced goods or services. For example, in *Arrow Fastener Co., Inc. v. Stanley Works*, 59 F.3d 384 (2d Cir. 1995), the court considered whether Stanley's "T50" series marks used for its high-power staple guns was confusingly similar to Arrow's registered trademark "T-50" for one of its own staple guns. The court held that it was not, given that purchasers of expensive pneumatic staplers used in the construction trades were sophisticated and not likely to be confused by similarity in the marks.

A consumer's sophistication does not always indicated the unlikelihood of confusion, however. For example, in *Wincharger Corp. v. Rinco, Inc.*, 297 F.2d 261 (C.C.P.A. 1962), the court considered whether applicant Rinco's "Rinco" mark, for use on precision electrical testing equipment, was confusingly similar to Wincharger's registered "Winco" mark for use on electrical generators. The court held that it was, reasoning that, while electrical technicians are "a discriminating group of people ... [b]eing skilled in their own art does not necessarily preclude their mistaking one trademark for another." Other courts have even held that sophisticated purchasers would be more likely to mistakenly infer an association between users based on the similarity of their marks. For example, in *Lois Sportswear, U.S.A., Inc. v. Levi Strauss & Co.*, 799 F.2d 867 (2d Cir. 1986), the court considered whether the "back-pocket stitching pattern" on Lois Sportswear's jeans was confusingly similar to the stitching pattern in which Levi Strauss held an incontestable trademark. Despite general agreement amongst the parties that "the typical buyer of 'designer' jeans is sophisticated with respect to jeans buying," the court held that "it is a sophisticated jeans consumer who is most likely to assume that the presence of appellee's trademark stitching pattern on appellants' jeans indicates some sort of association" between Levi Strauss and Lois, since only sophisticated consumers would even notice the stitching, and hence their similarity. However, the court also noted that "[i]t is quite possible of course to draw the opposite inference (no confusion) from the fact that these buyers are willing to pay almost $100 for a pair of jeans" in 1986.

d. Strength of Mark or Trade Dress

Stronger marks receive greater protection. *A & H Sportswear, Inc. v. Victoria's Secret Stores, Inc.*, 237 F.3d 198, 221 (3d Cir. 2000). For infringement purposes, "strength" has two dimensions: (1) "conceptual strength"—where the mark falls on the spectrum between generic and fanciful, and (2) "commercial strength"—the extent to which the mark is recognized and valued in the marketplace.

i. Conceptual Strength

In determining a mark's conceptual strength, the first step is to classify the mark as "descriptive" or "suggestive, arbitrary, or fanciful." Descriptive marks identify the ingredients, qualities or characteristics of the product or service, e.g., "Security Center." They are not inherently distinctive, and are protectable only if they have acquired secondary meaning. Suggestive, arbitrary or fanciful marks, on the other hand, are inherently distinctive, and do not require secondary meaning to be protected, although secondary meaning is relevant in determining their commercial strength.

A "descriptive" mark simply describes some characteristic or function of the goods or services to which they refer. For example, in *H-D Michigan, Inc. v. Top Quality Service, Inc.*, 496 F.3d 755 (7th Cir. 2007), the court considered whether a motorcycle club's trademarks "Hog" and "H.O.G." were generic or descriptive. The court held that, although the marks would be generic in reference to motorcycles, H-D's use of the marks—to describe members of the club who enjoy motorcycles—was descriptive. Unlike generic marks, descriptive marks can qualify for trademark protection provided that they have acquired secondary meaning, as where an otherwise descriptive product name comes to be uniquely associated with the original seller.

Suggestive marks are not directly descriptive, but rather stand an inferential step away from the goods, evoking their characteristics and qualities by provoking the consumer's imagination. In *Tumblebus Inc. v. Cranmer*, 399 F.3d 754 (6th Cir. 2005), the court analyzed the degree of distinctiveness in the mark "Tumblebus" used to market an on-site gymnastics center housed in a converted bus. Although elements of the mark were descriptive, since the center was housed in an actual "bus" and what the children did there could be described as "tumbling," the court held that the mark was suggestive. The court noted that the term "tumble" alone was insufficient to distinguish between the gymnastics taught on the bus and, "a mobile laundry service using tumble-dryers," such that the Tumblebus was consistently described in its advertisements as a "mobile gym on wheels" and a "bus filled with fun equipment bringing fitness to children at daycares, elementary and private schools." That demonstrated the sort of inferential step, requiring "the observer or listener to use imagination and perception to determine the nature of the goods," which qualifies a mark as suggestive.

Within the general category of suggestive marks, a particular mark may be relatively conceptually strong or weak. For example, in *Renaissance Greeting Cards, Inc. v. Dollar Tree Stores, Inc.*, 227 Fed. Appx. 239 (4th Cir. 2007), having concluded that the mark "Renaissance" for greeting cards was suggestive, the court analyzed the strength of the mark and concluded that it was relatively weak. Particularly persuasive to the court was that there were over 600 state and federally registered marks which incorporated the word renaissance, twenty three of which were in the same class of products.

Aside from frequency of usage in a particular category of goods, a mark's relative strength may be substantially weakened where it is self-laudatory. For example, in *A & H Sportswear, Inc. v. Victoria's Secret Stores, Inc.*, 237 F.3d 198 (3d Cir. 2000), the makers of a swimsuit sold under the trademark "Miraclesuit" brought a claim against Victoria's Secret, which had adopted the mark "Miracle Bra" for its product. The court held that the "Miraclesuit" mark was weakly suggestive—suggestive because both "miracle" and "suit" indirectly described some aspect of the bathing suit, and weak because of the wide use of the laudatory term "miracle" to describe other products. As the court concluded, "The short of it is that, whatever category of distinctiveness into which the mark falls, the multiple uses of MIRACLE in other markets is relevant to a determination of A & H's mark's strength." Another court was of similar opinion in *Stern's Miracle-Gro Products, Inc. v. Shark Products, Inc.*, 823 F. Supp. 1077 (S.D.N.Y. 1993). In that case, the court held that the mark "Miracle-Gro" for fertilizers was suggestive, but "not strongly" so.

Arbitrary or fanciful marks are accorded the highest degree of trademark protection, Although "an arbitrary mark may be classified as weak where there has been extensive third party use of similar marks on similar goods." In *Aber-*

crombie and Fitch Co. v. Moose Creek, Inc., previously discussed, Abercrombie alleged a likelihood of confusion between the trademarked moose emblem embroidered on its line of golf shirts and a similar moose emblem emblazoned on some of Moose Creek's golf shirts. Although the court determined that Abercrombie's moose logo was arbitrary—having nothing to do with golf shirts—it concluded that the mark was nevertheless weak in light of the "crowded field" of moose-branded apparel. The court was particularly persuaded by the fact that "a search for the term 'moose' on the Yahoo Shopping Internet web page under the category 'clothing'… yielded 4,051 results, each of which represents a distinct article of clothing."

ii. Commercial Strength

Commercial strength measures the marketplace recognition of the mark. The analysis used to determine commercial strength is essentially the same as the test for secondary meaning, although the issue is not whether the mark is entitled to protection, but how much protection it is entitled to. The senior user must show that "in the minds of the public, the primary significance of a product feature or term is to identify the source of the product rather than the product itself." *Stern's Miracle-Gro Products, Inc. v. Shark Products, Inc.*, 823 F. Supp. 1077, 1084 (S.D.N.Y. 1993). Common factors demonstrating meaning are (1) advertising expenditures, (2) consumer studies, (3) sales success, (4) unsolicited media coverage, (5) attempts at plagiarizing the mark, and (6) the length and exclusivity of the mark's use. In *Stern's Miracle-Gro*, the court determined "Miracle-Gro" was a strong mark even though it was "not strongly suggestive" based on compelling evidence of powerful secondary meaning.

> The Miracle-Gro mark has been exclusively used by Stern's for over 41 years.… During this period, the registered Miracle-Gro trademark has been widely featured in advertising, promotional and informational materials.… Moreover, in the past few years, Stern's also has been involved in various programs to serve the community, which have been publicized in the media. As a result of its forty-one years of effort, Stern's Miracle-Gro is now the largest selling brand of water soluble plant foods for lawn and garden use in the United States.… Miracle-Gro plant food is nationally distributed and sold in more than 40,000 retail stores in the United States, including K-Mart, Walmart, *sic*, Home Depot, and other major retailers.… Over twenty million containers of Miracle-Gro plant food, in various sizes, were sold in 1991.… This commercial success has been accompanied by signifi-

cant unsolicited media coverage.... Many gardeners listed in the Guinness Book of World Records attribute their success to Miracle-Gro and the product has been referred to in numerous news accounts.... Moreover, other companies have used the Miracle-Gro product in advertisements to analogize the characteristics of the plant food to its own product.

e. Direct Confusion

Direct confusion can result when a junior user adopts a mark similar or identical to that already claimed by a senior user, resulting in confusion among consumers as to either the origin of the goods or services sold under both marks or the relationship between the sellers. "The essence of a direct confusion claim is that a junior user of a mark attempts to free-ride on the reputation and goodwill of the senior user by adopting a similar or identical mark." *Lazzaroni USA Corp. v. Steiner Foods*, Slip Copy, 2006 U.S. Dist. Lexis 20962, 2006 WL 932345 (D.N.J.). At issue in *Lazzaroni* was the use of the surname of the family that had invented amaretti macaroons and sold them under the "Lazzaroni" and "Amaretti di Saronno" marks until 1984, when both the marks and the recipe were sold. In 2004, when the Lazzaroni family resumed selling "Amaretti di Saronno" cookies under their name, the current owners of the trademarks brought suit. Despite the defendant's denials, the court discerned a bald attempt to trade on their assignee's goodwill in the "family history" described on the defendant's packaging. That narrative read in part:

> Amaretti cookies were created by the Lazzaroni family way back in the Eighteenth century to celebrate the visit of the beloved Cardinal of Milan to the town of Saronno [where] they originated the renowned Amaretti di Saronno....

The court held that the proof of the defendant's attempted usurpation of goodwill, and consequent likelihood of confusion, were sufficient to justify a preliminary injunction against further use of the marks by the defendant.

The stronger the plaintiff's mark, the more likely that plaintiff is to prevail on a claim of direct confusion. This is because a claim that the defendant is trading on the plaintiff's goodwill is more plausible when the plaintiff's mark is abounding in goodwill and also because if consumer's are not aware of the plaintiff's mark, they are not likely to confuse it with the defendant's. For example, in *In-N-Out Burgers v. Chadders Restaurant*, Slip Copy, 2007 U.S. Dist. Lexis 47732, 2007 WL 1983813 (D.Utah), In-N-Out claimed that Chadders, a fast food restaurant in Utah, a state where In-N-Out has no presence, was infringing upon its registered trademarks "Protein® Style Burger, Animal® Style

Burger, 3 x 3® Burger, 4 x 4® Burger and Double Double®." Amongst other proofs, In-N-Out's general counsel testified that in response to complaints regarding Chadders from In-N-Out customers, he "traveled to Chadders Restaurant, viewed the premises and operations and ordered a meal not listed on its menu. He requested an 'Animal Style Double Double with Animal fries,' and his order was filled." The court had no difficulty finding that Chadder's use of the plaintiff's marks was likely to cause direct confusion, and enjoining further use of those marks.

By contrast, For example, in *MNI Management, Inc. v. Wine King, LLC*, 542 F. Supp. 2d 389, (D.N.J. 2008), the plaintiff operated a small chain of party stores under the name "Wine King," and claimed that defendant liquor store's use of the service mark "Wine King," though nearly 75 miles away, threatened to cause confusion among consumers. However, the court held the plaintiff was unable to demonstrate that its customer base and reputation either had expanded or would expand into the defendant's area. Without any risk that the defendant's could, let alone the risk that they would, trade on plaintiff's good will, there could not be any direct confusion between the marks.

f. Reverse Confusion

Reverse confusion claims focus on the danger that consumers will identify the senior user's goods or services as originating with the junior user, who's mark is more familiar. "The ultimate question in a reverse confusion claim is whether there is a likelihood of consumer confusion as to the source or sponsorship of a product." *A & H Sportswear, Inc. v. Victoria's Secret Stores, Inc.*, 237 F.3d 198 (3d Cir. 2000). Reverse confusion is more likely where the plaintiff's senior mark is commercially weak relative to the defendant's strong junior mark. For example, in *A & H Sportswear, Inc. v. Victoria's Secret Stores, Inc.*, 237 F.3d 198 (3d Cir. 2000), the plaintiff claimed that Victoria Secret's use of the mark "Miracle Bra" was likely to cause reverse confusion with the much less heavily promoted "Miraclesuit" mark under which the plaintiff sold swimsuits.

The injury alleged by plaintiffs in cases of reverse confusion is often different than the siphoning-off of good will and lost profits at issue in direct confusion cases. For example, in *Dreamwerks Production Group, Inc. v. SKG Studio*, 142 F.3d 1127 (9th Cir. 1998), the plaintiff was a sci-fi convention organizer operating under the mark "Dreamwerks" that alleged reverse confusion as a consequence of the adoption of the trademark "DreamWorks SKG" by a major film-production company. In that case, the plaintiff was concerned that it would "suffer ill will when people buy tickets under the misimpression that they are dealing with DreamWorks rather than Dreamwerks" or that its efforts to expand into related entertainment fields would be "foreclosed if Dream-Works gets there first." Most importantly, however, reverse confusion robs the senior user of control over its own trademark, as in *Dreamwerks*, where one of the plaintiff's major concerns was that "whatever goodwill it has built now rests in the hands of DreamWorks; if the latter should take a major misstep and tarnish its reputation with the public, Dreamwerks too would be pulled down."

In a reverse confusion case, courts apply the same factors that are relevant to direct confusion, although often with certain modifications or different weights accorded to each. For example, in *Attrezzi, LLC v. Maytag Corp.*, 436 F.3d 32 (1st Cir. 2006), the plaintiff held a state-registered trademark in the name "Attrezzi" for its retail business in "in fine kitchen products and services." When Maytag adopted the mark "Attrezzi" for use on a line of dishwashers, the plaintiff alleged a likelihood of reverse confusion, and the court held that "the source or extent of [confusion], the requirement of likely confusion is common both to the ordinary 'forward' [direct] confusion claim and the 're-verse' confusion variant urged in this case." The court proceeded to apply each factor of the First Circuit's test for confusion in almost the same manner as appropriate for a case of direct confusion, but noted that with regard to the strength of the plaintiff's mark, "the relatively greater strength of a junior user like Maytag may hurt, rather than help, its defense." With regard to that factor, the court concluded that the Maytag's vastly superior commercial strength resulted in an increased threat to the plaintiff from its adoption of an identical trademark for kitchenware-related goods, and justified a grant of broad injunctive relief to the plaintiff.

A substantial disparity between the commercial strengths of the marks at issue is not, however, a prerequisite to relief from infringement based on reverse confusion. In *A & H Sportswear v. Victoria's Secret*, discussed above, the district court had refused to entertain the plaintiff's reverse infringement claim on the grounds that its mark lacked sufficient "economic disparity" relative to Victoria's Secret's mark. The Third Circuit reversed, holding that economic disparity between the senior and junior user is merely a factor in evaluating a mark's commercial strength—it is not a threshold requirement.

g. Competitive Proximity, Similarity or "Relatedness"

Competitive proximity or similarity of the goods or services is a factor that bears directly on the degree of similarity needed to prove likelihood of confusion. In other words, the more similar the goods or services, the less similar the marks must be to support a finding likelihood of confusion. By the same token, where goods or services are different in nature or function, there must be a greater degree of similarity to cause a likelihood of confusion.

For example, in *Nautilus Group, Inc. v. ICON Health and Fitness, Inc.*, 372 F.3d 1330 (Fed. Cir. 2004), Nautilus and ICON, direct competitors in the home exercise equipment market, produced "essentially identical" resistance training systems featuring bendable rods. Nautilus's system was called "Bowflex" and ICON's was called "Crossbow." The district court found the marks were "somewhat similar" but not "necessarily confusing." But because it found that the products were virtually interchangeable, the court held that Nautilus prevailed on both factors—similarity of the marks and competitive proximity of the goods. The Federal Circuit affirmed, stating these two factors are often interdependent and that "the more closely related the goods are, the more likely consumers will be confused by similar marks."

Conversely, in *Checkpoint Systems, Inc. v. Check Point Software Technologies, Inc.*, 269 F.3d 270 (3d Cir. 2001), the plaintiff Checkpoint Systems specialized in products designed to prevent retail shoplifting by "tracking the physical location of goods," while the defendant, Check Point Software, marketed computer firewall software. Because neither parties' product could perform remotely the same function as the other's, the court concluded the products were neither similar nor related. Thus, even though the parties' marks were very similar, the court held there was no likelihood of confusion.

Even where goods are dissimilar in function, however, they may be otherwise related making confusion more likely. For example, in *International Kennel Club, Inc. v. Mighty Star, Inc.*, 846 F.2d 1079 (7th Cir. 1988), the plaintiff used its "International Kennel Club" mark was used in sponsoring dog shows, while the defendant used the "International Kennel Club" mark on dog toys. Because it found that buyers and users of each parties' goods were likely to encounter each other's goods, the court found that this created in their minds an assumption of common source, affiliation, or sponsorship. The defendant's identical mark was held to have infringed.

h. "Bridging the Gap"

Even if their products or services are not presently competitive, the senior or junior user may still intend to "bridge the gap" and expand into the other's market. Some courts will not find a likelihood of confusion unless such expansion is actually anticipated by consumers. For example, in *Lang v. Retirement Living Publishing Co., Inc.*, 949 F.2d 576 (2d Cir. 1991), the publisher of self-help books and tapes under the name "New Choices Press," brought a trade name infringement action against a magazine publisher that used name "New

Choices for the Best Years" for its magazine on retirement living. Although the plaintiff alleged an intent to expand into the defendant's market, the court noted that the plaintiff "provided no evidence that prospective purchasers would assume that New Choices Press would publish a magazine or other publication aimed at older adults." The court held the plaintiff's mere intent to expand, without evidence that consumers shared its anticipation, was insufficient to prove a likelihood of confusion. As explained by the court in *Buca, Inc. v. Gambucci's, Inc.*, 18 F. Supp. 2d 1193, 1210 (D.Kan. 1998), "the intent of the prior user to expand or its activities in preparation to do so, unless known by prospective purchasers, does not affect the likelihood of confusion."

However other courts will weigh one user's unanticipated intent to expand into the other's market as an independent factor. For example, in *Wendt v. Host International*, 125 F.3d 806 (9th Cir. 1997), the actors who played the characters Cliff and Norm on the television series "Cheers" brought actions for trademark infringement against the creator of animatronic robots based on their likenesses and placed in airport bars modeled on the Cheers set. John Ratzenberger, the actor who played Norm, offered evidence that "he would like to appear in advertisements for beer and has declined offers from small breweries in order to be available to a large brewery." The court held "[t]his factor therefore weighs in [the actors'] favor as the potential exists that in the future Ratzenberger's endorsement of other beers would be confused with his alleged endorsement of the beers sold at Host's bars."

i. Where the Goods or Services are Sold or Provided in Different Geographic Markets, the Extent to Which the Senior User's Mark Is Recognized in the Junior User's Territory

Registration of a trademark on the PTO's principal register is constructive notice of the registrant's claim of ownership and affords nationwide protection to registered marks, regardless of the areas in which the registrant actually uses the mark registered mark. 15 U.S.C. § 1072. Despite constructive notice, however, whether the senior user's mark is used or recognized in the junior user's territory is a factor in determining likelihood of confusion. For example, in *Dawn Donut Co. v. Hart's Food Stores, Inc.*, 267 F.2d 358 (2d Cir. 1959), the registrant produced and distributed wholesale donut and cake mixes under the registered mark "Dawn," while the defendant sold baked goods under the mark "Dawn" only within 45 miles of Rochester, New York, and without actual knowledge of the plaintiff's mark. Because the defendant's area of use was at its greatest extent 60 miles from any area in which the plaintiff used it's mark, the court held that "no likelihood of public confusion arises from the concurrent use of the mark ... in separate trading areas, and because there is no present likelihood that plaintiff will expand its retail use of the mark into defendant's market area, plaintiff is not now entitled to any relief ..." The *Dawn Donut* court made clear, however, that its holding did not give the junior users any permanent right to use the mark in its trading area. Because of the constructive notice of the registrant's ownership of the "Dawn" mark under the Lanham act, the plaintiff would be entitled to injunctive relief against the defendant's use of its mark should it expand, or should it be able to prove an intent to expand, its retail activities into the defendant's area at any time.

j. Intent — Whether the Junior User Intended to Deceive or Cause Confusion

Evidence that the junior user adopted its mark with the intent to cause confusion or deceive is another factor pointing to the likelihood of confusion. Such intent demonstrates the junior user's true opinion that confusion is likely. For example, in *Daddy's Junky Music Stores, Inc. v. Big Daddy's Family Music Center*, 109 F.3d 275, (6th Cir. 1997), the plaintiff operated a chain of used instrument stores in Ohio and contiguous states under the registered mark "Daddy's Junky Music Store," when the defendant opened a small retail instrument store in Delaware, Ohio, under the name "Big Daddy's Family Music Center." The district court dismissed the plaintiff's claim of infringement, finding consumer confusion unlikely, but the Sixth Circuit reversed, holding the trial court failed to consider circumstantial evidence of the defendant's intent to copy plaintiff's mark. The appellate court stated: "Intent is relevant because purposeful copying indicates that the alleged infringer, who has at least as much knowledge as the trier of fact regarding the likelihood of confusion, believes that his copying may divert some business from the senior user."

In *Kemp v. Bumble Bee Seafoods, Inc.*, 398 F.3d 1049 (8th Cir. 2005), Louis E. Kemp sold his seafood business to Oscar Meyer Foods Corporation, who sold it to Tyson Foods, Inc., who sold it to Bumble Bee. Bumble Bee and its predecessors spent $49 million promoting the mark "Louis Kemp" for use with seafood products and the mark developed significant recognition. Mr. Kemp then started a company that developed and sold precooked wild rice products. He marketed these products under the mark "Louis Kemp," explaining to a prospective business partner: "We could use the 'Louis Kemp' brand name where we can and want to, to take advantage of the considerable equity it possesses." The district court dismissed Bumble Bee's infringement claim, in part because it found that Mr. Kemp did not intend to trade on the goodwill Bumble Bee had built up in the "Louis Kemp" mark. The Eighth Circuit reversed, holding that, despite evidence that Mr. Kemp believed he had the contractual right to use the mark in connection with non-seafood products:

> His subjective opinions regarding his contract rights … in no way diminish the effect of his statement. He openly admitted his intention to market his products to take advantage of the considerable equity of the Oscar Meyer and Tyson investments. The only way to take advantage of this brand equity is to cause consumers to mistakenly believe there is, at a minimum, an association between the sources of the products.

Alleged infringers rarely admit, as did Mr. Kemp, their intent to confuse consumers or capitalize on the goodwill of another's mark. That intent is more often demonstrated by evidence that the defendant knew of plaintiff's prior use of the mark, and the subsequent inference that similarities between the senior and junior marks were the result of intentional copying. A defendant's knowledge of the plaintiff's prior use is often established by proof of the plaintiff's extensive advertising and long-term use of the protected mark. For example, in *Wynn Oil Co. v. American Way Service Corp.*, 943 F.2d 595 (6th Cir. 1991), the plaintiff had marketed a line of car-care products through car dealerships under the marks "Wynn's X-Tend" and "X-Tend" since the early 1970s. The plaintiff also promoted it's "X-Tend" mark on posters, banners, flags, ink pens, thermos jugs, jackets, shirts, and other clothing. When the defendant began marketing its own extended warranty program under the mark "The American Way X-TEND," the plaintiff claimed infringement. The defendant denied that he had copied, or even known of, the plaintiff's mark. However, the court held evidence that the "X-Tend" mark for care car products was "long in use … and widely advertised," in combination with proof that the defendant had "extremely close, even familial relationships with all car dealers in Michigan and his intimate knowledge of all aspects of their business" supported a finding of intentional infringement.

A defendant's intentional blindness regarding the existence of a prior mark can also support a finding of intent to confuse. *In Frehling Enterprises, Inc. v. International Select Group, Inc.*, 192 F.3d 1330 (11th Cir. 1999), the plaintiff, Frehling, had used the mark "Oggetti" (meaning "object" in Italian) in his decorative furniture business since 1975, and registered the mark in 1985. The defendant, ISG, had adopted the mark "Bell' Oggetti" ("beautiful object") for its line of prefabricated furniture in 1989, but did not conduct a trademark search before attempting to register its mark and continued to use the mark after registrations was refused because there was a potential for likelihood of confusion with Frehling's mark. The Eleventh Circuit held that "ISG's behavior displays an improper intent through intentional blindness and, given the demonstrated prevalence of this improper intent, we accordingly conclude that this factor weighs substantially in Frehling's favor" and reversed the district court's grant of summary judgment dismissing Frehling's complaint.

k. Actual Confusion

Evidence of actual confusion is highly probative in proving likelihood of confusion. For example, in *Lone Star Steakhouse & Saloon, Inc. v. Alpha of Virginia, Inc.*, 43 F.3d 922 (4th Cir 1995), the plaintiff alleged that its Lone Star trademark was infringed by the defendant's mark, "Lone Star Grill." Particularly persuasive to the court was evidence that:

> [N]umerous customers visiting the Lone Star Steakhouse restaurants presented coupons from Alpha's Lone Star Grill in Arlington, mistakenly believing that the restaurants were connected. Similarly, people telephoned the Lone Star Steakhouse restaurants in Centreville and Herndon to inquire about the Lone Star Grill in Arlington or to ask about whether the Centreville and Herndon restaurants were accepting the coupons from the Arlington restaurant. Alpha's bartenders and floor managers also testified that they had encountered instances of actual confusion among customers.

The district court entered a permanent injunction in favor of the plaintiff, which the Fourth Circuit affirmed, noting such evidence of actual confusion "is entitled to substantial weight as it provides the most compelling evidence of likelihood of confusion."

On the other hand, where there has been long-term use of the two marks in the same geographic area, an absence of actual confusion may indicate that confusion is unlikely. For example, in *Amstar Corp. v. Domino's Pizza, Inc.*, 615 F.2d 252 (5th Cir. 1980) the court held that use of the mark "Domino's Pizza" in connection with the sale of delivered pizza did not create likelihood of confusion in connection with plaintiff's use of trademark "Domino" for sugar sold in grocery stores, and used in individual packets in restaurants. Where the only evidence of actual confusion "amounted to two verbal inquiries as to whether 'Domino's Pizza' was related to 'Domino' sugar, and one misaddressed letter," the court held that "the fact that only three instances of actual confusion were found after nearly fifteen years of extensive concurrent sales under the parties' respective marks raises a presumption against likelihood of confusion in the future."

5. Defenses to Infringement Actions

a. Unregistered and Contestable Marks

Rights in trademark are acquired by use, not registration. However, registration has advantages in trademark infringement actions. A contestable mark is one that has been registered, but for less than five years and has, thus, not become uncontestable. Registration of a mark on the Principal Register is "prima facie evidence of the validity of the registered mark and of the registration of the mark, of the registrant's ownership of the mark, and of the registrant's exclusive right to use the registered mark in commerce." 15 U.S.C. § 1115(a). Unregistered marks have no such presumption.

In infringement cases involving contestable or unregistered marks, the defendant can defend on the basis that the plaintiff does not have a valid, enforceable trademark, by showing:

(1) the plaintiff has not used the mark commercially (discussed in Chapter Eight, section 5(c));

(2) the defendant has priority of use of the mark over the plaintiff (discussed in Chapter Eight, section 5(d)); or

(3) the mark is not distinctive—generally this means that the mark is merely descriptive and has not acquired secondary meaning (discussed in Chapter Eight, section 5(b)).

Defendants may also raise any of the defenses set forth in 15 U.S.C. § 1115(b) pertaining to incontestable marks, including abandonment, fair use, estoppel, laches and unclean hands.

It is also important to note that with all marks—unregistered, registered and incontestable—a defendant may also show that the mark has become generic and is not entitled to protection because it has ceased to be a trademark. For further discussion regarding generic marks and "genericide," see Chapter Eight, section 3(a) and (7)(a).

b. Incontestable Marks

Under 15 U.S.C. § 1065, if the resistant complies with the statutory formalities unchallenged, registered marks become incontestable five years after they are registered with the PTO. Once the mark has become incontestable "the registration shall be conclusive evidence of the validity of the registered mark, of the registration of the mark, of the registrant's ownership of the mark, and of the registrant's exclusive right to use the registered mark in commerce. 15 U.S.C. § 1115(b). Once a mark is incontestable, an infringement action cannot be defended on the ground that the mark is merely descriptive and has not acquired secondary meaning. Note, however, that even with an incontestable mark, the plaintiff in an infringement action must still prove likelihood of confusion.

Conclusive evidence of the right to use the registered mark based upon statutory incontestability under 15 U.S.C. § 1065 is subject to the following defenses or defects under § 1115(b):

(1) That the registration or the incontestable right to use the mark was obtained fraudulently;

(2) That the mark has been abandoned by the registrant;

(3) That the registered mark is being used to misrepresent the source of the goods or services it marks;

(4) That the allegedly infringing mark is the individual's name and is used fairly and in good faith to describe their goods or services, or the good's geographic origin;

(5) That the mark whose use by a party is charged as an infringement was adopted without knowledge of the registrant's prior use and has been continuously used from a date prior to (A) the date of constructive use of the mark (B) the registration of the mark if the application for registration is filed before the effective date of the Trademark Law Revision Act of 1988, or (C) publication of the registered mark under 15 U.S.C. § 1062(c); *provided that this defense or defect shall apply only for the area in which continuous prior use is proved*;

(6) That the allegedly infringing mark was registered and used prior to the registration under this chapter or publication under 15 U.S.C. § 1062(c) of the registered mark of the registrant, and not abandoned; *provided that this defense or defect shall apply only for the area in which the mark was used prior to registration or publication of the registrant's mark*;

(7) That the mark has been or is being used to violate the antitrust laws of the United States;

(8) That the mark is functional; or

(9) That equitable principles, like latches, estoppel, and acquiescence, are applicable.

If one of the defenses enumerated in § 1115(b) is established, registration constitutes only prima facie and not conclusive evidence of the owner's right to exclusive use of the mark. Thus, the defenses provide for a two step process—defeating the incontestable status of the mark, and then defending the infringement suit on the merits. Note, however, that courts often treat certain § 1115(b) defenses as complete defenses on the merits by compressing this two step process. For example, in *Venetianaire Corp. of America v. A & P Import Co.*, 429 F.2d 1079, 1081(2d Cir. 1970), the court stated that the "fair use" defense explicitly described in § 1115(b)(4) provides a complete defense to infringement. In addition abandonment under § 1115(b)(2), functionality under § 1115(b)(8), and equitable defenses under § 1115(b)(9) such as estoppel, and unclean hands are treated as complete defenses to infringement. This is not the case with all defenses. For example, with § 1115(b)(1) fraud in obtaining registration.

i. Section 1115(b)(1) — Fraud in Obtaining Registration

A defendant who proves that the registration or incontestable status of plaintiff's mark was obtained fraudulently should succeed in having the registration canceled and the claim under 15 U.S.C. § 1114 dismissed. However, assuming the owner still has a protectable interest in the mark, he may maintain an infringement action under 15 U.S.C.A. § 1125 for unregistered marks, as well as pursue common law claims for infringement and unfair competition. *In Orient Express Trading Co., Ltd. v. Federated Department Stores, Inc.*, 842 F.2d 650, 653 (2d. Cir. 1988), the court cancelled the plaintiff's mark after concluding the claimed dates of first use, and the claims regarding scope of use and continuous use had been "greatly exaggerated," amounting to fraud under § 1115(b)(1). The plaintiff still had priority in the mark, and the court allowed the claim under § 1115 as well as the common law and state law infringement and unfair competition claims to proceed.

ii. Section 1115(b)(2) — Abandonment

A defendant may also show that the plaintiff has abandoned its rights in the mark. Abandonment results from:

(1) non-use of the mark in with the intent not to continue its use, discussed in Chapter Eight, Section 7(b),

(2) an "assignment in gross" of the mark unaccompanied by the mark's goodwill, discussed in Chapter Eight, Section 8(a), or

(3) a "naked license" of the mark without sufficient quality control, discussed in Chapter Eight, Section 8(b).

iii. Section 1115(b)(3) — Misrepresentation of Source

Section 1115(b)(3) provides a limited unclean hands defense applicable only when the origin or source of goods distributed or services provided under the subject mark is misrepresented. The broader, equitable defense of unclean hands is available under section 1115(b)(9) and most defendants use the latter section.

iv. Section 1115(b)(4) — Fair Use

Section 1115(b)(4) sets forth the trademark fair use defense. It requires proof that the defendant (1) used the mark descriptively, rather than as a mark, and (2) used the mark fairly and in good faith.

A. Used Descriptively, Not as a Mark

In order to make out a fair use defense, the defendant must first prove that he used the term in "its descriptive sense" and not to identify his goods or services. In *Car-Freshener Corp. v. S.C. Johnson & Son, Inc.*, 70 F.3d 267, 269–70 (2d. Cir. 1995), the defendant's use of a pine-tree shape for its Glade Plug-Ins air fresheners was held to be a fair use of plaintiff's trademark in the pine-tree shape of it's automobile air fresheners that hang from rear view mirrors. The court stated: "Johnson's use of the pine-tree shape describes two aspects of its product. The pine tree refers to the pine scent of its air freshening agent. Furthermore, as a Christmas tree is traditionally a pine tree, the use of the pine-tree shape refers to the Christmas season, during which Johnson sells this item. Johnson's use of the pine-tree shape is clearly descriptive. There is no indication that Johnson uses its tree shape as a mark. Its pine-tree-shaped air fresheners come in boxes prominently bearing the "Glade Plug-Ins" trademark as well as Johnson's corporate logo. Each unit has Glade imprinted across the front of the product itself."

The language "used ... to describe the goods or services" in § 1115(b)(4) has been broadly construed and is not limited to words or images that describe particular characteristics of defendant's product or service." In *Cosmetically Sealed Industries, Inc. v. Chesebrough-Pond's USA Co.*, 125 F.3d 28, 30 (2d Cir. 1997), the defendant used the phrase "Seal it with a Kiss" with a promotion that encouraged customers to kiss a postcard wearing a sample of its Cutex "Color Splash" Lipstick and "Take this postcard and send it to the one you love!!" The court held the phrase "Seal it with a Kiss" was used in a "descriptive sense" and did not infringe on the plaintiff's mark for its lipstick "Sealed with a Kiss" because it described an action that the defendants hoped consumers would take in using their product.

The court also held "[t]he non-trademark use of the challenged phrase and the defendants' good faith are both evidenced by the fact that the source of the defendants' product is clearly identified by the prominent display of the defendants' own trademarks."

B. Used Fairly and in Good Faith

The used fairly and in good faith requirement examines whether the alleged infringer intended to trade on the goodwill of the trademark owner by creating confusion as to the source or sponsorship of the goods or services. In *KP Permanent Make-up v. Lasting Impressions I, Inc.*, 543 U.S. 111, 119–121 (2004), the Supreme Court held that the term "used fairly" in section 1115(b)(4) did not require the defendant to prove absence of confusion. Prior to that, there had been a split in the circuits as to whether a likelihood of confusion precluded the fair use defense. The Fifth, Sixth, and Ninth Circuits held that it did, and the Second, Fourth and Seventh Circuits held it did not. After *KP Permanent Make-up*, likelihood or absence of confusion is only a factor to be considered in the fair use defense. It is a matter of degree—a use is less likely to be found fair as the likelihood of confusion increases.

Efforts taken to avoid confusion by labeling, packaging or other displays that prominently identify the defendant as the source of the goods or services provide evidence of good faith. In *Zatarains, Inc. v. Oak Grove Smokehouse, Inc.*, 698 F.2d 786, 796 (5th Cir. 1983), the court held that the owner of the mark "Fish-Fri" for use with its coating mix could not prevent defendant's fair use of the term words "fish fry" in connection with a similar product. The court noted the defendant "consciously packaged and labeled their products in such a way as to minimize any potential confusion in the minds of consumers." While the plaintiff's coating was packages in cardboard boxes, the defendant's was sold in clear glassine packets prominently labeled with its own mark. Similarly, in *Cosmetically Sealed Industries, Inc. v. Chesebrough-Pond's USA Co.*, 125 F.3d 28, 30 (2d Cir. 1997), the court held the defendant's prominent display of its own trademarks as part of the promotion was evidence of the defendant's good faith use of the phrase "Seal It With A Kiss!!"

On the other hand, using packaging or labeling features that are similar to the plaintiff's can create an inference of lack of good faith. In *Venetianaire Corp. of America v. A & P Import Co.*, 429 F.2d 1079 (2d Cir. 1970), the distributor of mattress covers was aware of the registered mark "Hygient," displayed in a white cross on a green oval when it adopted the mark "Hygienic," which was displayed in white cross on red oval. The distributor also put its mark in same place on the package as the plaintiff's mark, and the mattress covers were retailed side-by-side in the same size wrapper. The court held the distributor was not entitled to claim fair use as a defense to infringement of plaintiff's trademark.

Generally, knowledge of a prior use of a mark does not, in itself demonstrate bad faith and defeat a fair use defense. However, absence of good faith may be inferred where a defendant, with knowledge of prior use, uses a trademarked term when there are adequate alternatives. In *Frito-Lay, Inc. v. Bachman Co.*, 704 F. Supp. 432, 436 (S.D.N.Y. 1989), the defendant marketed "Bachman's Ruffled All Natural Potato Chips" knowing of plaintiff's registered trademark in the term "Ruffles." The court stated it "is undisputed that other potato chip manufacturers use other terms to describe ridged potato chips, including 'ridged,' 'rippled,' and 'dip style.' Bachman is therefore not foreclosed from adopting a descriptive term for its potato chips because of Frito-Lay's right to exclusive use of 'Ruffles.' The availability of these other terms raises a question as to Bachman's asserted good faith."

The fair use defense is also available to those who use their own name in connection with their business. However, the right to use one's name as a mark is not absolute. If the junior user's name creates a likelihood of confusion courts may issue a limited injunction requiring them to disclaim any association with the senior user or to use their first and last names. For example, in *MacSweeney Enterprises, Inc. v. Tarantino*, 235 Cal. App. 2d 549 (1965) the court held that the defendants' use of their last name for their restaurant in Lake Tahoe, California infringed on plaintiff's mark "Tarantinos" for its restaurant in Fisherman's Warf, San Francisco, but suggested changing the name of the Lake Tahoe restaurant to "Joseph and Rose Tarantino."

v. Section 1115(b)(5) — Intermediate Junior User's Limited Area Defense

This section applies to an "intermediate junior user" — one who first uses a mark after the registrant's prior use, but before the registrant registered the mark if the application was made before November 13, 1989, or before the registrant applied for registration of the mark if the application was made after November 13, 1989. The intermediate junior user must have adopted the mark without knowledge of the prior use and continuously used the mark in a different geographic area than the prior user. 15 U.S.C. § 1115(b)(5).

Section 1115(b) does not provide a complete defense to infringement; rather, if the defendant satisfies the requirements, plaintiff's federal registration of the mark is no longer conclusive evidence of plaintiff's right to use the mark in defendant's geographic territory. In *Burger King of Florida, Inc. v. Hoots*, 403 F.2d 904 (7th Cir. 1968), plaintiffs opened their first "Burger King" restaurant in Florida in 1953. In 1957 defendants, without knowledge of plaintiffs' use of the mark, opened a restaurant called "Burger King" in Mattoon, Illinois and registered the mark under the Illinois Trademark Act. In 1961 plaintiffs opened a Burger King in Skokie, Illinois, and a certificate of registration was issued for the mark that same year. Thereafter, in 1962 defendant opened a second Burger King restaurant in Charleston, Illinois. The court held that "plaintiffs' federal registration of the trade mark 'Burger King' gave them the exclusive right to use the mark in Illinois except in the Mattoon market area ... where the defendants, without knowledge of plaintiffs' prior use, actually used the mark before plaintiffs' federal registration."

vi. Section 1115(b)(6) — Prior Use and Registration

Section 1115(b)(6) applies where the defendant's mark was registered, used, and not abandoned prior to the registration of plaintiff's mark. The defense applies only for the area in which defendant's mark was used prior to the registration or publication of plaintiff's mark. Section 1115(b)(6) has been mentioned in only a few published opinions, and then only in passing. *See Union Carbide Corp. v. Ever-Ready Inc.*, 531 F.2d 366, 374 n. 6 (7th Cir. 1976) (Section 1115(b)(6) "involves a situation where the alleged infringing mark was registered and used prior to the charging party's registration"); *U. S. Jaycees v. Chicago Jr. Ass'n of Commerce and Industry* 505 F. Supp. 998, 1001 n. 2 (N.D. Ill. 1981) ("As to the Eleventh Defense, prior use by the alleged infringer is a permitted defense under Section 1115(b)(6) only if the infringer's mark was also registered, which is not claimed by the Association.")

vii. Section 1115(b)(7) — Violation of United States Antitrust Laws

Some courts have suggested that section 1115(b)(7) provides a complete defense to infringement based on use of a registered mark to violate antitrust laws. *See Timken Roller Bearing Co. v. U.S.*, 341 U.S. 593, 599 n. 8 (1951) ("The reason for the penalty provision was that 'trade-marks have been misused have been used in connection with cartel agreements.' 92 Cong.Rec. 7872."). Similarly, the court in *General Motors Corp. v. Gibson Chemical & Oil Corp.*, 786 F.2d 105, 110 (2d Cir. 1986) held that an unlawful tying arrangement, which can be a defense to a trademark infringement action, see 15 U.S.C. § 1115(b)(7), conditions the sale or lease of one product on the purchase or lease of another separate product from the same seller. However, the legislative history of the Lanham Act indicates that a violation of section 1115(c)(7) simply negates the incontestable status of a registered mark. As Representative Lanham himself explained: "[P]roof of violation of the antitrust laws of the United States by a registrant in the use of his mark does not under this act destroy the validity of or the right of the registrant to continue to use the mark, but it places on him a burden of proof in the event of litigation which others do not have to carry, by diluting the weight the court is to give to his certificate of registration as evidence of ownership and the right to use the mark." *Helene Curtis Industries, Inc. v. Church & Dwight Co.*, 560 F.2d 1325, 1336 (7th Cir. 1977).

Still, courts have held that antitrust misuse of a mark may constitute an equitable unclean hands defense to infringement, but the defense is very narrow. For example, in *Phi Delta Theta Fraternity v. J.A. Buchroeder & Co.*, 251 F. Supp. 968 (W.D. Mo. 1966), the plaintiffs registered their insignias as trademarks for the purpose of unlawfully eliminating competition. The court held that such a use justified the application of the antitrust misuse defense and therefore denied relief for the infringement because of the doctrine of unclean hands.

However, the party invoking the defense must demonstrate that the trademark itself was being used as the primary means to engage in the antitrust activity. For example, in *R.J. Reynolds Tobacco Co. v. Premium Tobacco Stores, Inc.*, No. 99 C 1174, 2001 U.S. Dist. Lexis 8896, 2001 WL 747422 (N.D. Ill.), the defendant, Cigarettes Cheaper, alleged that R.J. Reynolds conspired with others to refuse to sell its trademarked products to the defendant and to refuse critical promotional support for these products while intentionally providing it to the defendant's competitors. Because the antitrust allegations related to the products bearing the trademark, and not to the use of the trademark itself, the court refused the antitrust misuse defense because it was not the trademark that was being misused.

viii. Section 1115(b)(8)—The Mark Is Functional

In 1998, Congress added functionality to the list of defenses to infringement of an incontestable mark after the Fourth Circuit had ruled that because functionality was not specifically enumerated in that section it could not be raised in an infringement action involving an incontestable mark. In *Wilhelm Pudenz, GmbH v. Littlefuse, Inc.*, 177 F.3d 1204 (11th Cir. 1999), the court applied § 1115(b)(8) retroactively; holding it was meant to clarify existing law and correct the flawed result reached by the Fourth Circuit."

Under the functionality doctrine, trademark protection does not extend to a product's functional shapes or features. For further discussion regarding functionality, see Chapter Eight, section (4)(b).

ix. Section 1115(b)(9)—Equitable Defenses

A. Estoppel—Laches, Acquiescence, Express Consent

The Lanham Act does not contain a statute of limitations. However, some federal courts apply the statute of limitations of the most analogous claim under state law as a complete bar to suit if that statute of limitations is not met. Others use the analogous state statute of limitations as a factor in determining of the claim is barred by laches. If a claim was filed within the state limitations period there is a strong presumption against laches, if it was filed after that period, the presumption is reversed. Then in determining if there is estoppel through laches, the court examines whether the plaintiff

(1) had knowledge of defendant's use of its marks and

(2) unreasonably delayed in taking action that

(3) resulted in prejudice to the defendant.

Determining unreasonable delay involves balancing the length of the delay with plaintiff's excuses for it. Resulting prejudice may be either economic or evidentiary. In *Joint Stock Society v. UDV North America, Inc.*, 53 F. Supp. 2d 692 (D.Del. 1999), the court held that a Russian distiller's claims of trademark infringement based on defendant's use of the name Smirnoff for vodka were barred by laches where the plaintiffs' predecessors knew the defendants had been marketing vodka for more than sixty years under the name Smirnoff and took no action to protect or enforce their trademark rights. The court held that the long delay was not excused by the alleged poverty of plaintiff's predecessors nor the "existence of the Iron Curtain and the tyranny of the Soviet State" since during that time they "did nothing. More troubling, they did not even try to do anything." The court held defendants had suffered both economic and evidentiary prejudice noting: "Over the last sixty years, the defendants have invested over $700 million in advertising, promoting, and marketing their vodka products under the Smirnoff name," and also "the defendants have suffered extreme evidentiary prejudice since, as the plaintiffs themselves admit, all of the central characters in this litigation have passed away; some over fifty years ago."

While laches involves the plaintiff's *inaction*, estoppel by acquiescence requires plaintiff's *action*, specifically:

(1) conduct on the part of the plaintiff that amounted to an express or implied assurance to the defendant that the plaintiff would not assert its trademark rights,

(2) delay between such assurance and the assertion of rights that

(3) resulted in prejudice to the defendant.

For example, in *ProFitness Physical Therapy Center v. Pro-Fit Orthopedic and Sports Physical Therapy P.C.*, 314 F.3d 62 (2d Cir. 2002), the plaintiff sent a cease and desist letter to the defendant, ProFit, asserting defendant's use of the name

"Pro-Fit Physical Therapy" infringed on the plaintiff's trade name. The defendant then sent the plaintiff a letter stating that to avoid "any confusion or further conflict" it had decided to change its name to "Pro-Fit Orthopedic and Sports Physical Therapy." The plaintiff did not respond, and the defendant sent a second letter stating if it did not hear from the plaintiff it would proceed with the proposed name change. The plaintiff did not respond and the defendant changed its name. About a year and a half later, the plaintiff sued the defendant for trademark infringement. The Second Circuit held plaintiff's continued silence in response to the defendant's proposed name change amounted to "an implicit assurance that trademark rights would not be asserted thereby reasonably inducing reliance by the defendant." However, it held the district court erred in holding plaintiff's acquiescence to defendant's use of the name in connection with its Queens location automatically extended to the use in connection with its later Manhattan location.

A plaintiff may counter the defenses of laches and acquiescence under the doctrine of progressive encroachment, which allows a plaintiff to wait to sue until it has a provable infringement claim against the defendant. This inquiry requires the court to evaluate and compare the likelihood of confusion (a) at the time plaintiff became aware of or acquiesced to defendant's use of its mark and (b) at the time plaintiff brought suit, and determine whether the defendant's expansion in the use of its mark led to a greater likelihood of confusion than its prior use.

One may also be estopped from maintaining an infringement action or obtaining relief where the plaintiff expressly consented to the defendant's use, for example through an assignment, license or settlement agreement. Estoppel based on express consent is essentially a straight contract issue. To apply, the use must be within the scope and duration of the consent given by the plaintiff.

B. Unclean Hands

A user may also be precluded from maintaining an infringement action or obtaining relief based on his inequitable conduct or "unclean hands." This defense is based on the rationale that "it is essential that the plaintiff should not in his trade mark, or in his advertisements and business, be himself guilty of any false or misleading representation." *Clinton J. Worden & Co. v. California Fig Syrup Co.*, 187 U.S. 516, 528 (1903). To constitute an unclean hands defense the plaintiff's conduct must be inequitable and must relate to the rights plaintiff seeks to enforce.

Typically the unclean hands defense applies where the plaintiff's mark or name is, in itself, deceptive. *See Worden v. California Fig Syrup Co.*, 187 U.S. 516 (name for laxative "Syrup of Figs" not protectable where product contained no figs or fig juice); *Haagen-Dazs, Inc. v. Frusen Gladje Ltd.*, 493 F. Supp. 73 (S.D.N.Y.

1980 (packaging and marketing theme which implied ice-cream produced in America was Scandinavian in origin not protectable); *Havana Club Holding, S.A. v. Galleon S.A.*, 203 F.3d 116 (2d Cir. 2000) ("Havana Club" label used with Panamanian-made rum not protectable). This is an issue of fact however, and names that appear deceptive may not be found so. See, e.g., *Japan Telecom, Inc. v. Japan Telecom America Inc.*, 287 F.3d 866 (9th Cir. 2002) (issue of fact existed regarding whether the trade name "Japan Telecon" for a California corporation was deceptive so as to support an unclean hands defense); *Holeproof Hosiery Co. v. Wallach Bros.*, 172 F. 859 (2d Cir. 1909) (name "Holeproof" used with socks was merely a "boastful and fanciful word" and did not support an unclean hands defense).

An example of a successful unclean hands defense is found in *Stray v. Devine's, Inc.*, 217 F. 2d 187 (7th Cir. 1954). There, the plaintiff, Dr. Nicholas Stray, marketed a foot cream under his own name in conjunction with the registered mark "Kule-Fut." When the defendant began selling foot cream under the mark "Devine's Kool-Foot Cream," the plaintiff brought suit for infringement. The court, however, held that the equitable doctrine of unclean hands barred Dr. Stray's claim since, as a chiropractor, he was not permitted under state law to hold himself out as a doctor to purchasers of the cream.

In cases where the mark or name is deceptive, plaintiff's inequitable conduct is directed toward the public. In addition, courts have also found unclean hands where the plaintiff has acted inequitably toward the defendant in relation to the trademark. *In Worthington v. Anderson*, 386 F.3d 1314 (10th Cir. 2004) the district court found plaintiffs' trademark infringement claims against their former partners were barred by unclean hands where defendants' continued use the mark in violation of an arbitration order was due in large part to plaintiffs failure to comply with its phase-out duties under that order. The Tenth Circuit affirmed stating: "The Worthingtons threw economic obstacles in the way of the Andersons' compliance with the arbitrator's decision awarding the trademark to the Worthingtons.... Where a plaintiff interferes with the defendant's ability to comply with his or her responsibilities, court of equity will not turn a blind eye to the net effect on the parties' equitable relationship."

Even where a plaintiff's conduct is deceptive or otherwise inequitable, it must be directly related to the trademark rights plaintiffs seeks to enforce in order for the unclean hands defense to apply. In *Fuddruckers, Inc. v. Doc's B.R. Others, Inc.*, 826 F.2d 837 (9th Cir. 1987), the plaintiff, an "upscale" hamburger chain, brought a trade dress infringement suit against a competitor. The defendant asserted an unclean hands defense alleging plaintiff had falsely described its hamburger meat as "ground steak." The district court rejected this defense and the Ninth Circuit affirmed noting that even assuming the allegation were true, the deception was not "a major part of the trade dress" and thus not material to the litigation. In *Flow Control Industries Inc. v. AMHI Inc.*, 278 F. Supp. 2d 1193 (W.D. Wash. 2003), the plaintiff sued for trademark infringement alleging that the defendants had used plaintiff's mark SKOFLO as a domain name and as a metatag—inserting it in the code of defendants' website so search engines such as Google would list defendant's website as an option to those searching for plaintiff's products. The defendants asserted that the plaintiff's claims were barred by unclean hands because plaintiff had also used defendant's mark as a metatag. The court disagreed, stating: "The fact that plaintiff may have infringed defendants'... trademark has nothing to do with the manner in which plaintiff obtained or used its SKOFLO mark.... Because plaintiff's alleged wrongdoing is unrelated to the right it seeks to enforce in this litigation, the doctrine of unclean hands does not apply." Rather, the defendants' remedy was a counterclaim for infringement.

6. Remedies for Trademark Infringement

The remedies for trademark infringement are injunctive relief, 15 U.S.C. § 1116, and monetary recovery, including defendant's profits, damages, and in "exceptional cases" attorney fees, 15 U.S.C. § 1117, and/or destruction of the infringing articles, 15 U.S.C. § 1118.

a. Injunctive Relief—15 U.S.C. § 1116

Injunctions are the most common form of relief awarded in trademark infringement suits. Section 1116(a) grants federal courts "the power to grant injunctions, according to the principles of equity and upon such terms as the court may deem reasonable" for infringement of federally registered marks. To receive injunctive relief, the prevailing "plaintiff must demonstrate (1) that it has suffered an irreparable injury; (2) that remedies available at law, such as monetary damages, are inadequate to compensate for that injury; (3) that, considering the balance of hardships between the plaintiff and defendant, a remedy in equity is warranted; and (4) that the public interest would not be disserved by a permanent injunction." *eBay Inc. v. MercExchange, L.L.C.*, 547 U.S. 388 (2006). Whether to grant an injunction is a matter of discretion for the district court, reviewable on appeal for abuse of discretion.

Some form of an injunction is generally awarded in cases of trademark infringement "to protect both the plaintiff and the public from the likelihood of future harm." Restatement (Third) of Unfair Competition § 35. com. b. The issue in most cases is the scope of injunctive relief.

In determining the scope of injunctive relief, courts focus on preventing the likelihood of confusion and the nature of infringing conduct. The greater the likelihood of confusion created by defendant's use, the broader the injunction will be. In *Perfumebay.com Inc. v. eBay, Inc.*, 506 F.3d 1165 (9th Cir. 2007), the court affirmed an injunction preventing plaintiff from using the terms perfumebay.com and perfume-bay.com noting eBay and Perfumebay's services are similar, as they both sell perfume on internet web sites and utilize search engines extensively for attracting customers.

Injunctions addressing similar marks or uses like this may be quite broad. In *Elvis Presley Enterprises v. Elvisly Yours, Inc.*, 936 F.2d 889 (6th Cir. 1991) the unauthorized sellers of Elvis Presley memorabilia were "permanently enjoined from using the name, likeness and image of Elvis Presley or any trademarks of the plaintiff or any trademarks confusingly similar thereto, for the purposes of the sale, distribution, marketing, advertising and licensing of unauthorized goods or services in the United States and its possessions and territories."

Injunctions are narrower and more specific where the infringing use involved noncompeting product or where the use was in a different geographic market, if the likelihood of confusion is less. In *Charles Jacquin Et Cie, Inc. v. Destileria Serralles, Inc.*, 921 F.2d 467 (3d Cir. 1990), the court granted an injunction that prevented plaintiff from using bottles shaped similarly to plaintiff's trade dress but only for cordials and specialty liquors as opposed to all liquors because those were the only type of products that competed with plaintiff's. In *Sweetarts v. Sunline, Inc.*, 436 F.2d 705 (8th Cir. 1971) an action between two candy makers using the name "SweeTarts", the appellate court reversed an injunction preventing the defendant from using the name in 11 states across the U.S. because there was insufficient evidence to show that the "SweeTarts" trademark was generally known or identified anywhere other than in Washington, Oregon and California.

Where the infringing use involves the defendant's own name, courts may issue qualified injunctions that allow the defendant to continue to use his personal name in some form, often with a disclaimer. In *Gucci v. Gucci Shops, Inc.*, 688 F. Supp. 916 (S.D.N.Y. 1988), the plaintiff, Paolo Gucci, grandson of the founder of the famous Gucci designer brand, was enjoined from using "Paolo Gucci" as a trademark or trade name based on likelihood of confusion with the Gucci trademark, but was allowed to identify himself as designer of products sold under a separate trademark which did not include the Gucci name. Mr. Gucci was also required to use a disclaimer notifying consumers that he "is no longer affiliated with any of the Gucci entities." Similarly, in *Emilio Pucci Societa a Responsibilita Limitata v. Pucci Corp.*, 10 U.S.P.Q. 2d 1541 (N.D. Ill.

1988), the defendant was required to display the name "Lawrence" prior to the name "Pucci" when advertising and selling its perfume and to include a disclaimer stating he was not associated with or related to Emilio Pucci.

Courts also have broad powers to issue qualified injunctions that allow prescribed uses accompanied by disclaimers, particularly when the balance of equities between the parties is close. In *Manhattan Industries, Inc. v. Sweater Bee by Banff, Ltd.*, 627 F.2d 628 (2d Cir. 1980), plaintiff began shipping merchandise under trademark "Kimberly" one day before defendant began using the mark. The court held that balancing of equities required that both plaintiff and manufacturers be allowed to use the "Kimberly" trademark; however, defendant would be required to use a "Kimberly" mark sufficiently distinct from that used by the plaintiff.

On the other hand, where the defendant's conduct has been particularly improper, a court may issue a broad injunction and enjoin actions that would otherwise be permissible. In *Kentucky Fried Chicken Corp. v. Diversified Packaging Corp.*, 549 F.2d 368 (5th Cir. 1977), the defendant's engaged in "an elaborate scheme for misleading franchisees into believing that [defendant] was connected with or approved by Kentucky Fried." Under these circumstances the Fifth Circuit held: "Even if [defendant] originally would have been entitled to use the marks, we hold that the unqualified injunction against their use is justified by [defendant's] history of improper behavior. An injunction can be therapeutic as well as protective. In fashioning relief against a party who has transgressed the governing legal standards, a court of equity is free to proscribe activities that, standing alone, would have been unassailable."

b. Monetary Recovery — 15 U.S.C. § 1117, Profits and Damages

Section 1117(a), allows a prevailing party in an infringement action "subject to the principles of equity, to recover (1) defendant's profits, (2) any damages sustained by the plaintiff, and (3) the costs of the action." Section 1117(a) further provides:

> The court shall assess such profits and damages or cause the same to be assessed under its direction. In assessing profits the plaintiff shall be required to prove defendant's sales only; defendant must prove all elements of cost or deduction claimed. In assessing damages the court may enter judgment, according to the circumstances of the case, for any sum above the amount found as actual damages, not exceeding three times such amount. If the court shall find that the amount of the re-

covery based on profits is either inadequate or excessive the court may, in its discretion, enter judgment for such sum as the court shall find to be just, according to the circumstances of the case. Such sum in either of the above circumstances shall constitute compensation and not a penalty. The court in exceptional cases may award reasonable attorney's fees to the prevailing party.

As with injunctive relief, the decision whether to award profits or damages is committed to the discretion of the trial court. *See Maier Brewing Co. v. Fleischmann Distilling Corp.*, 390 F.2d 117 (9th Cir.1968). At first glance, § 1117(a) may appear to provide some form of monetary relief as a matter of course. This is not the case, however, since the statute conditions the award of profits or damages on "principles of equity."

Since the prevailing party in an infringement action need only prove *likelihood* of confusion, an injunction may provide an adequate remedy. In such cases monetary relief will generally be denied. In *Aktiebolaget Electrolux v. Armatron Intern., Inc.* 999 F.2d 1 (1st Cir. 1993) the district court held defendant's "Leaf Eater" products that shredded leaves infringed upon plaintiff's "Weed Eater" mark used with its power trimmers and blower/vacuums. The court issued an injunction requiring defendant to use the term "Leaf Eater" only in conjunction with its "Flowtron" or "Vornado" logos, but declined to award plaintiff damages or profits. The First Circuit upheld the injunction noting: "otherwise similar marks are not likely to be confused where used in conjunction with the clearly displayed name and/or logo of the manufacturer." It affirmed the court's denial of monetary relief on the grounds (1) plaintiff failed to show actual harm, (2) the products did not directly compete such that defendant's profits would have gone to plaintiff absent the violation, and (3) defendant had not acted fraudulently or in bad faith.

i. Profits

An award of profits is a transfer of defendant's gain resulting from its infringing conduct to the plaintiff. Profits can be awarded to (1) prevent unjust enrichment, (2) compensate plaintiff for damages suffered as a result of the infringement, or (3) deter a willful infringer from infringing again. *Burndy Corp. v. Teledyne Industries, Inc.*, 748 F.2d 767 (2d Cir. 1984). Willful intent of the part of defendant is always a factor, and in some Circuits, a requirement for awarding profits.

In the Third, Fourth, Fifth, and Seventh Circuits, willful intent to infringe is merely a factor in determining whether to award profits. In *Quick Technologies, Inc. v. Sage Group PLC*, 313 F.3d 338 (5th Cir. 2002), the Fifth Circuit held that willfulness was an important factor, but not a prerequisite to an award of defendant's profits. The court listed six factors relevant to determining whether to award lost profits in a non-exclusive list:

(1) whether the defendant had the intent to confuse or deceive,

(2) whether sales have been diverted,

(3) the adequacy of other remedies,

(4) any unreasonable delay by the plaintiff in asserting his rights,

(5) the public interest in making the misconduct unprofitable, and

(6) whether it is a case of palming off.

The Fifth Circuit held that the district court erred in instructing the jury it should not reach the issue of awarding profits unless found willful infringement. However, it affirmed the court's denial of an award of profits because only the fourth and fifth factors were 'arguably applicable."

The Third Circuit followed *Quick Technologies* in *Banjo Buddies, Inc. v. Renosky*, 399 F.3d 168 (3d Cir. 2005) — a case involving competing fishing lure kits — plaintiff's "Banjo Minnow" and defendant's infringing "Bionic Minnow." The district court ordered the defendant to pay the plaintiff the net profits earned by the Bionic Minnow project, but its findings on bad faith and intent to infringe were equivocal. The court found that the defendant exhibited a lack of good faith and fair dealing by producing a nearly identical product in identical packaging, using the same primary marketing tool, an infomercial with similar content, and by claiming to be the developer of the Banjo Minnow in his marketing materials for the Bionic Minnow. The district court also found no evidence that the defendant deliberately intended to confuse consumers into believing that the Bionic Minnow was a Banjo Buddies product. The Third Circuit affirmed the award of profits. It concluded the willful intent factor was "neutral" and that the other 5 factors favored the award of profits. The defendant likely diverted sales as the lure kits were nearly identical and packaged nearly identically (factor two), which also supported a finding of palming off (factor six). Moreover, there were not other adequate remedies since the district court determined plaintiff's estimation of damages was speculative — thus unless profits were awarded, plaintiff would not be compensated for the infringement (factor three), and plaintiff did not delay in bringing suit (factor four). The Fourth Circuit adopted the *Quick Technologies* factors in *Synergistic International, LLC v. Korman*, 470 F.3d 162 (4th Cir. 2006), holding that willfulness is an important factor, but "not an essential predicate." In *Roulo v. Russ Berrie & Co., Inc.*, 886 F.2d 931, 941 (7th Cir.1989), the Seventh

Circuit stated "Other than general equitable considerations, there is no express requirement ... that the infringer willfully infringe ... to justify an award of profits.... Given the evidence of intentional imitation and the substantial similarity between the two card lines, the district judge's decision to instruct the jury that an award of profits would be appropriate was not an abuse of discretion."

In the Second, Eighth, Tenth and D.C. Circuits, willful intent to infringe is a mandatory prerequisite to awarding defendant's profits. In *The George Basch Co. v. Blue Coral, Inc.*, 968 F.2d 1532, 1534 (2d Cir. 1992), the court held that in order to justify an award of profits on any of the three theories of unjust enrichment, compensation for actual damages, or deterring a willful infringer from infringing again, "a plaintiff must establish that the defendant engaged in willful deception." Once this threshold is met, the court held these factors relevant:

(1) the degree of certainty that the defendant benefited from the unlawful conduct;

(2) availability and adequacy of other remedies;

(3) the role of a particular defendant in effectuating the infringement;

(4) plaintiff's laches; and

(5) plaintiff's unclean hands.

This was the approach of the Tenth Circuit in *Bishop v. Equinox International Corp.*, 154 F.3d 1220, 1223 (10th Cir. 1998) ("an award of profits requires a showing that defendant's actions were willful or in bad faith"), the Eighth Circuit in *Minnesota Pet Breeders, Inc. v. Schell & Kampeter, Inc.*, 41 F.3d 1242, 1247 (8th Cir. 1994) (profits may be awarded "[i]f a registered owner proves willful, deliberate infringement or deception"), and the D.C. Circuit in *ALPO Petfoods, Inc. v. Ralston Purina Co.*, 913 F.2d 958, 968 (D.C. Cir. 1990) ("an award based on a defendant's profits requires proof that the defendant acted willfully or in bad faith").

In the Ninth Circuit, willful infringement is not a prerequisite to an award profits based on compensation for plaintiff's actual damages. *Adray v. Adry-Mart, Inc.*, 76 F.3d 984, 991 (9th Cir.1995). However, if profits are awarded based on theories of unjust enrichment or deterrence, the plaintiff must establish the defendant's infringing conduct was willful. This is also the case in the First Circuit, *Tamko Roofing Products, Inc. v. Ideal Roofing Co., Ltd.*, 282 F.3d 23 (1st Cir. 2002) (award of defendant's profits "where the products *directly compete* does not require fraud, bad faith, or palming off" but "when the rationale for an award of defendant's profits is to deter some egregious conduct, willfulness is required."), and the Eleventh Circuit, *Burger King Corp. v. Mason*, 855 F.2d 779, 783 (11th Cir. 1988) ("Nor is an award of profits based on either unjust enrichment or deterrence dependent upon a higher showing of culpability on the part of the defendant, who is purposely using the trademark.")

In determining defendant's profits, the plaintiff need only prove gross sales of the infringing product(s), 15 U.S.C. § 1117(a), and doubts regarding the amount of sales will generally be resolved against the defendant. The defendant has the burden of proving any apportionment of those sales—which, if any, sales were not attributable to the infringing acts, as well as the burden of proving deductible costs from the gross sales such as overhead, certain operating expenses and taxes.

In addition if the court finds that the award of profits would be "either inadequate or excessive, the court may enter judgment for a sum that the court finds to be just under the circumstances." 15 U.S.C. §1117(a). Despite the statutory admonition "Such sum in either of the above circumstances shall constitute compensation and not a penalty," increases in profit awards have been based on both (1) difficulties in proving amounts, *see Playboy Enterprises, Inc. v. P.K. Sorren Export Co.*, 546 F. Supp. 987 (S.D. Fla. 1982) (doubling award to twice the amount of profits show where "the record strongly indicates that plaintiff's damages and defendants' profits were both greater than the amounts which were conclusively proven), and (2) defendant's egregious conduct, *see Holiday Inns, Inc. v. Airport Holiday Corp.*, 493 F. Supp. 1025 (N.D. Tex. 1980), *aff'd*, 683 F.2d 931(5th Cir. 1982) (profits and damages trebled based on defendant's "willful" and "flagrant" infringement).

ii. Damages

Recovery of damages for trademark infringement sounds in tort. "A prevailing plaintiff may recover damages as naturally and proximately result from the infringement of its mark." *Obear-Nester Glass Co. v. United Drug Co.*, 149 F.2d 671 (8th Cir. 1945). Such damages include:

- profits on lost sales;

- loss from reduction in the price of goods due to the infringing competition;

- damage to the reputation of the trademark owner's goods;

- damage to the trademark owner's business goodwill;

- expenses incurred in preventing, correcting or mitigating consumer confusion;

In order to recover damages for infringement, the plaintiff must show consumers were (1) actually confused or deceived by defendant's conduct, (2) causing injury. Actual confusion or deception may be proved by circumstantial evidence, however, including market surveys and analysis, or the defendant's misconduct." The plaintiff need not prove that defendant's conduct was intentional to recover damages, although he is more likely recover a higher award of damages on a lesser showing of proof in cases of intentional infringement. In *Zelinski v. Columbia 300, Inc.*, 335 F.3d 633 (7th Cir. 2003), plaintiff, a maker of high quality bowling balls under the name "Pin Breaker" prevailed in a trademark suit against the defendant, who was aware of the plaintiff's mark and yet knowingly sold balls labeled Pin Breaker in Pin Breaker boxes. Plaintiff testified that two people saw defendant's balls in Pin Breaker boxes and were possibly confused. The court held this evidence was not overwhelming but sufficient under the circumstances, stating: "The jury is entitled to use its common sense to reason that purchasers of Columbia's Pin Breaker balls were deceived. This is particularly the case when no amount of inspection would have revealed that Columbia—not Pin Breaker—manufactured the balls."

The plaintiff in *Zelinski* proved actual injury even though he wasn't producing bowling balls at either the time of infringement or the time of suit because he intended to resume use of his mark and would have to spend money on a curative advertising campaign. In *Otis Clapp & Son, Inc. v. Filmore Vitamin Co.*, 754 F.2d 738 (7th Cir. 1985), court also awarded damages for a curative advertising campaign, but refused an award of damages for "unrealized growth potential" based on lack of actual injury where the plaintiff failed to prove "a single lost sale" resulting from defendant's misconduct.

The standard for proving the proper amount of damages is lower than the standard for proving the *fact* of damages. Once a plaintiff has proven it was damaged by defendant's infringement, all that is required is substantial evidence in the record to permit a fact finder to draw reasonable inferences and make a fair and reasonable assessment of damages. Thus, in *Broan Mfg. Co., Inc. v. Associated Distributors, Inc.*, 923 F.2d 1232 (6th Cir. 1991), the court affirmed a jury's award of damages for future legal expenses in handling mistaken products liability claims resulting from defendant's infringement of its mark.

At the court's discretion, damage awards may be enhanced up to three times the amount found as actual damages, provided the award "shall constitute compensation and not a penalty." 15 U.S.C. §1117(a). Generally, courts require proof of intentional or willful infringement before enhancing damage awards. For example, in *Taco Cabana Int'l, Inc. v. Two Pesos, Inc.*, 932 F.2d 1113 (5th Cir. 1991), the court affirmed a judgment that was double the amount of the jury's award of $934,000 based upon "the evidence of brazen imitation and rapid market foreclosure." The Supreme Court affirmed, 505 U.S. 763 (1992).

iii. Damages — Counterfeit Marks

In cases of knowing, intentional counterfeiting, § 1117(b) requires courts to treble damages, unless they find extenuating circumstances. Thus, in *Larsen v. Terk Technologies Corp.*, 151 F.3d 140 (4th Cir. 1998), the court affirmed the district court's award of $217,779 in treble damages where the defendant "intentionally, willfully, knowingly, surreptitiously and fraudulently passed off counterfeit goods of inferior quality as Larsen's authentic Danish-made [designer CD holders] in violation of § 43(a) of the Lanham Act." A counterfeit mark is one that is "identical with, or substantially indistinguishable from" a valid mark. 15 U.S.C. 1115(B)(2). The court addressed extenuating circumstances under 1117(b) in *Gucci America, Inc. v. Rebecca Gold Enterprises, Inc.*, 802 F. Supp. 1048 (S.D.N.Y. 1992), "The most frequently cited extenuating circumstance is the hypothetical case of an 'unsophisticated individual, operating on a small scale, for whom the imposition of treble damages would mean that he or she would be unable to support his or her family.'" The *Gucci America* court affirmed the denial of treble damages because it found the infringement there was "limited in nature" — but it also affirmed an award of attorneys' fees to the prevailing party.

In addition, § 1117(c) allows a prevailing plaintiff in a counterfeiting action to elect statutory damages in lieu of actual damages. Statutory damages are (1) not less than $500 or more than $100,000 per counterfeit mark per type of goods or services sold, offered for sale, or distributed … or (2) if the court finds that the use of the counterfeit mark was willful, not more than $1,000,000 per counterfeit mark per type of goods or services sold, offered for sale, or distributed.…"

iv. Attorneys' Fees

Under 15 U.S.C. § 1117(a), in exceptional circumstances, the court may award reasonable attorneys' fees to the prevailing party. Exceptional cases are those where the acts of infringement were malicious, fraudulent, deliberate, or willful. Some courts require a showing of fraud or bad faith before attorneys' fees may be awarded under section 1117(a). So, for example, in *Texas Pig Stands, Inc. v. Hard Rock Cafe International, Inc.*, 951 F.2d 684 (5th Cir. 1992), the court reversed an award of attorneys' fees based on a jury verdict that the infringement was willful, stating: "While we do not condone Hard Rock's infringement, its actions do not approach 'deliberate pirating' or 'egregious conduct.'" Other courts hold that willful or deliberate conduct alone may support and award of attorney fees. *Tamko Roofing Products, Inc. v. Ideal Roofing Co., Ltd.*, 282 F.3d 23 (1st Cir. 2002) (collecting cases and discussing the two standards). In *Tamko Roofing*, the First Circuit, in affirming the award of attorney fees, enumerated myriad instances of defendant's knowing infringement in the face of repeated notices by the trademark owner and court orders. It concluded: "In combination, the facts above warrant the district court's conclusion that the initial infringement and continuing infringement, even in the face of court orders, was deliberate and willful and that equity required an award of fees."

v. Destruction of Infringing Articles

Under 15 U.S.C. § 1118, the court, in its discretion may order the destruction of all "labels, signs, prints, packages, wrappers, receptacles, and advertisements bearing the infringing mark" or the "word, term, name, symbol, device, combination thereof, designation, description, or representation that is the subject of the violation or any reproduction, counterfeit, copy or colorable imitation thereof, and all plates, molds, matrices and other means of making them."

For example, in *Playboy Enterprises, Inc. v. P. K. Sorren Export Co. Inc. of Florida*, 546 F. Supp. 987 (D.C. Fla. 1982), the defendant retailer that sold shirts with a rabbit head emblem that infringed Playboy Enterprises trademark was ordered to "all shirts in their possession or control bearing any infringing rabbit head design label and all infringing rabbit head design labels in their possession or control."

This remedy will not be ordered where the defendant is enjoined from further infringing activities and the court considers the injunction an adequate remedy. In *Kelley Blue Book v. Car-Smarts, Inc.*, 802 F. Supp. 278 (C.D. Cal. 1992), the court concluded the was a likelihood of confusion between plaintiff's "Kelley Blue Book" designation and defendants' "1-900-BLU-BOOK" and "1-800-BLUE-BOOK" designations in the California, Nevada, Arizona, Oregon and Hawaii, and enjoined defendants from using the phrase "blue book" or any confusingly similar phrase in those states. In light of this injunction it held that destruction of the defendant's infringing products was unnecessary.

The destruction order must be limited to infringing articles. In *Whittaker Corp. v. Execuair Corp.*, 953 F.2d 510 (9th Cir. 1992), the defendant Execuair, a surplus and replacement aircraft parts dealer, sold counterfeit versions of Whittaker parts, as well as genuine Whittaker parts and a variety of other aircraft parts. Judgment was entered in favor or Whittaker and Execuair was enjoined from further infringing activities. Execuair violated this injunction, and as a result the court ordered the destruction of it's entire inventory. The Ninth Circuit held this order was unauthorized under 15 U.S.C. § 1118 and modified the order to apply only to infringing goods.

7. Dilution

Dilution refers to the impairment of a "famous" mark's distinctiveness or reputation where no likelihood of confusion is created by defendant's use of its junior mark or trade name. On October 6, 2006, Congress enacted the Trademark Dilution Revision Act of 2006 ("TDRA") which amended the Federal Trademark Dilution Act enacted in 1996 ("FTDA"). The TDRA is codified in 15 U.S.C. § 1125(c) and provides:

> Subject to the principles of equity, the owner of a famous mark that is distinctive, inherently or through acquired distinctiveness, shall be entitled to an injunction against another person who, at any time after the owner's mark has become famous, commences use of a mark or trade name in commerce that is likely to cause dilution by blurring or dilution by tarnishment of the famous mark, regardless of the presence or absence of actual or likely confusion, of competition, or of actual economic injury.

15 U.S.C. § 1125(c)(1).

The Supreme Court held in *Moseley v. Victoria's Secret Catalogue, Inc.*, 537 U.S. 418, 432–33 (2003), that the FTDA required plaintiffs to prove actual dilution to prevail. The TDRA was enacted principally to legislatively overrule the *Moseley* decision and replace the actual dilution standard with a likelihood of dilution standard. Also, the Second Circuit, in *New York Stock Exchange, Inc. v. New York, New York Hotel LLC*, 293 F.3d 550 (2d Cir. 2002), had previously interpreted the FTDA as requiring a mark to be inherently distinctive to qualify for dilution protection, thus eliminating famous marks that had become distinctive through acquiring secondary meaning. Section 1125(c)(1) overruled this line of cases by expressly referring to a famous mark that is "distinctive, inherently or *through acquired distinctiveness....*"

To prevail on a dilution claim, the plaintiff must prove

(1) that its mark was famous as of a date prior to the first use of the [defendant's] mark and

(2) that [defendant's] use of its allegedly diluting mark creates a likelihood of dilution by blurring or tarnishment.

The TDRA applies to any claims for injunctive relief because such relief is prospective. The TDRA applies to claims for monetary damages if the defendant's mark or trade name likely to cause dilution was first used in commerce after October 6, 2006. If the mark or trade name was first used before October 6, 2006, the

FTDA applies. In *Adidas America, Inc. v. Payless Shoesource, Inc.*, 546 F. Supp. 2d 1029, 1066, (D.Or.) *rev'd on other grounds*, 166 Fed. Appx. 268 (9th Cir. 2006), the court applied the FTDA's actual dilution standard to Adidas' claims for monetary damages and the TDRA's likelihood of dilution standard to its claims for injunctive relief. The court held Adidas presented sufficient evidence that defendant's 4 stripe mark for shoes caused actual dilution of Adidas' famous three strip mark under the FTDA, and "because Adidas has proffered sufficient evidence to demonstrate actual dilution, it has necessarily satisfied the lesser standard of likelihood of dilution under the TDRA."

a. Famous Marks

A mark is famous where it is "widely recognized by the general consuming public of the United States as a designation of source of the goods or services of the mark's owner." 15 U.S.C. § 1125(c)(2)(A). This language eliminates protection for marks that have achieved only "niche fame" — fame in a particular market or geographic region where the defendant has used its mark in same market or region. Previously there had been a dispute among courts as to whether niche fame was sufficient. For example, in *Times Mirror Magazines, Inc. v. Las Vegas Sports News, LLC*, 212 F.3d 157 (3d Cir. 2000), the court stated: "Because a mark can be famous in a niche market where the mark has a high degree of distinctiveness within the market and where the plaintiff and defendant operate within or along side that market, we hold that the district court did not commit an obvious error by holding that the mark 'The Sporting News' was famous in its niche and therefore entitled to protection under the FTDA against [defendant's] use of a similar mark in the same market)." Conversely in *Star Markets, Ltd. v. Texaco, Inc.*, 950 F. Supp. 1030, 1034 n.5 (D.Haw. 1996), the court held that niche fame — the "big fish in a small pond" theory — is not persuasive for purposes of determining the fame of a mark for dilution purposes.

In determining whether a mark is famous, the court may consider all relevant factors, including:

(1) The duration, extent, and geographic reach of advertising and publicity of the mark, whether advertised or publicized by the owner or third parties;

(2) The amount, volume, and geographic extent of sales of goods or services offered under the mark;

(3) The extent of actual recognition of the mark; and

(4) Whether the mark is registered.

15 U.S.C. § 1125(c)(2)(A). In essence, the plaintiff must show its mark or trade name is truly prominent and renowned. *See , e.g., Louis Vuitton v. Haute Diggity Dog*, 507 F.3d at 267 (holding Louis Vuitton marks are famous "icons of high fashion"); *Nike, Inc. v. Nikepal Intern., Inc.*, 2007 WL 2782030 (E.D. Cal. September 18, 2007) (holding all four factors set forth in section 11(c)(2)(A) indicated the "Nike" name was famous); *compare Componentone, L.L.C. v. Componentart, Inc.*, 2007 U.S. Dist. Lexis 89772, 2007 WL 4302108 (W.D. Pa.) (holding the "ComponentOne" mark was not famous because "is well known only in its niche market — a specific segment of the computer information technology industry, namely, developers on the Windows, Borland, and Visual Studio platforms.").

b. Dilution by Blurring

Dilution by blurring occurs when defendants use of its mark impairs the distinctiveness of the famous mark. 15 U.S.C. § 1125(c)(2)(B). Distinctiveness involves the public's recognition that the famous mark identifies a single source of the product. In determining whether a mark or trade name is likely to cause dilution by blurring, the court may consider all relevant factors, including:

(1) The degree of similarity between the mark or trade name and the famous mark.

(2) The degree of inherent or acquired distinctiveness of the famous mark.

(3) The extent to which the owner of the famous mark is engaging in substantially exclusive use of the mark.

(4) The degree of recognition of the famous mark.

(5) Whether the user of the mark or trade name intended to create an association with the famous mark.

(6) Any actual association between the mark or trade name and the famous mark.

15 U.S.C. § 1125(c)(2)(B). Not every factor is relevant in every case, and not every blurring claim requires extensive discussion of the factors, but trial courts have been instructed by appellate courts to provide an indication of the factors found to be persuasive and explain why they are persuasive in order to allow effective appellate review.

In *Louis Vuitton Malletiers S.A. v. Haute Diggity Dog, LLC*, 507 F.3d 252 (4th Cir. 2007), the defendant marketed a "Chewy Vuitton" dog chew toys resembling a miniature handbag that "indisputably" evoked Louis Vuitton handbags of similar shape, design, and color. The district court granted defendant summary judgment on Louis Vuitton's dilution by blurring claim, but did not discuss any of the factors in section 1125(c)(2)(B). Rather, it simply stated "the famous mark's strength is not likely to be blurred by a parody dog toy product. Instead of blurring Plaintiff's mark, the success of the parodic use depends upon the continued association with Louis Vuitton." The Fourth Circuit rejected this reasoning: "parody is not automatically a complete defense to a claim of dilution by blurring where the defendant uses the parody as its own designation of source, i.e., as a trademark." It held the defendant's use of the mark as a parody was significant, however, and came to the same result as the district court—but by applying the factors set out in section 1125(c)(2)(B).

Regarding factors (2), (3) and (4) the court held the plaintiff's marks were "distinctive, famous, and strong: "The Louis Vuitton mark is well known and is commonly identified as a brand of the great Parisian fashion house, Louis Vuitton Malletier. ... It may not be too strong to refer to these famous marks as icons of high fashion." The strength of these factors contributed to the court's conclusion that the distinctiveness of the Louis Vuitton mark was not blurred by "Chewy Vuitton."

Also, significant to the court was that plaintiff's and defendant's marks were not sufficiently similar (factor (1)): "Haute Diggity Dog designed a pet chew toy to imitate and suggest, but not use, the marks of a high-fashion Louis Vuitton handbag. It used 'Chewy Vuitton' to mimic 'Louis Vuitton'; it used 'CV' to mimic 'LV'; and it adopted imperfectly the items of LVM's designs." Also, considering factors (5) and (6), "Haute Diggity Dog intentionally associated its marks, but only partially and certainly imperfectly, so as to convey the simultaneous message that it was not in fact a source of LVM products. Rather, as a parody, it separated itself from the LVM marks in order to make fun of them." Accordingly, the Fourth Circuit held defendant's marks did blur—impair the distinctiveness of Louis Vuitton's marks as unique identifier of their source.

The degree of similarity required in a dilution by blurring claim is likely to be greater that required in an infringement claim. Courts have held both the TDRA and the FTDA require the defendant's mark to be "identical, or nearly identical," to the famous mark. In *Century 21 Real Estate, LLC v. Century Ins. Group*, No. 03-0053-PHX-SMM, 2007 U.S. Dist. Lexis 9720, 2007 WL 484555 (D.Ariz.) the court noted: "Although the TDRA no longer requires actual dilution, the new law does not eliminate the requirement that the mark used by the alleged diluter be identical, nearly identical, or substantially similar to the protected mark."

c. Dilution by Tarnishment

Dilution by tarnishment occurs when the defendant's use of it's mark harms the reputation of the famous mark. 15 U.S.C. § 1125(c)(2)(C). The 1996 FTDA did not contain a provision regarding dilution by tarnishment, although many courts held the FTDA provided for such claims. *See Kraft Foods Holdings, Inc. v. Helm*, 205 F. Supp. 2d 942 (N.D. Ill. 2002) (Use of "King Velveeda" on "adult" content website dilution by tarnishing "Velveeta" for cheese products); *Hasbro, Inc. v. Internet Entertainment Group, Ltd.*, 40 U.S.P.Q.2d 1479, 1996 WL 84853 (W.D. Wash. 1996) ("Candyland" for children's board game diluted by tarnishment by "candyland.com" for an internet web site showing sexually explicit pictures); *Toys "R" Us, Inc. v. Akkaoui*, 40 U.S.P.Q.2d 1836, 1996 WL 772709 (N.D. Cal. 1996) (Toys 'R Us mark tarnished by use of Adults R Us as a domain name for an internet site selling "adult" products).

In *Moseley v. V Secret Catalogue, Inc.*, 537 U.S. 418 (2003), however, the Supreme Court indicated in dicta that the FTDA likely did not encompass dilution by tarnishment, because in contrast to many state statutes, the FTDA did not refer to "injury to business reputation." This led to the inclusion of a specific provision regarding dilution by tarnishment in the 2006 TDRA.

"Tarnishment occurs where a trademark is linked to products of shoddy quality, or is portrayed in an unwholesome or unsavory context, with the result that the public will associate the lack of quality or lack of prestige in the defendant's goods with the plaintiff's unrelated goods." *New York Stock Exchange, Inc. v. New York, New York Hotel LLC*, 293 F.3d 550, 558 (2d Cir. 2002) (internal quotations omitted). For example in *Original Appalachian Artworks, Inc. v. Topps Chewing Gum, Inc.*, 642 F. Supp. 1031, 1032 (N.D. Ga. 1986) the court concluded that the "Cabbage Patch Kids" mark was tarnished by "Garbage Pail Kids'" stickers [that] derisively depict dolls with features similar to Cabbage Patch Kids dolls in rude, violent and frequently noxious settings." In many cases the famous mark is placed in a sexual, crude, or illegal context. In *Eastman Kodak Co. v. Rakow*, 739 F. Supp. 116, 15 U.S.P.Q.2d 1631 (W.D.N.Y. 1989), the court found tarnishment and enjoined the defendant comedian from using the stage name Kodak because his "comedy act include[d] humor that relates to bodily functions and sex, and [he] use[d] crude, off-color language repeatedly." In *Coca-Cola Co. v. Gemini Rising, Inc.*, 346 F. Supp. 1183 (E.D.N.Y. 1972), the defendant's posters stating "Enjoy Cocaine" in the same script and red and white colors as used in Coca-Cola advertisements was held to have tarnished the Coca-Cola mark. Tarnishment is not limited to crude or illicit conduct, however. So, for example, in *New*

York Stock Exchange, Inc. v. New York, New York Hotel LLC, 293 F.3d 550 (2d Cir. 2002), the court held that a jury could find the plaintiff's marks were tarnished where New York themed Las Vegas casino used the words "New York, New York Slot Exchange" on a replica of the facade of the New York Stock Exchange Building.

d. Dilution Defenses

Section 1125(c)(3) contains specific defenses or "exclusions" to dilution by blurring or tarnishment:

(A) Any fair use, including a nominative or descriptive fair use, or facilitation of such fair use, of a famous mark by another person other than as a designation of source for the person's own goods or services, including use in connection with —

   (i) advertising or promotion that permits consumers to compare goods or services; or

   (ii) identifying and parodying, criticizing, or commenting upon the famous mark owner or the goods or services of the famous mark owner.

(B) All forms of news reporting and news commentary.

(C) Any noncommercial use of a mark.

i. Fair Use — Comparative Advertising, Parody, Comment or Criticism

As a threshold matter, the fair use defense will not apply if the mark is being used as a designation of source for the defendant's own goods and services, in other words, if it is being used as a trademark. In *Louis Vuitton v. Haute Diggity Dog*, 507 F.3d at 266–67, the court held that the defendant's purse shaped "Chewy Vuitton dog chew toy" that used "CV" instead of the "LV" did not qualify under the parody fair use defense because the defendant's parody of Louis Vuitton marks was being used as the defendant's trademark. However, it held that the defendant's use of the mark as a parody was significant in determining that the use was not likely to impair the Louis Vuitton's mark's distinctiveness.

The TDRA, like its predecessor the FTDA, specifically exempts comparative advertising from liability for dilution. Thus, a competitor is allowed to directly advertise that its product is better than a competitor's product.

Under the 1996 FTDA, parody and comment or criticism came within the general, noncommercial use defense. For example, in *Bally Total Fitness Holding Corp. v. Faber*, 29 F. Supp. 2d 1161, 1167 (C.D. Cal. 1998), the court held that use of "ballysucks" for a web site criticizing Bally health clubs was not a violation of the antidilution statute because it was not commercial use. Moreover "trademark owners may not quash unauthorized use of the mark by a person expressing a point of view." A similar result was reached in *Mattel, Inc. v. MCA Records, Inc.*, 296 F.3d 894 (9th Cir. 2002), where the court held the defendant's top 40 song entitled "Barbie Girl" that parodied the plaintiff's doll, Barbie, with lyrics such as "I'm a blonde bimbo girl, in a fantasy world, dress me up, make it tight, I'm your dolly," to be exempt from liability for dilution because it was not a "pure commercial use" since it did "more than propose a commercial transaction."

The 2006 TDRA, however, made parody and comment and criticism not used as a mark explicitly exempt from liability for dilution, in addition "any commercial use." 15 U.S.C.§ 1125(c)(3)(A)(ii) & (C). As of this writing, the only case to address TDRA's fair use defense, *Louis Vuitton v. Haute Diggity Dog, supra*, held it did not apply because defendant's parody was being used as its trademark. In *Smith v. Wal-Mart Stores, Inc.*, 537 F. Supp. 2d 1302 (N.D. Ga. 2008) the court entered a declaratory judgment that plaintiff's domain names "Walocaust.com" and "Wal-Quaeda" and its sales of T-Shirts with the term "Walocaust" was not subject to Wal-Mart's dilution claims because the plaintiff's uses were parodic, noncommercial speech protected by the First Amendment. The court did not apply the TDRA or address whether the plaintiff's parodies were used as a mark to identify the plaintiff's goods or services under § 1125(c)(3)(A).

ii. News Reporting and News Commentary, Commercial Use

The TDRA's section 1125(c)(3)(B) exempts "all forms of news reporting and news commentary." This exemption is identical to that in the FTDA. See 15 U.S.C. § 1125(c)(4)(C) (1996). The exemption was added to the FTDA at the request of the National Association of Broadcasters, who feared that the noncommercial use exemption might not be sufficient to cover news broadcasts. The TDRA's exemption for "any commercial use" in § 1125(c)(3)(C) is identical to that in the FTDA's § 1125(c)(4)(C).

iii. Statute of Limitations and Laches

Dilution claims arising under the 2006 TDRA and the 1996 FTDA are subject to the general 4-year statute of limitations set forth in 28 U.S.C. § 1658, enacted December 1, 1990, which provides: "Except as otherwise provided by law, a civil action arising under an Act of Congress enacted after the date of enactment of this section may not be commenced later than 4 years after the cause of action accrues." Also, since both acts apply "subject to the principles of equity" 15 U.S.C. § 1125(c)(1), equitable defenses, including laches and unclean hands are available to defendants. These defenses are discussed in detail in section 5(b)(ix) of this chapter.

e. Remedies

Under 15 U.S.C. § 1125, injunctive relief is the most common remedy for claims of dilution by blurring or tarnishment, an injunction against the offending use as provided in 15 U.S.C. § 1116. Profits and damages under 15 U.S.C. § 1117 as well as destruction of the offending articles under 15 U.S.C. § 1118 are also available, but only if the prevailing plaintiff proves the defendant, in cases of dilution by blurring, "willfully intended to trade on the recognition of the famous mark, and in cases of dilution by tarnishment, "willfully intended to harm the reputation of the famous mark." 15 U.S.C. § 1125(c)(5)(B). The TDRA applies to claims arising prior to its enactment where the plaintiff seeks prospective injunctive relief, but does not apply where the plaintiff seeks monetary damages.

For further discussion regarding remedies under §§ 1116, 1117, and 1118, see section 6 of this chapter.

f. State Anti Dilution Statutes

Currently there are 38 state dilution statutes, some of which protect against a "likelihood of dilution," while others prevent use of a famous mark that "causes dilution." Unlike the patent and copyright fields, state anti-dilution statutes are not preempted by the TDRA and its predecessor. House Report 104-374 (Nov. 30, 1995) state dilution statutes.

ALA. CODE § 8-12-17:	"likelihood of injury to business reputation or of dilution"
ALASKA STAT. § 45.50.180:	"A registrant that owns a mark that is famous in the state is entitled to an injunction against another's dilution of the mark."
ARIZ. REV. STAT. ANN. § 44-1448.01:	"causes dilution of the distinctive quality of the mark"

ARK. CODE ANN. § 4-71-213:	"causes dilution of the distinctive quality of the mark"
CAL. BUS. & PROF. CODE § 14330:	"likelihood of injury to business reputation or of dilution"
CONN. GEN. STAT. § 35-11i(c):	"causes dilution of the distinctive quality of the registrant's mark"
DEL. CODE ANN. tit. 6, § 3313:	"likelihood of injury to business reputation or of dilution"
FLA. STAT. § 495.151:	"likelihood of injury to business reputation or of dilution"
GA. CODE ANN. § 10-1-451:	"likelihood of injury to business reputation or of dilution"
HAW. REV. STAT. § 482-32:	"causes dilution of the distinctive quality of the famous mark"
IDAHO CODE ANN. § 48-512:	"likely to cause confusion or mistake or to deceive"
765 ILL. COMP. STAT. § 1036/65:	"causes dilution of the distinctive quality of the mark"
IND. CODE § 24-2-1-13.5:	"causes dilution of the distinctive quality of the mark"
IOWA CODE § 548.113:	"causes dilution of the distinctive quality of the owner's mark"
KAN. STAT. ANN. § 81-214:	"causes dilution of the distinctive quality of the mark"
LA. REV. STAT. ANN. § 51:223.1:	"likelihood of injury to business reputation or of dilution"
ME. REV. STAT. ANN. tit. 10, § 1530:	"likelihood of injury to business reputation or of dilution"
MASS. GEN. LAWS ch. 110H, § 12:	"likely to cause confusion or mistake or to deceive as to the source of origin"
MINN. STAT. § 333.285:	"causes dilution of the distinctive quality of the mark"
MISS. CODE ANN. § 75-25-25:	"causes dilution of the distinctive quality of the owner's mark"
MO. REV. STAT. § 417.061(1):	"likelihood of injury to business reputation or of dilution"
MONT. CODE ANN. § 30-13-334:	"causes dilution of the distinctive quality of the mark"
NEB. REV. STAT. § 87-140:	"causes dilution of the distinctive quality of the mark"

Nev. Rev. Stat. § 600.435:	"causes dilution of the mark"
N.H. Rev. Stat. Ann. § 350-A:12:	"likelihood of injury to business reputation or of dilution"
N.J. Stat. Ann. § 56:3-13.20:	"causes dilution of the distinctive quality of the owner's mark"
N.M. Stat. § 57-3B-10:	"causes dilution of the distinctive quality of the owner's mark"
N.Y. Gen. Bus. Law § 360-l:	"likelihood of injury to business reputation or of dilution"
Or. Rev. Stat. § 647.107:	"likelihood of injury to business reputation or of dilution"
54 Pa. Cons. Stat. § 1124:	"causes dilution of the distinctive quality of the mark"
R.I. Gen. Laws § 6-2-12:	"likelihood of injury to business reputation or of dilution"
S.C. Code Ann. § 39-15-1165:	"causes dilution of the distinctive quality of the registrant's mark"
Tenn. Code Ann. § 47-25-512:	"likely to cause confusion, mistake or deception as to the source of origin"
Tex. Bus. & Com. Code Ann. § 16.29:	"likely to injure a business reputation or to dilute the distinctive quality of a mark"
Utah Code Ann. § 70-3a-403:	"causes dilution of the distinctive quality of the mark"
Wash. Rev. Code § 19.77.160:	"causes dilution of the distinctive quality of the mark"
W. Va. Code § 47-2-13:	"causes dilution of the distinctive quality of the owner's mark"
Wyo. Stat. Ann. § 40-1-115:	"causes dilution of the distinctive quality of the owner's mark"

g. Cybersquatting

In 1999 Congress enacted the "Anti-cybersquatting Consumer Protection Act," or "ACPA," 15 U.S.C. § 1125(d), to prevent the registration of domain names that are the same or confusingly similar to trademarks or peoples' names. The purpose of the ACPA was to stop cybersquatters—people who would register several hundred Internet domain names with the purpose of later selling them to the legitimate owners of the mark." The elements of cybersquatting are:

(1) registering, using, or trafficking a domain name,

(2) that is confusingly similar to a registered or unregistered mark or dilutes a famous mark, with

(3) the bad faith intent to profit.

15 U.S.C. § 1125(d)(1)(A). The act also applies to "typosquatting" in which person registered domain names with intentional misspelling to divert internet traffic to their websites. As stated in *Shields v. Zuccarini*, 254 F.3d 476, 59 U.S.P.Q.2d 1207 (3d Cir. 2001), "A reasonable interpretation of conduct covered by the [ACPA's] phrase 'confusingly similar' is the intentional registration of domain names that are misspellings of distinctive or famous names, causing an Internet user who makes a slight spelling or typing error to reach an unintended site."

h. Gray Market Goods

"A gray-market good is a foreign-manufactured good, bearing a valid United States trademark, that is imported without the consent of the U.S. trademark holder." *K Mart Corp. v. Cartier, Inc.*, 486 U.S. 281, 285 (1988). Gray market goods are legitimately sold or distributed by the trademark holder or its licensee in a non-United States market, but when those same goods cross back into United States markets, they become gray-market goods. Typically, a gray market goods claim for trademark infringement or dilution arises when

(1) material differences exist between the goods sold by the trademark holder and its authorized or licensed dealers and those sold by the unauthorized dealer, and

(2) the unauthorized dealer sells the materially different trademarked goods so that it is likely to cause consumer confusion and dilute the strength of the trademark owner's mark.

The material difference prong is a threshold requiring only a showing that consumers would be likely to consider the differences between the foreign and domestic products to be significant when purchasing the product. Those sort of differences would erode the goodwill of the domestic source. Material differences may be physical or non-physical. For example, in *Societe Des Produits Nestle, S.A. v. Casa Helvetia, Inc.*, 982 F.2d 633, 635 (1st Cir.1992), differences in ingredients, quality control, variety, composition, and price between chocolates that were manufactured in Italy and chocolate manufactured in Venezuela that both bore the same "Perugina" trademark were found to be material. In

Lever Bros. Co. v. United States, 877 F.2d 101, 103 (D.C. Cir. 1989), differences in the packaging of Sunlight dishwashing liquid meant to be distributed in the United States and Sunlight dishwashing liquid meant to be distributed in the United Kingdom were material: the U.S. bottle was shaped like an "hourglass," while the U.K. bottle was shaped like a "cylindrical drum," and the U.K. label included a "royal emblem" and the statement "By Appointment to Her Majesty the Queen." In *Bourdeau Bros., Inc. v. International Trade Com'n,* 444 F.3d 1317 (Fed. Cir. 2006), differences in lighting configuration, hitch mechanisms, safety labels and service plans between European and North American forage harvesters considered material. Once the plaintiff meets the material difference threshold, the plaintiff must prove the elements required for infringement, or dilution by blurring or tarnishment.

Checkpoints

- The elements of an infringement action are (1) proof of a valid mark entitled to protection and (2) proof that the defendant's use is likely to cause confusion.

- Proving validity of a mark requires showing that the owner of the mark (1) used it commercially, (2) is the senior user (has priority in the mark), and (3) that the mark has distinctiveness (either inherent or acquired).

- Junior marks that are likely to cause confusion as to the source of goods or services will be found to infringe.

- Junior marks that are likely to deceive as to the affiliation or sponsorship will be found to infringe.

- The factors considered in determining likelihood of confusion include (1) the similarity of the appearance, sound, and meaning of the marks; (2) similarity in marketing and distribution; (3) the sophistication of the relevant consumers; (4) the strength of the mark; (5) the competitive proximity or similarity of the goods or services; (6) likelihood the owners will "bridge the gap" by expanding into the other user's market; (7) recognition of the mark in the other user's geographic territory; (8) the intent to deceive or cause confusion; and (9) proof of actual confusion.

- The strength of the mark is determined by both its conceptual strength — descriptive marks are the weakest, then suggestive, arbitrary, and fanciful the strongest — and by its commercial strength — market recognition and how strongly the goods or services are associated with the mark.

- When considering relatedness, the more similar the competing goods or services, the less similar the marks must be to support a finding of infringement.

- Reverse confusion is where goods bearing a weak senior mark are confused as originating with the owner of a stronger junior mark.

- Incontestable status provides conclusive evidence of the mark's validity and the registrant's ownership and exclusive right to use the mark. However, 15 U.S.C. § 1115 provides a list of defenses to infringement of incontestable (and other) marks including fraud in obtaining the registration, abandonment, misrepresentation of source, fair use, limited area and prior use defenses, violation of antitrust laws, functionality of the mark, and equitable defenses such as estoppel and unclean hands.

- In addition to the defenses available to incontestable marks, defenses to infringement of unregistered and contestable marks include showing that the plaintiff's mark is invalid because it is not used commercially, has subordinate priority to the defendant's, or is not distinctive. Additional defenses are available that are applicable to all marks, even incontestable ones.

- A defendant may also show that an incontestable, contestable, or unregistered mark has become generic and is not entitled to protection because it has ceased to be a trademark.

- Remedies for trademark infringement include injunctions, profits, damages, attorneys' fees, and destruction of the infringing articles.

- Injunctions are the most common remedy for trademark infringement. To receive an injunction, trademark owners must show (1) that they have suffered irreparable injury, (2) that money damages are inadequate, (3) a balance of the hardships, and (4) that the public interest would not be disserved.

- Monetary recovery — is available as measured by the infringer's profits or the plaintiff's actual damages and the court may treble damages at its discretion. In exceptional cases, the prevailing party is entitled to attorneys' fees.

- For intentional counterfeit marks, treble damages are awarded or the plaintiff may choose to receive statutory damages in lieu of actual damages.

- Trademark dilution occurs when a famous mark's distinctiveness (dilution by blurring) or reputation (dilution by tarnishment) is impaired by a junior mark even where there is no likelihood of confusion.

- To prevail on a dilution claim, the plaintiff must show that (1) the mark is famous (widely recognized) and (2) the defendant's use caused a likelihood of dilution by blurring or tarnishment.

- Dilution defenses include fair use (such as comparative advertising, criticism, and parody; news reporting and commentary) and other basic defenses such as the statute of limitations and equitable defenses.

- Dilution remedies are the same as the remedies available for trademark infringement with injunctions being the most common.

- Cybersquatting is the registering, using, or trafficking in domain names that are confusingly similar to or dilutes a famous mark with the bad faith intent to profit. Cybersquatting and typosquatting are prohibited.

- Gray market goods are foreign manufactured goods bearing a valid United States trademark that are imported into the United States without the consent of the trademark owner. Gray market goods give rise to claims for infringement and, if the goods are of a lower quality and the mark is famous, also for dilution.

Mastering Intellectual Property Checklist

Trade Secrets

❏ Trade secret protection is derived from state common law and draws heavily from the following three sources: the Restatement (First) of Torts § 757, the Uniform Trade Secrets Act, and the Restatement (Third) of Unfair Competition § 39.

❏ Trade secret law protects proprietary information for as long as it remains secret (rather than for a fixed term like patents and copyrights).

❏ Eligible subject matter is information that: (1) is not a matter of general knowledge and is not readily ascertainable; (2) is commercially valuable or gives the holder an economic advantage because of its secrecy; and (3) is guarded by reasonable means to maintain its secrecy.

❏ Misappropriation can be committed by: acquiring a trade secret through improper or wrongful means; disclosing a trade secret that was acquired wrongfully, in breach of a duty, or by mistake; or using a trade secret that was acquired wrongfully, in breach of a duty, or by mistake.

❏ Defenses to misappropriation include a valid licensing agreement; that the information was not actually secret; and discovery by proper means, such as independent invention, reverse engineering, discovery under a license, observation of public use, and discovery through published literature.

❏ Remedies for trade secret misappropriation include injunctions, damages, attorneys' fees, and punitive damages. Misappropriation might also result in criminal penalties, including prison sentences and fines as high as $5,000,000.

❏ Licensing allows the trade secret holder to share and profit from the information without compromising its secrecy, and licensing agreements often include provisions related to updates and technical support, renewal rights, confidentiality and non-disclosure agreements, exclusivity of the license, and residual rights.

❏ Trade secrets can serve as collateral. Security interests in trade secrets attach and are perfected as "general intangibles" under Article 9 of the Uniform Commercial Code.

Patents

❏ Patent law provides inventors a limited monopoly on qualifying inventions that allows them to exclude others from making, using, selling, offering to sell, or importing their invention.

❏ Any process, product, design, or plant that meets the statutory requirements may be patented. However, abstract ideas, the laws of nature, and naturally occurring phenomena cannot be patented.

❏ *Utility patents*, the most common type of patent, expire twenty years from the application date, and are available for processes, machines, articles of manufacture, and combinations of matter.

❏ *Design patents* expire fourteen years from the date of issue and are available for non-functional ornamental designs.

❏ *Plant patents* expire twenty years from the application date and are available for asexually propagated plants.

❏ *Utility*, found in 35 U.S.C. § 101, requires that in order to be patentable, an invention must be capable of producing a practical or commercial benefit and must be operable and reduced to practice.

❏ *Novelty*, found in 35 U.S.C. § 102, requires that in order to be patentable, an invention must differ from prior art. Under § 102, inventors are not entitled to a patent if they did not personally invent the claimed invention, or they abandoned, suppressed, or concealed the invention.

❏ The *statutory bar*, also found in 35 U.S.C. § 102, bars patenting if the invention was patented, described in a printed publication, in public use, or sold prior to the "critical date," which is one year before the patent application was filed.

❏ *Non-obviousness*, found in 35 U.S.C. § 103, is similar to novelty and requires that in order to be patentable, an invention must be more than a trivial advance over prior art. Obviousness is determined by whether the invention would be obvious to a hypothetical artisan of ordinary skill in the art given all of the prior art. Or, in the case of design patents, by the ordinary designer.

❏ *Secondary considerations*, such as commercial success, a long felt but unsolved need, and the failure of others, and *synergism*, the combination of obvious elements in such a way that the whole exceeds the sum of the parts, indicate non-obviousness and might enable a patent to issue in an otherwise close case.

❏ Patent holders can assign or license their patents and use them as collateral in secured transactions. Filing the necessary security documents under the applicable state-law Uniform Commercial Code and filing with the Patent and Trademark Office is prudent to ensure perfection of a security interest in a patent.

❏ Provisional applications do not require claims and allow patent applicants to gain the priority of the provisional filing date when they eventually file a non-provisional application.

❏ The specification discloses the invention, enables a skilled artisan to make the invention, shows that the inventor accomplished the invention at the time of the application filing, and sets out the best mode for carrying out the invention.

❏ Claims specifically define the scope of the patent and distinguish the invention from the prior art and are construed in light of the specification.

❏ Patent applicants are under a duty of candor toward the PTO and violations can invalidate the patent.

❏ A patent holder may obtain a reissue patent to correct innocent error but cannot use the reissue process to correct a breach of the duty of candor or to extend the patent to cover improvements developed after the initial patent issued.

❏ There are two types of reexaminations, *ex parte* and *inter partes*, that allow a challenge to the validity of the patent after additional prior art is brought to light. *Ex parte* reexaminations have minimal participation from third parties whereas *inter partes* reexaminations require the challenger to actively participate in the proceedings.

❏ When the claims contained in a patent application interfere with those of another application or an existing patent, that priority dispute is generally settled through an interference proceeding.

❏ United States District courts have original and exclusive jurisdiction over any civil action arising under the patent laws. On appeal, jurisdiction lies in the United States Court of Appeals for the Federal Circuit. The Federal Circuit applies its own law to patent matters and the law of the circuit in which the originating district court sits for non-patent matters in the case.

❏ Infringement includes any unauthorized manufacture, use, sale, offer to sell, or importation into the United States of any patented article. Infringement is a strict liability cause of action; the intent of the infringer is only relevant in the determination of damages.

❏ In conducting an infringement analysis, the court construes the claims of the patent and then determines if the allegedly infringing device "reads on" every limitation of the claims, either identically or under the doctrine of equivalents.

❏ The doctrine of equivalents broadens the scope of patent protection to cover insubstantial or trivial nonfunctional changes that do not literally infringe. An element is equivalent to a limitation of a patent claim if it performs substantially the same function in substantially the same way to obtain substantially the same result as the claim limitation.

❏ Direct infringement is the manufacture, use, sale, or importation of the infringing device and requires that the accused device meet every limitation of the claim, either literally or under the doctrine of equivalents.

❏ Indirect infringement includes both contributory infringement and inducement to infringement and requires direct infringement as a prerequisite to liability.

❏ Contributory infringement occurs when one sells a material component of another's patented invention that is not itself a staple article or commodity of commerce suitable for substantial non-infringing use.

❏ Inducement to infringement occurs when one actively induces another to engage in direct infringement.

❏ Common defenses to infringement include invalidity of the patent, misuse, shop rights, prior use, safe harbors, and nonpatent defenses including that the accused device did not infringe or lapse of the statute of limitations.

❏ Defendants asserting patent invalidity carry the burden of proof but may use any of the grounds required for patentability to make the challenge such as by negating novelty, non-obviousness, utility.

❏ Misuse is generally asserted as a defense when the patent holder has allegedly abused the patent monopoly with a tying arrangement by requiring the purchase of unpatented goods with the patent or conditioning the grant of a license upon acceptance of another different license or some similar tying arrangement or unlawful restraint of competitive trade.

❏ Shop rights grant an employer the right to use an invention patented by an employee under equitable circumstances, such as when the employer provided the material and the employee developed the invention in the course of their employment.

❏ Injunctions are the most common remedy for patent infringement and are issued on equitable principles identical to those for nonpatent injunctions. To receive an injunction, patentees are required to show that they have suffered irreparable injury, that money damages are inadequate, balance of the hardships, and that the public interest would not be disserved.

❏ Patent holders may also receive money damages for their lost profits if they can prove them with requisite certainty but more often the measure of damages is a reasonable royalty. A reasonable royalty is calculated by what a willing licensor and licensee would bargain for in a hypothetical negotiation.

❏ The court may treble the damages in a case of willful infringement or bad faith, but cannot increase damages as a compensatory measure.

❏ In exceptional cases, such as those involving willful infringement, inequitable conduct, or vexatious litigation, the prevailing party in a patent infringement action may receive an award of its reasonable attorneys' fees.

Copyrights

❏ All original works of authorship are copyrightable. Section 102 provides a nonexclusive list of copyrightable works including literary works, musical works, dramatic works, pictorial, graphic, and sculptural works, motion pictures and other audio visual works, sound recordings, and architectural works.

❏ Copyright protects only the expression of an idea, not the underlying idea, procedure, process, system, method of operation, concept, principle, or discovery.

❏ Copyright protection extends to all original works of authorship fixed in any tangible medium of expression, now known or later developed, from which they can be perceived, reproduced, or otherwise communicated, either directly or with the aid of a machine or device. This is known as the "fixation" requirement.

❏ A work must be the independent creation of the author and display at least minimal creativity in order to be eligible for a copyright: the "originality" requirement.

❏ Purely utilitarian works cannot be copyrighted, but if conceptual separability exists then the aesthetic or expressive aspects of a utilitarian work can be copyrighted.

❏ The "merger doctrine" applies when an idea necessarily involves certain forms of expression, in which case those forms of expression cannot be copyrighted.

❏ Joint works are works prepared by two or more authors with the intention that their contributions be merged into inseparable parts of a unitary whole. The contributions need not be equal, but each must be independently copyrightable. Co-authors of joint works are treated as tenants in common and each has the exclusive rights found in § 106 and may independently license the work.

❏ Works for hire are works prepared by an employee within the scope of their employment or a commissioned work if the parties expressly agree that it is a work for hire; but they cannot make it a work for hire retroactively.

❏ For authors or joint authors, copyright protection lasts for the life of the last surviving author plus an additional seventy years; for works before January 1, 1978, copyrights last twenty eight years with an option to renew it for another sixty seven years; for anonymous, pseudonymous, and works for hire copyright protections expire after the earlier of ninety five years after the first publication or 120 years after the date of their creation.

❏ Some or all of the author's rights can be assigned or licensed. An exclusive transfer requires a written embodiment but a nonexclusive transfer need not be evidenced by a writing.

❑ The termination right allows authors to recapture their work and cancel any assignments and licenses.

❑ Copyright holders can use their interest as collateral in secured transactions and are perfected by a filing with the Copyright Office.

❑ Copyright protection of a work attaches upon the work's creation, but to enforce the copyright against infringers and to recover statutory damages or attorneys' fees the copyright must be registered.

❑ Under the 1909 Copyright Act, the failure to place notice precluded protection, but under the 1976 Act, the lack of notice only limited remedies and reduced damages. After the revisions in the wake of Berne, notice is irrelevant to copyright protections and remedies for works created after 1989, except as it relates to the innocent infringer defense.

❑ The exclusive rights under the copyright act include the right to reproduce the work; prepare derivative works; distribute copies through sale, rental, lease, or lending of the work; perform the work publicly; display the work publicly; and perform the work publicly via digital audio transmission.

❑ The right to reproduction allows the copyright holder to prevent others from making an unauthorized copy or phonorecord.

❑ The right to derivative works allows the copyright holder to prevent others from making unauthorized translations, dramatizations, fictionalizations, motion picture adaptations, abridgments, and other transformative works.

❑ The right to distribution allows the copyright holder to prevent others from selling, renting, leasing, or lending the work.

❑ The "first sale doctrine" limits the copyright holder's right of distribution by providing an exception so that once a copyrighted article is sold without restriction, the distribution rights no longer prevent further distributions of that same article.

❑ The right to performance allows the copyright holder to prevent others from publicly performing the work, but there are exceptions for nonprofit groups, religious services, and charity fundraisers.

❑ The right to display allows the copyright holder to prevent others from publicly displaying the copyrighted work, but the face-to-face exception allows the public display of the work at the place where the work is located.

❑ Copyright infringement occurs whenever another engages in activities otherwise reserved for the copyright owner without permission.

❑ To prevail in a copyright infringement suit, the plaintiff must show that there is a valid copyright, one that is original and fixed in a tangible medium of expression. Also, the mark must be registered (or denied registration) in order to bring suit.

❑ Copying can be proven directly if possible, or through circumstantial evidence. To indirectly prove copying, one must show that the alleged infringer had access to the protected work and that the accused work is substantially similar to the protected work.

❑ Access is the reasonable opportunity to view, hear, or experience the protected work. Access can be shown by possession of a copy of the work, inferred based on interaction with those in possession of the work, presumed when the work has been widely disseminated or mass produced, or inferred when the two works are strikingly similar when considered against the diversity in the marketplace.

❑ Substantial similarity is determined through tests that objectively and subjectively compare the copyrighted work with the alleged infringing work.

❑ Secondary infringement liability exists for those who induce, cause, or materially contribute to the infringement of another.

❑ Defenses to infringement include fair use; independent creation; uses for educational purposes, in the course of worship, or for free public concerts and charitable fundraisers; and copies for personal use and software backups, among others.

❑ Fair use is an equitable doctrine that acts as an affirmative defense. Fair use is determined by balancing four factors: the purpose and character of the use, including if it is a commercial or non-profit use; the nature of copyrighted work; the amount and substantiality of the portion used in relation to work as a whole; and the effect of the use upon the market for or value of the copyrighted work.

❑ The types of fair use are transformative works, which borrow from the earlier work to produce a new work and includes parody, and non-transformative works, those that are direct copies of the original work, such as works reproduced for criticism or educational purposes.

❑ Copyright infringement remedies include injunctions, impoundment, monetary damages, and attorneys' fees. Criminal penalties are also available in cases of willful infringement fr commercial advantage or personal financial gain.

❑ Injunctions issue after meeting the traditional four part test: a showing of irreparable harm; that money damages are inadequate; a balancing of the hardships; and that the public interest is not disserved. Courts can order the impoundment and destruction of infringing articles as an additional non-monetary remedy.

❑ Monetary damages are available for lost profits, lost royalties, loss of good will, and the like.

❑ Infringers profits may be ordered if the profits are greater than the actual damages, but double recovery is not allowed.

❑ Statutory damages are available in lieu of actual damages/infringers profits, and may be awarded in an amount of $750–$30,000 per infringement (as low as $200 for innocent infringement and up to $150,000 if willful infringement), as set by the court.

❑ Attorneys' fees and costs are awardable to the prevailing party if the infringement was willful or if the suit was frivolous or brought in bad faith.

Moral Rights

❑ Moral rights are a set of protections for authors and their works that secure artists control over their works and allow them some control over their reputations. Traditionally they have not been widely recognized in the United States.

❑ Moral rights remain with the author, even if the copyright in the work is assigned, and last as long as the work exists.

❑ The right of integrity allows artists to prevent changes to their work.

❑ The right of attribution allows artists to identify their work as their own.

❑ The right of disclosure allows artists control over whether and how their work is shared with the public.

❑ The right of withdrawal allows artists to remove their previously disclosed work from the public if the work truly misrepresents their convictions or is obsolete and would thereby damage their reputations.

❏ Some jurisdictions also recognize additional artists' rights beyond the core moral rights, described above, called the *droit de suite*, which include the right to collect a fee upon resale of their work.

❏ The Visual Artists Rights Act (VARA) is the primary United States protection of moral rights, but it is strictly limited to works of visual art. VARA protects the rights of attribution and integrity, and even allows visual artists to prevent the destruction of their work if the work is of a "recognized stature."

❏ Artists that still hold the copyright to their work can use copyright protections to enforce some moral rights, such as by using the copyright prohibition on derivative works to enforce the moral right of integrity and the copyright protections of performance and display to protect the moral right of disclosure.

❏ Some states have enacted laws that provide moral rights protections beyond the scope of VARA.

Trademarks

❏ A trademark is any distinctive mark, symbol, device, or emblem used by a business to identify and distinguish its goods from those of others and that enables consumers to identify products and their source.

❏ Trademarks are protected by both state and federal law.

❏ Trademark protection is also available for service marks, collective marks, certification marks, and trade dress.

  ❏ A service mark is used by a company to identify and accumulate goodwill toward specific intangibles such as services.

  ❏ A collective mark distinguishes membership in an association, union, or other group.

  ❏ A certification mark is used by third parties to guarantee that certified goods or services meet certain criteria.

  ❏ Trade dress is the nonfunctional overall appearance of a product's design as presented in the marketplace, including the decor, packaging, wrappers, and labels.

    ❏ *De facto* functionality exists where the elements of the design are arbitrary or superfluous. *De facto* functional marks and trade dress are eligible for protection.

❏ *De jure* functionality exists where the overall appearance is the consequence of entirely and necessarily utilitarian considerations. *De jure* marks or trade dress are not eligible for protection.

❏ There are four categories of trademarks arranged in ascending order according to their strength: (1) generic, (2) descriptive (including deceptively misdescriptive), (3) suggestive, and (4) arbitrary or fanciful.

❏ Generic marks are never distinctive and are not eligible for protection.

❏ Descriptive and deceptively misdescriptive marks are eligible for protection only if they acquire secondary meaning, but primarily geographically deceptively misdescriptive marks adopted after 1993 are ineligible for trademark protection.

❏ Suggestive marks are inherently distinctive and are eligible for protection.

❏ Arbitrary and fanciful marks are inherently distinctive, eligible for protection, and considered the strongest type of mark.

❏ Trademarks must be distinctive—they must serve the purpose of identifying the origin of the goods or services—in order to be eligible for protection. Distinctiveness may be obtained inherently, as with suggestive, arbitrary, fanciful marks, or through use once the mark has obtained secondary meaning, as with some descriptive marks.

❏ A mark must actually be in use, or the mark holder must have a bona fide intent to use the mark in commerce, in order to be protected.

❏ Priority in a mark is typically given to the first party to use the mark in commerce (the "senior user"). The standard of use is minimal, but must be continuous from its first instance until ownership is asserted in order to preserve the user's priority.

❏ Rights in a trademark are acquired by use, not registration, but federal registration is prima facie evidence of validity, the registrant's ownership of the mark, and the registrant's exclusive right to use the mark in commerce. Registration also provides constructive notice of the registrant's claim to the mark, thereby foreclosing any claims of innocence or good faith by later or "junior users."

❏ Certain marks are barred from registration, including those that are generic, deceptive, primarily geographically deceptively misdescriptive, immoral, scandalous, or disparaging. Marks that are confusingly similar with a prior mark or marks comprised of government insignia are also barred.

❏ A registered mark confers a nationwide right of priority against any subsequent users.

❏ After being registered and in continuous use without challenge for five years and the filing of an affidavit to that effect, the mark becomes "incontestable." Incontestable status provides conclusive evidence of the mark's validity and the registrant's ownership and exclusive right to use the mark.

❏ Registration of a mark can be cancelled at any time, even if it is incontestable, if the mark has become generic or if registration was procured by fraud.

❏ A mark that does not meet all of the requirements for registration on the Principal Register, but that is capable of distinguishing the applicant's goods or services, may be registered on the PTO's Supplemental Register.

❏ Registration on the Supplemental Register is not evidence of the mark's validity, but it enables the registrant to satisfy some foreign home registration requirements, creates federal jurisdiction for disputes involving the mark, and will establish priority if the mark ever becomes eligible for registration on the Principal Register.

❏ Abandonment is non-use with intent to not resume use. Non-use within the United States for three consecutive years is prima facie evidence of abandonment, but such evidence may be rebutted by showing that the non-use was excusable and that the owner intended to resume the use within a reasonable time. Additionally, assignments in gross and naked licensing may lead to a finding of abandonment.

❏ Trademarks can be sold (assigned) and licensed, but are subject to special rules because the mark also represents the goodwill associated with the mark.

❏ An assignment of the mark without the associated goodwill is an assignment in gross and is invalid (and may also lead to a finding of abandonment).

❏ Licensing of a mark is permitted only if the owner of the mark retains sufficient control over the quality and consistency of the goods or services provided. Otherwise, the trademark owner may be found to have abandoned the mark through a naked license.

❏ Trademarks can provide valuable collateral for secured transactions, but perfecting a security interest in the mark without also perfecting and interest in the goodwill could lead to an invalid assignment in gross. Failure to perfect an interest in a business's trademarks can greatly decrease the value of a secured party's collateral.

❏ The elements of an infringement action are (1) proof of a valid mark entitled to protection and (2) proof that the defendant's use is likely to cause confusion.

❏ Proving validity of a mark requires showing that the owner of the mark (1) used it commercially, (2) is the senior user (has priority in the mark), and (3) that the mark has distinctiveness (either inherent or acquired).

❏ Junior marks that are likely to cause confusion as to the source of goods or services will be found to infringe.

❏ Junior marks that are likely to deceive as to the affiliation or sponsorship will be found to infringe.

❏ The factors considered in determining likelihood of confusion include (1) similarity of the appearance, sound, and meaning of the marks; (2) similarity in marketing and distribution; (3) the sophistication of the relevant consumers; (4) the strength of the mark; (5) the competitive proximity or similarity of the goods or services; (6) likelihood the owners will "bridge the gap" by expanding into the other market; (7) recognition of the mark in the other user's geographic territory; (8) the intent to deceive or cause confusion; and (9) proof of actual confusion.

❏ The strength of a mark is determined by both its conceptual strength (descriptive marks are the weakest, then suggestive, arbitrary, and fanciful the strongest) and its commercial strength (market recognition and how strongly the goods or services are associated with the mark).

❏ When considering relatedness, the more similar the competing goods or services, the less similar the marks must be to support a finding of infringement.

❏ Reverse confusion occurs where goods or services bearing a weak senior mark are confused as originating from, affiliation with or sponsorship by the owner of a stronger junior mark.

❏ Incontestable status provides conclusive evidence of the mark's validity and the registrant's ownership and exclusive right to use the mark. However 15 U.S.C. § 1115 provides defenses to infringement of incontestable (and other) marks including fraud in obtaining the registration, abandonment, misrepresentation of source, fair use, limited area and prior use defenses, violation of antitrust laws, functionality of the mark, and equitable defenses such as estoppel and unclean hands.

❏ In addition to the defenses available to incontestable marks, defenses to infringement of unregistered and contestable marks include showing that the plaintiff's mark (1) is invalid because it is not used commercially, (2) has subordinate priority to the defendant's, or (3) is not distinctive.

❏ A defendant may also show that an incontestable, contestable, or unregistered mark has become generic and is not entitled to protection because it has ceased to be a trademark.

❏ Remedies for trademark infringement include injunctions, profits, damages, attorneys' fees, and destruction of the infringing articles.

❏ Injunctions are the most common remedy for trademark infringement. Injunctions are applied on equitable principles identical to those for other injunctions. To receive an injunction, trademark owners must show (1) that they have suffered irreparable injury, (2) that money damages are inadequate, (3) a balance of the hardships, and (4) that the public interest would not be disserved.

❏ Monetary recovery—is available as either the infringer's profits, or the plaintiff's actual damages, and the court may treble damages at its discretion. In exceptional cases, the prevailing party is entitled to attorneys' fees.

❏ Treble damages are awarded in cases of intentional counterfeiting, or the plaintiff may choose to receive statutory damages in lieu of actual damages.

❏ Trademark dilution occurs when a famous mark's distinctiveness (dilution by blurring) or reputation (dilution by tarnishment) is impaired by a junior mark, even where there is no likelihood of confusion.

❏ To prevail on a dilution claim, the plaintiff must show that (1) the mark is famous (widely recognized) and (2) the defendant's use caused a likelihood of dilution by blurring or tarnishment.

❏ Dilution defenses include fair use (such as comparative advertising, criticism, and parody; news reporting and commentary) and other basic defenses such as the statute of limitations and equitable defenses.

❏ Dilution remedies are the same as remedies available for trademark infringement, and injunctions are the most common remedy.

❏ Cybersquatting is the registering, using, or trafficking in domain names that are confusingly similar to or dilutes a famous mark with the bad-faith intent to profit. Cybersquatting and "typosquatting" (which is similar to cybersquatting but involves domain names that are comprised of common misspellings of famous marks) are prohibited.

❏ Gray market goods are foreign manufactured goods bearing a valid United States trademark that are imported into the United States without the consent of the trademark owner. Gray market goods give rise to claims for infringement and, if the goods are of a lower quality and the mark is famous, also for dilution.

Index